Multimedia Technologies: Designs, Tools and Applications

Multimedia Technologies: Designs, Tools and Applications

Edited by
Kyle Baldwin

www.willfordpress.com

Published by Willford Press,
118-35 Queens Blvd., Suite 400,
Forest Hills, NY 11375, USA

ISBN: 978-1-68285-687-1

Cataloging-in-Publication Data

Multimedia technologies : designs, tools and applications / edited by Kyle Baldwin.
   p. cm.
Includes bibliographical references and index.
ISBN 978-1-68285-687-1
1. Multimedia systems. 2. Multimedia systems--Design. 3. Multimedia communications.
I. Baldwin, Kyle.
QA76.575 .M85 2019
006.7--dc23

For information on all Willford Press publications
visit our website at www.willfordpress.com

Contents

Permissions

List of Contributors

Index

Preface

Over the recent decade, advancements and applications have progressed exponentially. This has led to the increased interest in this field and projects are being conducted to enhance knowledge. The main objective of this book is to present some of the critical challenges and provide insights into possible solutions. This book will answer the varied questions that arise in the field and also provide an increased scope for furthering studies.

Any content, which integrates different content forms such as audio, animations, interactive content, images, and video to convey a message is known as multimedia. It can be displayed, recorded, played and accessed by devices or tools like mobile phones, tablets, computers, televisions, etc. The two broad categories of multimedia technology are linear and non-linear. Linear multimedia technologies refer to the content progression without viewer navigational control whereas non-linear multimedia employs interactivity to control progression, like in video games. The usage of multimedia technology is constantly growing. It is used in advertising, journalism, designing video games, animations like VFX, computer-based education, etc. It is also used in technical fields like mathematical and scientific research, medicine and engineering. This book traces the progress in the field of multimedia technology and highlights some of its key designs and tools. Such selected concepts that redefine this vast subject have been presented herein. Those with an interest in multimedia technology and its applications would find this book helpful.

I hope that this book, with its visionary approach, will be a valuable addition and will promote interest among readers. Each of the authors has provided their extraordinary competence in their specific fields by providing different perspectives as they come from diverse nations and regions. I thank them for their contributions.

Editor

Block Compressed Sensing of Images Using Adaptive Granular Reconstruction

Ran Li, Hongbing Liu, Yu Zeng, and Yanling Li

School of Computer and Information Technology, Xinyang Normal University, Xinyang 464000, China

Correspondence should be addressed to Ran Li; liran358@163.com

Academic Editor: Patrizio Campisi

In the framework of block Compressed Sensing (CS), the reconstruction algorithm based on the Smoothed Projected Landweber (SPL) iteration can achieve the better rate-distortion performance with a low computational complexity, especially for using the Principle Components Analysis (PCA) to perform the adaptive hard-thresholding shrinkage. However, during learning the PCA matrix, it affects the reconstruction performance of Landweber iteration to neglect the stationary local structural characteristic of image. To solve the above problem, this paper firstly uses the Granular Computing (GrC) to decompose an image into several granules depending on the structural features of patches. Then, we perform the PCA to learn the sparse representation basis corresponding to each granule. Finally, the hard-thresholding shrinkage is employed to remove the noises in patches. The patches in granule have the stationary local structural characteristic, so that our method can effectively improve the performance of hard-thresholding shrinkage. Experimental results indicate that the reconstructed image by the proposed algorithm has better objective quality when compared with several traditional ones. The edge and texture details in the reconstructed image are better preserved, which guarantees the better visual quality. Besides, our method has still a low computational complexity of reconstruction.

1. Introduction

Nyquist frequency sampling theorem is the theoretical basis of traditional image coding (such as JPEG and JPEG 2000), which requests that the number of image transformations is the total number of pixels at least. The full transformation of image results in a large amount of calculations, but most of transformation coefficients are discarded during encoding, which causes the waste of energy consumption. Due to a high computational complexity and a low utilization rate of energy consumption, the traditional image coding is not suitable for the application requiring a light load, for example, wireless sensor network node with the limited energy consumption [1] and remote sensing imaging [2]. In addition, since a few transformation coefficients contain most of useful information, the quality of image reconstruction can be degraded severely once these important coefficients lose; thus it is also challenging for the fault-tolerant mechanism in the wireless communication [3]. Compressed Sensing (CS) [4, 5] transforms the signal with the sub-Nyquist rate, and it can still accurately recover the signal, which motivates the

image CS as a new image coding scheme [6]. The CS random sampling can be regarded as the partial image transformation, and it compresses image by dimensionality reduction while transforming image. Due to the advantage of saving mostly the costs of image coding, the image CS attracts lots of academic interests.

Many researchers are dedicated to improving the rate-distortion (RD) performance of image CS; the popular method explores the adaptive sparse representation model to improve the convergence performance of minimum l_1-norm reconstruction [7, 8]; for example, Chen et al. [9] use the spatial correlation to establish Multiple-Hypotheses (MH) prediction model and recover the more sparse residual to improve the reconstruction quality; Becker et al. [10] proposed the NESTA algorithm based on the first-order analysis to solve the minimum Total Variation (TV) model, which ensures the speediness and robustness of the sparse decomposition; Zhang et al. [11] exploit the nonlocal self-similarity existing in the group of blocks to express the concise sparse representation model; Wu et al. [12] introduce the local autoregressive (AR) model to trace the nonstationary statistical property of image. For above-mentioned methods, the improvement of RD performance is at the expense of the high computational complexity, which results in the fact that the reconstruction time rises rapidly as the dimensionality of image increases; for example, the AR algorithm proposed by Wu et al. [12] requires 1 hour to reconstruct an image with size of 512 × 512 pixels, which makes this method lose the value of application. Compared with the above methods which ignore the computational complexity but pursue the high reconstruction quality, Gan [13] and Mun and Fowler [14] proposed the Smoothed Projected Landweber (SPL) algorithm with a low computational complexity to ensure the better RD performance. However, the SPL algorithm adopts a fixed sparse representation basis (e.g., DCT and wavelet basis) which cannot change adaptively according to the image content in the process of iteration; therefore the potential to improve the reconstruction quality is not developed completely. The Principal Component Analysis (PCA) [15] is the optimal orthogonal transformation matrix to remove spatial redundancy of image; our previous work [16] uses PCA to update continually the sparse representation basis at each SPL iteration. Adapted by the image statistical property, the PCA-based SPL algorithm guarantees the performance improvement. The defect of our previous work is that we ignore the stationary local structural characteristic of image when learning PCA matrix. This defect suppresses the performance improvement of PCA decorrelation, which results in the degradation of reconstructed image by the SPL algorithm.

Aimed at the problem that PCA cannot exploit the stationary local structural characteristic of image to update the sparse representation basis at each SPL iteration, this paper proposes the adaptive reconstruction algorithm based on Granular Computing (GrC) theory [17]. The proposed method divides the image into several granules, in which any granule is a set of image patches with the similar structural characteristic. We use PCA to learn the corresponding optimal representation basis of each granule so as to obtain the efficient hard-thresholding shrinkage. Experimental results show that the proposed algorithm can improve the RD performance of image CS and achieve the better subjective visual quality.

This paper will explore the adaptive granular reconstruction in block CS of images. First of all, we briefly introduce the background of block CS and GrC-based clustering, and then we describe the adaptive reconstruction algorithm in detail. Afterward, the experimental results are shown and discussed, and finally we make a conclusion on the paper.

2. Background

2.1. Image Block CS. When applied in image acquisition, CS has high time and space complexity, which may be computationally expensive for some real-world systems. Hence, most of existing image CS approaches [9, 13, 14, 16] split the images into nonoverlapping blocks, and, at the decoder, each block is recovered independently in the recovery algorithm. To the best of our knowledge, the pioneering work of block CS was proposed by Gan [13]. This work was further extended by Gan

[13] and Mun and Fowler [14] to improve the performance of block CS. Block CS framework is described as follows. First of all, an $I_c \times I_r$ image $\mathbf{x}$ with $N = I_c I_r$ pixels is divided into n small blocks with size of $B \times B$ pixels each. Let $\mathbf{x}_i$ represent the vectorized signal of the ith block ($i = 1, 2, \ldots, n$; $n = N/B^2$) through raster scanning. Construct $B^2 \times B^2$ random Gaussian matrix, and get orthogonal matrix $\mathbf{\Omega}$ by orthonormalizing the Gaussian matrix. Then, we randomly pick $M_B(\ll B^2)$ rows from $\mathbf{\Theta}$ to produce the block measurement matrix $\mathbf{\Phi}_B$. Finally, the corresponding observation vector $\mathbf{y}_i$ of each block is obtained by measuring $\mathbf{x}_i$ with $\mathbf{\Phi}_B$ as follows:

$$\mathbf{y}_i = \mathbf{\Phi}_B \mathbf{x}_i. \tag{1}$$

There are M CS observed values for the original image ($M = n \times M_B$), and the total measurement matrix $\mathbf{\Phi}$ is a block diagonal matrix, in which each diagonal element is $\mathbf{\Phi}_B$; that is,

$$\mathbf{\Phi} = \begin{bmatrix} \mathbf{\Phi}_B & & & \\ & \mathbf{\Phi}_B & & \\ & & \ddots & \\ & & & \mathbf{\Phi}_B \end{bmatrix}. \tag{2}$$

The block CS can compute an initial image to accelerate the reconstruction process by adopting the linear Minimum Mean Square Error (MMSE) criterion. The MMSE solution of image block can be computed as follows:

$$\widehat{\mathbf{x}}_i^{(0)} = \mathbf{R}_{xx} \mathbf{\Phi}_B^T \left(\mathbf{\Phi}_B \mathbf{R}_{xx} \mathbf{\Phi}_B^T \right)^{-1}, \quad i = 1, \ldots, n$$

$$\mathbf{R}_{xx}$$

$$= \begin{bmatrix} 1 & \rho & \cdots & \rho^{\sqrt{2}(B-1)} \\ \rho & 1 & \cdots & \rho^{\sqrt{(B-2)^2+(B-1)^2}} \\ \vdots & \vdots & \ddots & \vdots \\ \rho^{\sqrt{2}(B-1)} & \rho^{\sqrt{(B-2)^2+(B-1)^2}} & \cdots & 1 \end{bmatrix}, \tag{3}$$

in which ρ ranges from 0.9 to 1. We set ρ and B to be 0.95 and 32, respectively, by experience.

When reconstructing image, we can construct the relationship model between the block observation vector $\mathbf{y}_i$ and a whole image $\mathbf{x}$:

$$\mathbf{y} = \begin{bmatrix} \mathbf{y}_1 \\ \mathbf{y}_2 \\ \vdots \\ \mathbf{y}_n \end{bmatrix} = \begin{bmatrix} \mathbf{\Phi}_B & & & \\ & \mathbf{\Phi}_B & & \\ & & \ddots & \\ & & & \mathbf{\Phi}_B \end{bmatrix} \begin{bmatrix} \mathbf{x}_1 \\ \mathbf{x}_2 \\ \vdots \\ \mathbf{x}_n \end{bmatrix} = \mathbf{\Phi} \cdot \mathbf{E} \mathbf{x}$$

$$= \mathbf{\Theta} \mathbf{x}, \tag{4}$$

in which $\mathbf{E}$ is the elementary matrix to rearrange the column vectors block by block to a raster scanning column vector of image, and $\mathbf{\Theta} = \mathbf{\Phi} \cdot \mathbf{E}$. The minimum l_1-l_2 norm reconstruction model can be constructed by using (4) as follows:

$$\hat{\mathbf{x}} = \arg\min_{\mathbf{x}} \left\{ \|\mathbf{y} - \mathbf{\Theta}\mathbf{x}\|_2^2 + \lambda \|\mathbf{\Psi}\mathbf{x}\|_1 \right\}, \qquad (5)$$

in which $\| \cdot \|_1$ and $\| \cdot \|_2$ denote l_1 and l_2 norm, respectively, $\mathbf{\Psi}$ is the sparse representation basis, and λ is the fixed regularization factor. Equation (5) can be solved by using the SPL algorithm with a low computational complexity; in particular $\mathbf{\Psi}$ can be updated flexibly at each SPL iteration. Therefore, the PCA can be used to learn the adaptive sparse representation basis.

2.2. GrC-Based Clustering.
GrC is proposed by Zadeh in 1979, and he said that the information granule exists widely in our daily life and it can be viewed as an abstraction of actual object. Granulating, organization, and causality are three important concepts of GrC [18]; that is, the granulating divides a whole of the object into several parts, the organization combines several parts into a whole by some specific operators, and the causality is used to model the relationship between the cause and its result. In the above, there is a natural relation between GrC and clustering. The training set can be regarded as the object, and each sample in training set is defined as a single granule. From the above views, we can see that the granulating and organization correspond to the clustering and its inverse, respectively, and the causality describes the internal relation between samples. Different from the traditional clustering method (e.g., K-means [19]), the GrC-based clustering chooses a variety of shapes to flexibly represent a granule, and the relationship between granules can be modeled by using the more mature algebraic system; therefore the GrC-based clustering has better generalization ability.

Although the group of points in training set has irregular shape, their borders can be better distinguished by GrC-based clustering, since GrC can express the granule as various shapes, for example, hyperdiamond, hypersphere, and hyperbox. The vector form of granule is denoted as $\mathbf{G} = (\mathbf{c}, \mathrm{gr})$, in which $\mathbf{c}$ is the center of granule and gr is the granularity. Denote $\mathbf{c}_i$ as a point contained in the granule $\mathbf{G}$, and the granularity of $\mathbf{G}$ is computed by

$$\mathrm{gr} = \max_i \|\mathbf{c} - \mathbf{c}_i\|_p, \qquad (6)$$

in which $\|\cdot\|_p$ is p-norm to measure the distance. The different distance measure represents the different shape of granule; for example, $p = 1$ expresses the corresponding granule as hyperdiamond granule, $p = 2$ expresses the corresponding granule as hypersphere, and $p = \infty$ expresses the corresponding granule as hyperbox granule. The operators between granules include the merge operator $\vee$ and the decomposing operator $\wedge$. The merge operator $\vee$ is to merge two smaller granules into a big one, and the decomposition operator $\wedge$ is to decompose a big granule into two smaller ones, in which the merge operator $\vee$ is used to cluster the samples in the training set. The merge granules of two granules $\mathbf{G}_1 = (\mathbf{c}_1, r_1)$ and $\mathbf{G}_2 = (\mathbf{c}_2, r_2)$ are merged as a new granule:

$$\mathbf{G}_1 \vee \mathbf{G}_2 = \frac{1}{2} \left(\mathbf{P} + \mathbf{Q}, \|\mathbf{P} - \mathbf{Q}\|_p \right), \qquad (7)$$

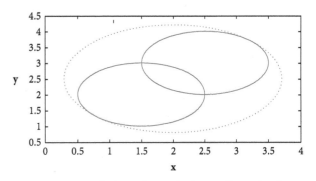

FIGURE 1: Merging of spherical granules in two-dimensional space.

in which

$$\mathbf{P} = \mathbf{c}_1 - \frac{r_1}{\|\mathbf{c}_{12}\|_p},$$

$$\mathbf{Q} = \mathbf{c}_2 + \frac{r_2}{\|\mathbf{c}_{12}\|_p}, \qquad (8)$$

$$\mathbf{c}_{12} = \mathbf{c}_2 - \mathbf{c}_1.$$

Figure 1 illustrates the merging of two spherical granules $\mathbf{G}_1 = (1.0, 2.0, 2.0)$ and $\mathbf{G}_2 = (2.5, 2.5, 2.5)$ in the two-dimensional space, and their merging result is $\mathbf{G}_1 \vee \mathbf{G}_2 = (1.75, 2.25, 1.75)$.

According to the vectorized representation of granule, the relation between granules inevitably involves the relation between vectors, but the partial order relation between vectors is not consistent with inclusion relation between granules. Therefore, we regard that the fuzzy inclusion relation exists between granules. When merging granules, we measure the fuzzy inclusion relation as follows:

$$\mu(\mathbf{G}_1, \mathbf{G}_2) = \frac{v(\mathbf{G}_2)}{v(\mathbf{G}_1 \vee \mathbf{G}_2)}, \qquad (9)$$

in which $v(\mathbf{G}) : \mathbf{G} \to R$ is a mapping from the space of granule to the space of real numbers, and this mapping $v(\mathbf{G})$ uses the following formula:

$$v(\mathbf{x}) = \sum_i \sin\left(\frac{\pi x_i}{2}\right). \qquad (10)$$

Aimed to the training set $\mathbf{S}$ in the clustering problem, we construct an algebra system $\langle \mathbf{G}, \mu \rangle$, which is made up of the granule set $\mathbf{G}$, the fuzzy inclusion relation $\mu(\cdot, \cdot)$, and merge operator $\vee$. By the fuzzy inclusion relation between granules, we control the granule merging and divide gradually $\mathbf{S}$ into a number of granules in order for each granule to be corresponding to a category. Figure 2 shows the GrC-based clustering results of spherical and square granules in the two-dimensional space; we can see that the GrC performs the granule merging by using the fuzzy inclusion relation and the granularity, which guarantees the better clustering performance; in particular the control of inclusion relation is very beneficial to distinguish the ownership of the training samples in the border. In a natural image signal, some relations exist between image blocks in the spatial domain.

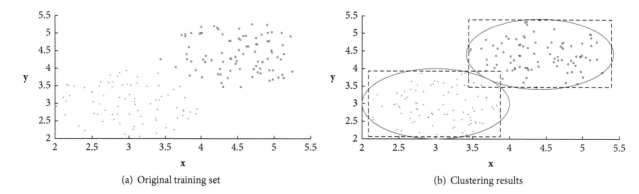

(a) Original training set

(b) Clustering results

FIGURE 2: GrC clustering results of spherical and square granules in two-dimensional space.

Depending on this experience, the GrC-based clustering divides automatically a whole image into several regions including blocks according to the image content. In each cluster, the structure feature of any block is very similar to others; thus it is more conducive to find the sparse representation basis adapted to the fixed data pattern.

3. Adaptive Granular Reconstruction

3.1. SPL Iteration. In the framework of block CS, the convex optimization algorithm (e.g., NESTA [10]) can be only used to independently reconstruct each block. However, the varying block sparsity results in the uneven qualities of reconstructed blocks due to the different local structure characteristics of image. The uneven reconstructed qualities bring about lots of blocking artifacts. In addition, the small block size restricts the performance of block reconstruction, which makes the reconstructed image contain a lot of noises. Aimed to the above problem, Gan [13] proposed the image reconstruction algorithm based on SPL iteration by combining Projection Onto Convex Set (POCS), hard-thresholding shrinkage, and wiener filtering. The SPL algorithm guarantees the better reconstruction performance with a low computational complexity. The flow of SPL algorithm is presented as shown in the following

The Flow of SPL Iteration

Task. Find the optimal solution $\widehat{\mathbf{x}}$ of model (5).

> *Input*: block CS observation vector $\mathbf{y}_i$, $i = 1, 2, \ldots, n$; block measurement matrix $\boldsymbol{\Phi}_B$; sparse representation basis $\boldsymbol{\Psi}$; regularization factor λ for hard thresholding.
>
> *Initialization*: set the initial MMSE linear estimator $\widehat{\mathbf{x}}_i^{(0)} = \mathbf{R}_{xx}\boldsymbol{\Phi}_B^T(\boldsymbol{\Phi}_B\mathbf{R}_{xx}\boldsymbol{\Phi}_B^T)^{-1}$, $i = 1, 2, \ldots, n$.
>
> *Main iteration*: increment k by 1, and apply these steps:
>
> (i) Weiner filtering: the Winner filter with 3×3 sliding window is performed to process $\widehat{\mathbf{x}}^{(k)}$ as follows:
>
> $$\widehat{\overline{\mathbf{x}}}^{(k)} = \text{Wiener}\left(\widehat{\mathbf{x}}^{(k)}, [3 \; 3]\right). \tag{11}$$

(ii) POCS: the filtered image is projected into the convex set $\mathbf{C}$; that is,

$$\overline{\mathbf{x}}_i^{(k)} = \widehat{\overline{\mathbf{x}}}_i^{(k)} + \boldsymbol{\Phi}_B^T\left(y_i - \boldsymbol{\Phi}_B\widehat{\overline{\mathbf{x}}}_i^{(k)}\right), \quad i = 1, \ldots, n. \tag{12}$$

(iii) Hard-thresholding shrinkage: transform $\overline{\mathbf{x}}^{(k)}$ by using the sparse representation basis $\boldsymbol{\Psi}$, and perform the hard-thresholding shrinkage as follows:

$$\underline{\mathbf{x}}^{(k)} = \boldsymbol{\Psi}\overline{\mathbf{x}}^{(k)}.$$

$$\sigma^{(k)} = \frac{\text{median}\left(\left|\underline{\mathbf{x}}^{(k)}\right|\right)}{0.6745}$$

$$\widetilde{\mathbf{x}}^{(k)} = \text{Threshold}\left(\underline{\mathbf{x}}^{(k)}, \lambda\right) \tag{13}$$

$$= \begin{cases} \underline{\mathbf{x}}^{(k)}, & \left|\underline{\mathbf{x}}^{(k)}\right| > \lambda\sigma^{(k)}\sqrt{2\log N} \\ 0, & \text{else}, \end{cases}$$

$$\widehat{\mathbf{x}}^{(k)} = \boldsymbol{\Psi}^{-1}\widetilde{\mathbf{x}}^{(k)}$$

(iv) POCS: perform the POCS operator again:

$$\widehat{\mathbf{x}}_i^{(k+1)} = \widehat{\mathbf{x}}_i^{(k)} + \boldsymbol{\Phi}_B^T\left(\mathbf{y}_i - \boldsymbol{\Phi}_B\widehat{\mathbf{x}}_i^{(k)}\right), \quad i = 1, \ldots, n. \tag{14}$$

(v) Stopping rule: stop when $|D^{(k+1)} - D^{(k)}| < \varepsilon$, where $D^{(k)} = \|\widehat{\mathbf{x}}^{(k)} - \overline{\mathbf{x}}^{(k-1)}\|_2/\sqrt{N}$; ε is the stopping tolerance.

Output: the reconstructed image $\widehat{\mathbf{x}}$.

Due to the presence of blocking artifacts and noise in the MMSE linear estimator, we firstly use the 3×3 Wiener filter to reduce the blocking artifacts and smoothen the image. Afterward, the filtered image is projected to the convex set $\mathbf{C} = \{\mathbf{x}_i : \mathbf{y}_i = \boldsymbol{\Phi}_B\mathbf{x}_i, i = 1, \ldots, n\}$ again, and the transformation coefficients on the sparse representation basis $\boldsymbol{\Psi}$ are shrunk by the hard thresholding to eliminate further noises. Finally, the POCS is performed again to enforce the image into the convex set $\mathbf{C}$. Repeat the above flow until meeting the stopping criterion. In the process of hard-thresholding shrinkage, the solution is not sparse due to the existence of noises. We can get the more sparse transformation coefficients by enforcing the noise components to 0.

3.2. GrC-Based PCA Hard-Thresholding Shrinkage.

Whether the hard-thresholding shrinkage can eliminate the noises effectively is important for the reconstruction performance of SPL iteration. Gan [13] performs the hard-thresholding operator in the overlapping block DCT and the undecimated wavelet domain, but they cannot better capture the directional characteristics (e.g., point, line, and edge) so as to degrade the reconstructed quality of image. To overcome the above defects, Mun and Fowler [14] proposed the bivariate shrinkage based on directional transform (e.g., contour and double-tree wavelet), which achieves some performance improvements. The above-mentioned methods focus the useful information as much as possible on a few transformation coefficients by constructing some specific wavelets and remove lots of transform coefficients with little information to suppress noises. According to [20], when performing the hard-thresholding shrinkage, it is more effective to capture the important information by learning the dictionary adapted by image content than by constructing the specific wavelet. However, the dictionary learning algorithms (e.g., K-SVD algorithm [21]) have a high computational complexity; therefore the dictionary learning algorithm is not suited to the SPL iteration requiring a low computational complexity. Our previous work [16] proposed the PCA-based hard-thresholding shrinkage to suppress noises. These methods extract the image patches from the noisy image as samples and perform the PCA to train the orthogonal transformation matrix which removes the spatial correlation. Since the PCA matrix can better separate useful components and useless noises existing in image, the hard-thresholding shrinkage gets some performance improvements. In addition, the PCA-based hard-thresholding shrinkage has a low computational complexity; thus it is so suitable to SPL iteration. Due to the fact that the image has only locally stationary statistics and varying structural characteristics globally, the training set composed by global patches will generate a single PCA matrix with the poor ability to extract the sparse coefficients. Depending on the local stationary statistics of image, it is more practical to divide the global patches into several subsets which contain the patches with similar structural characteristics, and PCA is used to generate the sparse representation basis of each subset. These PCA matrices are specialized to some particular structure characteristics; thus they guarantee that all samples in subset have the more sparse representations.

According to the above-mentioned viewpoints, we firstly cluster image patches before using PCA to learn the sparse representation basis. K-means [19] is a popular clustering algorithm, but it requires setting the number of clusters in advance, so that the training set cannot be classified adaptively in terms of the data pattern. Due to the nonstationary statistical characteristics of image, a large difference exists between the structure features of patches; thus K-means is not appropriate for the classification of image patches. The GrC does not need to set a fixed number of clusters, and it can achieve the suitable number of clusters by controlling the threshold of granularity to merge the granules depending on the fuzzy inclusion relation between granules. Therefore, we use the GrC to cluster image patches according to the data pattern of training set. The steps of GrC-based PCA hard-thresholding shrinkage are described as follows.

Step 1. We extract all m patches with the size of $d = W_p \times W_p$ from the noisy image $\bar{\mathbf{x}}^{(k)}$ and denote these patches as $\mathbf{p}_i$ ($i = 1, \ldots, m$). The upper-left pixel of patch $\mathbf{p}_i$ is corresponding to the ith pixel; thus each pixel is corresponding to a patch. There are overlapping pixels between patches, and those pixels beyond the border of image cannot be extracted; that is, $m = (I_c - W_p) \times (I_r - W_p)$.

Step 2. We use $\mathbf{p}_i$ as the finest atom to constitute the training set $\mathbf{S}$ and set the control parameter ρ of granularity. The merge operator $\vee$ is used to merge the granule conditionally until all training samples are contained in some granule, and finally each granule corresponds to a category. The flow of clustering is shown in the following.

The Flow of Dividing the Training Set $\mathbf{S}$ Using GrC Clustering

Task. Merge the samples in $\mathbf{S}$ into several granules according to the specified conditions.

> *Input*: the training set $\mathbf{S} = \{\mathbf{p}_1, \mathbf{p}_2, \ldots, \mathbf{p}_m\}$ and the threshold T of granularity.
>
> *Initialization*: use the m samples in $\mathbf{S}$ to induce m granule atoms; that is, the sample $\mathbf{p}_l$ corresponds to the hyperbox granule atom $\mathbf{G}_l = \{\mathbf{p}_l, \mathbf{p}_l, 0\}$, in which the first entry is the starting point, the second entry is the terminal point, and the third entry is the granularity. In the above, we obtain the initial hyperbox granule set $\mathbf{GS} = \{\mathbf{G}_1, \mathbf{G}_2, \ldots, \mathbf{G}_L\}$, $L = m$.
>
> *Main iteration*: increment i by 1 to m, and apply these steps:

> (i) Compute the fuzzy inclusions between $\mathbf{G}_i$ and other granules of $\mathbf{GS}$; that is, $\mu_{il} = \mu(\mathbf{G}_i, \mathbf{G}_l)$, $l = 1, \ldots, L$.
>
> (ii) Select the index Q of granule with the maximum fuzzy inclusion; that is, $Q = \arg \min_l \mu_{il}$.
>
> (iii) Compute the granularity $\rho_i = \|\mathbf{G}_i - \mathbf{G}_Q\|_2$, and judge whether to merge granules $\mathbf{G}_i$ and $\mathbf{G}_Q$: if $\rho_i \le T$, $\mathbf{G}_i$ and $\mathbf{G}_Q$ are merged into a new granule $\mathbf{G}_i \vee \mathbf{G}_Q$; otherwise $\mathbf{G}_i$ is still a member in $\mathbf{GS}$.
>
> (iv) Update the training set $\mathbf{S}$, that is, to remove $\mathbf{p}_i$ from $\mathbf{S}$.
>
> (v) Stop the above iteration once $\mathbf{S}$ is empty.

> *Output*: hyperbox granule set $\mathbf{GS}$.

By this flow, we can get the granule set $\mathbf{GS} = \{\mathbf{G}_1, \mathbf{G}_2, \ldots, \mathbf{G}_L\}$ composed of L granules.

Step 3. We compute the $d \times d$ covariance matrix $\boldsymbol{\Sigma}_l$ of the lth granule $\mathbf{G}_l$ as follows:

$$\boldsymbol{\Sigma}_l = \frac{1}{|\mathbf{G}_l|} \sum_{\mathbf{p}_i \in \mathbf{G}_l} \mathbf{p}_i \mathbf{p}_i^T - \overline{\mathbf{p}}\, \overline{\mathbf{p}}^T,$$

$$\overline{\mathbf{p}} = \frac{1}{|\mathbf{G}_l|} \sum_{\mathbf{p}_i \in \mathbf{G}_l} \mathbf{p}_i, \tag{15}$$

in which $|\mathbf{G}_l|$ is the number of samples in $\mathbf{G}_l$.

Step 4. We compute the eigenvalues $\lambda_1 \geq \cdots \geq \lambda_d$ of $\boldsymbol{\Sigma}_l$ and their corresponding normalized eigenvectors $\mathbf{e}_1, \mathbf{e}_2, \ldots, \mathbf{e}_d$.

Step 5. The eigenvectors are used to construct the orthogonal transformation matrix $\boldsymbol{\Gamma}_l = [\mathbf{e}_1, \mathbf{e}_2, \ldots, \mathbf{e}_d]$, and we transform each patch into $\boldsymbol{\Gamma}_l$ domain as follows:

$$\widehat{\mathbf{p}}_i = \boldsymbol{\Gamma}_l^T \cdot \mathbf{p}_i. \tag{16}$$

Step 6. The hard-thresholding shrinkage is performed as follows:

$$\widehat{\widehat{\mathbf{p}}}_i = \begin{cases} \widehat{\mathbf{p}}_i, & |\widehat{\mathbf{p}}_i| \geq \lambda\sigma \\ 0, & \text{else,} \end{cases}$$

$$\sigma = \frac{\text{median}\,(|\widehat{\mathbf{p}}|)}{0.6745}, \tag{17}$$

$$\widehat{\mathbf{p}} = \left[\widehat{\mathbf{p}}_1^T, \widehat{\mathbf{p}}_2^T, \ldots, \widehat{\mathbf{p}}_{|\mathbf{G}_l|}^T \right].$$

Step 7. The thresholding coefficients $\widehat{\widehat{\mathbf{p}}}_i$ are transformed inversely into the pixel domain; that is,

$$\widetilde{\mathbf{p}}_i = \boldsymbol{\Gamma}_l \cdot \widehat{\widehat{\mathbf{p}}}_i. \tag{18}$$

Step 8. We combine all patches into a whole image after shrinking all patches in $\mathbf{G}_l$. Because of the existence of overlapped area between patches, these pixels in overlapped area are computed by averaging all pixel values at the same position.

By the above flow, each granule corresponds to a PCA matrix, and the additional computational complexity $O(m \cdot W_p^2)$ is from the GrC clustering. Therefore, the GrC-based PCA learning algorithm maintains a low computational complexity when compared with the computations of learning global PCA matrix.

4. Experimental Results and Analysis

The performances of proposed algorithm are evaluated on the five 512×512 test images *Lenna*, *Barbara*, *Parrot*, *Leaves*, and *House* including the varying smooth, edge, and texture components. Its parameter settings are described as follows: the regularization factor λ is 2.5, the stopping tolerance ε of SPL iteration is 0.01, the patch size W_p is 7, and the threshold T of granularity is 0.03. On one hand, we evaluate the performance of hard-thresholding shrinkage based on the

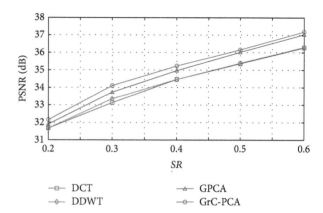

FIGURE 3: The comparison of hard-thresholding shrinkage performances under the different sparse representation bases.

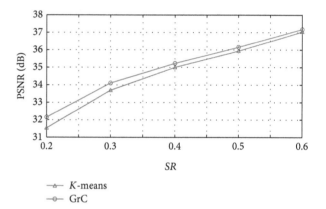

FIGURE 4: The comparison of hard-thresholding shrinkage performances under the different clustering methods.

different sparse representation bases. The proposed algorithm uses the GrC-based PCA basis, which is abbreviated to GrC-PCA, and we select the comparing bases including DCT basis, Double-Tree Discrete Wavelet Transform (DDWT) basis, and Global PCA basis (GPCA). On the other hand, we compare the reconstruction performance of proposed algorithm with the MH based SPL (MH_SPL) algorithm [9], the NESTA algorithm with the minimum TV (NESTA_TV) [10], and the Group-based Sparse Recovery (GSR) algorithm [11]. In all experiments, the block size B is 32; the preset total measurement rate SR is set from 0.2 to 0.6. The Peak Signal-to-Noise Ratio (PSNR) is used to evaluate the objective performance, and all PSNR values are averaged over 5 trials, since the quality of reconstruction can vary due to the randomness of random transformation matrix $\boldsymbol{\Phi}_B$. All experiments run under the following computer configuration: Intel(R) Core(TM) i7 @ 3.40 GHz CPU, 8 GB RAM, Microsoft Windows 7 32 bits, and MATLAB Version 7.6.0.324 (R2008a).

4.1. Performance Comparison of Hard-Thresholding Shrinkage. Figure 3 presents the average RD performance on the five test images of the SPL algorithm with the hard-thresholding shrinkages based on DCT, DDWT, GPCA, and GrC-PCA.

(a) NESTA_TV

(b) MH_SPL

(c) GSR

(d) Proposed

FIGURE 5: Comparison of visual qualities using the different methods to reconstruct *Lenna* image when the measurement rate is 0.3.

We can see that our GrC-PCA basis obtains the highest PSNR value among all bases at any measurement rate, and particularly it has about 1 dB gains compared to the DCT basis. Our GrC-PCA basis exploits the local stationary structural characteristics of image; thus the PSNR of GrC-PCA basis is 0.2 dB larger than GPCA basis. Figure 4 shows the performance of hard-threshold shrinkage using different clustering algorithms. We can see that the RD performance degrades once using the traditional K-means algorithm. However, the PSNR value obtains the obvious improvement at any measurement rate when using the GrC-based clustering method; particularly when the measurement rate is 0.2, the PSNR gain of GrC-PCA is around 0.6 dB.

4.2. Comparison of Reconstruction Performance. To evaluate the RD performance of our GrC-PCA-based SPL algorithm, we select the popular reconstruction algorithms as benchmarks, and they include MH_SPL [9], NESTA_TV [10], and GSR [11]. Table 1 lists the average PSNR value on the five test images when the measurement rate ranges from 0.2 to 0.4. We can see that our method obviously outperforms

TABLE 1: Comparison of average PSNR values of the 5 test images using the different methods.

Reconstruction algorithm	Measurement rate SR			
	0.2	0.3	0.4	Average
MH_SPL	31.62	33.52	34.82	33.32
NESTA_TV	28.56	30.89	32.15	30.53
GSR	32.56	34.82	35.95	34.44
Proposed	32.12	34.08	35.21	33.80

MH_SPL and the NESTA_TV, and it obtains the PSNR gain of 0.48 dB and 3.27 dB, respectively. However, when compared with the GSR algorithm, the proposed algorithm in this paper deteriorates 0.64 dB on average, which results from the fact that the GSR uses both the local stationary statistics of image and nonlocal similarities of patches. Therefore, the GSR obtains more sparse representation compared to GrC-PCA. However, it can be observed from Table 2 that the GSR algorithm has a high computational complexity, and it requires 2542.65 s to reconstruct *Lenna* on average, but our algorithm

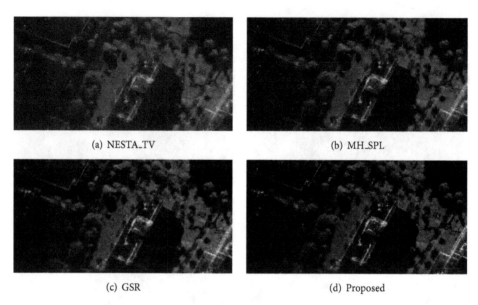

(a) NESTA_TV

(b) MH_SPL

(c) GSR

(d) Proposed

FIGURE 6: Comparison of visual qualities using the different methods to reconstruct *Kirtland* image when the measurement rate is 0.3.

TABLE 2: Comparison of consumed times when using the different methods to reconstruct *Lenna* image.

Reconstruction algorithm	Measurement rate *SR*			
	0.2	0.3	0.4	Average
MH_SPL	6.59	12.52	15.88	11.66
NESTA_TV	44.98	44.63	44.81	44.81
GSR	2272.15	2519.23	2836.56	2542.65
Proposed	32.05	30.61	27.95	30.20

requires only 30.20 s. In the above, when considering both the reconstruction quality and computational complexity, the proposed algorithm is more practical than GSR. Compared with the DDWT-based MH_SPL algorithm, our algorithm increases 18.54 s on average, which results from the fact that PCA needs to relearn the sparse representation basis at each iteration, so that the proposed algorithm obtains the PSNR improvement at the cost of computational complexity. Figure 5 shows the visual qualities of reconstructed *Lenna* using the different algorithms when the measurement rate is 0.3; we can see that the reconstructed image by NESTA_TV contains lots of blocking artifacts, and MH_SPL algorithm eliminates the blocking artifacts but introduces the noises. However, our algorithm gets the subjective visual quality similar to the GSR algorithm. Figure 6 shows the visual qualities of reconstructed remote sensing image *Kirtland* using the different algorithms when the measurement rate is 0.3. It can be observed that our method provides better visual quality for the remote sensing application when compared the other reconstruction algorithms.

5. Conclusion

In this paper, we use the GrC-based clustering to improve the performance of PCA-based hard-thresholding shrinkage in the SPL iteration. Considering the local stationary statistical property, the image is firstly decomposed into some granules. Since GrC can divide adaptively the training set according to the data pattern, the samples in granule have the similar structure. Then, the PCA is performed to learn the sparse representation basis dedicated to the granule, and the patches in granule are shrunk by the hard thresholding using PCA matrix. Finally, all patches merge into a whole image. The experimental results show that the proposed algorithm has better RD performance and guarantees the better subjective visual quality of reconstructed image with a low computational complexity.

Competing Interests

The authors declare that there are no competing interests regarding the publication of this paper.

Acknowledgments

This work was supported in part by the National Natural Science Foundation of China under Grants nos. 61501393 and 61572417, in part by the Key Scientific Research Project of Colleges and Universities in Henan Province of China under Grant no. 16A520069, and in part by Youth Sustentation Fund of Xinyang Normal University under Grant no. 2015-QN-043.

References

[1] P. Guo, J. Wang, B. Li, and S. Lee, "A variable threshold-value authentication architecture for wireless mesh networks," *Journal of Internet Technology*, vol. 15, no. 6, pp. 929–936, 2014.

[2] J. Wu, F. Liu, L. C. Jiao, and X. Wang, "Compressive sensing SAR image reconstruction based on Bayesian framework and evolutionary computation," *IEEE Transactions on Image Processing*, vol. 20, no. 7, pp. 1904–1911, 2011.

[3] S. Xie and Y. Wang, "Construction of tree network with limited delivery latency in homogeneous wireless sensor networks," *Wireless Personal Communications*, vol. 78, no. 1, pp. 231–246, 2014.

[4] E. J. Candes, J. Romberg, and T. Tao, "Robust uncertainty principles: exact signal reconstruction from highly incomplete frequency information," *IEEE Transactions on Information Theory*, vol. 52, no. 2, pp. 489–509, 2006.

[5] D. L. Donoho, "Compressed sensing," *IEEE Transactions on Information Theory*, vol. 52, no. 4, pp. 1289–1306, 2006.

[6] C. Deng, W. Lin, B.-S. Lee, and C. T. Lau, "Robust image coding based upon compressive sensing," *IEEE Transactions on Multimedia*, vol. 14, no. 2, pp. 278–290, 2012.

[7] X. Gao, M. Yu, J. Wang, and J. Wei, "l_0 sparsity for image denoising with local and global priors," *Advances in Multimedia*, vol. 2015, Article ID 386134, 9 pages, 2015.

[8] S. Xiao, "Deblurring by solving a TV^p-Regularized optimization problem using split bregman method," *Advances in Multimedia*, vol. 2014, Article ID 906464, 11 pages, 2014.

[9] C. Chen, E. W. Tramel, and J. E. Fowler, "Compressed-sensing recovery of images and video using multihypothesis predictions," in *Proceedings of the 45th Asilomar Conference on Signals, Systems and Computers (ASILOMAR '11)*, pp. 1193–1198, Pacific Grove, Calif, USA, November 2011.

[10] S. Becker, J. Bobin, and E. J. Candes, "NESTA: a fast and accurate first-order method for sparse recovery," *SIAM Journal on Imaging Sciences*, vol. 4, no. 1, pp. 1–39, 2011.

[11] J. Zhang, D. Zhao, and W. Gao, "Group-based sparse representation for image restoration," *IEEE Transactions on Image Processing*, vol. 23, no. 8, pp. 3336–3351, 2014.

[12] X. Wu, W. Dong, X. Zhang, and G. Shi, "Model-assisted adaptive recovery of compressed sensing with imaging applications," *IEEE Transactions on Image Processing*, vol. 21, no. 2, pp. 451–458, 2012.

[21] M. Aharon, M. Elad, and A. Bruckstein, "K-SVD: an algorithm for designing overcomplete dictionaries for sparse representation," *IEEE Transactions on Signal Processing*, vol. 54, no. 11, pp. 4311–4322, 2006.

[13] L. Gan, "Block compressed sensing of natural images," in *Proceedings of the International Conference on Digital Signal Processing*, pp. 403–406, 2007.

[14] S. Mun and J. E. Fowler, "Block compressed sensing of images using directional transforms," in *Proceedings of the 2009 16th IEEE International Conference on Image Processing (ICIP '09)*, pp. 3021–3024, Cairo, Egypt, November 2009.

[15] C. A. Deledalle, J. Salmon, and A. Dalalyan, "Image denoising with patch based PCA: local versus global," in *Proceedings of the 22nd British Machine Vision Conference*, pp. 1–10, 2011.

[16] R. Li and X. Zhu, "A PCA-based smoothed projected Landweber algorithm for block compressed sensing image reconstruction," in *Proceedings of the 4th International Conference on Image Analysis and Signal Processing (IASP '12)*, pp. 1–6, November 2012.

[17] L. A. Zadeh, *Fuzzy Sets and Information Granulation*, North Holland, Amsterdam, The Netherlands, 1979.

[18] L. A. Zadeh, "Toward a theory of fuzzy information granulation and its centrality in human reasoning and fuzzy logic," *Fuzzy Sets and Systems*, vol. 90, no. 2, pp. 111–127, 1997.

[19] C. M. Bishop, *Pattern Recognition and Machine Learning*, Springer, New York, NY, USA, 2006.

[20] M. Elad and M. Aharon, "Image denoising via sparse and redundant representations over learned dictionaries," *IEEE Transactions on Image Processing*, vol. 15, no. 12, pp. 3736–3745, 2006.

Efficient Gabor Phase Based Illumination Invariant for Face Recognition

Chunnian Fan,[1,2] **Shuiping Wang,**[1,2] **and Hao Zhang**[2]

[1]*Jiangsu Engineering Center of Network Monitoring, Nanjing University of Information Science and Technology, Nanjing 210044, China*
[2]*School of Computer and Software, Nanjing University of Information Science and Technology, Nanjing 210044, China*

Correspondence should be addressed to Chunnian Fan; yuuqingnuist@163.com

Academic Editor: Haoran Xie

This paper presents a novel Gabor phase based illumination invariant extraction method aiming at eliminating the effect of varying illumination on face recognition. Firstly, It normalizes varying illumination on face images, which can reduce the effect of varying illumination to some extent. Secondly, a set of 2D real Gabor wavelet with different directions is used for image transformation, and multiple Gabor coefficients are combined into one whole in considering spectrum and phase. Lastly, the illumination invariant is obtained by extracting the phase feature from the combined coefficients. Experimental results on the Yale B and the CMU PIE face database show that our method obtained a significant improvement over other related methods for face recognition under large illumination variation condition.

1. Introduction

Face recognition has attracted much interest for its wide application. Although great progress has been made according to related researches [1, 2], many issues still remain unresolved, including varying illumination, pose, and expression problems. The varying illumination problem is intractable yet crucial and has to be dealt with. The illumination can change face appearance dramatically and thus will seriously affect the performance of face recognition system [3]. To address this problem, researchers have proposed many approaches, and these methods are mainly classified into three groups.

(1) Illumination Preprocessing. These approaches adopt image processing to remove lighting effects from face images to obtain illumination normalized face images [4, 5]. Tan and Triggs [6] proposed a preprocessing chain which combines Gamma correction (GC) and difference of Gaussian (DoG) with contrast equalization. It eliminates most of illumination effects while still preserving needed essential appearance details. Fan and Zhang [7] presented a homomorphic filtering (HF) based illumination normalization algorithm and obtained promising results. Recently, Lee et al. compensated

illumination using orientated local histogram equalization (OLHE), which encoded rich information on the edge orientations [8]. Illumination preprocessing methods are simple, effective, and efficient. However, they could not resolve extreme uneven illumination variations completely [3].

(2) Face Modeling. Illumination variations are mainly generated from the 3D shape of human faces under various lighting directions. A generative 3D face model has been constructed to render face images with different poses and illumination. Belhumeur et al. [9, 10] proposed an illumination cone named generative model, which uses an illumination convex cone to represent face images set with changing illumination conditions under fixed pose. They first construct an illumination convex cone using a great deal of images with varying lighting and then use a low-dimensional linear subspace to represent the cone approximated. Basri and Jacobs [11] found that a 9D linear subspace could approximate the set of images of a convex Lambertian object with varying lighting very well. These methods need images of the same subject with varying lighting and 3D shape information for training. However, these needs could not be met in real world. Therefore, the application of these methods is limited.

(3) Illumination Invariant Extraction. This kind of approach is the mainstream, which tries to extract illumination-robust facial features. Many methods are based on the Lambertian illumination model. In that model, a face image $f(x, y)$ under illumination conditions is generally regarded as a product $f(x, y) = i(x, y)r(x, y)$, where $r(x, y)$ is the reflectance component and $i(x, y)$ is the illumination component at each point (x, y) [12]. The objective is to extract the reflectance component $r(x, y)$, which is considered as the intrinsic information specific to each class. However, it is difficult to calculate the reflectance and the illuminance component from real images. A common assumption is that $i(x, y)$ varies slowly and mainly lies in low frequencies, while $r(x, y)$ can change abruptly and typically lies in high frequencies. Under this assumption, Jobson et al. [13] proposed the multiscale retinex (MSR) method which estimated the reflectance component as the ratio of the image and its low-pass version that served as estimate for the illumination component. Wang et al. [14] used a similar idea (with a different local filter, namely, the weighted Gaussian filter) in the Self Quotient Image (SQI), which was very simple and could be applied to any single image. However, the used weighted Gaussian filter can hardly keep sharp edges in low frequency illumination fields, and it needs experience and time to select proper parameter. Aiming at solving this problem, Chen et al. [15] replaced the weighted Gaussian filter by Logarithmic Total Variation (LTV) to improve SQI. In 2009, Zhang et al. [16] presented a wavelet-based illumination invariant method (WD), which extracted denoised high frequency component in wavelet domain as the reflectance component. Inspired by this, Cheng et al. [17] and Xie et al. [18] presented two similar illumination invariant extraction methods in the nonsubsampled Contourlet transform (NSCT) domain. In 2011, Chen et al. [19] utilized the scale invariant property of natural images to derive a Wiener filter approach to best separate the illumination invariant features from an image. Cao et al. [20] proposed a wavelet-based illumination invariant extraction approach while taking the correlation of neighboring wavelet coefficients into account in 2012. Recently, Song et al. [21] presented a novel illumination invariant, histogram-based descriptor, and Faraji and Qi [22] proposed a novel illumination invariant using logarithmic fractal dimension-based complete eight local directional patterns. Experiments show that these methods have achieved very good results. Chen et al. [23] revealed that the direction of the image gradient is insensitive to changes of illumination. Based on this, Zhang et al. [24] introduced the Gradientfaces method, which used the arctan of the ratio between y- and x-gradient of an image as Gradientfaces. Chen and Zhang [25] improved the Gradientfaces method by proposing multidirectional orthogonal gradient phase faces method.

Recent studies confirm that the phase also contains a lot of effective information for image feature extraction, comparing with the magnitude [26]. Based on this, Sao and Yegnanarayana [27] presented a 2D Fourier phase based face image representation, and Cheng et al. [28] presented a novel illumination invariant method, namely, multiscale principal contour direction (MPCD). Inspired by the above mentioned, based on Gabor wavelet's excellent visual physiology background and its powerful ability as a feature descriptor, we present a novel illumination invariant extraction method based on the Gabor wavelet phase (GF) in this paper. We first preprocess the face image by using a homomorphic filtering (HF) based illumination normalization algorithm [7]. Then a set of 2D real Gabor wavelet with different directions is used for image transformation. Finally, multiple Gabor coefficients are combined into one whole in considering both spectrum and phase information and the illumination invariant is obtained by extracting the phase feature from the combined coefficients. The 2D symmetric real Gabor wavelet is chosen in our method, which aims not only at avoiding the complexity of complex calculations, but also at fitting the symmetry of the face image itself.

The rest of this paper is organized as follows. Section 2 presents the proposed method in detail. The experimental results and our conclusions are shown in Sections 3 and 4, respectively.

2. Algorithm Description

Researchers have found that Gabor functions have the capability of modeling simple cells in the visual cortex of mammalian brains [29]. Thus, image analysis using Gabor functions is similar to perception in the human visual system. Frequency and orientation representations of Gabor filters are similar to those of the human visual system, and they are particularly appropriate for texture representation and discrimination.

In recent years, the Gabor wavelet transform has been widely used as an effective element in face recognition [26, 30–34]. Gabor wavelet transform is insensitive to external environment factors such as illumination, facial expressions, gestures, and occlusion [35]. For this reason, it has been widely used to extract robust facial feature. Most existing Gabor feature-based methods usually use the Gabor magnitude features and discard the phase features. However, studies have shown that the phase information contains a number of effective image features, and it is insensitive to illumination variation. Inspired by this, the Gabor phase features are extracted as illumination invariants in this paper.

The proposed illumination invariant extraction method consists of three steps. Firstly, a homomorphic filtering based illumination normalization method [7] is used to preprocess the face images. Secondly, a set of 2D real Gabor wavelet with different directions is used for image transformation. Lastly, multiple Gabor coefficients are combined into one whole in considering both spectrum and phase information, and the illumination invariant is obtained by extracting the phase feature from the combined coefficients.

2.1. Illumination Normalization. We use the method presented in the literature [7], which combines homomorphic filtering and histogram equalization. In our paper, this illumination normalization method is called HF + HQ for short. This preprocessing greatly corrects the uneven illumination effects.

2.2. 2D Gabor Wavelet Transform. Different Gabor wavelets can be obtained by using different kernel functions. In order to avoid the complexity of complex calculations, and to fit the symmetry of the face image itself, the 2D symmetric real Gabor wavelet is chosen in our method. The kernel function used in this paper is the following.

$$G(x, y, \theta_k, f)$$

$$= \exp\left(-\frac{1}{2}\left(\left(\frac{x'}{s_x}\right)^2 + \left(\frac{y'}{s_y}\right)^2\right)\right)\cos\left(2\pi f x'\right), \quad (1)$$

$$x' = x\cos\theta_k + y\sin\theta_k,$$

$$y' = y\cos\theta_k - x\sin\theta_k,$$

where f is the frequency of the sinusoidal function, s_x and s_y represent the spatial scaling coefficient along x- and y-axes, respectively, and θ_k is the orientation of Gabor filter. θ_k is defined by this formula.

$$\theta_k = \frac{\pi}{n}(k-1), \quad k = 1, 2, \ldots, n. \quad (2)$$

Here, n determines the number of the filter's orientation, and we set $n = 8$ in this paper. If s_x and s_y are selected, after the Gabor wavelet transform of an gray face image $f(x, y)$, we have

$$C(x, y, \theta_k, f) = f(x, y) \otimes G(x, y, \theta_k, f). \quad (3)$$

Here, $\otimes$ indicates convolution of the two functions. $C(x, y, \theta_k, f)$ is denoted as $C_{\theta_k, f}$ for short. All the Gabor wavelet transformed coefficients are denoted as follows.

$$\left\{C_{\theta_k, f}\right\}, \quad f = 0, 2, 4, 8, 16, 32; \quad k = 1, 2, \ldots, 8. \quad (4)$$

Figure 1 illustrates the spectrograms of a face image under the same frequency ($f = 0$) and 8 different orientations (θ_k).

2.3. Illumination Invariant Extraction. After 2D Gabor wavelet transforming, the set $\{C_{\theta_k, f}\}$ includes all the spectrum information under different orientations. In order to take the phase information into account, we define the complex wavelet coefficients as follows.

$$\overline{C}_{\theta_k, f} = C_{\theta_k, f} e^{i\theta_k}. \quad (5)$$

Then, summing up all the complex coefficients under the same frequency (f) aiming at reducing feature dimension, we have

$$S_f = \sum_{\theta_k = \pi/8}^{7\pi/8} \overline{C}_{\theta_k, f}. \quad (6)$$

The phase feature is calculated by this formula.

$$\Lambda_f(x, y) = \arctan\left|\frac{\text{Im}\left(S_f(x, y)\right)}{\text{Re}\left(S_f(x, y)\right)}\right|. \quad (7)$$

Here, $\text{Re}(S_f(x, y))$ and $\text{Im}(S_f(x, y))$ are the real and imaginary part of $S_f(x, y)$, respectively. In this paper, the phase feature $\Lambda_f(x, y)$ is considered as the illumination invariant. Figure 2 shows the illumination normalized face images and the obtained illumination invariant.

3. Experimental Results

In this section, the performance of the proposed method (GF) is compared with the existing methods including MSR, WD, LTV, Gradientfaces, and MPCD using Yale B [36] and CMU PIE [37]. Firstly, we present different illumination invariants in image form. Then, we compare their recognition performance by using Eigenfaces under the same experimental conditions. According to the FERET testing protocol [38], the Tops 1 and 3 recognition rate are tested.

3.1. Comparison of the Different Illumination Invariants. To prove the efficiency of different methods, Figure 3 shows some original images in the Yale B and their corresponding illumination invariants. As can be seen from the images, the GF method has removed most effects of the illumination variation and greatly reduced the intraclass difference.

3.2. Experimental Results for the Yale B. The face database of Yale B has 10 different persons, and each person has 9 poses, and each pose is captured by 64 different illumination conditions. In our experiments, the frontal images are used. And, based on the angle of light source direction, these images are classified into five subsets. They are subset 1 (0–12°), subset 2 (13°–25°), subset 3 (26°–50°), subset 4 (51°–77°), and subset 5 (others) [39]. All images are cropped and rescaled to 192×168 pixels with strict alignment. The five images of each subset (each row) for one person are shown in Figure 4, and their illumination invariants are extracted by GF method.

Firstly, we select subset 1 as the training set and others as the testing set. As can be seen from Figures 5 and 6 the proposed method (GF) outperforms MSR, WD, and LTV, and GF obtains outstanding results similar to the Gradientfaces and the MPCD method. The average Top 1 recognition rate is nearly 99%.

Secondly, subset 4 is selected as the training set, and others are used as testing set. Figures 7 and 8 show the recognition rates. It is clearly seen that the performance of GF is far greater than others and achieves 100% recognition rate on each testing subset.

Thirdly, for the training set, we randomly choose 10 images for each person, namely, subset r, and the others are used for testing. To achieve a credible result, the result is averaged over 50 random splits. The experiment results are presented in Figures 9 and 10. It can be observed that the recognition rate of GF is higher than the other methods, and the performance is quite similar to that of the Gradientfaces and the MPCD, and it reaches a 100% recognition rate on every testing subset except subset 2.

The experiments are implemented using different training sets. It is clearly seen that the proposed method obtains excellent results under different conditions, and this demonstrates its robustness to illumination.

3.3. Experimental Results for the CMU PIE. The CMU PIE face database [37] contains images of 68 persons with various poses, illuminations, and expressions. In our experiments,

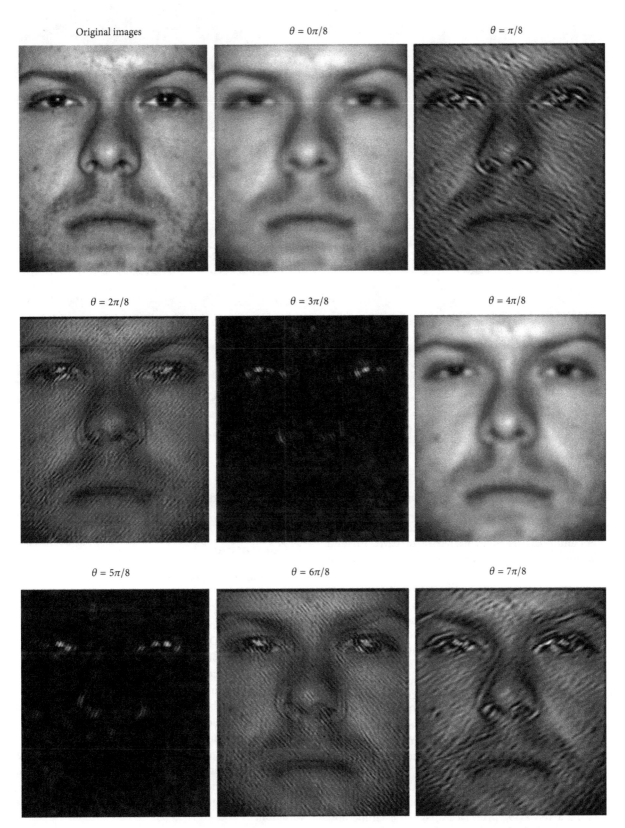

FIGURE 1: The Gabor spectrogram of a face image.

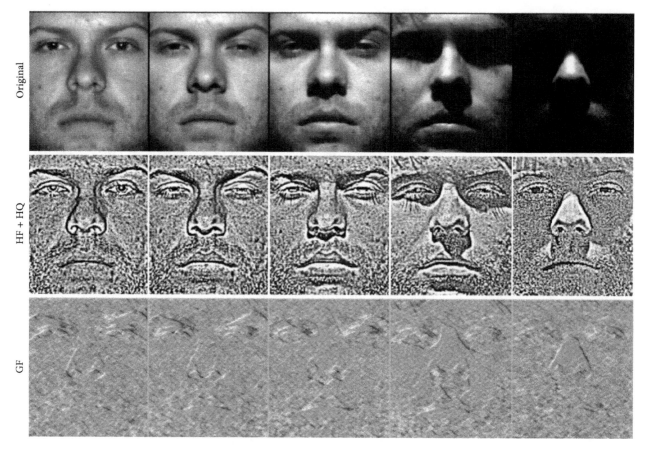

FIGURE 2: Examples of the HF + HQ processed images and the extracted illumination invariant.

the illumination subset (C27) is used, and C27 has 21 different illuminations for each person. All images used in our experiments are cropped and rescaled to 64 × 64 pixels. 21 different illumination images of a person on CMU PIE and their illumination invariants extracted by GF are shown in Figure 11.

The experiments on CMU PIE are divided into two sections. In Section 1, the first 3, 4, and 5 images of each person are selected as the training set and others as the testing set, respectively. Table 1 shows the recognition results of Section 1. In Section 2, we randomly choose 3, 4, and 5 images of each person as training set and others as testing set, respectively. To achieve a credible result, the result is averaged over 50 random splits. The recognition results of Section 2 are tabulated in Table 2. From Tables 1 and 2, it can be seen that the proposed method outperforms all other methods and consistently achieves a high recognition rate, which strongly shows its outstanding efficacy in relation to varying illumination.

Run time is also critical in real application. To evaluate the computational complexity of each method, the run time of processing a 168 × 192 pixel face image of each method is presented in Table 3. The hardware platform is 2.6 GHz P4 with 2G memory. Table 3 shows that the proposed method only needs 37 ms to process a face image, which shows that it can process face images in real time and thus it is able to

handle large face databases. MSR, LTV, and MPCD are slower than our method.

4. Conclusion

In this paper, we propose an efficient Gabor phase based illumination invariant extraction method. We first normalize face images using a homomorphic filter-based preprocessing method to preeliminate effects of the illumination changes. Then, a set of 2D real Gabor wavelet with different directions is used for image transformation, and multiple Gabor coefficients are combined into one whole in considering both spectrum and phase. Lastly, the illumination invariant is obtained by extracting the phase feature from the combined coefficients. The proposed method does not need 3D face shape information or a bootstrap for training. And the extracted illumination invariant contains more essential discriminant information while greatly reducing the effect of illumination changes at the same time. Experimental results show its effectiveness and robustness to different illumination variation.

Conflicts of Interest

The authors declare that they have no conflicts of interest.

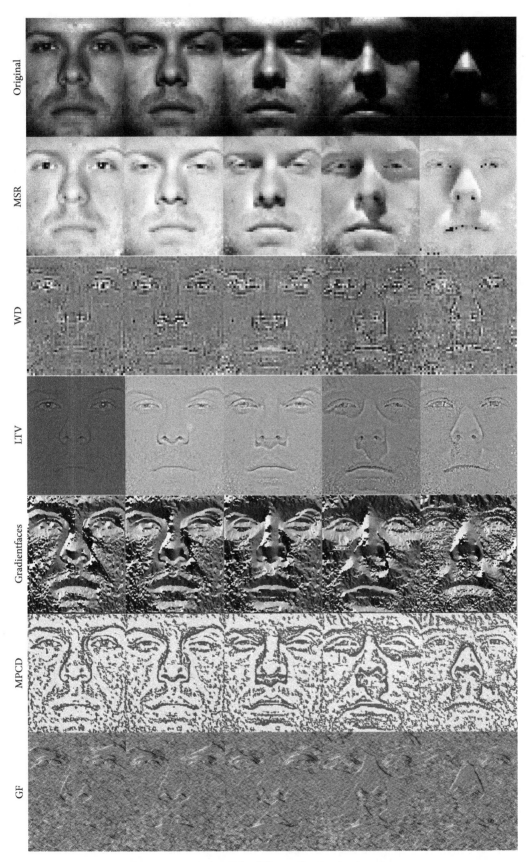

FIGURE 3: Examples of the different illumination invariants.

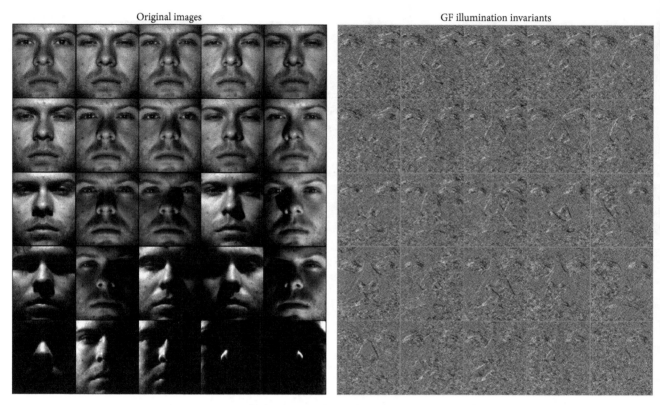

FIGURE 4: Images of subsets 1–5 and their illumination invariants using GF.

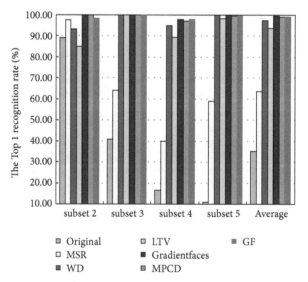

FIGURE 5: Comparisons on the Top 1 recognition rate (the subset 1 used as the training set).

TABLE 1: Comparison on the recognition rate of different illumination invariants in Section 1.

Recognition rate (%)	Training set	Original	MSR	WD	LTV	Gradientfaces	MPCD	GF
	3	37.61	51.33	89.36	89.78	91.04	89.99	94.54
Top 1	4	39.57	63.24	91.81	93.56	95.87	92.79	96.08
	5	43.21	72.90	96.15	96.15	99.16	96.64	97.34
	3	47.20	61.20	95.52	94.82	97.13	95.73	99.44
Top 3	4	50.49	71.99	97.48	96.99	99.02	97.55	99.51
	5	54.41	79.90	98.81	98.32	99.86	99.30	99.93

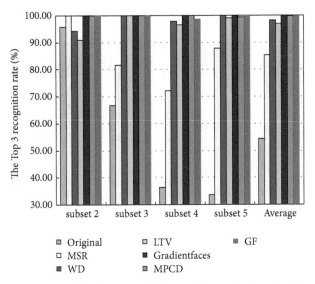

FIGURE 6: Comparisons on the Top 3 recognition rate (the subset 1 used as the training set).

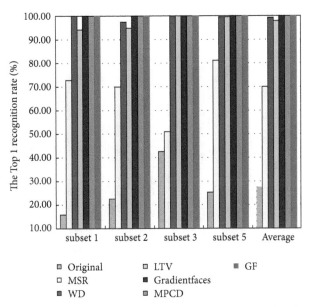

FIGURE 7: Comparisons on the Top 1 recognition rate (the subset 4 used as the training set).

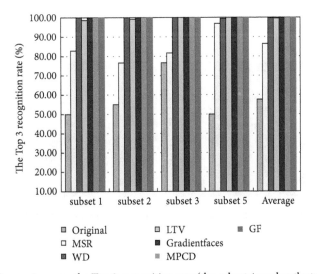

FIGURE 8: Comparisons on the Top 3 recognition rate (the subset 4 used as the training set).

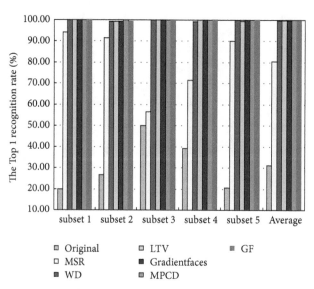

FIGURE 9: Comparisons on the Top 1 recognition rate (the subset r used as the training set).

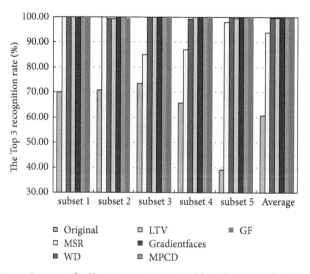

FIGURE 10: Comparisons on the Top 3 recognition rate (the subset r used as the training set).

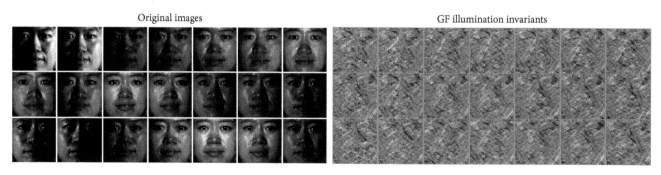

FIGURE 11: Images of a person in C27 and their illumination invariants using GF.

TABLE 2: Comparison on the recognition rate of different illumination invariants in Section 2.

Recognition rate (%)	Training set	Original	MSR	WD	LTV	Gradientfaces	MPCD	GF
	3	40.94	80.23	99.08	98.90	99.22	99.21	99.67
Top 1	4	42.17	84.50	99.68	99.37	98.46	99.24	99.84
	5	42.86	87.26	99.78	99.46	99.95	99.58	99.83
	3	53.60	87.85	99.66	99.55	99.93	99.75	99.93
Top 3	4	55.59	91.16	99.89	99.79	99.98	99.87	99.96
	5	56.38	92.75	99.93	99.80	99.98	99.93	99.96

TABLE 3: Comparison on the run time of different illumination invariants.

Method	MSR	WD	LTV	Gradientfaces	MPCD	GF
Time (ms)	171	36	59	22	97	37

Acknowledgments

This work is supported by the Natural Science Foundation of the Jiangsu Higher Education Institutions of China under Grant 17KJB520021, Jiangsu Government Scholarship for Overseas Studies, Training Projects of Undergraduate Practice Innovation funded by Nanjing University of Information Science and Technology, and a Project Funded by the Priority Academic Program Development of Jiangsu Higher Education Institution.

References

[1] W. Zhao, R. Chellappa, P. J. Phillips, and A. Rosenfeld, "Face recognition: a literature survey," *ACM Computing Surveys*, vol. 35, no. 4, pp. 399–458, 2003.

[2] P. J. Phillips, W. T. Scruggs, A. J. O'Toole et al., "FRVT 2006 and ICE 2006 large-scale experimental results," *IEEE Transactions on Pattern Analysis and Machine Intelligence*, vol. 32, no. 5, pp. 831–846, 2010.

[3] Y. Adini, Y. Moses, and S. Ullman, "Face recognition: the problem of compensating for changes in illumination direction," *IEEE Transactions on Pattern Analysis and Machine Intelligence*, vol. 19, no. 7, pp. 721–732, 1997.

[4] S. Shan, W. Gao, B. Cao, and D. Zhao, "Illumination normalization for robust face recognition against varying lighting conditions," in *Proceedings of the IEEE International Workshop on Analysis and Modeling of Faces and Gestures (AMFG '03)*, pp. 157–164, IEEE, Nice, France, October 2003.

[5] M. Savvides and B. V. Kumar, "Illumination Normalization Using Logarithm Transforms for Face Authentication," in *Audio- and Video-Based Biometric Person Authentication*, vol. 2688 of *Lecture Notes in Computer Science*, pp. 549–556, Springer, Guildford,UK, 2003.

[6] X. Tan and B. Triggs, "Enhanced local texture feature sets for face recognition under difficult lighting conditions," *IEEE Transactions on Image Processing*, vol. 19, no. 6, pp. 1635–1650, 2010.

[7] C.-N. Fan and F.-Y. Zhang, "Homomorphic filtering based illumination normalization method for face recognition," *Pattern Recognition Letters*, vol. 32, no. 10, pp. 1468–1479, 2011.

[8] P.-H. Lee, S.-W. Wu, and Y.-P. Hung, "Illumination compensation using oriented local histogram equalization and its application to face recognition," *IEEE Transactions on Image Processing*, vol. 21, no. 9, pp. 4280–4289, 2012.

[9] P. N. Belhumeur and D. J. Kriegman, "What Is the Set of Images of an Object under All Possible Illumination Conditions?" *International Journal of Computer Vision*, vol. 28, no. 3, pp. 245–260, 1998.

[10] A. S. Georghiades, P. N. Belhumeur, and D. J. Kriegman, "From few to many: illumination cone models for face recognition under variable lighting and pose," *IEEE Transactions on Pattern Analysis and Machine Intelligence*, vol. 23, no. 6, pp. 643–660, 2001.

[11] R. Basri and D. W. Jacobs, "Lambertian reflectance and linear subspaces," *IEEE Transactions on Pattern Analysis and Machine Intelligence*, vol. 25, no. 2, pp. 218–233, 2003.

[12] B. Horn, *Robot Vision*, McGraw-Hill, New York, NY, USA, 1986.

[13] D. J. Jobson, Z.-U. Rahman, and G. A. Woodell, "A multiscale retinex for bridging the gap between color images and the human observation of scenes," *IEEE Transactions on Image Processing*, vol. 6, no. 7, pp. 965–976, 1997.

[14] H. Wang, S. Z. Li, and Y. Wang, "Face recognition under varying lighting conditions using self quotient image," in *Proceedings of the 6th IEEE International Conference on Automatic Face and Gesture Recognition (FGR '04)*, pp. 819–824, Seoul, Korea, May 2004.

[15] T. Chen, W. Yin, X. S. Zhou, D. Comaniciu, and T. S. Huang, "Total variation models for variable lighting face recognition," *IEEE Transactions on Pattern Analysis and Machine Intelligence*, vol. 28, no. 9, pp. 1519–1524, 2006.

[16] T. Zhang, B. Fang, Y. Yuan et al., "Multiscale facial structure representation for face recognition under varying illumination," *Pattern Recognition*, vol. 42, no. 2, pp. 251–258, 2009.

[17] Y. Cheng, Y. Hou, C. Zhao, Z. Li, Y. Hu, and C. Wang, "Robust face recognition based on illumination invariant in nonsubsampled contourlet transform domain," *Neurocomputing*, vol. 73, no. 10-12, pp. 2217–2224, 2010.

[18] X. Xie, J. Lai, and W.-S. Zheng, "Extraction of illumination invariant facial features from a single image using nonsubsampled contourlet transform," *Pattern Recognition*, vol. 43, no. 12, pp. 4177–4189, 2010.

[19] L.-H. Chen, Y.-H. Yang, C.-S. Chen, and M.-Y. Cheng, "Illumination invariant feature extraction based on natural images statistics Taking face images as an example," in *Proceedings of the 2011 IEEE Conference on Computer Vision and Pattern Recognition, CVPR 2011*, pp. 681–688, Colorado Springs, Colo, USA, June 2011.

[20] X. Cao, W. Shen, L. G. Yu, Y. L. Wang, J. Y. Yang, and Z. W. Zhang, "Illumination invariant extraction for face recognition using neighboring wavelet coefficients," *Pattern Recognition*, vol. 45, no. 4, pp. 1299–1305, 2012.

[21] T. Song, K. Xiang, and X.-Y. Wang, "Face recognition under varying illumination based on gradientface and local features," *IEEJ Transactions on Electrical and Electronic Engineering*, vol. 10, no. 2, pp. 222–228, 2015.

[22] M. R. Faraji and X. Qi, "Face recognition under varying illuminations using logarithmic fractal dimension-based complete eight local directional patterns," *Neurocomputing*, vol. 199, pp. 16–30, 2016.

[23] H. F. Chen, P. N. Belhumeur, and D. W. Jacobs, "In search of illumination invariants," in *Proceedings of the IEEE Conference on Computer Vision and Pattern Recognition (CVPR '00)*, vol. 1, pp. 254–261, Hilton Head Island, SC, USA, June 2000.

[24] T. Zhang, Y. Y. Tang, B. Fang, Z. Shang, and X. Liu, "Face recognition under varying illumination using gradientfaces," *IEEE Transactions on Image Processing*, vol. 18, no. 11, pp. 2599–2606, 2009.

[25] X. Chen and J. Zhang, "Illumination robust single sample face recognition using multi-directional orthogonal gradient phase faces," *Neurocomputing*, vol. 74, no. 14-15, pp. 2291–2298, 2011.

[26] B. Zhang, S. Shan, X. Chen, and W. Gao, "Histogram of Gabor phase patterns (HGPP): a novel object representation approach for face recognition," *IEEE Transactions on Image Processing*, vol. 16, no. 1, pp. 57–68, 2007.

[27] A. K. Sao and B. Yegnanarayana, "On the use of phase of the Fourier transform for face recognition under variations in illumination," *Signal, Image and Video Processing*, vol. 4, no. 3, pp. 353–358, 2010.

[28] Y. Cheng, C. L. Wang, Z. Y. Li, Y. K. Hou, and C. X. Zhao, "Multiscale principal contour direction for varying lighting face recognition," *IEEE Electronics Letters*, vol. 46, no. 10, pp. 680–682, 2010.

[29] J. G. Daugman, "Uncertainty relation for resolution in space, spatial frequency, and orientation optimized by two-dimensional visual cortical filters," *Journal of the Optical Society of America A: Optics and Image Science, and Vision*, vol. 2, no. 7, pp. 1160–1169, 1985.

[30] L. Wiskott, J.-M. Fellous, N. Krüger, and C. von der Malsburg, "Face recognition by elastic bunch graph matching," *IEEE Transactions on Pattern Analysis and Machine Intelligence*, vol. 19, no. 7, pp. 775–779, 1997.

[31] C. Liu and H. Wechsler, "Gabor feature based classification using the enhanced Fisher linear discriminant model for face recognition," *IEEE Transactions on Image Processing*, vol. 11, no. 4, pp. 467–476, 2002.

[32] W. Zhang, S. Shan, W. Gao, X. Chen, and H. Zhang, "Local gabor binary pattern histogram (LGBPHS): a novel non-statistical model for face representation and recognition," in *Proceedings of the 10th IEEE International Conference on Computer Vision (ICCV '05)*, pp. 786–791, Beijing, China, October 2005.

[33] S. Xie, S. Shan, X. Chen, X. Meng, and W. Gao, "Learned local Gabor patterns for face representation and recognition," *Signal Processing*, vol. 89, no. 12, pp. 2333–2344, 2009.

[34] Á. Serrano, I. Martín De Diego, C. Conde, and E. Cabello, "Analysis of variance of Gabor filter banks parameters for optimal face recognition," *Pattern Recognition Letters*, vol. 32, no. 15, pp. 1998–2008, 2011.

[35] J. C. Goswami and A. K. Chan, *Fundamentals of Wavelets: Theory, Algorithms, and Applications*, Wiley, Hoboken, NJ, USA, 2nd edition, 2010.

[36] K.-C. Lee, J. Ho, and D. J. Kriegman, "Acquiring linear subspaces for face recognition under variable lighting," *IEEE Transactions on Pattern Analysis and Machine Intelligence*, vol. 27, no. 5, pp. 684–698, 2005.

[37] T. Sim, S. Baker, and M. Bsat, "The CMU pose, illumination, and expression (PIE) database," in *Proceedings of the 5th IEEE International Conference on Automatic Face and Gesture Recognition*, pp. 46–51, Washington, DC, USA, May 2002.

[38] P. J. Phillips, H. Wechsler, J. Huang, and P. J. Rauss, "The FERET database and evaluation procedure for face-recognition algorithms," *Image and Vision Computing*, vol. 16, no. 5, pp. 295–306, 1998.

[39] S. Du and R. Ward, "Wavelet-based illumination normalization for face recognition," in *Proceedings of the IEEE International Conference on Image Processing, ICIP 2005*, vol. 2, pp. 954–957, Genoa, Italy, September 2005.

3

Moving Object Detection for Dynamic Background Scenes Based on Spatiotemporal Model

Yizhong Yang, Qiang Zhang, Pengfei Wang, Xionglou Hu, and Nengju Wu

School of Electronic Science & Applied Physics, Hefei University of Technology, Hefei, China

Correspondence should be addressed to Yizhong Yang; yangyizhong@hfut.edu.cn

Academic Editor: Deepu Rajan

Moving object detection in video streams is the first step of many computer vision applications. Background modeling and subtraction for moving detection is the most common technique for detecting, while how to detect moving objects correctly is still a challenge. Some methods initialize the background model at each pixel in the first N frames. However, it cannot perform well in dynamic background scenes since the background model only contains temporal features. Herein, a novel pixelwise and nonparametric moving object detection method is proposed, which contains both spatial and temporal features. The proposed method can accurately detect the dynamic background. Additionally, several new mechanisms are also proposed to maintain and update the background model. The experimental results based on image sequences in public datasets show that the proposed method provides the robustness and effectiveness in dynamic background scenes compared with the existing methods.

1. Introduction

Recently, background modeling and subtraction became the most popular technique for moving object detection in computer vision, such as object recognition and traffic surveillance [1–9].

Compared to optical flow [10, 11] and interframe difference algorithms [12], background subtraction algorithm needs less computation and performs better, and it is more flexible and effective. The idea of background subtraction is to differentiate the current image from a reference background model. These algorithms initialize a background model at first to represent the scene with no moving objects and then detect the moving objects by computing the difference between the current frame and the background model. Dynamic background is a challenge for background subtraction, such as waving tree leaves and ripples on river. In the past several years, many background subtraction algorithms have been proposed, and most of them focus on building more effective background model to handle dynamic background as follows:

(1) Features: texture and color [13–15]

(2) Combining methods: combining two or more background models as the new model [16]

(3) Updating the background model [17]

In this paper, a new pixelwise and nonparametric moving object detection method is proposed. Background model is built by the first N_1 frames and sampling m times in 3×3 neighborhood region randomly. On the one hand, spatiotemporal model represents dynamic background scenes well. On the other hand, a new update strategy makes the background model fit the dynamic background. In addition, the proposed method can deal with ghost well. Experimental results show that the proposed method can efficiently and correctly detect the moving objects from the dynamic background.

This paper is organized as follows. In the next section, an overview of existing approaches of background subtraction is presented. Section 3 describes the proposed method in detail, and then Section 4 provides the experimental results and comparison with other methods. Section 5 includes conclusions and further research directions.

2. Related Work

In this section, some background subtraction methods will be introduced, which are divided into parametric and nonparametric models.

For parametric models, the most commonly used method is Gaussian Mixture Model (GMM) [18]. Before GMM, a per-pixel Gaussian model was proposed [19], which calculated the mean and standard deviation for each pixel at first and then compared the probability with a certain threshold of each pixel to classify the current pixel as background or foreground. But this Gaussian model cannot deal with noise and dynamic situation. GMM was proposed to solve these problems. GMM usually set three-to-five Gaussian models for each pixel and updated the model after matching. Several papers [20, 21] improved the GMM method to be more flexible and efficient in recent years.

In contrast to parametric models, nonparametric models are commonly set up by the collection of the observed pixel values or neighborhood pixel values of each pixel. Kernel Density Estimation (KDE) [22] was proposed to open the door of hot research of nonparametric methods. In [13], a clustering technique was proposed to set up a nonparametric background model. The background model's samples of each pixel were clustered into the set of code words. In [23], Wang et al. chose to include large number (up to 200) of samples in the background model. Since the background models set up by [13, 23] are only based on temporal information, they cannot deal with dynamic background scenes well without the spatial information. In ViBe [24, 25], a random scheme was introduced to set up and update background models. They initialized the background model from the first frame, and the model elements were sampled from the collection of each pixel's neighborhood randomly. ViBe shows robustness and effectiveness for dynamic background scenes in a sense. In order to improve ViBe further, Hofmann et al. [17] proposed an adaptive scheme to automatically tune the decision threshold based on previous decisions made by the system. However, the background models set up by [17, 24, 25] are only based on spatial information. The lack of temporal information makes it hard to deal with time-related situation well. In [26], a modified Local Binary Similarity Pattern (LBSP) descriptor was proposed to set up the background model in feature space. It calculated the LBSP descriptor by absolute difference which is different from LBP. What is more, intra-LSBP and inter-LSBP were calculated in the same predetermined pattern to capture both texture and intensity changes. The change detection results from LSBP proved efficiency against many complex algorithms. Reference [27] improved LSBP in threshold area and combined with ViBe method to detect motion. The improvement was obviously in noisy and blurred regions. Reference [28] proposed spatiotemporal background model by integrating the concepts of a local feature-based approach and a statistical approach into a single framework; the results show that it can deal with illumination and dynamic background scenes well. These algorithms contain both temporal information and spatial information, resulting in not bad performance.

Initialization and update strategy are important steps common for background modeling. As for initialization, some background subtraction methods initialized the background models with pixel values at each pixel in the first N frames [16]. However, it was not effective for dynamic background situation because of the lack of neighboring pixel information. Reference [24] initialized from the first frame by choosing the neighborhood pixel values as sample randomly.

However, it initialized the background model by only one frame. In addition, it sampled 20 pixels as the background model in the field of current pixel neighborhood. However, there were only 8 pixels in neighborhood, which inevitability resulted in repeated selection. Then it would affect segmentation decision because of the ill-considered model. Reference [29] proposed a different method to initialize the background model. Every element of the model contained pixel value and an efficacy C_k, and the element with the least value of C_k will be removed or updated. However, element with the least value of C_k might not be the worst element in dynamic background scenes. As for update strategy, in [24], when a pixel has been classified as background, a random process determined whether this pixel was used to update the corresponding pixel model. It was workable but too blind to update the model well.

Herein, a nonparametric model collecting both the history and the neighborhood pixel values is presented to improve the performance for dynamic background scenes. The proposed method, based on spatiotemporal model, collects pixel values as sample from the history and neighborhood of a pixel, and the model elements are sampled from neighborhood region in the first N_1 frames. As for update strategy, the range of randomness is decreased to increase the accuracy. All above methods proposed are different from other methods based on spatiotemporal model.

3. Spatiotemporal Model for Background

Normally, a background model can fit only one kind of scenes and it is difficult to get a universal background model which can deal with all the complex and diverse scenes. Some background subtraction methods combine the different models or features like texture together to get universal models. These methods regard every frame as the most complex scenes and result in a large amount of calculation. As for this question, this paper proposes a novel and simple method to model background for dynamic background scenes, and the idea is employed to initialize the model. Next, the details of our spatiotemporal model will be introduced. The diagram of the proposed method is shown in Figure 1.

3.1. Initialization. The proposed method initializes background model from the first N_1 frames. First of all, the spatial model $BN(x_i)$ can be initialized by picking out pixel value randomly in the neighborhood of x_i for m times at each frame, and m is less than 8.

$$BN_1(x_i) = \{I_1(x_i), I_2(x_i), \ldots, I_m(x_i)\}$$

$$BN_2(x_i) = \{I_{m+1}(x_i), I_{m+2}(x_i), \ldots, I_{2m}(x_i)\}$$

$$BN_{N_1}(x_i)$$

$$= \left\{I_{(N_1-1)\times m+1}(x_i), I_{(N_1-1)\times m+2}(x_i), \ldots, I_{N_1\times m}(x_i)\right\}. \quad (1)$$

Then these spatial background models are integrated together to construct spatiotemporal model $B(x_i)$:

$$B(x_i) = \left\{BN_1(x_i), BN_2(x_i), \ldots, BN_{N_1}(x_i)\right\}. \quad (2)$$

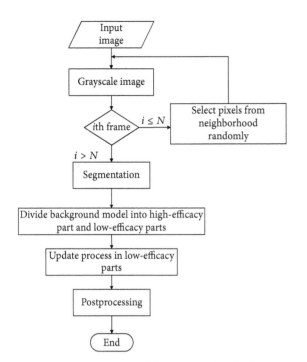

FIGURE 1: Diagram of the proposed method.

For the convenience of record,

$$B(x_i) = \{I_1, I_2, I_3, \ldots, I_N\}, \quad N = N_1 \times m. \quad (3)$$

As for the value of N_1, N, m will be discussed in Section 4 later. The spatial information and the temporal information are integrated, and the combined idea is used here without large amount of computation. The proposed background model is proved to be effective.

3.2. Segmentation Decision.
Since the proposed model only consists of grayscale value of pixel, the segmentation decision is simple in our single model. It just compares the distance between the current pixel and the pixel in the background model, and the formula is shown as follows:

$$F(x_i)$$
$$= \begin{cases} 1 & \#\{dist(I(x_i), B_k(x_i)) < R(x_i)\} < \#_{min} \\ 0 & else, \end{cases} \quad (4)$$

where $B_k(x_i)$ represents the kth element in model $B(x_i)$. $\#_{min}$ defines the least number of elements in background model meeting the threshold condition. If $F(x_i) = 1$, it implies that the pixel belongs to foreground, and conversely, the pixel belongs to background.

3.3. Updating Process.
Background changes all the time in dynamic background scenes, so it is necessary to update the background model regularly to fit the dynamic background. In this section, update of the spatiotemporal model and adaptive update of decision threshold will be described in detail.

3.3.1. Update of the Spatiotemporal Model. The proposed method divides the model elements into two parts, high-efficacy part and low-efficacy part. The elements which meet the formula $dist(I(x_i), B_k(x_i)) < R(x_i)$ belong to high-efficacy part, and the rest belong to low-efficacy part. Then the random strategy will be conducted in the range of these elements belonging to low-efficacy part. What is more, learning rate T is determined by experiments to fit the proposed method better.

3.3.2. Update of the Neighborhood. Background pixels always exist together in some regions, so the neighborhood of a pixel may be background pixels if this pixel has been classified as background. However, it may not be true in the edge region. In conclusion, pixels in neighborhood region of a background pixel are more likely to be background pixels compared with other pixels. So the background model of neighborhood pixel will be updated as well with the same method introduced in Section 3.3.1. After the update process, parameter $\#_{min}$ will become $\#_{min}$-1 when segmentation decision is conducted in neighborhood, which is just like adaptive update.

The update method above is a memoryless update strategy. The samples in the background model at time t are preserved after the update of the pixel model with the probability $(N - 1)/N$. For any further time $t + dt$, this probability formula is shown as follows:

$$P(t, t + dt) = \left(\frac{N-1}{N}\right)^{(t+dt)-t}. \quad (5)$$

This formula can also be written as follows:

$$P(t, t + dt) = e^{-\ln(N/(N-1))dt}, \quad (6)$$

where $P(t, t + dt)$ denotes the probability after time dt, and it shows that the expected remaining lifespan of any sample value of the model decays exponentially.

4. Experiments and Results

In this section, a series of experiments are conducted to analyze the parameter setting and evaluated the performance of the proposed method with others. Here, we first express our gratitude to changedetection.net [34], which provides the datasets for our experiments. The datasets include six test videos on the category of dynamic background and several objective indexes for evaluating performance quantitatively:

$$Recall = \frac{TP}{TP + FN}$$

$$Precision = \frac{TP}{TP + FP}$$

$$F\text{-Measure} = \frac{2 \times Precision \times Recall}{Precision + Recall}$$

$$FPR = \frac{FP}{FN + FP}$$

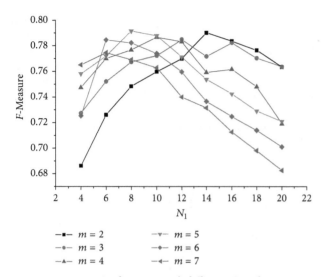

FIGURE 2: Performance with different N_1 and m.

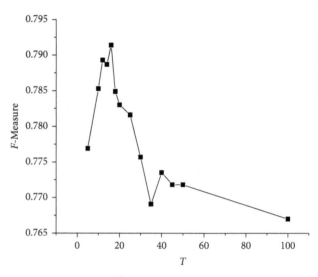

FIGURE 3: Performance with different T value.

$$FNR = \frac{FN}{TP + FN}$$

$$PWC = 100 \times \frac{FN + FP}{TP + FN + FP + TN},$$

$$(7)$$

where True Positive (TP) is the number of correctly classified foreground pixels and True Negative (TN) is the number of correctly classified background pixels. On the other hand, False Positive (FP) is the number of background pixels that is incorrectly classified as foreground and False Negative (FN) is the number of foreground pixels that is incorrectly classified as background pixel in background subtraction method. The data above are used to calculate Recall, Precision, and F-Measure. Recall represents the percent of the correctly detected foreground relative to the ground truth foreground. Precision represents the percent of the correctly detected foreground relative to the detected foreground including true foreground and false foreground. F-Measure is a comprehensive index of Recall and Precision, which is primarily used to evaluate the performance of different parameters and different methods.

The proposed method is implemented in C++ programming language with opencv2.4.9 on a core i3 CPU with 3.0 GHz and 2 G RAM.

4.1. Parameter Setting. It was mentioned in Section 3 that we initialized the model from N_1 frames and sampled elements from neighborhood randomly m times. We conducted a series of experiments on the adjustment of m and N_1 with the fixed parameter, learning rate T and $\#_{min}$, and without postprocessing.

It is clear that performance with parameter m from 5 to 6 and N_1 from 6 to 10 are better in Figure 2. Further experiments tested with different parameters are shown in Table 1. Performance with different T value is shown in Figure 3.

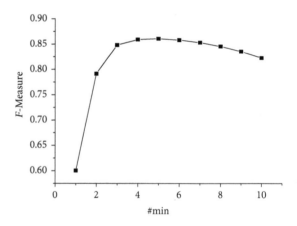

FIGURE 4: Performance with different $\#_{min}$.

TABLE 1: Further experiments to choose $N1$ and m.

F-M	N_1				
	6	7	8	9	10
m					
5	0.7720	0.7855	0.7914	0.7788	0.7878
6	0.7844	0.7736	0.7822	0.7765	0.7739

$N_1 = 8$ and $m = 5$ are the best choices, and $N = N_1 \times m = 40$ is also a desired parameter for small computational burden.

The parameters T and $\#_{min}$ will be determined by experiments with fixed N_1 and m. The experiment result of selecting T can be seen in Figure 3 and the experiment result of selecting $\#_{min}$ can be seen in Figure 4.

After these kinds of experiments (Figures 3 and 4), the parameters were set as follows:

(1) $N_1 = 8, m = 5, N = 40$.

(2) $T = 16$.

FIGURE 5: Comparison of the dynamic situation. (a) The thirteenth frame of "Overpass" video. (b) The detection result of [13]. (c) The detection result of the proposed method.

FIGURE 6: Comparison of ghost elimination. (a) and (b): the first and fiftieth frames of "Highway" video, respectively. (c) The detection result of the fiftieth frame by ViBe. (d) The detection result of the fiftieth frame by the proposed method.

(3) $\#_{\min} = 5, R = 20$.

(4) A median filter step was applied, and it can be seen that, in Table 2, a 9×9 window behaves better. The median filter is a step to make the results better, while, compared with other algorithm, this step is removed.

4.2. Comparison with Other Methods.
Figures 5(b) and 5(c) show the detection results of [13] and the proposed method from the input frame (a), respectively. The waving tree leaves in (a) are the dynamic background. Since [13] is a temporal-only model method, the background model lacks the neighborhood pixel information, which will regard the dynamic background as moving objects. The proposed method considers both temporal information and spatial information, setting up the background model from the first 8 frames and sampling 5 times in the 3×3 neighborhood region randomly. Therefore, the performance in dynamic background scenes is better than [13].

Figure 6 shows the detection results of ViBe [24] and the proposed method. Since ViBe [24] sets up the background model only based on spatial information, time-related situation such as ghost may exist. As shown in Figure 6(c), it sets up background model just from the first frame and regards all pixels in it as background pixels without moving objects. If there are some moving objects in first frame and the

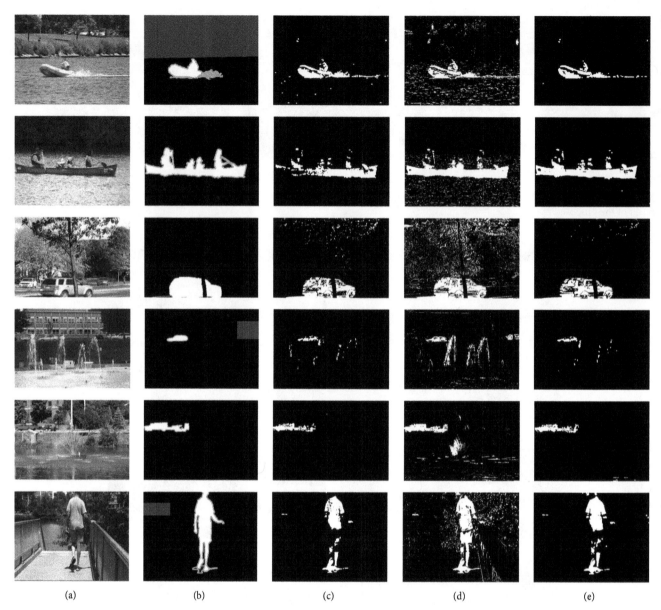

| (a) | (b) | (c) | (d) | (e) |

FIGURE 7: Comparison of the detection results. (a) Input frames of the six videos of "dynamic background" in changedetection.net, and they are the 2000th frame in "Boats," the 955th frame in Canoe, the 1892th frame in Fall, the 1147th frame in "Fountain01," the 745th frame in "Fountain02," and the 2462th frame in "Overpass" from top to bottom. (b) Ground truth of (a). (c) Results of ViBe. (d) Results of CodeBook. (e) Results of the proposed method.

TABLE 2: Performance of proposed method with postprocessing.

Size	3×3	5×5	7×7	9×9	11×11
F-Measure	0.8690	0.8813	0.8879	0.8888	0.8881

moving objects move away (the fiftieth frame (b)), they will be detected as ghosts (cars marked in red rectangles in (c)). The background model of the proposed method contains not only spatial information but also temporal information, so it can recognize the moving objects from first frame. Therefore, ghost can be well eliminated.

The proposed method focuses on building and updating more effective background model to deal with dynamic background scenes. The public dynamic background video datasets from changedetection.net, which are "Boats" with 7999 frames, "Canoe" with 1189 frames, "Fall" with 4000 frames, "Fountain01" with 1184 frames and "Fountain02" with 1499 frames, "Overpass" with 3000 frames, are used to conduct the experiments. For fair comparison, the results of the proposed method do not use any postprocessing. ViBe [24] and CodeBook [13] are two classical methods for background segmentation, so we conducted comparison between the proposed method and them. Experimental results are shown in Figure 7.

(a) (b) (c) (d)

FIGURE 8: Detection results of other categories. (a) and (c): input test video; (b) and (d): detection results. The first row is the "Bad Weather" category, the second row is the "Baseline" category, the third row is the "Thermal" category, the fourth row is "Intermittent Object Motion" category and "Turbulence" category, the fifth row is "Low Framerate" category and "Night Videos" category, and the sixth row is "Camera Jitter" category and "PTZ" category.

Beyond dynamic background scenes, the results of other categories in changedetection.net are shown in Figure 8. It can be seen that the proposed method performs well in several different categories, such as "Bad Weather," "Baseline", "Thermal," and "Intermittent Object Motion." But in other categories, the proposed method performs not very well. For example, in "PTZ" category, after the camera moves, the proposed method needs a rather long time to learn the new background by the update process, which may result in

false detection during this process. However, although the proposed method is not a universal method, it can deal with most scenes satisfactorily.

The quantitative comparison results of "dynamic background" category between the proposed method and more other background subtraction methods are shown in Table 3. Among these methods, ViBe [24] is a nonparameter algorithm, from which the proposed method is derived. LOBSTER [27] and Multiscale Spatiotemporal BG Model [30]

TABLE 3: Comparison of performance between the proposed method and others.

Methods	Recall	FPR	FNR	PWC	PRE	F-Measure
ViBe [24]	0.7222	0.0104	0.2778	1.2796	0.5346	0.5652
LOBSTER [27]	0.7670	0.0180	0.0023	1.9984	0.5923	0.5679
Multiscale Spatiotemporal BG Model [30]	0.7392	0.0095	0.2608	1.1365	0.5515	0.5953
EFIC [31]	0.6667	0.0144	0.3333	0.9154	0.6849	0.5779
TVRPCA [32]	0.56	—	—	—	0.74	0.61
AAPSA [33]	0.6955	0.0011	0.3045	0.4992	0.7336	0.6706
Proposed method without postprocessing	0.6692	0.5322	0.3318	1.2762	0.6084	0.6213
Proposed method with postprocessing	0.7296	0.2773	0.2704	0.2800	0.8755	0.7960

are spatiotemporal background modeling algorithms, which are similar to the proposed method. EFIC [31] is a popular method in changedetection.net. TVRPCA [32] is an advanced RPCA based method, which is also designed for dynamic background scenes. As shown in Table 3, AAPSA [33] has the highest F-Measure for its autoadaptive strategy. Expect AASPA, in the aspect of F-Measure, the proposed method gets the highest score. Herein, although the proposed method's F-Measure is not the highest, it can deal with not only dynamic background scenes well but also ghost elimination.

5. Conclusion

In this paper, a novel change detection method of nonparametric background segmentation for dynamic background scenes is proposed. The background model is built by sampling 5 times in 3×3 neighborhood region randomly from first 8 frames. The samples of background model are separated to high-efficacy part and low-efficacy part, and the samples in low-efficacy part will be replaced randomly. The update strategy which replaces sample in low-efficacy part can continuously optimize the background model. It can be seen from the experimental results that the proposed method is robust in dynamic background scenes and ghost elimination compared to other methods.

Conflicts of Interest

The authors declare that there are no conflicts of interest regarding the publication of this paper.

Acknowledgments

This work was supported by the National Natural Science Foundation of China under Grant 61401137 and Grant 61404043 and the Fundamental Research Funds for the Central Universities under Grant J2014HGXJ0083.

References

[1] I. Haritaoglu, D. Harwood, and L. S. Davis, "W4: real-time surveillance of people and their activities," *IEEE Transactions on Pattern Analysis and Machine Intelligence*, vol. 22, no. 8, pp. 809–830, 2000.

[2] E. Stringa and C. S. Regazzoni, "Real-time video-shot detection for scene surveillance applications," *IEEE Transactions on Image Processing*, vol. 9, no. 1, pp. 69–79, 2000.

[3] L. Li, Y. H. Gu, M. K. H. Leung, and Q. Tian, "Knowledge-based fuzzy reasoning for maintenance of moderate-to-fast background changes in video surveillance," in *Proceedings of the 4th IASTED International Conference Signal and Image Processing*, 2002.

[4] Z. Zivkovic and F. van der Heijden, "Efficient adaptive density estimation per image pixel for the task of background subtraction," *Pattern Recognition Letters*, vol. 27, no. 7, pp. 773–780, 2006.

[5] C. Schmidt and H. Matiar, "Performance evaluation of local features in human classification and detection," *Iet Computer Vision*, vol. 2, no. 28, pp. 236–246, 2008.

[6] L. Maddalena and A. Petrosino, "A self-organizing approach to background subtraction for visual surveillance applications," *IEEE Transactions on Image Processing*, vol. 17, no. 7, pp. 1168–1177, 2008.

[7] C. Guo and L. Zhang, "A novel multiresolution spatiotemporal saliency detection model and its applications in image and video compression," *IEEE Transactions on Image Processing*, vol. 19, no. 1, pp. 185–198, 2010.

[8] P. Sun, S. Xia, G. Yuan, and D. Li, "An overview of moving object trajectory compression algorithms," *Mathematical Problems in Engineering*, vol. 2016, Article ID 6587309, 13 pages, 2016.

[9] C. I. Patel, S. Garg, T. Zaveri, and A. Banerjee, "Top-down and bottom-up cues based moving object detection for varied background video sequences," *Advances in Multimedia*, vol. 2014, Article ID 879070, 20 pages, 2014.

[10] J. L. Barron, D. J. Fleet, and S. S. Beauchemin, "Performance of optical flow techniques," *International Journal of Computer Vision*, vol. 12, no. 1, pp. 43–77, 1994.

[11] S. Denman, C. Fookes, and S. Sridharan, "Improved simultaneous computation of motion detection and optical flow for object tracking," in *Proceedings of the Digital Image Computing: Techniques and Applications, DICTA 2009*, pp. 175–182, December 2009.

[12] R. Liang, L. Yan, P. Gao, X. Qian, Z. Zhang, and H. Sun, "Aviation video moving-target detection with inter-frame difference," in *Proceedings of the 2010 3rd International Congress on Image and Signal Processing, CISP 2010*, pp. 1494–1497, October 2010.

[13] K. Kim, T. H. Chalidabhongse, D. Harwood, and L. Davis, "Real-time foreground-background segmentation using codebook model," *Real-Time Imaging*, vol. 11, no. 3, pp. 172–185, 2005.

[14] K. Wilson, "Real-time tracking for multiple objects based on implementation of RGB color space in video," *International*

Journal of Signal Processing, Image Processing and Pattern Recognition, vol. 9, no. 4, pp. 331–338, 2016.

[15] M. Heikkilä and M. Pietikäinen, "A texture-based method for modeling the background and detecting moving objects," *IEEE Transactions on Pattern Analysis and Machine Intelligence*, vol. 28, no. 4, pp. 657–662, 2006.

[16] B. Yin, J. Zhang, and Z. Wang, "Background segmentation of dynamic scenes based on dual model," *IET Computer Vision*, vol. 8, no. 6, pp. 545–555, 2014.

[17] M. Hofmann, P. Tiefenbacher, and G. Rigoll, "Background segmentation with feedback: The pixel-based adaptive segmenter," in *Proceedings of the 2012 IEEE Computer Society Conference on Computer Vision and Pattern Recognition Workshops, CVPRW 2012*, pp. 38–43, June 2012.

[18] G.-A. Bilodeau, J.-P. Jodoin, and N. Saunier, "Change detection in feature space using local binary similarity patterns," in *Proceedings of the 10th International Conference on Computer and Robot Vision, CRV 2013*, pp. 106–112, May 2013.

[19] C. R. Wren, A. Azarbayejani, T. Darrell, and A. P. Pentland, "P finder: real-time tracking of the human body," *IEEE Transactions on Pattern Analysis and Machine Intelligence*, vol. 19, no. 7, pp. 780–785, 1997.

[20] P. Kaewtrakulpong and R. Bowden, *An Improved Adaptive Background Mixture Model for Realtime Tracking with Shadow Detection*, Springer, USA, 2002.

[21] D.-S. Lee, "Effective Gaussian mixture learning for video background subtraction," *IEEE Transactions on Pattern Analysis and Machine Intelligence*, vol. 27, no. 5, pp. 827–832, 2005.

[22] A. Mittal and N. Paragios, "Motion-based background subtraction using adaptive kernel density estimation," in *Proceedings of the 2004 IEEE Computer Society Conference on Computer Vision and Pattern Recognition, 2004, CVPR 2004*, vol. 2, no. 2, pp. 302–309, Washington, DC, USA.

[23] H. Wang and D. Suter, "A consensus-based method for tracking: Modelling background scenario and foreground appearance," *Pattern Recognition*, vol. 40, no. 3, pp. 1091–1105, 2007.

[24] O. Barnich and M. Van Droogenbroeck, "ViBe: a universal background subtraction algorithm for video sequences," *IEEE Transactions on Image Processing*, vol. 20, no. 6, pp. 1709–1724, 2011.

[25] M. Van Droogenbroeck and O. Paquot, "Background subtraction: experiments and improvements for ViBe," in *Proceedings of the IEEE Computer Society Conference on Computer Vision and Pattern Recognition Workshops*, vol. 71, no. 6, pp. 32–37, IEEE, Providence, RI, USA, June 2012.

[26] G. A. Bilodeau, J. P. Jodoin, and N. Saunier, "Change detection in feature space using local binary similarity patterns," in *Proceedings of the International Conference on Computer & Robot Vision*, vol. 10, no. 1, pp. 106–112, 2013.

[27] P.-L. St-Charles and G.-A. Bilodeau, "Improving background subtraction using Local Binary Similarity Patterns," in *Proceedings of the 2014 IEEE Winter Conference on Applications of Computer Vision, WACV 2014*, pp. 509–515, March 2014.

[28] S. Yoshinaga, A. Shimada, H. Nagahara, and R.-I. Taniguchi, "Object detection based on spatiotemporal background models," *Computer Vision and Image Understanding*, vol. 122, no. 5, pp. 84–91, 2014.

[29] B. Wang and P. Dudek, "A fast self-tuning background subtraction algorithm," in *Proceedings of the 2014 IEEE Conference on Computer Vision and Pattern Recognition Workshops, CVPRW 2014*, pp. 401–404, June 2014.

[30] X. Lu, "A multiscale spatio-temporal background model for motion detection," in *Proceedings of the IEEE International Conference on Image Processing*, pp. 3268–3271.

[31] G. Allebosh, F. Deboeverie, P. Veelaert, and W. Philips, "EFIC: Edge based Forground background segmentation and interior classification for dynamic camera viewpoints," in *Advanced Concepts for Intelligent Vision Systems (ACTIVS)*, pp. 433–454, 2015.

[32] X. Cao, L. Yang, and X. Guo, "Total variation regularized rpca for irregularly moving object detection under dynamic background," *IEEE Transactions on Cybernetics*, vol. 46, no. 4, pp. 1014–1027, 2016.

[33] G. Ramírez-Alonso and M. I. Chacón-Murguía, "Auto-adaptive parallel SOM architecture with a modular analysis for dynamic object segmentation in videos," *Neurocomputing*, vol. 175, pp. 990–1000, 2016.

[34] N. Goyette, P.-M. Jodoin, F. Porikli, J. Konrad, and P. Ishwar, "changedetection.net: a new change detection benchmark dataset," in *Proceedings of the 2012 IEEE Computer Society Conference on Computer Vision and Pattern Recognition Workshops, CVPRW 2012*, pp. 1–8, June 2012.

4

Nonintrusive Method Based on Neural Networks for Video Quality of Experience Assessment

Diego José Luis Botia Valderrama and Natalia Gaviria Gómez

Engineering Department, Universidad de Antioquia, Medellín, Colombia

Correspondence should be addressed to Diego José Luis Botia Valderrama; diego.botia@gmail.com

Academic Editor: Stefanos Kollias

The measurement and evaluation of the QoE (Quality of Experience) have become one of the main focuses in the telecommunications to provide services with the expected quality for their users. However, factors like the network parameters and codification can affect the quality of video, limiting the correlation between the objective and subjective metrics. The above increases the complexity to evaluate the real quality of video perceived by users. In this paper, a model based on artificial neural networks such as BPNNs (Backpropagation Neural Networks) and the RNNs (Random Neural Networks) is applied to evaluate the subjective quality metrics MOS (Mean Opinion Score) and the PSNR (Peak Signal Noise Ratio), SSIM (Structural Similarity Index Metric), VQM (Video Quality Metric), and QIBF (Quality Index Based Frame). The proposed model allows establishing the QoS (Quality of Service) based in the strategy *Diffserv*. The metrics were analyzed through Pearson's and Spearman's correlation coefficients, RMSE (Root Mean Square Error), and outliers rate. Correlation values greater than 90% were obtained for all the evaluated metrics.

1. Introduction

The assessment of quality in digital video systems is a topic of great interest to the telecommunications companies that hope to increase the quality to their users. The QoE (Quality of Experience) is the degree of user's satisfaction with any kind of multimedia service. This concept has been defined in different ways by various authors. Liu et al. [1] suggested that QoE involves two aspects:

(i) The monitoring of the user's experience online.

(ii) The service control to ensure that QoS (Quality of Service) can satisfy the user's requirements.

QoE is an extension of QoS, since the former provides information about the services delivery from point of view of the end users. QoE refers to personal preferences of users and so seeks to assess the subjective perception of the received service [2, 3]. However, this perception is influenced, by the network performance in terms of QoS and video encoding parameters. Different methodologies proposed in the literature aim at estimating subjective Quality of Experience, through the assessment of different metrics of video quality generally using objective methods.

In the implementation of digital television platforms (e.g., IPTV and DVB), some important restrictions can affect the management and proper operation of the network. Some of these are

(i) the large amount of bandwidth the user should contract,

(ii) the limitation of internal buffers in routers and STB (Set Top Box), which can generate problems such as packet loss that are critical on video or audio transmission,

(iii) the type of video compression format, which will reduce the channel use without affecting the quality,

(iv) other items that should be installed and properly configured, such as the last mile link used and the admission control class used.

Different researches have proposed quality assessment models for video streams and measurement strategies in order to identify the optimal values for each metric guaranteeing the experience of the viewer.

According to Winkler [4], there are projects for QoE assessment: VQEG (Video Quality Experts Group), QoSM (Quality of Service Metrics) from ATIS IPTV Interoperability Forum, and specific metrics such as those oriented to packets, a bitstream, hybrids, and images metrics [5–8]; but these are more complex, and the correlation methods have not yet been applied for real time services assessment. Other works propose a new relationship between KPIs (Key Performance Indexes) with QoE assessment on mobile environments, but it can be applied in other scenarios as fixed broadband networks focused particularly on telecommunications providers [9].

One of the main problems on the estimation of the video subjective quality is the lack of proper estimation or correlation models. These must guarantee results with accuracy but in many cases heavily depend on objective metrics [10–12]. Also, the correlation models in QoE metrics are not accurate and reliable.

According to [13], three strategies were developed to perform the estimation of video quality. The first one is to apply a subjective assessment with a selected group of people; the main drawback of the evaluations is the cost and time. The second one is the objective quality metrics assessment for video, in which the principal disadvantage is the low correlation with regard to subjective quality metrics [14]; in addition, such metrics obviate the network and content parameters. The last one is to use machine learning methods to analyse the objective and subjective assessment but the major drawback is the difficult for configuring and testing; furthermore, some methods may fail whether a suitable design and optimal parameter selection are not performed.

According to Kuipers et al. [15], the minimum threshold of accepted quality is a MOS (Mean Opinion Score) value of 3.5. The subjective tests (such as MOS) are widely useful in assessing the users satisfaction due to its accuracy; however, the application of them is still very complex due to the high consumption of time and money; therefore, they are impractical for tasks of testing in network devices, and a controlled environment is required is required (in some cases, its implementation are complex).

Also if we want to develop traffic management techniques in real time, it is necessary to find a relationship among them and the objective metrics, measurable by the network equipment.

Objective methods are based on algorithms for the assessment of video quality, making them less complex and, furthermore, can be performed on controlled simulation environments. The objective metrics are supported in mathematical models that approximate themselves to the Human Vision System (HVS) behavior and, therefore, try to estimate as accurately as possible the true QoE. However, the perception of each viewer is highly influenced by the quality of the data network, expressed by the QoS parameters [26]. A lot of proposals for assessing QoE metrics have been created to define the user's experience. ITU-T has carried out standards for some of them [27, 28].

Due to complex factors such as the HVS, different kinds of solutions such as the implementation of machine learning techniques have been proposed. Some of the most used methods are Artificial Neural Network (ANN), fuzzy logic based on rules, neural-fuzzy networks (e.g., ANFIS), support vector machines (SVM), Gaussian processes, and genetic algorithm, among others. Nonintrusive QoE estimation methods for video are mainly based on application layer and network parameters.

Models as artificial neural networks have been little studied for estimation and prediction of video quality. For the evaluation of nonintrusive methods, we decided to employ two methods of machine learning: BPNN feedforward and RNN (Random Neural Network). We assess the output of each system, estimated MOS versus expected MOS. In each case, the fit of the correlation, determined by Pearson and Spearman rank order correlation coefficients, RMSE (Root Mean Square Error), and Outliers Ratio were calculated. The expected MOS was calculated from the VQM (Video Quality Metric), SSIM (Structural Similarity Index Metric), PSNR (Peak Signal Noise Ratio), and QIBF (Quality Index Based Frame) metrics.

This paper presents the key objective and subjective quality metrics and introduces a nonintrusive QoE assessment methodology based on machine learning techniques, showing its main features and functionality. Afterwards, the developed testbed is explained; both results obtained as their analyses are presented. Finally the main conclusions and further works will be shown.

2. Related Works

2.1. Methods for Quality of Experience Assessment. In spite of all proposals for objective metrics, they are always not close to the human perception, due to the fact that the perception is highly influenced by the performance of the network, defined in terms of QoS parameters. According to [29, 30], the objective metrics are computational models that predict the image quality perceived by any person and can be classified as intrusive and nonintrusive methods, as shown in Figure 1.

The Subjective Pseudo Quality Assessment model or PSQA (Pseudo Subjective Quality Assessment) is an example of nonintrusive method (NR). This model uses an RNN (Random Neural Network) [31–33] to learn and recognize the relationship between video and the characteristics of the network with the quality perceived by users.

Initially, for the training process of the RNN, a database is required which contains different sequences to assess the distortions generated by several QoS and coding parameters. Afterwards, the training of the RNN with any video sequence is evaluated in order to validate the MOS measure.

2.2. QoE Metrics

2.2.1. PSNR and MSE Metrics. The PSNR (Peak Signal Noise Ratio) and MSE (Mean Square Error) metrics are the most frequently applied ones [11]. They assess the quality of the received video sequence and, thus, can be mapped on a subjective scale PSNR aiming to compare pixel-by-pixel and frame-by-frame the quality of the received image with the

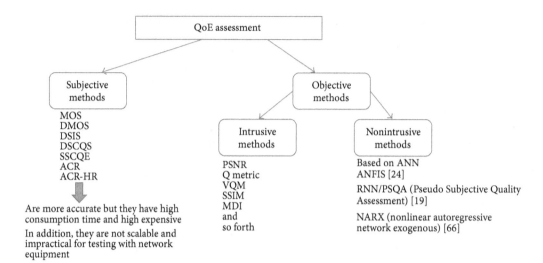

FIGURE 1: Methods for Quality of Experience assessment.

source image. It is the most known FR (Full Reference) metric. If we consider frames with a size of $M \times N$ pixels and 8 bits/sample, the PSNR can be calculated using (1) according to [34, 35] as follows:

$$\text{PSNR} = 20$$

$$\cdot \log_{10}\left(\frac{255}{\sqrt{(1/(M \times N))\sum_{i=0}^{M-1}\sum_{j=0}^{N-1}\|Y_s(i,j) - Y_d(i,j)\|^2}}\right), \quad (1)$$

where $Y_s(i, j)$ denotes a pixel in the (i, j) position of the original frame and $Y_d(i, j)$ refers to the pixel located at (i, j) position of the frame reconstructed in the receiver side. Around 255 elements are the maximum value that the pixel can take (255 for 8-bit images). The denominator is known as MSE or Mean Square Error, which is the mean square of the differences among the grey level values of the pixels into the pictures or sequences Y_s and Y_d.

Since several studies have used this mapping, PSNR is limited by the image content and it is not able to identify artifacts due to packet loss. In addition, the measure does not always correlate with the real user's perception due to the fact that a pixel-by-pixel comparison is carried out without performing an analysis of the image structural elements (e.g., contours or specific distortions introduced by either encoders or transmitting devices on the network or spatial and temporal artifacts). Therefore, some metrics are proposed to generate the extraction and analysis of the features and artifacts into video sequences such as SSIM metric [36].

2.2.2. SSIM Metric. Assuming that the human visual perception is highly adapted for extracting structures from a scene, SSIM (Structural Similarity Index) calculates the mean, variance, and covariance between the transmitted and received frames [37]. To apply SSIM, three components (luminance, contrast, and structural similarities) are measured and combined into one value called SSIM index ranging between −1 and 1, where a negative or 0 value indicates zero

correlation with the original image and 1 means that it is the same image [35].

According to Wang et al. [38], SSIM gives a good approximation of the image distortion due to changes in the measurement of structural information. On the video sequences, this metric considers a wide range of scenes complexity, in terms of movement, spatial details, and color. According to Wang et al. [37], this metric uses a structural distortion measure instead of the error. The above is focused on the human vision system to extract structural information from the visual field and ignored the extraction of errors. Therefore, a calculation of the structural distortion should give a better correlation with subjective metrics. In [39, 40], a simple and effective algorithm was proposed to calculate the SSIM index.

Let x be the original signal, $x = \{x_i \mid i = 1, 2, \ldots, N\}$, and let y be the distorted signal, $y = \{y_i \mid i = 1, 2, \ldots, N\}$; the similarity structure index is given by

$$\text{SSIM} = \frac{(2\overline{xy} + C1)(2\sigma_{x,y} + C2)}{\left[(\overline{x})^2 + (\overline{y})^2 + C1\right]\left(\sigma_x^2 + \sigma_y^2 + C2\right)}, \quad (2)$$

where is the mean of x, is the mean of y, and are the variances of x and y, is the covariance of x and y, and C1 and C2 are constant values. The SSIM value can be defined as

$$\text{SSIM}(x, y) = [l(x, y)]^\alpha [c(x, y)]^\beta [s(x, y)]^\gamma, \quad (3)$$

where $l(x, y), c(x, y)$, and $s(x, y)$ are comparison functions of the luminance, contrast, and structure components, and the parameters α, β, and $\gamma > 0$ are constants. SSIM(x, y) is the quality assessment index. For more details see [39].

2.2.3. VQM Metric. The NTIA VQM metric (Video Quality Metric) [39] considers two image inputs, the original and processed video, in which the quality levels are verified through the human vision system and some subjective aspects. This metric divides the image into sequences of space-temporal

TABLE 1: Comparative table of the main QoE metrics.

Metric	Standard	Class	Estimate	Type
PSNR		Objective	Pixel-by-pixel comparison between reference image and compressed image.	FR
VQM (Video Quality Metric)	NTIA	Objective	Sequences are divided into temporal-space blocks. Calculate the orientation of each block using spatial luminance gradient. Score tends to 0 (best). Assess blurring, global noise, block distortion, and color distortion	RR
SSIM (Structural Similarity Index)		Objective	Find the mean, variance, and covariance within a frame and combine them in a distortion map. Use luminance, contrast, and structure similarity. Use decimal value from 0 to 1 (high correlation with original picture).	FR
MOS	ITU-T P.800	Subjective	Subjective scale from 1 (poor) to 5 (good).	NA

blocks, measuring elements like blurring, general noise, block distortion, color distortion, and mix among them into a single metric. The score closer to 0 is considered the best possible value. According to Wang [41], this metric shows a good correlation with subjective methods and has also been adopted by ANSI as a standard for the assessment of video quality.

In Table 1, the comparative table of the main QoE metrics is summed up, which is used in this work.

2.2.4. New Mapping QoE Metrics. Zinner et al. [42] proposed a framework for the assessment of the QoE by using streaming video systems. On the other hand, Botia et al. [16] proposed a new mapping among the PSNR, SSIM, VQM, and MOS metrics, shown in Table 2. In our simulations, we calculated the average of each MOS for all video sequences with the value of each FR metric from Table 2 and then we obtained the expected MOS.

2.2.5. QIBF Metric. Serral-Garcia et al. [43] propose a framework called PBQAF (Profile Based QoE Assessment Framework). This framework defines three states for frames (correct, altered, and lost) through the analysis of the payload. Moreover, a mapping is performed to generate and associate the quality index. This metric is calculated from payload of the received packets, associated with a PLR (Packet Loss Rate) in particular. Equation (4) shows the quality function to generate the mapping function M:

$$Q(f) = M(\text{PLR}(f)), \qquad (4)$$

with PLR(f) being the packet loss rate of the frame f. The mapping function is given by

$$M(x) = 1 - x, \qquad (5)$$

where x shows the ratio of lost frames; therefore, when a high packet loss rate is measured, the quality index will be lower and tends to be 0. Thus, the final quality of the video stream into a set of quality values $q(fx)$ for particular frames is given by

$$Q_f = \{q(f_1), \ldots, q(f_n)\}, \qquad (6)$$

where $f_{1,\ldots,n}$ is the set of all frames in the video stream. From Botia et al. [44], a mapping between QIBF (Quality Index

TABLE 2: Mapping among QoE metrics (SSIM, PSNR, VQM, and MOS) [16].

MOS	PSNR (dB)	SSIM	VQM
5 (excellent)	≥37	≥0.93	<1.1
4 (good)	≥31–<37	≥0.85–<0.93	≥1.1–<3.9
3 (fair)	≥25–<31	≥0.75–<0.85	≥3.9–<6.5
2 (poor)	≥20–<25	≥0.55–<0.75	≥6.5–<9
1 (bad)	<20	<0.55	≥9

TABLE 3: QIBF versus MOS mapping [16].

MOS	QIBF value
5 (excellent)	≥0.85
4 (good)	≥0.65–< 0.85
3 (fair)	≥0.45–< 0.65
2 (poor)	≥0.25–< 0.45
1 (bad)	<0.25

Based Frame) metric and MOS metric is proposed for each frame *class I/P/B*; that is, each frame is equivalent to one class. In (7), the QIBF is given by

$$\text{QIBF}(\text{seq}, \text{nt}) = \sum_{f=1}^{F} \frac{1 - \text{NFL}(f)}{3} - \alpha, \qquad (7)$$

where F is the maximum number of frames, seq is the sequence of actual video to be evaluated, nt refers to the class network applied over the transmitted sequence (*BestEffort* or *Diffserv*), NFL(f) is the number of frames ($I/P/B$) lost, determined by the set of MPEG images, and α is an adjustment factor set to 0.05, obtained from several developed tests.

The factor 1/3 in (7) is defined through 3 classes of frames used in the tests. As NFL$(f) \in [0, 100]$, the value of NFL is divided by 100 in order to define NFL$(f) \in [0, 1]$ and, therefore, to calculate QIBF(seq, nt) $\in [0, 1]$. The demonstration is shown in Appendix A.

Table 3 shows the proposed mapping between quality index and MOS metric, where QIBF$(f) \in [0, \ldots, 1]$ and, as observed in Table 3, for an index value QIBF$(f) > 0.65$, a good value for the MOS metric is obtained, indicating a video sequence with a minimum of artifacts.

(a) News TVE

(b) Winter tree

(c) Mass

(d) Highway

FIGURE 2: Screenshots from video sequences assessed.

3. Simulation Testbed

For our test, a testbed is built up to use a simulation software tool *NS-2* and the framework *Evalvid* for assessing a set of video sequences. The results obtained from FR/RR metrics are evaluated to find the possible correlation with subjective metrics using machine learning techniques.

In the simulation, we used a selection of different video raw uncompressed sequences in format *YUV* with color mode or sampling 4 : 2 : 0, encoded with the ffmpeg and main concept software tools, to adapt them to different bitrates and GOP (Group of Pictures) lengths. Four video sequences were initially assessed with different levels of movement, encoded in the MPEG-4 format, which were adapted to be transmitted by a simulated IP network.

Figure 2 illustrates some screenshots of the evaluated videos (News of the Spanish Public *TV*, Mass, Highway and Winter Tree), converted and encoded at a resolution of 720 × 480 pixels (standard definition) under the NTSC standard, with frame rate of 30 fps. For each video stream, several parameters were combined as length of the GOP (10, 15, and 30), the bit rates recommended *by* DSL Forum [45] (1.5, 2, 2.5, and 3 Mbps), and packet loss rate for both networks (*BestEffort* and *Diffserv* using the congestion control algorithm, *WRED*), which produced 385 different video sequences for testing [16].

The generated video traces were adapted to be sent to the data network through the encapsulation of each packet with an MTU (Maximum Transfer Unit) of 1024 bits, using the RTP protocol (Real Time Transport Protocol) with *MP4trace* software tool. Considering the simulation tool *NS-2* and *Evalvid* framework [46], the sender and receiver trace files that were created, to calculate the sent and received lost frames and packets, delays, and jitters. The above facilitates the analysis of each video sequence for both implemented scenarios (*BestEffort* and *Diffserv* data networks).

The Evalvid framework also supports PSNR and MOS metrics and has a modular structure, making it easily adaptable to any simulation environment. MSU VQMT software tool [47] allows getting the Y-PSNR, SSIM, and VQM metrics values through the original reference video and received video with distortion.

The simulation scenario is composed of a video sender (server for video on demand) and 9 cross-traffic sources, which consist of *CBR* and *On-Off* traffic sources. The network is based on dumbell topology [48] (see Figure 3). In our test, we send several video packets over a network with congestion and will be allowed to test the defined QoS scheme (*Diffserv with WRED*). The MPEG-4 video flow is complete with background *On-Off* traffic flows, which has an exponential distribution with an average packet size of 1500 bytes, burst time of 50 ms, idle time of 0.01 ms, and sending rate of 1 Mbps [16, 44]. The access network is represented by a video receiver (simulating a last mile with ADSL2), with a bandwidth link of 10 Mbps and several receiving nodes (sink) for cross traffic with a bandwidth of 10 Mbps for each one. Transmission distortions were simulated at different PLR (Packet Loss Rate). The traffic behavior and QoE metrics were tested with several error rates over a link established between the core and edge routers, using a loss model with uniform distribution at rates of 0%, 1%, 5%, and 10% and delay of 5 ms. Tables 4 and 5 show the main parameters used in the simulation and encoding.

4. Implementation of Nonintrusive Methods to Estimate Video Quality by Objective and Subjective Metrics

For the evaluation of nonintrusive methods, we decided to use two machine learning methods (BPNN feedforward and Random Neural Network). These methods have been used in different environments described in the next section. To

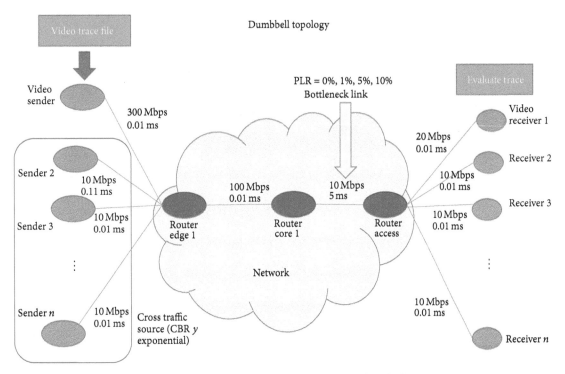

FIGURE 3: Simulation scenery with NS-2 and Evalvid.

TABLE 4: Encoder parameters.

GOP length	10, 15, and 30 frames
Frame rate	30 fps
Bitrate	1.5, 2, 2.5, and 3 Mpbs
GOP sequence	IPBBPBBPBBP...
Resolution	NTSC 720 × 480 p
Video color mode	YUV (4 : 2 : 0)

TABLE 5: Simulation parameters.

Bandwidth link	10/100 Mbps
Link delay	0.01 ms–5 ms
Buffer size	50
Tail behavior	DropTail/WRED random early detection
Packet size	1052 bytes (8 bytes UDP and 20 bytes IP)
Max fragment size	1024 bytes
PLR, loss model with uniform distribution	0%, 1%, 5%, and 10% and delay of 5 ms

assess the output of each system, we considered the following: estimates MOS versus expected MOS, where the latter is computed through the mapping of PSNR, VQM, SSIM, and QIBF metrics (see Tables 1 and 2).

In each case, the correlation adjustment was calculated, determined by the Pearson correlation coefficient and RMSE to estimate the error. The general methodology is presented in Figure 4 [26, 49].

Initially, the video sequences in RAW-format were obtained and they were codified in MPEG-4/AVC-format. Each sequence was sent through an IP-simulated network. The above is based on "BestEffort" and "Diffserv" where each FR/RR metric is calculated and their respective values are mapped. In this manner, average MOS value is obtained by using Tables 2 and 3. Considering the codification values, the kind of QoS network and the obtained FR/RR metrics allow building the input database for training two neural networks.

MATLAB software suite was used for BPNN, using the Neural Networks Toolbox. For RNNs case, we used the QoE-NNR software tool [50]. From 385 different sequences at different configured parameters, around 70% were used as training data and the remaining 30% as test and validation data. Finally, obtaining the estimated MOS value, the correlation is calculated with respect to the average MOS value. The given results of machines learning will be presented and discussed.

Table 7 shows a brief state of the art where several papers assess QoE using neural networks as PNN (Probabilistic Neural Network), BPNN (Backpropagation Neural Network), RNN (Random Neural Network), and ANFIS (Adaptive Neurofuzzy Inference System). Works, using a few video sequences, do not show resolutions or codec information and apply low resolutions (for mobile devices). Codec formats more used are H.264 and MPEG-4 AVC. We found that PSNR, SSIM, and VQM metrics are frequently applied and few works use 2 metrics or more. In our case, we were using 5 different metrics and 4 video sequences with motion levels in each scene. Finally, the machine learning based on neural networks (RNN, BPNN, and ANFIs) is used in these works. The results show a good performance of the MOS estimation.

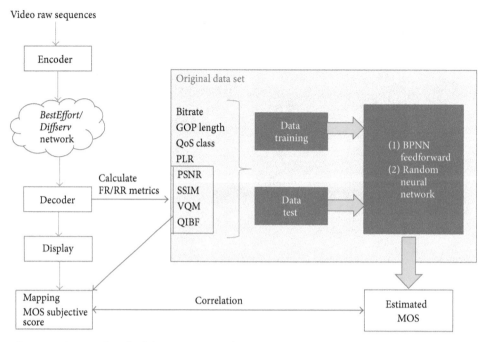

FIGURE 4: Proposed methodology to estimate the MOS metric using machine learning techniques.

However, they are defined by few input parameters, only assessing 1 or 2 video sequences in low resolution(s). They do not compare with other kinds of ANNs and, in most cases, the Pearson correlation coefficient was <0.90.

4.1. Case 1. Implementation of a Feedforward Artificial Neural Network with Backpropagation. The ANNs are a paradigm for processing information inspired by the human neural system. Usually, ANNs are composed of a large number of highly interconnected processing elements called neurons, which work together to solve problems [13]. The base is the creation of a neural network also called MLP (Multilayer Perceptron), usually divided into 3 or *N*-layers.

The first layer contains neurons connected to the input vector data; the second layer is called the hidden layer and incudes a set of synapses and a number of weights W_{ij} and some activating functions defined for exciting or inhibiting each neuron, generating a response. According to Rubino et al. [51], if the number of hidden neurons is low, it can have large training and generalization errors due to the underfitting. Otherwise, if there are many neurons in the hidden layer, low training errors may occur, but high generalization errors may appear, causing the undesired effect of overtraining (overfitting) and high variance. The third layer is the output layer directly connected to the hidden layer where data vectors of each estimated output will be obtained. Multiple layers of neurons with nonlinear transfer functions (such as tangential-sigmoid) allow the ANNs learning the linear and nonlinear relationships between the inputs (PLR, GOP, bitrate, QoS class, QIBF, PSNR, SSIM, and VQM) and the desired output vectors (MOS). The structure of Backpropagation Neural Network is shown in Figure 5.

ANNs type feedforward are the most commonly used ones to perform estimation of subjective metrics. Several works propose different models based on ANN [52–58]. These approaches are generally applied on mobile systems or with low resolutions (QCIF or CIF); furthermore, these works obviate the network parameters or video objective metrics. In most cases, one or two metrics as input to the network are used, and the results from Pearson's autocorrelations almost always are below 0.90.

According to Ding et al. [52], the neural network can be used to obtain mapping functions between objective quality assessment and subjective quality assessment indexes. This affirmation allows the understanding of the usefulness of the ANN to analyse the estimated MOS and the proposed model presented in this research.

In that case, the network training was carried out through several parameters, which will turn into input variables. As stated, the objective parameters may affect the video quality. After training, an evaluation with a set of test data (96 sequences) will be performed in order to reach the corresponding network validation. The idea is to reach the lowest error and to be able to correlate the estimated MOS by ANN versus the average MOS computed from the objective metrics defined by Tables 1 and 2.

For the case of study, we want to build the estimated MOS function, defined by

$$\text{MOS\_Est} = f(x_1, x_2, \ldots, x_n), \qquad (8)$$

where $\{x_1, x_2, \ldots, x_n\}$ are the input parameters established by bitrate, packet loss rate, GOP length, QoS class (1 for *BestEffort* and 2 for *Diffserv*), SSIM, PSNR, VQM, and QIBF.

Like a human being, the ANN system needs a learning phase and another one for validation and testing to establish when the neural network generalized its learning for any data set. For this process, the network is trained through a training

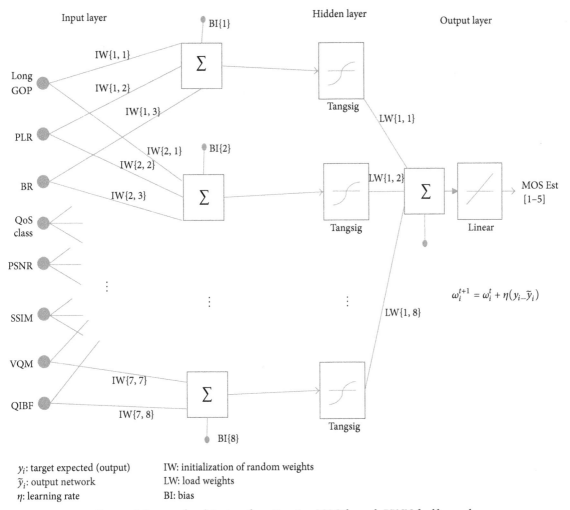

FIGURE 5: Proposed architecture for estimating MOS through BPNN feedforward.

algorithm and the lowest possible error is computed through the cost function MSE (Mean Square Error). In that case, we used an iterative gradient descent algorithm or other learning algorithms to achieve convergence to a target value (target), that is, to calculate the minimum training error of the network.

According to Ries et al. [59], in the multilayer network MLP, with a wide variety of nonlinear continuous activation functions on the hidden layers, one of these layers, which contain a largely arbitrary number of neurons, is sufficient to satisfy the property called universal approach. This allowed defining the neural network with a single hidden layer (with 20 neurons) satisfying the outputs (estimated MOS and desired MOS), calculated from the mapping of objective metrics. One of the major drawbacks is to find the right number of hidden neurons due to factors such as the quantity of input/output neurons, the number of training cases, the amount of noise in the output and input, the used architecture, the learning algorithms, and the kind of activation functions in the neurons on the hidden layer.

An empirical methodology was performed starting with 16 neurons in the hidden layer equal to twice of input neurons and a new neuron to reach the objective function with the

training algorithm Levenberg-Marquardt was added in each training and testing cycle. This is a widely used algorithm to solve the problem of least squares.

The proposed BPNN feedforward architecture is shown in Figure 6. In the input and output layer, the neurons have a linear activation function (*purelin*). In the hidden layer after various tests, the lowest training error was obtained with 20 neurons with function tangent-sigmoid activation (*tansig*).

After performing several iterations and resetting the weights in the training stage, the best performance is obtained as shown in Figure 7.

In Figure 8, the validation stage is illustrated. As shown, a good fit between the output data of the network and the desired MOS is obtained. An analysis of the linear regression between them is performed. The relationship is established between the estimated value by the BPNN (y variable) and desired data (x variable). The representation is given by the following classical linear equation:

$$y = mx + b. \qquad (9)$$

According to Pearson correlation parameter between the estimated MOS by BPNN and the expected MOS, a linear fit of 96.72% and a RMSE of 0.1977 were obtained. Figure 9

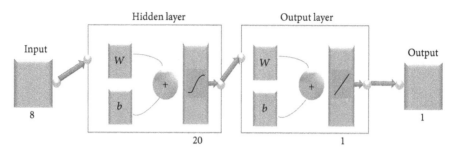

FIGURE 6: Neural Network feedforward 3-layer architecture.

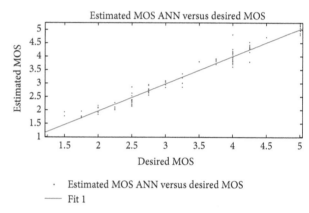

FIGURE 9: Estimated ANN MOS versus expected MOS.

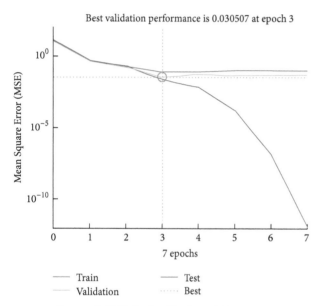

FIGURE 7: MSE obtained in the training stage.

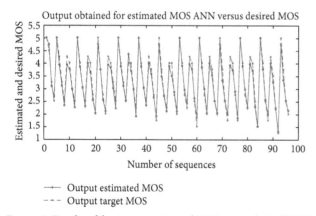

FIGURE 8: Results of the output, estimated MOS versus desired MOS.

shows the output of the correlation obtained. The results establish that the feedforward neural network allowed a good generalization with data used for validation and full linear relationship.

4.2. Implementation of a Random Neural Network (RNN) through PSQA Methodology. This kind of network captures with great accuracy and robustness mapping functions,

where several parameters are involved. According to Casas et al. [60], such networks have been used on multiple engineering fields, highlighting and solving NP-complete optimization problems, generating textures in images problems, video and image compression algorithms, and classification problems for perceived quality of voice and video over IP, which make them ideal for its application in QoE assess. Appendix B explains in detail the RNNs and the main parameters used in these networks. The RNNs are a cross between neural networks and queuing networks. By definition, RNNs are sets of ANNs formed by a range of interconnected neurons. These neurons exchanged instantly signals which travel from one neuron to another and send signals from and to the environment. Each neuron is associated with an integer random variable associated with a potential. The potential of a neuron i at time t is defined by $q_{i(t)}$. If the potential of the neuron i is positive, the neuron is excited and randomly sends signals to other neurons or to the environment according to Poisson process of rate r_i. The signals can be positive (+) or negative (−). The RNN has a three-tier architecture. Thus, the set of neurons $R \in \{1, \ldots, N\}$ is split into 3 subsets: the input neuron set, the set of hidden neurons, and the output neurons. An output $\vec{Y}^{(k)}$ is generated when the input is $\vec{X}^{(k)}$; therefore, $\vec{Y}^{(k)}$ = MOSs, for $k = 1, \ldots, K$, the set of weights for step k.

According to Casas et al. [60], it is necessary to apply a methodology to assess the Quality of Experience based on the use of network parameters (probability of packet loss, delay,

TABLE 6: General overview of the correlations obtained for the study cases.

Correlation	PCC	SROCC	RMSE	OR
Y-PSNR versus MOS BPNN	0.9303	0.9713	0.2882	0.5833
VQM versus MOS BPNN	0.9412	0.9707	0.2647	0.1979
SSIM versus MOS BPNN	0.9446	0.9733	0.257	0.1483
QIBF versus MOS BPNN	0.937	0.9711	0.2739	0.1562
Y-PSNR versus MOS_{psqa}	0.9698	0.9873	0.1796	0.5833
VQM versus MOS_{psqa}	0.9645	0.9900	0.1948	0.1666
SSIM versus MOS_{psqa}	0.9497	0.9889	0.2319	0.1354
QIBF versus MOS_{psqa}	0.9254	0.9853	0.2824	0.1354

Note: PCC (Pearson correlation coefficient) for prediction accuracy.
SROCC (Spearman rank order correlation coefficient) for monotonicity.
RMSE (Root Mean Square Error) for correlation quality assessment.
OR (Outlier Ratio) for consistence.

jitter, etc.) and video parameters (encoding, bitrate, frame rate, GOP length, etc.), which will become input parameters. Based on these criteria, a mapping function between these parameters and subjective quality value defined by the MOS metric can be generated. To perform this task, the author proposes the methodology PSQA (Pseudo Subjective Quality Assessment), which uses the RNNs to learn the mapping between the parameters and perceived quality [51].

This methodology is characterized by its accuracy; it allows generating automatic evaluations in real time which is efficient and can be applied with many kinds of media codec and under different parameters and network conditions. Also, it can be extended for comparison with objective metrics, generating more accurate correlations [61].

The RNN is considered as a supervised learning machine, which uses multimedia and network characteristics and the expected MOS values. If in the training stage a relationship of the input parameters through the objective metrics and the expected output is found, it is possible to estimate and/or predict the subjective values with a higher level of accuracy. Due to the RNNs features, they are perfect to generate good assessments for a wide variation of all parameters that affect the quality [51]. Therefore, it is an accurate model, fast, and with low computational cost. To develop the proposed study case, RNN feedforward 3-layer architecture, proposed by Mohamed and Rubino [61], is implemented. QoE-RNN software tool was used to estimate the MOS value through the use of a RNN. This tool has LGPL license and was developed in the programming language-C [50].

The whole process is presented in Figure 10, where video sequences transmitted over the network are assessed by comparing the target average MOS. Thus, depending on the QoS strategy implemented, the MOS values associated to each objective metrics (PSNR, VQM, SSIM, and QIBF) are set and are defined by MOS_{obj} and so the average MOS (MOS_p) that is the target value of the RNN is calculated. MOS_p is expressed as shown in the following equation [26]:

$$MOS_p = \sum_{i=1}^{N} \frac{MOS_{obj}}{N}, \quad (10)$$

where MOS_{obj} refers to the MOS for each objective metric and N is the total of samples.

The input parameters are chosen and, with the MOS_{psqa} obtained from the network, the corresponding correlation analysis is performed.

The number of boundary iterations is 2000 and the network topology is defined by 9 input neurons, 10 neurons in the hidden layer, and one output neuron. In different conducted tests, the best fit is achieved with 10 neurons in the hidden layer.

Using MATLAB, an analysis of the linear correlation between the expected MOS and MOS_{psqa} is performed. A good linear fit is found by the Pearson coefficient R^2 at 0.9812 and RMSE at 0.1412. In Figure 11, this correlation is shown.

The general summary of all correlations obtained from each study case is presented in Table 6.

The performance of perceptual quality metrics depends on its correlation with the results of objective metrics. Thus, the accuracy in the estimation of subjective metrics with respect to issues such as prediction accuracy, monotonicity, and consistency is evaluated. This guarantees a high reliability in the subjective assessment of video quality over a range of video test sequences with different artifacts. The assessment methods are proposed by the Video Quality Experts Group (VQEG) [62]. Four statistical measurements are applied to evaluate the video quality metrics performance: Pearson correlation coefficient (PCC), Spearman's rank order correlation coefficient (SROCC), Mean Square Error (RMSE), and Outlier Ratio (OR) [63, 64].

As shown in the results of Table 6, the correlations between MOS_{psqa} metrics were certainly good with objective metrics, with high Spearman coefficient proving high linear trend in all cases. The generalization was very high and we noted the consistency, accuracy, and monotonicity results. In the simulations performed, we observed that the VQM, SSIM, and QIBF metrics are highly correlated and are close to the users' perception (established by the MOS metric).

For all cases, the correlation reached values higher than 90%, and the correlation between the objective and subjective metrics in each case presents an excellent linear behavior. Accordingly, the metrics as VQM, SSIM, and QIBF are largely related to the subjectivity established by MOS. Also

TABLE 7: Papers with machine learning methods for assessing QoE.

Paper	# video sequences	Resolution	Code c	SSIM	VQM	PSRN	MSE	BR	FR	PLR	Q value (decodificables frames rate)	QP	Playout interruptions	Delay	Jitter	BW	MLBS	GOP	Machine learning	Assess MOS/DMOS?	Correlation performance PCC	SROCC	RMSE	OR
He et al. [17], 2012	1	QCIF	MPEG4			X				X				X	X		X	X	Probabilistic Neural Network (PNN)	Yes	0.9286	No	No	No
Kipli et al. [18], 2012	N/D	No data	No data	X		X	X												BPNN	Yes	0.891	No	No	No
Singh et al. [19], 2012	4	HD-720p	H.264			X				X		X	X	X					RNN	Yes	No	No	0.37	No
Lia et al. [20], 2011	4	No data	No data																BPNN	No	No	No	No	No
Khan at al. [21], 2010	6	QCIF	H.264					X	X								X		ANFIS	Yes	0.8717	No	0.2812	No
Du et al. [22], 2009	1	SD	No data			X				X				X	X	X	X		BPNN	Yes	No	No	No	No
Piamrat et al. [23], 2009	1	No data	H.264			X				X							X		PSQA with RNN	Yes	R = 0.8056 for MOS predicted versus MOS	No	RMSE = 0.1846 for MOS predicted versus MOS	No
Khan et al. [24], 2008	3	CIF	MPEG4					X	X	X	X					X			ANFIS	Yes	Measure and R = 0.9229 for Q predicted versus Q measure	No	measure and RMSE = 0.06234 for Q predicted versus Q measure	No
Rubino et al. [25], 2004	Only VoIP	No data	No data							X							X		RNN	No	No	No	No	No

BR: bitrate, FR: frame rate, PLR: Packet Loss Rate, QP: Quantization Parameter, BW: bandwidth, MLBS: Mean Loss Burst Size, GOP: Group of Pictures, PCC: Pearson correlation coefficient, SROCC: Spearman rank order correlation coefficient, RMSE: Root Mean Square Error, and OR: Outlier Ratio.

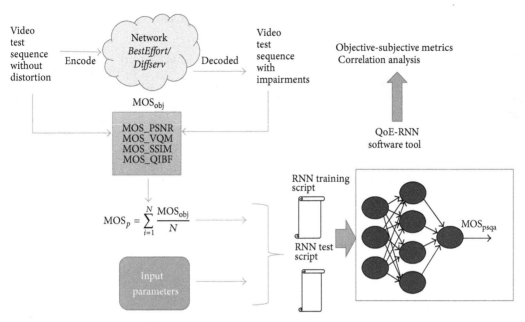

FIGURE 10: Employed methodology for the implementation of PSQA with the RNN.

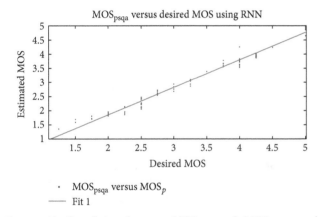

FIGURE 11: Correlation between MOS_{psqa} and MOS expected through the RNN.

it was observed that the results of the BPNN feedforward indicate a good generalization for estimated MOS against every assessed objective metrics, although it was slightly higher for applying the RNN. The RNN with PSQA provides a better correlation with the predicted values for MOS. The strategy generated by the nonintrusive model based on machine learning methods was shown to be accurate and highly flexible. It allows the estimation of subjective MOS values by relating them with FR (Full Reference) and RR (Reduced Reference) chosen for the research.

5. Conclusion

In this work, we obtained excellent correlation values between the objective and subjective QoE metrics through the use of nonintrusive methods. The accuracy, consistency, and monotonicity were validated with the analysis of Pearson's and Spearman's correlations, outliers rate, and RMSE (Roots Mean Square Error). One of the main limitations of the objective and subjective methods is the lack of complete methodologies to analyze the accuracy of QoE. Therefore, this problem was addressed in order to propose a new methodology that allows finding new correlations between objective and subjective metrics. To improve the analysis, the machine learning techniques were proposed through backpropagation artificial neural networks and Random Neural Networks to enhance the approach of the estimation of human perception. In different performed simulations, we observed that VQM, SSIM, and QIBF metrics are highly correlated and are close to the user perception (determined by the MOS metric). Unlike previous works, we developed a general correlation model which uses network and coding parameters applied to several video sequences. Analyzing the results from learning machines, the BPNNs and RNNs generated high correlations with objective metrics, obtaining PCC values higher than 90% and low error rates. The consistency of correlations between the metrics through outliers was calculated with low values. We conclude that the application of nonintrusive methods allows us to generate more accurate approaches to human perception. In addition, telecommunications providers can use this methodology for estimating the QoE of users and improve their data network architectures and/or global settings on their platforms, optimize the QoS, and employ better encoding mechanisms. The development of new models for the assessment of QoE is a top research topic according to the state of the art. The topics that are being currently working include

(i) development of new objective metrics, which are easy to apply and can be mapped accurately to the true perception of the viewer,

(ii) the close relationship of all QoS factors which affect the QoE,

(iii) new transmission strategies over highly congested data networks that can have a greater impact on transmission environments for streaming video over the internet which affect the user experience on the multimedia content over the next generation mobile devices,

(iv) the application of new kinds of video codecs specifically aimed at *HD* (*H.265/MPEG-DASH*, Dynamic Adaptive Streaming over *HTTP*) [65],

(v) the application of different methodologies based on machine learning techniques especially those related to artificial neural networks, neurofuzzy networks, support vector machines, and genetic algorithms.

Appendices

A. Proof of QIFB Metric

Let QIBF(seq, nt) be a QIBF metric $[0, 1]$; (7) fulfills the following axioms:

(P.1) [Maximum] If QIBF(seq, nt) = 1 for all $f = \{1, 2, 3\}$, with 1 being equivalent to I, 2 equivalent to P, and 3 equivalent to B, the MOS index is excellent; MOS = 5.

(P.2) [Minimum] If QIBF(seq, nt) = 0 for all $f = \{1, 2, 3\}$, with 1 being equivalent to I, 2 equivalent to P, and 3 equivalent to B, the MOS index is bad; MOS = 1.

(P.3) [Resolution] $QIBF_1$(seq, nt) < $QIBF_2$(seq, nt) for all $f = \{1, 2, 3\}$, with 1 being equivalent to I, 2 equivalent to P, and 3 equivalent to B, if $NFL_1(1) > NFL_2(1)$; $NFL_1(2) > NFL_2(2)$; and $NFL_1(3) > NFL_2(3)$.

(P.4) [Symmetry] $QIBF_1$(seq, nt) = $QIBF_2$(seq, nt) for all $f = \{1, 2, 3\}$, with 1 being equivalent to I, 2 equivalent to P, and 3 equivalent to B, if $NFL_1(1) = NFL_2(1) = NFL_1(2) = NFL_2(2) = NFL_1(3) = NFL_2(3)$.

Proof. (P.1) Considering NFL(1) = NFL(2) = NFL(3) = 0 for all $f = \{1, 2, 3\}$ and supposing that $\alpha = 0$, then QIBF(seq, nt) = 1. If $\alpha = 0.05$ as real adjustment, then QIBF(seq, nt) = 0.95 but this value can be approached at 1 in order to get a better evaluation of MOS. Therefore, as QIBF(seq, nt) = 1, the MOS score is around 5 as maximum value.

(P.2) If NFL(1) = NFL(2) = NFL(3) = 1 (maximum lost) for all $f = \{1, 2, 3\}$ and supposing that $\alpha = 0$, then QIBF(seq, nt) = 0. If $\alpha = 0.05$ as real adjustment, then QIBF(seq, nt) = 0.05 but this value can be approached at 0 in order to get a better evaluation of MOS. Therefore, as QIBF(seq, nt) = 0, the MOS score is around 1 as minimum value.

(P.3) Assuming $NFL_1(1) > NFL_1(2) > NFL_1(3)$ and $NFL_2(1) > NFL_2(2) > NFL_2(3)$, these relations are rewritten as

$$NFL_1(1) > NFL_2(1) > NFL_1(2) > NFL_2(2)$$
$$> NFL_1(3) > NFL_2(3). \tag{A.1}$$

Taking into account $QIBF_1$(seq, nt) and $QIBF_2$(seq, nt),

$$QIBF_1(\text{seq}, \text{nt}) = \sum_{f=1}^{F} \frac{1 - NFL_1(f)}{3} - \alpha,$$
$$QIBF_2(\text{seq}, \text{nt}) = \sum_{f=1}^{F} \frac{1 - NFL_2(f)}{3} - \alpha. \tag{A.2}$$

Then,

$$QIBF_2(\text{seq}, \text{nt}) - QIBF_1(\text{seq}, \text{nt})$$

$$= \left[\sum_{f=1}^{F} \frac{1 - NFL_2(f)}{3} - \alpha \right]$$

$$- \left[\sum_{f=1}^{F} \frac{1 - NFL_1(f)}{3} - \alpha \right], \tag{A.3}$$

$$QIBF_2(\text{seq}, \text{nt}) - QIBF_1(\text{seq}, \text{nt})$$

$$= \sum_{f=1}^{F} \frac{1 - NFL_2(f)}{3} - \sum_{f=1}^{F} \frac{1 - NFL_1(f)}{3}.$$

If $NFL_1(1) > NFL_2(1) > NFL_1(2) > NFL_2(2) > NFL_1(3) > NFL_2(3)$, it is obtained that

$$QIBF_2(\text{seq}, \text{nt}) > QIBF_1(\text{seq}, \text{nt}) \longleftrightarrow$$

$$\sum_{f=1}^{F} \frac{1 - NFL_2(f)}{3} > \sum_{f=1}^{F} \frac{1 - NFL_1(f)}{3}. \tag{A.4}$$

Therefore, it is found that $QIBF_1$(seq, nt) < $QIBF_2$(seq, nt) in which if $NFL_2\{1, 2, 3\}$ is monotonically decreased, the loss is also decreased and $NFL_1\{1, 2, 3\}$ is monotonically decreased if the loss is also increased. Thus, $QIBF_1$(seq, nt) < $QIBF_2$(seq, nt) is a sufficient condition.

(P.4) If $NFL_1(1) = NFL_2(1) = NFL_1(2) = NFL_2(2) = NFL_1(3) = NFL_2(3)$, it is obvious that $QIBF_1$(seq, nt) = $QIBF_2$(seq, nt) where the quantity of loss is the same. $\square$

B. Random Neural Network

The RNNs are a cross between neural networks and queuing networks. By definition, RNNs are sets of ANNs comprising a series of interconnected neurons. These neurons exchange signals which instantly travel from one neuron to another and send signals from and to the environment. Each neuron is associated with an integer random variable and these are associated with a potential. The potential of a neuron i at time t is defined by $q_i(t)$. If the potential of the neuron i is positive, the neuron is excited and randomly it sends signals to other neurons or to the environment according to Poisson's process with rate r_i. The signals may be positive (+) or negative (−). Thus, the probability that the signal sent from neuron i to neuron j is positive is denoted by $P_{i,j}^+$, and the probability that the signal is negative is denoted by.

The probability that the signal goes to the environment is denoted by d_i. If N is the number of neurons, for all $i = \{1, \ldots, N\}$, then d_i is expressed as shown in

$$d_i + \sum_{j=1}^{N} \left(p_{i,j}^+ + p_{i,j}^\pm \right) = 1. \tag{B.1}$$

Therefore, when a neuron receives a positive signal from another neuron or from the environment, its potential is increased by 1. If a negative potential signal is received, it decreases by one. When a neuron sends a positive or negative signal, its potential decreases in a unit.

The flow of positive signals arriving from the environment to the neuron i is Poisson's process with a λ_i^+ or λ_i^- rate. It is thus possible to have $\lambda_i^+ = 0$ and $\lambda_i^- = 0$ for any neuron i. To have an active network, (B.2) is needed:

$$\sum_{i=1}^{N} \left(\lambda_i^+ \right) > 0. \tag{B.2}$$

If g_i is defined as the equilibrium probability for neuron i in excitation state then, (B.3) is considered:

$$g_i = \lim_{t \to \infty} P \left(q_i(t) > 0 \right). \tag{B.3}$$

In (B.3), if Poisson's process for the potential of the neurons $\overrightarrow{q(t)} = \{q_1(t), \ldots, q_N(t)\}$ is ergodic, the network is defined as a stable and satisfies the conditions for a nonlinear system.

In RNNs, the purpose of the learning process is to obtain the values of R_i and probabilities $P_{i,j}^+$ and $P_{i,j}^-$. The above allows obtaining the weights of the connections between the neurons i, j, as shown in

$$\begin{aligned} \omega_{i,j}^+ &= R_i P_{i,j}^+, \\ \omega_{i,j}^- &= R_i P_{i,j}^-. \end{aligned} \tag{B.4}$$

From (B.4), the set of weights on the network topology is initialized with arbitrary positive values and K iterations that are performed to modify the weights. For $k = 1, \ldots, K$, the set of weights for the step k is calculated from the set of weights at step $k - 1$. Let $R^{(k-1)}$ be the network obtained after step $k - 1$ defined by weights $\omega_{i,j}^{+(k-1)}$ and $\omega_{i,j}^{-(k-1)}$; then, the set of inputs rates (positive external signals) on $R^{(k-1)}$ for $X_i^{(k)}$ will get a network that allows generating an output $\vec{Y}^{(k)}$ when the input is $\vec{X}^{(k)}$; therefore, $\vec{Y}^{(k)} = $ MOSs.

The RNN has a three-tier architecture. Thus, the set of neurons $R \in \{1, \ldots, N\}$ is split into three subsets: the set of input neuron, the set of hidden neurons, and the set of output neurons. The input neurons receive positive signals from the outside. For each node i, $d_i = 0$. For the output nodes $\lambda_i^+ = 0$, $d_i > 0$. The intermediate nodes are not directly connected to the environment, for any hidden neuron i, $\lambda_i^+ = \lambda_i^- = d_i = 0$.

There are several video sequences with different parameters for the case study, where a set of training data and another set of test data are selected. In (B.5), S denotes the set of training sequences, where each sequence is defined by α_n and S' refers to the set of validation sequences. Moreover, P is the set of parameters λ that affects each sequence, where

$$\begin{aligned} S &= \{\alpha_1, \alpha_2, \ldots, \alpha_S\}, \\ S' &= \{\alpha_1', \alpha_2', \ldots, \alpha_S'\}, \\ P &= \{\lambda_1, \lambda_2, \ldots, \lambda_n\}. \end{aligned} \tag{B.5}$$

The value of the parameter λ_p in the sequence α_S is defined by V_{ps} where $V = (V_{ps})$, where s is a matrix $s = 1, 2, \ldots, S$. Each sequence α_S receives a score MOSs $\in [1, \ldots, 5]$. Moreover, for the sequences $\alpha_S' \in S'$, a function $f(V_{1S}, V_{2S}, \ldots, V_{ps}) \approx$ MOSs is obtained and the training process is completed. Otherwise, we can try with more data or change some parameters of the RNN and proceed to build a new function f.

Conflict of Interests

The authors declare that there is no conflict of interests regarding the publication of this paper.

Acknowledgment

This research was developed as part of the macroproject "System of Experimental Interactive Television" for the Research and Innovation Center (Regional Alliance of Applied ICT-Artica) with code 1115-470-22055 and project no. RC584 funded by Colciencias and MinTIC.

References

[1] L.-Y. Liu, W.-A. Zhou, and J.-D. Song, "The research of quality of experience evaluation method in pervasive computing environment," in *Proceedings of the 1st International Symposium on Pervasive Computing and Applications*, pp. 178–182, IEEE, Urumqi, China, August 2006.

[2] S. Mohseni, "Driving Quality of Experience in mobile content value chain," in *Proceedings of the 4th IEEE International Conference on Digital Ecosystems and Technologies (DEST '10)*, pp. 320–325, Dubai, United Arab Emirates, April 2010.

[3] A. Devlic, P. Kamaraju, P. Lungaro, Z. Segall, and K. Tollmar, "Towards QoE-aware adaptive video streaming," in *Proceedings of the IEEE/ACM International Symposium on Quality of Service*, Portland, Ore, USA, February 2015, http://people.kth.se/~devlic/publications/IWQoS15.pdf.

[4] S. Winkler, "Standardizing quality measurement for video services," *IEEE COMSOC MMTC E-Letter*, vol. 4, no. 9, 2009.

[5] S. Winkler, "Video quality measurement standards—current status and trends," in *Proceedings of the 7th International Conference on Information, Communications and Signal Processing (ICICS '09)*, Macau, China, December 2009.

[6] K. Seshadrinathan and A. C. Bovik, "Motion tuned spatio-temporal quality assessment of natural videos," *IEEE Transactions on Image Processing*, vol. 19, no. 2, pp. 335–350, 2010.

[7] H. R. Sheikh and A. C. Bovik, "Image information and visual quality," *IEEE Transactions on Image Processing*, vol. 15, no. 2, pp. 430–444, 2006.

[8] A. K. Moorthy and A. C. Bovik, "A motion compensated approach to video quality assessment," in *Proceedings of the 43rd Asilomar Conference on Signals, Systems and Computers*, pp. 872–875, Pacific Grove, Calif, USA, November 2009.

[9] K. Radhakrishnan and L. Hadi, "A study on QoS of VoIP networks: a random neural network (RNN) approach," in *Proceedings of the Spring Simulation Multiconference (SpringSim '10)*, Society for Computer Simulation International, Orlando, Fla, USA, April 2010.

[10] S. Winkler and P. Mohandas, "The evolution of video quality measurement: from psnr to hybrid metrics," *IEEE Transactions on Broadcasting*, vol. 54, no. 3, pp. 660–668, 2008.

[11] F. Boavida, E. Cerqueira, R. Chodorek et al., "Benchmarking the quality of experience of video streaming and multimedia search services: the content network of excellence," in *Proceedings of the 23rd National Symposium of Telecommunications and Teleinformatics (KSTiT '08)*, Institute of Telecommunication and Electrical Technologies of University of Technology and Life Sciences, Bydgoszcz, Poland, September 2008.

[12] P. Casas, A. Sackl, R. Schatz, L. Janowski, J. Turk, and R. Irmer, "On the quest for new KPIs in mobile networks: the impact of throughput fluctuations on QoE," in *Proceedings of the IEEE International Conference on Communication Workshop (ICCW '15)*, pp. 1705–1710, London, UK, June 2015.

[13] M. Ries and J. R. Kubanek, "Video Quality Estimation for mobile streaming applications with neural networks," in *Proceedings of the Measurement of Speech and Audio Quality in Networks Workshop (MESAQIN '06)*, Prague, Czech Republic, June 2006.

[14] O. Nemethova, M. Ries, E. Siffel, and M. Rupp, "Quality assessment for H.264 coded low rate and low resolution video sequences," in *Proceedings of the IASTED International Conference on Communications, Internet and Information Technology (CIIT '04)*, pp. 136–140, St. Thomas, Virgin Islands, November 2004.

[15] D. Kuipers, R. Kooij, D. Vleeshauwer, and K. Brunnstrom, "Techniques for measuring quality of experience," in *Wired/Wireless Internet Communications*, vol. 6074 of *Lecture Notes in Computer Science*, pp. 216–227, Springer, Berlin, Germany, 2010.

[16] D. Botia, N. Gaviria, D. Jiménez, and J. M. Menéndez, "An approach to correlation of QoE metrics applied to VoD service on IPTV using a diffserv network," in *Proceedings of the 4th IEEE Latin-American Conference on Communications (IEEE LATINCOM '12)*, Cuenca, Ecuador, November 2012.

[17] Y. He, C. Wang, H. Long, and K. Zheng, "PNN-based QoE measuring model for video applications over LTE system," in *Proceedings of the 7th International ICST Conference on Communications and Networking in China (CHINACOM '12)*, pp. 58–62, Kunming, China, August 2012.

[18] K. Kipli, M. Muhammad, S. Masra, N. Zamhari, K. Lias, and D. Azra, "Performance of Levenberg-Marquardt backpropagation for full reference hybrid image quality metrics," in *Proceedings of International Conference of Muti-Conference of Engineers and Computer Scientists (IMECS '12)*, Hong Kong, March 2012.

[19] K. D. Singh, Y. Hadjadj-Aoul, and G. Rubino, "Quality of experience estimation for adaptive Http/Tcp video streaming using H.264/AVC," in *Proceedings of the 9th Anual IEEE Consumer Communications and Networking Conf. Multimedia and Entertainment Networking and Services (CCNC '12)*, pp. 127–131, Las Vegas, Nev, USA, January 2012.

[20] Q. Lia, J. Yangb, L. He, and S. Fan, "Reduced-reference video quality assessment based on bp neural network model for packet networks," *Energy Procedia*, vol. 13, pp. 8056–8062, 2011, Proceedings of the International Conference on Energy Systems and Electric Power (ESEP '11).

[21] A. Khan, L. Sun, E. Ifeachor, J.-O. Fajardo, F. Liberal, and H. Koumaras, "Video quality prediction models based on video content dynamics for H.264 video over UMTS networks," *International Journal of Digital Multimedia Broadcasting*, vol. 2010, Article ID 608138, 17 pages, 2010.

[22] H. Du, C. Guo, Y. Liu, and Y. Liu, "Research on relationship between QoE and QoS based on BP neural network," in *Proceedings of the IEEE International Conference on Network Infrastructure and Digital Content (IC-NIDC '09)*, pp. 312–315, Beijing, China, November 2009.

[23] K. Piamrat, C. Viho, A. Ksentini, and J.-M. Bonnin, "Quality of experience measurements for video streaming over wireless networks," in *Proceedings of the 6th International Conference on Information Technology: New Generations (ITNG '09)*, pp. 1184–1189, IEEE, Las Vegas, Nev, USA, April 2009.

[24] A. Khan, L. Sun, and E. Ifeachor, "An ANFIS-based hybrid video quality prediction model for video streaming over wireless networks," in *Proceedings of the 2nd International Conference on Next Generation Mobile Applications, Services, and Technologies (NGMAST '08)*, pp. 357–362, Cardiff, Wales, September 2008.

[25] G. Rubino and M. Varela, "A new approach for the prediction of end-to—end performance of multimedia streams," in *Proceedings of the International Conference on Quantitative Evaluation of Systems (QUEST '04)*, pp. 110–119, IEEE CS Press, University of Twente, Enschede, The Netherlands, September 2004.

[26] P. Goudarzi, "A no-reference low-complexity QoE measurement algorithm for H.264 video transmission systems," *Scientia Iranica Transactions: Computer Science & Engineering and Electrical Engineering*, vol. 20, no. 3, pp. 721–729, 2013.

[27] ITU-T, "Subjective video quality assessment methods for multimedia applications," Recommendation P.910, International Telecommunication Union, Geneva, Switzerland, 1999.

[28] ITU-T, *Recommendation, QoE Requirements in Consideration of Service Billing for IPTV Service*, UIT-T FG-IPTV, International Telecommunication Union, Geneva, Switzerland, 2006.

[29] P. Casas, P. Belzarena, I. Irigaray, and D. Guerra, "A user perspective for end-to-end quality of service evaluation in multimedia networks," in *Proceedings of the 4th International IFIP/ACM Latin American Conference on Networking (LANC '07)*, San José, Costa Rica, 2007.

[30] P. Casas, P. Belzarena, and S. Vaton, "End-2-end evaluation of IP multimedia services, a user perceived quality of service approach," in *Proceedings of the 18th ITC Specialist Seminar on Quality of Experience (ITEC '08)*, Karlskrona, Sweden, May 2008.

[31] R. Immich, P. Borges, E. Cerqueira, and M. Curado, "QoE-driven video delivery improvement using packet loss prediction," *International Journal of Parallel, Emergent and Distributed Systems—Smart Communications in Network Technologies*, vol. 30, no. 6, pp. 478–493, 2015.

[32] M. Kailash and D. Padma, "An overview of quality of service measurement and optimization for voice over internet protocol implementation," *International Journal of Advances in Engineering & Technology*, vol. 8, no. 1, pp. 2053–2063, 2015.

[33] S. Timotheou, "The random neural network: a survey," *The Computer Journal*, vol. 53, no. 3, pp. 251–267, 2010.

[34] K. Kilkki, "Next generation internet and QoE," in *Presentation at EuroFGI IA.7.6 Workshop on Socio-Economic Issues of NGI*, Santander, Spain, June 2007.

[35] ITU. FG-IPTV.DOC-0814, Quality of Experience Requirements for IPTV Services, 2007.

[36] E. Cerqueira, L. Veloso, M. Curado, and E. Monteiro, *Quality Level Control for Multi-User Sessions in Future Generation Networks*, University of Coimbra INESC Porto, Coimbra, Portugal, 2008.

[37] Z. Wang, A. C. Bovik, H. R. Sheikh, and E. P. Simoncelli, "Image quality assessment: from error visibility to structural similarity," *IEEE Transactions on Image Processing*, vol. 13, no. 4, pp. 600–612, 2004.

[38] D. Wang, W. Ding, Y. Man, and L. Cui, "A joint image quality assessment method based on global phase coherence and structural similarity," in *Proceedings of the 3rd International Congress on Image and Signal Processing (CISP '10)*, vol. 5, pp. 2307–2311, IEEE, Yantai, China, October 2010.

[39] M. Vranješ, S. Rimac-Drlje, and D. Žagar, "Objective video quality metrics," in *Proceedings of the 49th International Symposium ELMAR*, Faculty of Electrical Engineering, University of Osijek, Zadar, Croatia, September 2007.

[40] Z. Wang and A. C. Bovik, "A universal image quality index," *IEEE Signal Processing Letters*, vol. 9, no. 3, pp. 81–84, 2002.

[41] Y. Wang, *Survey of Objective Video Quality Measurements*, EMC Corporation, Hopkinton, Mass, USA, 2004, ftp://ftp.cs.wpi.edu/pub/techreports/pdf/06-02.pdf.

[42] T. Zinner, O. Abboud, O. Hohlfeld, T. Hossfeld, and P. Train-Gia, "Towards QoE management for scalable video streaming," in *Proceedings of the 21st ITC Specialist Seminar on Multimedia Applications Traffic, Performance and QoE*, Miyazaki, Japan, March 2010.

[43] R. Serral-Garcia, Y. Lu, M. Yannuzzi, X. Masip-Bruin, and F. Kuipers, *Packet Loss Based Quality of Experience of Multimedia Video Flows, Crente de Recerca d'Arquitectures Avancades de Xarxes (Politencic University of Cataluña), Spain*, Delft University of Technology, Delft, The Netherlands, 2009, http://personals.ac.upc.edu/rserral/research/techreports/psnr_mos.pdf.

[44] D. Botia, N. Gaviria, J. Botia, D. Jiménez, and J. M. Menéndez, "Improved the quality of experience assessment with quality index based frames over IPTV network," in *Proceedings of the 2nd International Conference on Information and Communication Technologies and Applications (ICTA '12)*, Orlando, Fla, USA, 2012.

[45] DSL Forum, "Triple play services quality of experience requierements and machanism," Working Text WT-126 version 0.5, 2006.

[46] J. Klaue, B. Rathke, and A. Wolisz, "EvalVid—a framework for video transmission and quality evaluation," in *Proceedings of the 13th International Conference on Modelling Techniques and Tools for Computer Performance Evaluation*, pp. 255–272, Urbana, Ill, USA, September 2003.

[47] D. Vatolin, "MSU Video Metric Quality Tool," MSU Graphics and media Lab, 2012, http://compression.ru/video/quality_measure/video_measurement_tool_en.html, Rusia.

[48] P. Subramanya, K. Vinayaka, H. Gururaj, and B. Ramesh, "Performance evaluation of high speed TCP variants in dumbbell network," *IOSR Journal of Computer Engineering*, vol. 16, no. 2, pp. 49–53, 2014.

[49] D. Botia, N. Gaviria, D. Jiménez, and J. M. Menéndez, "Strategies for improving the QoE assessment over iTV platforms based on QoS metrics," in *Proceedings of the IEEE International Symposium on Multimedia (ISM '12)*, pp. 483–484, Irvine, Calif, USA, December 2012.

[50] QoE-RNN Tool, 2011, http://code.google.com/p/qoe-rnn/.

[51] G. Rubino, M. Varela, and J.-M. Bonnin, "Controlling multimedia QoS in the future home network using the PSQA metric," *The Computer Journal*, vol. 49, no. 2, pp. 137–155, 2006.

[52] W. Ding, Y. Tong, Q. Zhang, and D. Yang, "Image and video quality assessment using neural network and SVM," *Tsinghua Science and Technology*, vol. 13, no. 1, pp. 112–116, 2008.

[53] A. Bouzerdoum, A. Havstad, and A. Beghdadi, "Image quality assessment using a neural network approach," in *Proceedings of the 4th IEEE International Symposium on Signal Processing and Information Technology*, pp. 330–333, Rome, Italy, December 2004.

[54] J. Choe, K. Lee, and C. Lee, "No-reference video quality measurement using neural networks," in *Proceedings of the 16th International Conference on Digital Signal Processing (DSP '09)*, pp. 1–4, IEEE, Santorini-Hellas, Greece, July 2009.

[55] X. Zhang, L. Wu, Y. Fang, and H. Jiang, "A study of FR video quality assessment of real time video stream," *International Journal of Advanced Computer Science and Applications*, vol. 3, no. 6, 2012.

[56] C.-H. Kung, W.-S. Yang, C.-Y. Huan, and C.-M. Kung, "Investigation of the image quality assessment using neural networks and structure similarty," in *Proceedings of the International Symposium on Computer Science*, vol. 2, no. 1, p. 219, August 2010.

[57] C. Wang, X. Jiang, F. Meng, and Y. Wang, "Quality assessment for MPEG-2 video streams using a neural network model," in *Proceedings of the IEEE 13th International Conference on Communication Technology (ICCT '11)*, pp. 868–872, IEEE, Jinan, China, September 2011.

[58] P. Reichl, S. Egger, S. Moller et al., "Towards a comprehensive framework for QOE and user behavior modelling," in *Proceedings of the 17th International Workshop on Quality of Multimedia Experience (QoMEX '15)*, pp. 1–6, IEEE, Pylos-Nestoras, Greece, May 2015.

[59] M. Ries, J. Kubanek, and M. Rupp, "Video quality estimation for mobile streaming applications with neural networks," in *Proceedings of the Measurement of Speech and Audio Quality in Networks Workshop (MESAQIN '06)*, Prague, Czech Republic, June 2006.

[60] P. Casas, D. Guerra, and I. Bayarres, "Perceived Quality of Service in Voice and Video Services over IP," School of Engineering, Universidad de la República, End of career project, Electrical Engineering—Plan 97, Telecommunications, Uruguay, 2005.

[61] S. Mohamed and G. Rubino, "A study of real-time packet video quality using random neural networks," *IEEE Transactions on Circuits and Systems for Video Technology*, vol. 12, no. 12, pp. 1071–1083, 2002.

[62] VQEG, "Video Quality Experts Group, Final Report from the VQEG on the validation of Objective Models of Video Quality Assessment, Phase II," 2003, http://www.its.bldrdoc.gov/vqeg/vqeg-home.aspx.

[63] S. Winkler, *Digital Video Quality—Vision, Models and Metrics*, John Wiley & Sons, 2005.

[64] A. Bath, I. Richardson, and S. Kannangara, *A New Perceptual Quality Metric for Compressed Video*, The Robert Gordon University, Aberdeen, Scotland, 2007.

[65] M. Alreshoodi, J. Woods, and I. K. Musa, "Optimising the delivery of Scalable H.264 Video stream by QoS/QoE correlation," in *Proceedings of the IEEE International Conference on Consumer Electronics (ICCE '15)*, pp. 253–254, IEEE, Las Vegas, Nev, USA, January 2015.

[66] A. Kuwadekar and K. Al-Begain, "User centric quality of experience testing for video on demand over IMS," in *Proceedings of the 1st International Conference on Computational Intelligence, Communication Systems and Networks (CICSYN '09)*, pp. 497–504, Indore, India, July 2009.

5

Image Encryption Performance Evaluation Based on Poker Test

Shanshan Li and Weiyang Sun

School of Information Engineering, Chang'an University, Middle Section of Nan'er Huan Road, Xi'an 710064, China

Correspondence should be addressed to Shanshan Li; sputnik@126.com

Academic Editor: Deepu Rajan

The fast development of image encryption requires performance evaluation metrics. Traditional metrics like entropy do not consider the correlation between local pixel and its neighborhood. These metrics cannot estimate encryption based on image pixel coordinate permutation. A novel effectiveness evaluation metric is proposed in this paper to address the issue. The cipher text image is transformed to bit stream. Then, Poker Test is implemented. The proposed metric considers the neighbor correlations of image by neighborhood selection and clip scan. The randomness of the cipher text image is tested by calculating the chi-square test value. Experiment results verify the efficiency of the proposed metrics.

1. Introduction

The accelerating growth of personal smart devices and Internet makes it easy to distribute, share, and exchange digital image data via various sorts of open networks. It is simple to access these image data when they are transmitted via open networks. In this case, image data security has become a crucial issue because some of the image content needs to be kept confidential. Image encryption is an effective solution to guarantee image data security. The encryption process converts the original image into another incomprehensible image. The ideal cipher text image is not intelligible. Such a cipher text image could be stored or transmitted across insecure networks without content leaking to anyone except the intended recipient. Since images have certain characteristics such as bulk data size and high intercorrelation, image encryption schemes focus on destroying the correlation between neighbor pixels. This requires that cipher text image should appear as meaningless noises.

Since image encryption has attracted extensive attention, various encryption schemes have been proposed in recent years. As a result, efficient image encryption performance evaluation is desired. To evaluate the encryption performance helps optimizing parameter setting as well as improving encryption scheme [1]. Subjective preference test provides several cipher text images and asks the observers to find out the one that they consider to be best performed. The subjective test is intuitive and straightforward. However, it is inconvenient, time-consuming, and expensive. Hence, it has led to a rising demand for objective evaluations. Image encryption destroys the correlation between neighbor pixels. Cipher text image should be nonrelative to the original plain text image and appear like meaningless noise. As a result, there are two kinds of objective evaluation metrics. The first kind tries to estimate the relation between cipher text image and plain text image. Correlation coefficient is a metric of this kind, which calculates the correlation coefficient between pixels in the same location in the plain text and cipher text images [2]. Another widely used metric is the deviation from identity, which measures the deviation of the histogram of the encrypted image from the histogram of the ideally encrypted image [3]. This kind of objective metrics requires the knowledge of reference image. The other kind focuses on randomness test of cipher text image. This kind of objective metrics does not need the plain text image as reference [4]. The nonreference objective encryption performance evaluation is more practical because the reference image is not always available. Several statistical tests for randomness could be employed to evaluate image encryption performance, such as approximate entropy and block frequency [5]. These evaluations usually require transformation of image to bit stream.

This paper proposes a nonreference objective metric to evaluate the image encryption performance. The novel metric is based on Poker Test with consideration of pixel neighborhood relationships. First traditional objective criterions are discussed. Then, Poker Test is introduced. The novel metric is described. Finally, performance of the metric is evaluated to check the effectiveness in Section 5.

2. Traditional Metrics

When an image encryption scheme is proposed, several performance analyses will be implemented to estimate the effectiveness of novel encryption scheme. The most widely used evaluation criterions include encryption quality and Shannon entropy.

2.1. Encryption Quality. The encryption quality is designed to measure the change rate of pixel values when encryption is applied to an image [6]. Higher change in pixel value indicates the image encryption and the encryption quality to be more effective. The encryption quality is expressed in terms of total changes in pixels values between the plain text image and the cipher text image.

Let P and C denote the plain text image and cipher text image, respectively. Assume $H_l(P)$ and $H_l(C)$ are the numbers of occurrences for each gray level l in the plain text image and cipher text image; the total gray level is L. Encryption quality is defined as follows:

$$\text{EQ} = \frac{\sum_{l=0}^{L-1} |H_l(P) - H_l(C)|}{L}. \tag{1}$$

The encryption quality could not estimate encryption based on image pixel coordinate permutation. The pixel positions shuffle without values changing makes no difference between $H_l(P)$ and $H_l(C)$. In this case, encryption quality could not evaluate the performance of encryption. Moreover, encryption quality requires the knowledge of plain text image P, which is not always available.

2.2. Shannon Entropy. Shannon entropy or information entropy is a measurement of uncertainty. The greater value of entropy indicates the system is more random. When a random variable's probability distributes equally, the Shannon entropy will be the biggest. If the Shannon entropy of a cipher text image approaches the theoretical peak value, the encryption will be considered as effective [7].

Assume the probability of pixel value l is $h(l)$ and the total gray level is L; Shannon entropy of the image is calculated by

$$\text{SE} = 6 - \sum_{l=0}^{L-1} h(l) \log_2(h(l)). \tag{2}$$

Shannon entropy requires no reference image. However, it cannot evaluate the encryption based on pixel position shuffle either. The neighbor correlations of pixels are not considered.

2.3. Autocorrelation. Autocorrelation is the cross-correlation of a signal with itself at different points in time [8]. Pixels in

meaningful image are correlative in horizontal, vertical, and diagonal directions. Effective image encryption destroys the correlation among adjacent pixels. Thus, two-dimensional autocorrelation values could be adopted to evaluate the performance of image encryption. As the correlation between adjacent pixels is the focus, normalized autocorrelation values of one pixel shifted on these three directions are employed as the measurement of image encryption quality. That means the center of the mask image is shifted from the center of original image with one pixel. The normalized 2D autocorrelation of image I is defined as

$$\text{NA}(i, j) = \frac{\sum_{r,c} \left(I(r,c) - \bar{I}\right)\left(I(r-i, c-i) - \bar{I}\right)}{\sqrt{\sum_{r,c}\left(I(r,c) - \bar{I}\right)^2 \left(I(r-i, c-i) - \bar{I}\right)^2}} \tag{3}$$

in which $I(r,c)$ is the pixel value in image I at position (r,c). $\bar{I}$ is the mean value of the image. If the size of the image is $R * C$, NA will be a matrix with size of $(2R-1) * (2C-1)$. The normalized autocorrelation value with one-pixel shift is the value in matrix NA at position of $(R, C+1)$, $(R+1, C)$, and $(R+1, C+1)$.

2.4. Gap Test. The gap test is used for testing randomness of a sequence. It is concerned with the number of gaps in any particular class of digits [9]. The elements of the sequence are classified into two categories: the elements with values between zero and upper bound, marked as 0, and the elements with other values, marked as 1. The continuous zeros are defined as "gap." The length of zero gaps is counted. Then the chi-square statistic is calculated by

$$G = \sum_j \frac{\left(n_j - np_j\right)^2}{np_j} \tag{4}$$

in which n_j is the number of zero gaps of length j and p_j is the probability of the length of zero gaps equal to j. p_j is calculated by $p_j = p^j(1-p)^2$, where p is the probability that the element belongs to category 0.

3. Poker Test

Poker Test is a randomness test. It treats numbers grouped together as a poker's hand. The hands obtained are compared to what is expected. The classical Poker Test consists of using all possible categories obtained from poker that uses hands of five numbers. In practice, Poker Test can be applied without being restricted to hands of five numbers. For cryptography application, four numbers are more convenient to deal with bit streams [10].

National Institute of Standards and Technology designed randomness test FIP 140-2 with Poker Test as the second test [11]. The Poker Test in FIP 140-2 is defined as follows: a single bit stream of 20,000 consecutive bits shall be divided into 5,000 nonoverlapping parts. These parts are called nibbles [12]. One nibble consists of 4 bits. The numbers of occurrences of each of the $2^4 = 16$ possible values are counted

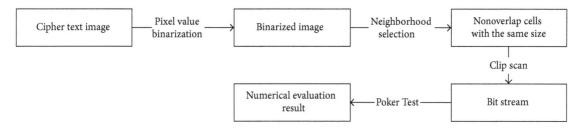

FIGURE 1: Flowchart of encryption performance evaluation of proposed metric.

and stored. The Poker Test determines whether these nibbles appear approximately in the same frequency. The chi-square test is employed to evaluate the randomness by formula

$$X = \frac{16}{5000} \sum_{i=0}^{15} \left(f(i) \right)^2 - 5000 \qquad (5)$$

in which $f(i)$ is the number of the ith possible values. It is obvious that Poker Test deals with bit stream and the number of the streams is constrained. A cipher image is a two-dimensional matrix with unknown size and integer values of elements. These issues require being addressed if we try to evaluate the randomness of cipher text image by the Poker Test.

4. Novel Metric

Image encryption destroys the correlation between neighbor pixels. Cipher text image should appear like meaningless noise as much as possible. Effective image encryption should generate randomness like cipher text image. The novel encryption performance evaluation metric is based on randomness test of cipher text image and pixel neighborhood correlations. Figure 1 provides the flowchart of encryption performance evaluation by proposed novel metric.

4.1. Pixel Value Binarization. The cipher text image consists of pixels with integer decimal values. The values need to be binarized for Poker Test because there are too many possible combinations for pixel values. The cipher text image can be converted into a binary image by tossing coin formula [13]

$$b(i, j) = \begin{cases} 1, & p(i, j) \geq \overline{p} \\ 0, & \text{else} \end{cases} \qquad (6)$$

in which $p(i, j)$ is the pixel value at position (i, j) and $\overline{p}$ denotes the average value of all pixels in the cipher text image.

After the binarization, an image with binary pixel values is obtained.

4.2. Neighborhood Selection. The binarized cipher text image is divided into small cells that have the same size. One cell covers a local neighborhood. The size of cell is flexible, which is related to the neighborhood selection. Generally using 8-neighborhood of current pixel corresponds to a $3 * 3$ size cell.

A $2 * 2$ size cell considers the adjacent pixels in the horizontal, vertical, and diagonal direction. It is another neighborhood selection. Besides these two kinds of size, one-dimensional sizes like $1 * 3$ or $3 * 1$ are also workable. If the cipher text image size cannot be divided with no remainder by the cell size, the remainder of last rows and columns will be abandoned in the succeeding procedures. The reason is that cell size is small. Thus, the remainders are also not big. The small sizes of remainders have little influence on the randomness property of the whole image.

The size of neighborhood selection affects the bit segment of bit stream. Different size generates different length of bit segment. The possible combination numbers of the bit segments are also different. This will lead to the difference of chi-square value because the number of possible occurrences influences the value. In this case, the evaluation procedure should be kept consistent with neighborhood selection when estimating encryption schemes. Otherwise, the results make no sense.

4.3. Bit Stream Production. After neighborhood selection, small cells with the same size are acquired. The cell is two-dimensional in most cases. Thus, it is required to convert these cells into bit stream for Poker Test. The cells are clip scanned to produce bit segments. Figure 2 shows the schematic of clip scan. This kind of scan makes adjacent pixels in a cell still adjacent in the output bit segment. The procedure keeps neighborhood correlations of binarized cipher text image as much as possible. The segments construct a bit stream, which is going to be used in Poker Test.

4.4. Poker Test. The bit stream consists of bit segments. These bit segments have the same length of $M * N$, in which M and N are the numbers of cell rows and columns. There will be 2^{M*N} possible values of these segments. For each possible value, the number of occurrences is counted. This processing produces a histogram of 2^{M*N} bins. If the original pixel value is used to run the Poker Test, there will be 256^{M*N} bins for an 8-bit grey image. The computational cost is vast if the binarization step is skipped. Image has bulk data size. Thus the number of these occurrences is big enough, which is suitable for further statistic test. Chi-square test is employed to evaluate the similarity of observed and expected data. The expected data distributes evenly according to the hypothesis: "the occurrence of every possible value is the same." The random distributed bit stream supports the hypothesis.

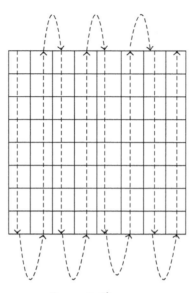

FIGURE 2: Clip scan.

The observed occurrence of possible value i is assumed as $O(i)$; the expected occurrence of every possible value is

$$E(i) = \frac{1}{2^{M*N}} \sum_{i=0}^{2^{M*N}-1} O(i). \qquad (7)$$

Then the chi-square value is calculated by

$$\chi^2 = \sum_{i=0}^{2^{M*N}-1} \frac{(O(i) - E(i))^2}{E(i)}. \qquad (8)$$

The computed value approximately follows the chi-square distribution with $2^{M*N} - 1$ degree of freedom. When the neighborhood is selected, the numbers of M and N are fixed and the degree of freedom is fixed. The more random distributed bit stream has smaller result value from (6), which means the cipher text image is more random-like. In this case, the encryption scheme that produces the cipher text image performs better.

5. Experiment

5.1. Evaluation of Pixel Position Encryption. Arnold's cat map is a chaotic map. It could be employed to encrypt image by transforming pixel positions [14]. The encrypted image randomizes the original one with enough iteration. There are quite a number of image encryption algorithms based on Arnold's cat map [15, 16]. Usually pixel value scrambling is combined with the position transformation to improve the security.

In this section, the classical Arnold's cat map image encryption algorithm is adopted to verify the proposed performance evaluation metric. The pixel in position (i, j) of

the original image is transformed to position (x, y) in the cipher text image by

$$\begin{bmatrix} x \\ y \end{bmatrix} = \begin{bmatrix} i + j \\ i + 2j \end{bmatrix} \quad \mod n \qquad (9)$$

in which n is the number of rows or columns of the image. The transformation could be iterated to gain more random-like results. However, if the iteration goes beyond necessary, the original image will be recovered. Figure 3 shows Arnold's cat map encryption result of $124 * 124$ image *Lena* with different iterations. The pixels rapidly degenerate into a chaos by iteration number five. Then the appearance of ciphered image is less random-like by iterations seven and eight. After that, the pixels again show chaos like at iterations nine and ten. When (9) is iterated more than 12 times, the cipher text images show some pattern. At iteration 15, the cipher text image is the same as the original plain text image.

Because there is no pixel value confusion processing in this encryption, the histogram of any ciphered image in Figure 3 is kept the same as the histogram of the original. Thus, the encryption quality calculated by (1) will be zero for every ciphered image. And the Shannon entropy calculated by (2) will be the same for every image in Figure 3.

The proposed metric is affected by the neighborhood selection as mentioned in former section. Table 1 lists the evaluation results of Figure 3 by the proposed novel metric with different neighborhood selections. Figure 4 presents the curve of evaluation value with respect to iteration number. It could be observed that the evaluation result curves are shaped like W. This is consistent with the impression of cipher image randomness in Figure 3. The middle bounce in the curve is not clear as neighborhood size is growing. This phenomenon appears because of the evaluation value growing at the first and last iteration. However, the evaluation results in Table 1 indicate the changing trends are the same in every column: decreasing, a little bounce off the bottom, decreasing again, and then increasing.

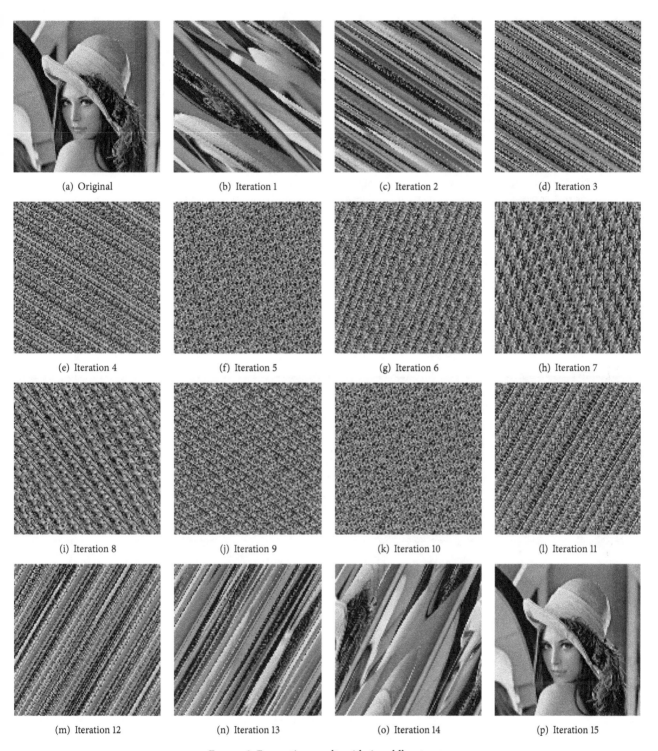

(a) Original   (b) Iteration 1   (c) Iteration 2   (d) Iteration 3

(e) Iteration 4   (f) Iteration 5   (g) Iteration 6   (h) Iteration 7

(i) Iteration 8   (j) Iteration 9   (k) Iteration 10   (l) Iteration 11

(m) Iteration 12   (n) Iteration 13   (o) Iteration 14   (p) Iteration 15

FIGURE 3: Encryption results with Arnold's cat map.

The novel metric ranks these cipher images performance by evaluation results' descending order as in Table 2. The poorest performance is considered to be cipher text image at iterations 1 and 14. This is consistent with the impression in Figure 3. The best performance of cipher image varies as the neighborhood selection changes. That is because the W shaped curve has two valleys. The ranking results demonstrate that the novel metric is efficient to evaluate the encryption performance. Moreover, the evaluation result is little affected by the neighborhood selection.

As the selection of neighborhood varies, the processing time for evaluation changes. Table 3 provides the time cost of novel metric with different neighborhood selection. It is clear that the time cost decreased as neighborhood area increased.

TABLE 1: The evaluation results of Figure 3 with different neighborhood selections.

Iteration	1×3	3×1	2×2	2×3	3×2	3×3	3×4	4×3	4×4	4×5	5×4
1	*1.385719*	1.196775	*3.347191*	*11.99883*	11.63813	75.55482	*480.2665*	413.79	*5323.014*	*65296.32*	58423.71
2	0.734746	0.360651	1.543533	4.922365	3.755407	19.79392	92.41148	79.89103	793.5749	8690.154	6602.61
3	0.120514	**0.027534**	0.304063	1.000514	0.659406	3.073698	14.45406	9.230866	117.1537	1612.963	2851.851
4	0.0273	0.043753	0.039836	0.191264	0.15016	0.906664	**5.316007**	5.184159	79.54323	**1487.938**	1525.824
5	0.047465	0.035306	0.048886	0.216916	0.163809	1.072634	5.757189	5.579702	80.82056	1540.979	1597.809
6	0.027789	0.028205	**0.0344**	**0.105016**	0.221175	0.975154	5.873823	6.071595	**77.55626**	1703.891	1828.916
7	0.027089	0.264011	0.283531	0.470944	0.695101	1.582503	5.62027	7.268365	87.91688	1707.679	1696.313
8	0.043775	0.057244	0.203925	0.426553	0.518664	1.632874	7.273436	7.253152	96.00669	1919.844	2014.56
9	**0.025219**	0.038816	0.055798	0.137621	0.208002	0.896879	8.510775	**5.037098**	79.82708	1616.752	2294.92
10	0.055899	0.032103	0.061117	0.228405	**0.148219**	1.015378	5.736905	5.255154	80.82056	1525.824	1514.458
11	0.027194	0.027806	0.045033	0.141306	0.161313	**0.879123**	5.336291	5.564489	82.38175	1575.077	**1442.474**
12	0.033834	0.121355	0.291464	0.564086	0.934649	2.592457	9.190297	10.09295	96.43247	1798.607	1559.922
13	0.301445	0.672199	1.310661	3.284809	4.448776	17.09745	61.50843	80.58577	577.9887	4556.741	5522.846
14	1.023181	*1.591066*	3.282402	10.75702	*12.68549*	72.00784	391.0057	*462.9641*	4649.005	54479.73	*61140.17*

TABLE 2: Performance ranking of cipher text image by descending order in Figure 3 with different neighborhood selections.

Ranking number	1×3	3×1	2×2	2×3	3×2	3×3	3×4	4×3	4×4	4×5	5×4
1	9	3	6	6	10	11	4	9	6	4	11
2	7	11	4	9	4	9	11	4	4	10	10
3	11	6	11	11	11	4	7	10	9	5	4
4	4	10	5	4	5	6	10	11	10	11	12
5	6	5	9	5	9	10	5	5	5	3	5
6	12	9	10	10	6	5	6	6	11	9	7
7	8	4	8	8	8	7	8	8	7	6	6
8	5	8	7	7	3	8	9	7	8	7	8
9	10	12	12	12	7	12	12	3	12	12	9
10	3	7	3	3	12	3	3	12	3	8	3
11	13	2	13	13	2	13	13	2	13	13	13
12	2	13	2	2	13	2	2	13	2	2	2
13	14	1	14	14	1	14	14	1	14	14	1
14	1	14	1	1	14	1	1	14	1	1	14

TABLE 3: Time cost of 124 * 124 image with different neighborhood selections.

Time cost (s)	1×3	3×1	2×2	2×3	3×2	3×3	3×4	4×3	4×4	4×5	5×4
	0.7323	0.708	0.597	0.4365	0.4407	0.3298	0.2946	0.2897	0.2613	0.2598	0.2486

It is because small neighborhood fragments the image area, which increases clip scan processing times. Since the evaluation result is affected little by the neighborhood selection, bigger area neighborhood is recommended. However, as the neighborhood area is growing, the numbers of possible combinations of the bit segment will grow exponentially. That causes high burden on computer memory. In this case, the area neighborhood should not be too big. Thus, the recommended neighborhood is 4 × 4, 4 × 5, and 5 × 4.

Normalized autocorrelation values with one-pixel shift on different directions are employed to measure the encryption performance in Figure 3 as a comparison. The center of the mask image is shifted from the center of original image one pixel in horizontal, vertical, and diagonal directions. Tables 4 and 5 present the evaluation results and performance ranking of autocorrelation. Because minus one value of autocorrelation indicates strong minus correlative, the absolute value in Table 4 is used to produce the ranking result in Table 5. The last several rows of vertical direction in Table 5 show there is a problem when evaluating the poorest performed cipher images. It is clear in Figure 3 that cipher images of iterations 1 and 14 are the poorest performed with iterations 2 and 13 after them. However, the vertical directional normalized autocorrelation ranks cipher image 13 in a high position. It is even higher than cipher image with iterations 3 and 8. This is not consistent with the visual impression in Figure 3.

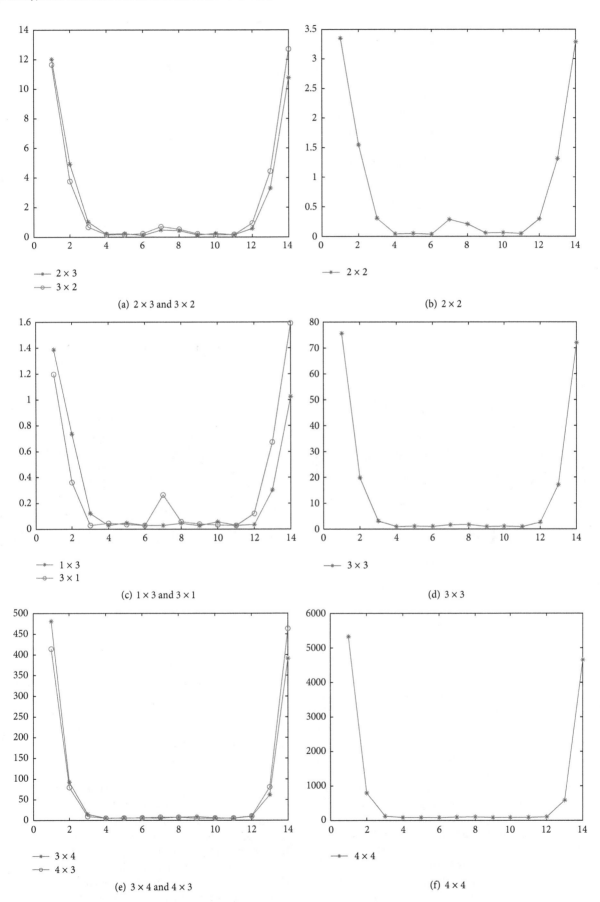

(a) 2×3 and 3×2

(b) 2×2

(c) 1×3 and 3×1

(d) 3×3

(e) 3×4 and 4×3

(f) 4×4

FIGURE 4: Continued.

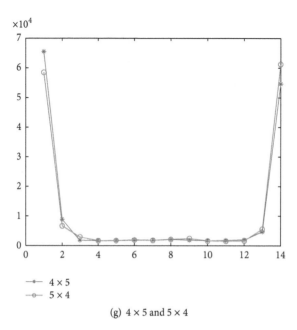

(g) 4×5 and 5×4

FIGURE 4: Evaluation result value curve with different neighborhood selection.

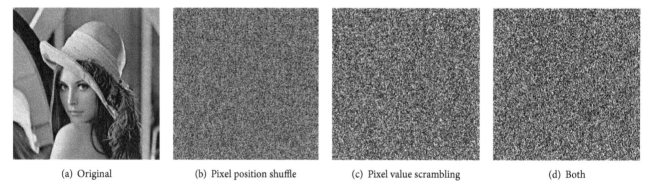

(a) Original   (b) Pixel position shuffle   (c) Pixel value scrambling   (d) Both

FIGURE 5: Encryption results with pixel value scrambling and position shuffle.

Another comparison is presented by the gap test. The cipher text images are stretched to a vector column by column to perform the gap test. As the cipher text images in Figure 3 are with 8-bit grey levels, the upper bound is set to be 51, 128, and 179 for the elements classification. The three values are 20%, 50%, and 70% of the maximum grey level. Then the chi-square is calculated by (4) as the evaluation. Tables 6 and 7 present the evaluation results and performance ranking. The gap tests have some problems when evaluating the four poorest performed cipher text images. When the upper bound value is set to be 20% of the maximum value, cipher text image of iteration 2 is ranked in a high position compared to iteration 7. When the upper bound value is set to be 70% of the maximum value, cipher text images of iterations 1, 2, and 13 are ranked even higher than cipher images with iterations 10 and 5. This is not consistent with the visual impression.

5.2. Evaluation of More Sophisticated Encryption. In this section, image encryptions with pixel value scrambling and position shuffle are used to verify the novel evaluation metric. The plain text image is first encrypted by Vigenere cipher to scramble its pixel grey level, and then the pixel positions are shuffled. Coupled logistic map is employed to produce the pseudorandom sequences for the encryption [17]. The plain text image and cipher text images are shown in Figure 5. Figure 5(b) is the cipher text image with only position shuffle. Figure 5(c) is the cipher text image with only pixel value scrambling processing; Figure 5(d) is the cipher text image with both processing. The keys are the same. The complex processing brings higher security. Thus, Figure 5(d) should be evaluated as the best performed.

The evaluation results for Figures 5(b), 5(c), and 5(d) by the proposed metric and other metrics are provided in Table 8. It is clear that the proposed metric with different neighborhood selection gives Figure 5(d) the lowest value. That means the cipher text image encrypted both by pixel scrambling and by position shuffle is considered as the best encrypted. All of the proposed metrics also score Figure 5(b)

TABLE 4: The evaluation results of Figure 3 by normalized autocorrelation on different directions.

Iteration	Horizontal	Vertical	Diagonal
1	0.77962	0.729447	0.865807
2	0.57696	0.423958	0.706407
3	0.214836	0.064253	0.415315
4	0.026138	−0.06878	0.062199
5	−0.04489	−0.00844	−0.06562
6	−0.03496	0.026926	−0.00918
7	0.01608	0.364424	0.025746
8	0.101325	0.091398	0.349932
9	0.024626	−0.06663	0.094174
10	−0.04724	−0.00661	−0.06211
11	−0.01579	0.018661	−0.00866
12	0.080648	0.25252	0.01943
13	0.419839	0.577335	0.243791
14	0.672049	0.819787	0.55581

TABLE 6: The evaluation results of Figure 3 by gap test with different upper bound value.

Iteration	20%	50%	70%
1	52503.25	7808.829	367.5231
2	47752.74	4465.835	209.8415
3	43252.68	1820.068	259.5888
4	41304.9	1747.163	451.1019
5	44715.45	1527.501	468.2339
6	43627.67	1364.194	362.027
7	48866.78	3543.446	162.4724
8	43643.1	2268.268	249.9645
9	41271.27	1787.271	459.0743
10	44687.99	1501.879	476.4293
11	43458.54	1339.975	367.6016
12	46925.5	2605.323	217.2968
13	50898.11	5734.178	265.2439
14	54496.37	8954.634	479.1238

TABLE 5: Performance ranking of cipher text image by descending order in Figure 3 with normalized autocorrelation in different directions.

Ranking number	Horizontal	Vertical	Diagonal
1	10	11	11
2	5	6	7
3	11	12	9
4	6	7	4
5	3	10	6
6	9	4	5
7	4	5	10
8	8	9	12
9	12	13	8
10	7	8	3
11	2	3	13
12	13	14	2
13	1	2	14
14	14	1	1

TABLE 7: Performance ranking of cipher text image by descending order in Figure 3 with different upper bound value gap test.

Ranking number	20%	50%	70%
1	9	11	7
2	4	6	2
3	3	10	12
4	11	5	8
5	6	4	3
6	8	9	13
7	10	3	6
8	5	8	1
9	12	12	11
10	2	7	4
11	7	2	9
12	13	13	5
13	1	1	10
14	14	14	14

as the poorest performed. This is consistent with the performance analysis. Normalized autocorrelation assigns Figure 5(c) the smallest absolute value except vertical direction. The gap test also has some problems when evaluating Figures 5(c) and 5(d). In the last column, Figure 5(b) has the same entropy as the original plain text image while Figures 5(c) and 5(d) have the same entropy. This is because their grey level histograms distribute the same.

6. Conclusion

This paper proposes a nonreference objective metric to evaluate the image encryption performance. The novel metric considers pixel neighborhood relationships. Poker Test is employed to test the randomness of the cipher text image. The metric can efficiently estimate encryption based on image pixel coordinate permutation. The experiment recommends several neighborhood selections.

Competing Interests

The authors declare that there is no conflict of interests regarding the publication of this paper.

Acknowledgments

The project is supported by National Natural Science Foundation of China (Grant nos. 61402051 and 51278058), the 111 Project (no. B14043), Natural Science Basic Research Plan in Shaanxi Province of China (Program no. 2016JM6076), and the Young Scientists Fund of Natural Science Foundation of Shaanxi Province (Program no. 2015JQ6239).

TABLE 8: Evaluation results of the cipher text image in Figure 5.

	The proposed metric			Normalized autocorrelation			Gap test			Entropy
	3×3	4×5	5×4	Horizontal	Vertical	Diagonal	20%	50%	70%	
Figure 5(b)	0.337	325.96	322.42	0.0627	−0.075	−0.061	172290	2504.5	2221.7	7.4442
Figure 5(c)	0.071	320.85	321.63	0.0009	−0.006	0.0023	91872	2666.9	17.1381	7.9967
Figure 5(d)	0.066	320.45	320.25	−0.003	0.0028	0.0081	94411	2823.1	14.51	7.9967

References

[1] L. Tong, F. Dai, Y. Zhang, and J. Li, "Visual security evaluation for video encryption," in *Proceedings of the 18th ACM International Conference on Multimedia (MM '10)*, pp. 835–838, ACM, October 2010.

[2] J. Ahmad and F. Ahmed, "Efficiency analysis and security evaluation of image encryption schemes," *Computing*, vol. 23, p. 25, 2010.

[3] C. Chattopadhyay, B. Sarkar, and D. Mukherjee, "Encoding by DNA relations and randomization through chaotic sequences for image encryption," http://arxiv.org/pdf/1505.01795.pdf.

[4] X.-F. Zhang and J.-L. Fan, "Two new digital image encryption effect evaluation criterions," *Computer Science*, vol. 37, no. 2, pp. 264–268, 2010.

[5] L. Wang, W. Meilin, D. Kui, and Z. Xuecheng, "Scalable truly random number generator," in *Proceedings of the World Congress on Engineering*, vol. 1, London, UK, July 2015.

[6] A. H. M. Ragab, O. S. Farag Allah, A. Y. Noaman, and K. W. Magld, "Encryption quality evaluation of robust chaotic block cipher for digital imaging," *International Journal of Recent Technology and Engineering*, vol. 2, no. 6, pp. 4–9, 2014.

[7] S. Chapaneri, R. Chapaneri, and T. Sarode, "Evaluation of chaotic map lattice systems for image encryption," in *Proceedings of the International Conference on Circuits, Systems, Communication and Information Technology Applications (CSCITA '14)*, pp. 59–64, IEEE, Mumbai, India, April 2014.

[8] C. Yuganya, "2D cross correlation multi-modal image recognition," *Journal of Global Research in Computer Science*, vol. 4, no. 4, pp. 13–17, 2013.

[9] E. Bofinger and V. J. Bofinger, "The gap test for random sequences," *The Annals of Mathematical Statistics*, vol. 32, pp. 524–534, 1961.

[10] W. M. F. Abdel-Rehim, I. A. Ismail, and E. Morsy, "Testing randomness: the original poker approach acceleration using parallel MATLAB with OpenMP," *Computer Science and Engineering*, vol. 5, no. 2, pp. 25–29, 2015.

[11] Federal Information Processing Standard (FIPS), "Security requirements for cryptographic modules," PUB 140-2, 2001.

[12] S.-J. Xu, X.-B. Chen, R. Zhang, Y.-X. Yang, and Y.-C. Guo, "An improved chaotic cryptosystem based on circular bit shift and XOR operations," *Physics Letters A*, vol. 376, no. 10-11, pp. 1003–1010, 2012.

[13] R. Kadir and M. A. Maarof, "Randomness analysis of pseudorandom bit sequences," in *Proceedings of the International Conference on Computer Engineering and Applications (IPCSIT '11)*, vol. 2, Singapore, 2011.

[14] G. Peterson, "Arnold's cat map," Math 45-Linear algebra, 1997, http://pages.physics.cornell.edu/~sethna/teaching/562_S03/HW/pset02_dir/catmap.pdf.

[15] Z.-G. Ma and S.-S. Qiu, "An image cryptosystem based on general cat map," *Journal of China Institute of Communications*, vol. 24, no. 2, pp. 51–57, 2003.

[16] A. Kanso and M. Ghebleh, "A novel image encryption algorithm based on a 3D chaotic map," *Communications in Nonlinear Science and Numerical Simulation*, vol. 17, no. 7, pp. 2943–2959, 2012.

[17] S. Li, Y. Zhao, B. Qu, and J. Wang, "Image scrambling based on chaotic sequences and Veginère cipher," *Multimedia Tools and Applications*, vol. 66, no. 3, pp. 573–588, 2013.

6

A Distortion-Free Data Hiding Scheme for Triangular Meshes Based on Recursive Subdivision

Yuan-Yu Tsai[1,2]

[1]*Department of M-Commerce and Multimedia Applications, Asia University, Taichung 413, Taiwan*
[2]*Department of Medical Research, China Medical University Hospital, China Medical University, Taichung 404, Taiwan*

Correspondence should be addressed to Yuan-Yu Tsai; yytsai@asia.edu.tw

Academic Editor: Balakrishnan Prabhakaran

This study adopts a triangle subdivision scheme to achieve reversible data embedding. The secret message is embedded into the newly added vertices. The topology of added vertex is constructed by connecting it with the vertices of located triangle. For further raising the total embedding capacity, a recursive subdivision mechanism, terminated by a given criterion, is employed. Finally, a principal component analysis can make the stego model against similarity transformation and vertex/triangle reordering attacks. Our proposed algorithm can provide a high and adjustable embedding capacity with reversibility. The experimental results demonstrate the feasibility of our proposed algorithm.

1. Introduction

Reversible data hiding algorithms [1–12] can recover the marked media to original one after the secret message is correctly extracted. The important media, such as those for medical or military applications, can apply such algorithms to carry the secret message. Therefore, researches on reversible data hiding have been springing up quickly in recent years.

Even though reversible image data hiding is a very hot research issue, algorithms for 3D models have not been intensively studied. Besides, most reversible data hiding algorithms for 3D models usually directly extended the ones for images to 3D models. For example, Jhou et al. [4] applied histogram modification on 3D models. They first calculate the gravity center of the input model and the embedding order for each vertex is then determined based on its distance to the center. Thereafter, the last d-digit of all coordinate values is used for histogram construction. The message is embedded into the coordinate values whose last d-digit is located at the peak point of the histogram. Chuang et al. [1] employed the Helmert transformation to raise the robustness against similarity transformation attacks. Their algorithm performs data embedding on the normalized distance between each vertex and the model center. Huang and Tsai [3] used the difference between each vertex and its neighboring ones

for histogram construction. Experimental results prove that their proposed algorithm can achieve higher embedding capacity, acceptable distortion, and greater robustness. Nevertheless, Wu and Dugelay [9] proposed a reversible data hiding algorithm based on difference expansion. They first predict a vertex position by calculating the center of its traversed neighbors. The secret message is then embedded by expanding the difference between the predicted and the original coordinate values. Zhu et al. [12] expand half aforementioned prediction difference to embed the watermark. Their proposed algorithm can provide lower distortion and controllable distortion. In contrast to above methods, Ji et al. [5] expand the distance ratio for data embedding to raise the robustness against noise attacks. Wu and Wang [10] first form a sequence of vertices by adopting a mesh traversal strategy. The secret message is embedded into the difference between every two adjacent vertices based on difference expansion and difference shifting.

Recently, Jung and Yoo [6] proposed the first interpolation-based reversible data hiding algorithm for images. Some improved algorithms [7, 8] are then proposed to improve its performance. The interpolation-based reversible data hiding algorithms first enlarged the input image to cover image based on their proposed interpolation scheme.

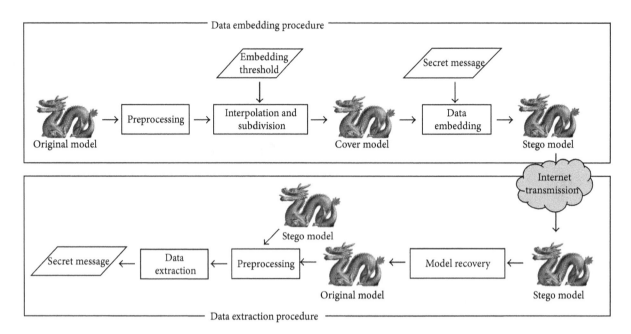

FIGURE 1: A flowchart of the proposed algorithm.

The secret message is embedded into the newly added interpolated pixels. In other words, more secret message can be embedded with larger magnifying factors. Because the pixels in the input image are not altered in the data embedding procedure, the input image can be recovered without any error. However, above proposed algorithm is currently applicable to grayscale images.

Similar interpolation concept for 3D models is so-called subdivision surface, representing a smooth surface via a recursive subdivision process on each given coarse polygonal face into smaller ones. Although some watermarking algorithms [13, 14] are operated on subdivision surface, they are either nonblind or irreversible or have low embedding capacity limited by the refinement process of subdivision surface.

This study extends the interpolation idea to triangular meshes. The algorithm first generates newly added vertices with the message embedded within one corresponding triangle. We then construct their topology with the vertices of located triangle. To raise the total embedding capacity, a recursive subdivision mechanism, terminated by a given criterion, is employed. Finally, a principal component analysis [15] makes our stego model against similarity transformation and reordering attacks.

This rest of this paper is organized as follows: Section 2 details the proposed technique; Section 3 presents a discussion on the experimental results; and, finally, Section 4 offers a conclusion and directions for future research.

2. Proposed Method

This section details the proposed distortion-free data hiding algorithm for triangular meshes. A triangle subdivision approach is performed on triangle meshes and the

secret message is embedded into the newly added vertices. Because the original vertex is not altered during the entire data embedding procedure, the original triangle meshes can be recovered without any error. Further, a recursive subdivision is employed to raise the embedding capacity. A given criterion terminates the recursion, considering the fixed number precision for representing the stego model. For being robust against the similarity transformation and vertex/triangle reordering attacks, a principal component analysis is used to solve this issue. Figure 1 shows a flowchart of the proposed algorithm. The following sections describe the proposed algorithm.

2.1. Data Embedding Procedure. This section details the data embedding procedure. The procedure begins by preprocessing the topological information of the input triangular meshes. The model information can be also derived in this process. Each vertex and each triangle are then sorted with the help of the normal vector and the principal axis. The data embedding process generates three barycentric weights and two of them are with the secret message embedded. The final triangle subdivision process takes above data-embedded weights as input to produce a newly added vertex and the triangle is subdivided into three smaller ones. The embedding capacity can be further improved significantly by recursive subdivision. Finally, the stego model is generated after processing each triangle. For simplicity, this study illustrates the proposed technique using 2D triangles. However, this can be easily extended to a 3D space.

2.1.1. Preprocessing Process. The relative information about the original triangular meshes is obtained in this process. Assume the triangular meshes consist of N_V vertices and N_T triangles. A principal component analysis is performed

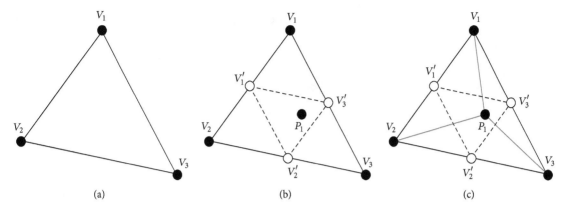

FIGURE 2: One example for data embedding process.

on the triangular meshes and one PCA coordinates system is generated. Obviously, the new coordinates system has a new origin, PCA_O, which is a gravity center of the triangular meshes, and three principal axes, called PCA_X, PCA_Y, and PCA_Z. Each vertex V_i is sorted according to the angle between the principal axis P_Z and the vector $\overrightarrow{V_i\text{PCA}_O}$. Each triangle T_i is also sorted according to the angle between the principal axis P_Z and the vector $\overrightarrow{C_{T_i}\text{PCA}_O}$, where C_{T_i} is the gravity center of the triangle T_i. The sorted result is the processing order for data embedding.

2.1.2. Data Embedding Process.

According to the processing order for each triangle, the data embedding process is initialized. Assume a triangle T (see Figure 2(a)) is constructed by three vertices, V_1, V_2, and V_3 and two series of B-bit secret message B_1 and B_2 are prepared for embedding. Three weights can be generated using (1) and the sum of them equals one, where $\text{SM}_{10}^{B_i}$ is the decimal value converted from B-bit binary secret message. For avoiding the unbalanced subdivision for each triangle, three temporary vertices V_1', V_2', and V_3' are first generated by (2) (see Figure 2(b)) and then sorted according to the angle between the principal axis P_Z and the vector $\overrightarrow{V_i'\text{PCA}_O}$. Assume that VS_1, VS_2, and VS_3 are the sorted results. A new point P_1, within the located triangle T, is then obtained based on the concept of barycentric coordinates using (3). The vertex P_1 is now with $2B$-bit secret message embedded (see Figure 2(b)). Consider

$$\alpha_1 = \frac{\text{SM}_{10}^{B_1}}{2^B},$$

$$\alpha_2 = (1 - \alpha_1) \times \frac{\text{SM}_{10}^{B_2}}{2^B}, \qquad (1)$$

$$\alpha_3 = 1 - \alpha_1 - \alpha_2,$$

$$V_{1_r}' = \frac{\left(V_{1_r} + V_{2_r}\right)}{2},$$

$$V_{2_r}' = \frac{\left(V_{2_r} + V_{3_r}\right)}{2},$$

$$V_{3_r}' = \frac{\left(V_{3_r} + V_{1_r}\right)}{2},$$

$$\text{where } r = x, y, z, \qquad (2)$$

$$P = \alpha_1 \text{VS}_1 + \alpha_2 \text{VS}_2 + \alpha_3 \text{VS}_3. \qquad (3)$$

2.1.3. Triangle Subdivision Process.

After the new point P_1 is generated, we then construct its topology with original vertices of located triangle T. The triangle $T_{V_1V_2V_3}$ is subdivided into three smaller triangles $T_{P_1V_1V_2}$, $T_{P_1V_1V_3}$, and $T_{P_1V_2V_3}$ (see Figure 2(c)). The first iteration for data embedding is now finished.

Following above rules, we can subdivide each smaller triangle again to raise the embedding capacity. However, considering the number precision of the stego model, the triangle cannot be subdivided infinitely. Therefore, some criteria can be adopted for terminating the recursive triangle subdivision, such as total embedding capacity, the area of subdivided triangle, or the number of subdivision iteration. In this study, we adopt the ratio R between the average triangle area AA of the triangular meshes and the area of subdivided triangle A_{ST} as the termination criterion. The triangle subdivision process is continued only when the area of subdivided triangle A_{ST} is larger than R times of the average area ($A_{\text{ST}} \geq R \times \text{AA}$).

First, we sort three subdivided triangles and process each triangle sequentially. For example, in Figure 3(a), the triangle $T_{P_1V_1V_2}$ is assumed to be the next processing triangle. We then pick one additional point P_2 again using (1), (2), and (3) and then construct its topology with three vertices of located triangle. Three smaller triangles are then generated. The recursive triangle subdivision process is continued until the termination condition is reached. For example, in Figure 3(b), the triangle $T_{P_1P_2V_1}$ cannot be subdivided because its surface area termination condition is assumed to be reached. Otherwise, an insufficient number precision for representing the vertex coordinates of stego model may result in the failure of data extraction. Figure 3(c) shows the example subdivided result for the triangle $T_{P_1P_2V_2}$. After processing the residual

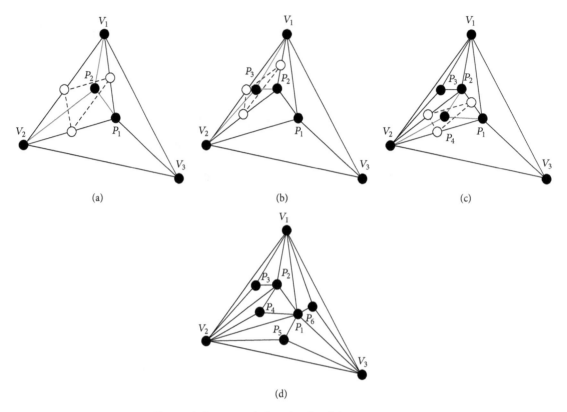

FIGURE 3: One example for triangle subdivision process.

triangles $T_{P_1V_2V_3}$ and $T_{P_1V_1V_3}$ recursively, one example stego model is shown in Figure 3(d).

2.2. Data Extraction Procedure.

After the receiver obtained the stego model, the data extraction procedure is initialized to extract the secret message following the below steps. Because each added vertex is derived from the barycentric weights of planar triangle, the distance between the vertex and its located triangle equals 0. Therefore, we first remove all the added vertices to reconstruct the original triangular meshes and a principal component analysis is then performed to obtain the original PCA coordinates system. Thus, the data extraction order for each triangle T_i can be obtained with the help of the angle between the principal axis P_Z and the vector $\overrightarrow{C_{T_i}\mathrm{PCA}_O}$.

Next, we adopt an iterative process to extract the secret message. It is obvious that the number of neighboring vertices for each added vertex is 3. Therefore, each iteration consists of four steps, including finding the added vertex, calculating its barycentric weights, extracting the secret message, and recovering the triangle. Above steps iteratively continue until all added vertices are removed. For example, in Figure 4(a), vertices P_3, P_5, and P_6 are found in the first iteration because of its three neighboring vertices. Take vertex P_3, for example, we can calculate its three barycentric weights. However, only two of them are with the secret message embedded. By checking the processing order of vertices V_1, V_2, and P_2, fortunately, we can obtain first two barycentric weights to extract secret message. Equation (4) shows the barycentric

weight calculation formula, where VS_1, VS_2, and VS_3 are the sorted results of three vertices of the processing triangle and P' is the processing vertex for data extraction. Equation (5) is used to extract two series of B-bit secret message. Because the secret message is embedded according to the angle between the normal of the triangle and principal axis, we then first recover three smaller triangles into a bigger one by removing the vertex and its neighboring relationship. Two series of B-bit secret message are then attached to the recovered angle. The first iteration is finished and current triangular meshes are shown in Figure 4(b). In the next iteration, vertices P_2 and P_4 are processed, whereas two triangles are recovered (see Figure 4(c)). Finally, vertex P_1 is processed (see Figure 4(d)) and the original triangle is recovered. The data extraction procedure is finished. Consider

$$\alpha_1 = \frac{\Delta P'\mathrm{VS}_2\mathrm{VS}_3}{\Delta\mathrm{VS}_1\mathrm{VS}_2\mathrm{VS}_3},$$

$$\alpha_2 = \frac{\Delta P'\mathrm{VS}_1\mathrm{VS}_3}{\Delta\mathrm{VS}_1\mathrm{VS}_2\mathrm{VS}_3}, \tag{4}$$

$$\alpha_3 = \frac{\Delta P'\mathrm{VS}_1\mathrm{VS}_2}{\Delta\mathrm{VS}_1\mathrm{VS}_2\mathrm{VS}_3},$$

$$\mathrm{SM}_{10}^{B_1} = \left\lfloor \alpha_1 \times 2^B \right\rfloor,$$

$$\mathrm{SM}_{10}^{B_2} = \left\lfloor \frac{(\alpha_2 \times 2^B)}{(1 - \alpha_1)} \right\rfloor. \tag{5}$$

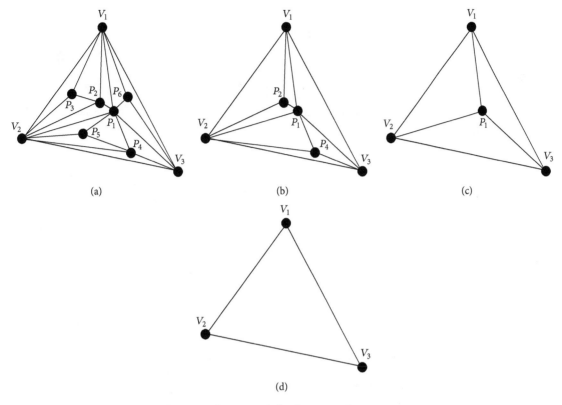

FIGURE 4: One example for data extraction process.

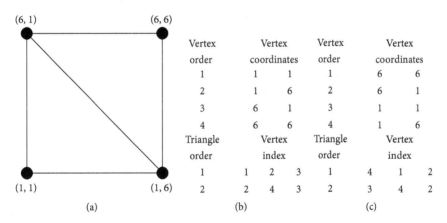

Vertex order	Vertex coordinates		Vertex order	Vertex coordinates	
1	1	1	1	6	6
2	1	6	2	6	1
3	6	1	3	1	1
4	6	6	4	1	6
Triangle order	Vertex index			Triangle order	Vertex index		
1	1	2	3	1	4	1	2
2	2	4	3	2	3	4	2

(a)   (b)   (c)

FIGURE 5: Examples of vertex reordering attacks.

2.3. Robustness Assessment. This section discusses the robustness of the proposed method. In this study, a principal component analysis is adopted to determine the processing order for each vertex and each triangle. In the beginning of the data extraction procedure, each added vertex can be removed because it is located on the triangle constructed by its neighboring vertices. The original cover model can be reconstructed and the same PCA coordinates system is obtained. Because the PCA coordinates system is robust against the rotation and translation operations, our stego model can resist above two attacks. Further, the barycentric weights are invariant before and after scaling operations; the same weights can be obtained.

Reordering attacks [3] modify the vertex/triangle representation orders in the model file but do not affect the appearance of 3D models. Figure 5 gives a 2D example of reordering attacks both on vertices and on triangles. The model in Figure 5(a) consists of four vertices and two triangles. Two examples for representing the model are shown in Figures 5(b) and 5(c). One of them can be the reordering attack of the other one. Although their vertex and triangle orders are different, the visual effects are the same. When performing our proposed data embedding and extraction procedure, each vertex and each triangle are sorted according to the angle between the normal vector and principal axis. The reconstructed extraction order is the same as the embedding

Bunny   Cow   Hippo

Solid shaded visual effects

Solid wireframe shaded result

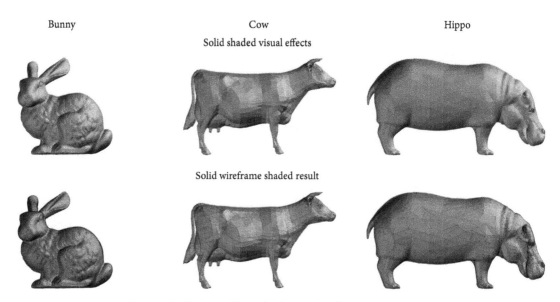

FIGURE 6: The visual effects for three triangular meshes.

order. Thus, our stego model can be robust against reordering attacks.

However, unlike watermarking algorithms with higher robustness against some intentional attacks, the proposed data embedding algorithm can provide more embedding capacity but with less robustness. Noise attacks cause some random disturbances on the vertex coordinates of 3D models. Even a noise attack for each vertex with small intensity can affect the integrity of extracted secret message. Some vertices with secret message embedded may be classified as ones without message embedded. However, if only part of vertices in the stego model is under the noise attack, we still have a chance to extract partial secret message. Finally, lossy compression attacks quantize the vertex coordinates, introduce new vertices, remove original vertices, or modify the topological relationship between vertices. The attacks seriously affect the generation of principal axis and the extraction order for each vertex is different from its embedding order. The extraction of the secret message from the attacked model fails.

3. Experimental Results

This section presents the experimental results obtained from three 3D triangular meshes, called "bunny," "cow," and "hippo." Table 1 shows the mesh information, including the number of vertices, N_V, the number of triangles, N_T, and model size (represented by the diagonal length DL_{BV} of the bounding volume), of each mesh. We also show the file size for each test model, stored in PLY file format, for later comparing the one of each stego model. Microsoft Visual C++ programming language was used to implement the proposed algorithm on a personal computer with an Intel® Core™ i7-6700K processor and 16 GB memory. Figure 6 shows the solid and solid wireframe shaded results for each cover triangular mesh. The embedded secret message was a

TABLE 1: Information about three triangular meshes.

Model name	N_V	N_T	DL_{BV}	File size
Bunny	34834	69541	25.02	2366 KB
Cow	2903	5804	12.71	179 KB
Hippo	23105	46202	60.00	1572 KB

randomly generated 0/1 bit string. The parameter B is set as 10.

This section first presents the visual effects for three stego models. We also show the close-up views for each model for a better comparison. Second, this section also presents the embedding capacity for three triangular meshes with different embedding thresholds R. Thereafter, the triangle area distribution for each mesh is shown to know the position of the embedding threshold. This section next presents the robustness assessment for our stego models. Finally, a comparison of this algorithm with current outstanding nonreversible/reversible algorithms demonstrates the feasibility of the proposed method.

Figure 7 shows the visual effects for three triangular meshes with secret message embedded. From Figures 6 and 7, the cover and stego models with different number of vertices and triangles can have the same rendering results. The reason is that the entire data embedding procedure makes all the added vertices and triangles being located on the original triangle. No influence is caused for visual effects. Figure 8 shows the close-up views of different meshes with different embedding thresholds, enabling a better comparison. Obviously, a close-up view for the wireframe shaded result of each model is quite different especially for small embedding threshold.

Table 2 shows the embedding capacity, number of processed triangles, and final number of vertices/triangles for

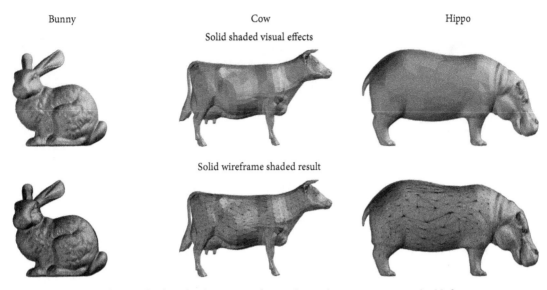

FIGURE 7: The visual effects for three triangular meshes with secret message embedded.

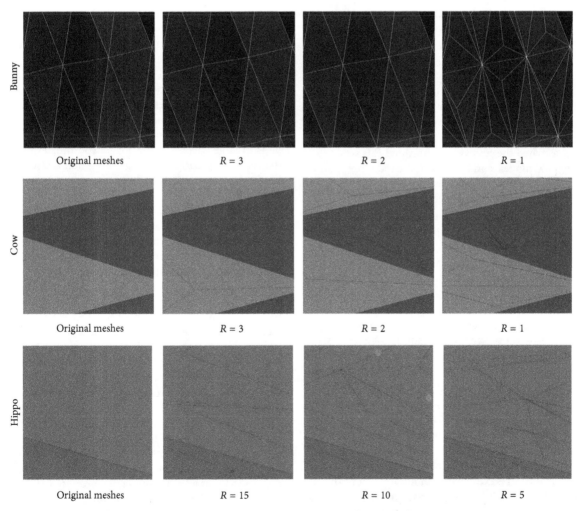

FIGURE 8: The close-up views for three triangular meshes with secret message embedded.

TABLE 2: The embedding capacity, number of processed triangles, and the number of vertices and triangles in the stego model.

Model name	Bunny			Cow			Hippo		
AA	0.008226			0.018753			0.065556		
R	1	2	3	1	2	3	5	10	15
Embedding capacity	525180	12760	1460	64820	19500	7960	88880	34680	19660
Number of processed triangles	25706	604	72	1842	753	342	1340	677	456
Vertex number, N_V'	61093	35472	34907	6144	3878	3301	27549	24839	24088
Triangle number, N_T'	121969	70727	69597	12286	7754	6600	55090	49670	48168
File size	4179 KB	2410 KB	2371 KB	383 KB	241 KB	204 KB	1882 KB	1693 KB	1641 KB

each test model. With the increase of the embedding threshold, the number of triangles which can be processed is less and the embedding capacity is decreased. Because each added vertex can be with $2B$-bit secret message embedded, the total embedding capacity equals $2B \times (N_V' - N_V)$. Further, the file size of each stego model is increased because of storing the coordinate values of newly added points and their topological relationship. Figure 9 shows the histogram of the area distribution of each triangle for different models. We also indicate the position of the embedding threshold R to show the located region used for data embedding. For each example in Figure 9, each triangle located at the gray region cannot be with message embedded because the embedding criterion is not reached. With the increasing of the embedding threshold, the number of embeddable triangles decreases and less secret message can be embedded. Only the triangle with an area located at the blue region can perform data embedding when the embedding threshold R is set as 3 for the bunny/cow models and is set as 15 for the hippo model. More triangles can be processed with message embedded with smaller threshold. For example, when the embedding threshold R is set as 2 for the bunny/cow models and is set as 10 for the hippo model, the triangles with an area located within the green region can be additionally used for data embedding.

This section next presents the robustness assessment for our proposed algorithm. As mentioned above, each added vertex is derived from the barycentric weights of planar triangle; the distance between the vertex and its located triangle equals 0. Therefore, we can reconstruct the original model by removing all the added vertices. The same PCA coordinates system is then obtained and the extraction order for each vertex is determined with no error. Further, to test the robustness of our scheme, we randomly rotate, translate, and uniformly scale each 3D stego model. Figure 10 shows the visual effects after similarity transformation attacks. The experimental results show that no error is in the extracted secret message. However, the number precision of the stego model must be increased properly under downscaling attack. For reordering attacks, vertices and triangles in the model file were reordered randomly for several times according to the scenario illustrated in Section 2.3. The embedded secret message can be extracted without any error. That is, the proposed scheme is robust against reordering attacks. For the experiment of our proposed method under noise attacks, we add random noise within the interval $[-\sigma, \sigma]$ to all the three coordinates of p percentage of vertices in

TABLE 3: The ratio of the vertices for correct message extraction after noise attacks with different parameters.

σ	p				
	10	20	30	40	50
1.0×10^{-4}	46.84%	19.73%	7.42%	2.70%	0.91%
5.0×10^{-5}	49.85%	23.04%	10.04%	4.13%	1.81%
1.0×10^{-5}	69.19%	48.49%	33.31%	22.75%	15.72%
5.0×10^{-6}	84.48%	71.96%	60.12%	48.98%	41.00%
1.0×10^{-6}	99.65%	99.42%	99.22%	99.05%	98.89%

the model and record the ratio R of the vertices for correct message extraction, where σ is the amplitude of noise. Table 3 shows the experimental results of bunny model under above scenarios. Other test models have similar results. As the value of parameter p increases, the ratio of the vertices for correct message extraction is apparently lower. Further, when the value of parameter σ is larger, indicating that each vertex can be with larger displacement for its coordinates, the ratio of the vertices for correct message extraction is also lower. As a result, the proposed algorithm has weak resistance to noise attacks.

Finally, this section compares the proposed algorithm with other existing outstanding algorithms in terms of embedding capacity, robustness, processed domain, and reversibility (Table 4). From the aspect of embedding capacity, Huang et al. introduced the permutation steganography for data embedding; each vertex can be with $\log_2 n!/n$-bit message embedded in the representation domain. However, the original orders for each vertex and triangle cannot be recovered after the message is embedded. Huang and Tsai proposed a reversible data hiding scheme for 3D polygonal models based on histogram shifting. The embedding capacity is unsatisfactorily only from 0.09 to 0.51 bit per vertex. Ji et al. adopted the difference expansion to achieve reversible data embedding with the embedding capacity of 1.01 to 1.09 bit per vertex. Our proposed algorithm derives the newly added points for data embedding; each can be with $2B$-bit secret message embedded. From the aspect of robustness, four algorithms are all robust against similarity transformation (ST) attacks. Huang et al.'s proposed algorithm can withstand similarity transformation attacks since the representation order of vertices and polygons is not modified after translation, scaling, and rotation attacks. The distance ratio in Ji et al.'s proposed method is invariant after the

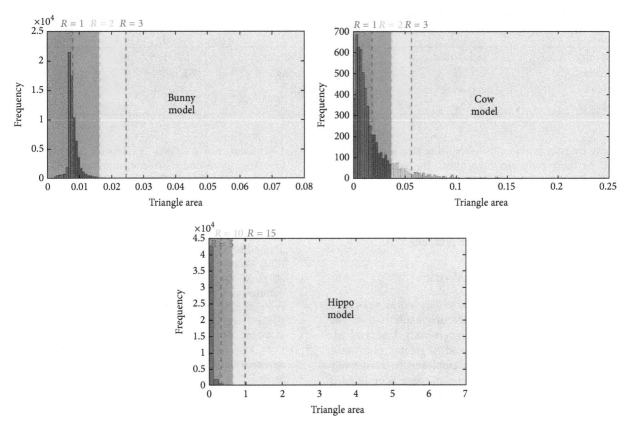

FIGURE 9: The histogram of the area distribution of each triangle for different models and the position of the embedding threshold R.

Rotating attacks

Translation attacks

Scaling attacks

FIGURE 10: The visual effects of stego models after similarity transformation attacks.

TABLE 4: A comparison of the methods of Huang et al. [16], Huang and Tsai [3], and Ji et al. [5] and the current method.

Algorithm	[16]	[3]	[5]	Our approach
Capacity (bpv)	$\approx \log_2 n!/n$	0.09~0.51	1.01~1.09	$2B$
Robustness	ST	ST, reordering	ST, noising	ST, reordering
Domain	Representation	Spatial	Spatial	Spatial
Reversibility	No	Yes	Yes	Yes

similarity transformation attacks. Noising attack can be also resisted in their proposed algorithm. The remaining two algorithms employ principal component analysis to make their algorithms robust against similarity transformation attacks. Our proposed algorithm can additionally be robust against reordering attack, because each processing vertex and each triangle are determined by the principal axis.

4. Conclusions and Future Work

This study proposes a novel reversible data hiding algorithm for 3D triangular meshes based on recursive subdivision. The proposed algorithm can provide reversibility, high embedding capacity, no visual distortion, and the greater robustness. For each triangle, a threshold is employed to recursively subdivide the triangle and the secret message is embedded into the added vertex. A principal component analysis can help the stego model against similarity transformation and vertex reordering attacks. The experimental results in this study demonstrate the feasibility of the proposed technique for reversible data hiding.

However, in the future, we hope to integrate the concept of subdivision surface to generate high-quality smooth meshes. Further, a novel systematic way to determine the appropriate threshold R is also an interesting problem deserving investigation. Finally, improvements on raising the robustness against cropping or noising attacks may be considered.

Competing Interests

The author declares that there are no competing interests regarding the publication of this paper.

Acknowledgments

This work was supported by Ministry of Science and Technology of Taiwan under Grant nos. MOST 103-2221-E-468-021 and MOST 104-2218-E-468-001.

References

[1] C.-H. Chuang, C.-W. Cheng, and Z.-Y. Yen, "Reversible data hiding with affine invariance for 3D models," in *Proceedings of the IET International Conference on Frontier Computing. Theory, Technologies and Applications*, pp. 77–81, Taichung, Taiwan, August 2010.

[2] I. J. Cox, M. L. Miller, J. A. Bloom, J. Fridrich, and T. Kalker, *Digital Watermarking and Steganography*, Morgan Kaufmann, Burlington, Mass, USA, 2nd edition, 2008.

[3] Y.-H. Huang and Y.-Y. Tsai, "A reversible data hiding scheme for 3D polygonal models based on histogram shifting with high embedding capacity," *3D Research*, vol. 6, no. 2, article 20, pp. 1–12, 2015.

[4] C.-Y. Jhou, J.-S. Pan, and D. Chou, "Reversible data hiding base on histogram shift for 3D vertex," in *Proceedings of the 3rd International Conference on Intelligent Information Hiding and Multimedia Signal Processing (IIHMSP '07)*, vol. 1, pp. 365–370, IEEE, Kaohsiung, Taiwan, November 2007.

[5] H. Ji, X. Yang, C. Zhang, and X. Gao, "A new reversible watermarking of 3D models based on ratio expansion," in *Proceedings of the 3rd International Congress on Image and Signal Processing (CISP '10)*, pp. 3899–3903, Yantai, China, October 2010.

[6] K.-H. Jung and K.-Y. Yoo, "Data hiding method using image interpolation," *Computer Standards & Interfaces*, vol. 31, no. 2, pp. 465–470, 2009.

[7] C.-F. Lee and Y.-L. Huang, "An efficient image interpolation increasing payload in reversible data hiding," *Expert Systems with Applications*, vol. 39, no. 8, pp. 6712–6719, 2012.

[8] Y.-Y. Tsai, J.-T. Chen, Y.-C. Kuo, and C.-S. Chan, "A generalized image interpolation-based reversible data hiding scheme with high embedding capacity and image quality," *KSII Transactions on Internet and Information Systems*, vol. 8, no. 9, pp. 3286–3301, 2014.

[9] H.-T. Wu and J.-L. Dugelay, "Reversible watermarking of 3D mesh models by prediction-error expansion," in *Proceedings of the IEEE 10th Workshop on Multimedia Signal Processing (MMSP '08)*, pp. 797–802, Cairns, Australia, October 2008.

[10] D. Wu and G. Wang, "A reversible watermarking scheme for 3D meshes," in *Active Media Technology: 5th International Conference, AMT 2009, Beijing, China, October 22–24, 2009. Proceedings*, vol. 5820 of *Lecture Notes in Computer Science*, pp. 513–521, Springer, Berlin, Germany, 2009.

[11] C.-Y. Yang, "Reversible data hiding using two marked images based on adaptive coefficient-shifting algorithm," *Advances in Multimedia*, vol. 2012, Article ID 473896, 9 pages, 2012.

[12] A. Zhu, C. Zhang, X. Yang, and X. Gao, "An efficient 3D information hiding algorithm based on sampling concepts," in *Proceedings of the 3rd International Congress on Image and Signal Processing (CISP '10)*, vol. 3, pp. 1171–1175, Yantai, China, October 2010.

[13] X. Feng, "A novel watermarking for 3D subdivision mesh," *International Journal of Advancements in Computing Technology*, vol. 4, no. 15, pp. 66–73, 2012.

[14] G. Lavoué, F. Denis, and F. Dupont, "Subdivision surface watermarking," *Computers and Graphics*, vol. 31, no. 3, pp. 480–492, 2007.

[15] A. C. Rencher, *Methods of Multivariate Analysis*, John Wiley & Sons, New York, NY, USA, 2nd edition, 2002.

[16] N.-C. Huang, M.-T. Li, and C.-M. Wang, "Toward optimal embedding capacity for permutation steganography," *IEEE Signal Processing Letters*, vol. 16, no. 9, pp. 802–805, 2009.

7

Enhancement of Video Streaming in Distributed Hybrid Architecture

Soumen Kanrar[1,2] and Niranjan Kumar Mandal[2]

[1]*Vehere Interactive Pvt. Ltd., Calcutta, West Bengal 700053, India*
[2]*Vidyasagar University, West Bengal 721102, India*

Correspondence should be addressed to Soumen Kanrar; soumen.kanrar@veheretech.com

Academic Editor: Martin Reisslein

Pure Peer to Peer (P2P) network requires enhancing transportation of chunk video objects to the proxy server in the mesh network. The rapid growth of video on demand user brings congestion at the proxy server and on the overall network. The situation needs efficient content delivery procedure, to the video on demand viewer from the distributed storage. In general scenario, if the proxy server does not possess the required video stream or the chunk of that said video, then the same can be smoothly and rapidly streamed to the viewer. This paper has shown that multitier mesh shaped hybrid architecture composed of P2P and mesh architecture increase the number of requests served by the dynamic environment in comparison with the static environment. Optimized storage finding path search reduces the unnecessary query forward and hence increases the size of content delivery to the desired location.

1. Introduction

The efficient traffic flow of information is a key element in current technology and business environment. This traffic flow is controlled by a complex network architecture and supported communication infrastructure. High-speed network transport mechanism serves as enabling technologies for new classes of communication service such as multimedia and video on demand. The smooth transport of chunk video objects over the network is a challenging issue. Lots of literature address this issue with various concepts based on content driven network (CDN), pure Peer to Peer network, and hybrid as mix of "CDN and Peer to Peer network" [1]. How to design an efficient P2P VOD system with high utilization of bandwidth and low maintenance cost remains an open challenge [2]. The demand for streaming video over a low bit rate channel is increasing in a fast pace for many applications like the newscast, video conferencing, distance learning, video game, entertainment, and so forth. Some sort of traffic and congestion control, admission control, packet drop, needs to be considered due to the characteristic of the video traffic.

However, a major bottleneck is the timely delivery of a large amount of data through a very limited bandwidth. The issue directly involves how efficiently the overlay network adapts to the dynamic topology. The video content is pushed from the origin storage server to the peer nodes in the tree-shaped overlay network. Conceptually tree based overlay network is the address followed by multitree streaming approach tree [3, 4]. Here the topology dynamically changes with the multiple subtrees in place of one single tree [4, 5]. However, the mesh based chunk delivery approach gives the better result for both video on demand and the live video streaming. The latter concepts give better performance as observed in PPlive and Livesky [6]. In mesh shaped overlay network, the peers pull "video objects" from the neighboring peer [7]. The pull operation is done by the buffer map between the peers. To achieve the quality of service, chunk of "video object" delivery delays have to be handled efficiently. Quality of Experience (QoE) is defined in [8] as "the overall acceptability of an application as perceived subjectively by end user." In general, HTTP streaming has a bad QoS (quality of service) but a good QoE (Quality of Experience), because HTTP used reliable mode of transportation. This so happened for QoS (quality of service). The considered parameters are packet loss rate and packet delay and so forth. So it is highly required to enhance HTTP/TCP streaming as a major technology for media transformation [9]. In adaptive bit streaming, the media file is fragmented into small segments or chunks of same duration with the request to some specific time unit [10]. During the adaptive bit streaming, each chunk is decoded independently enabling seamless transport from one quality to another when network conditions are being changed frequently. The playout of a chunk is finished. Video player can start playing the next chunk with a different quality. So, for the adaptive bit streaming, lossy compression is a better option for video on demand [11]. The delay occurs due to the search for a chunk of "video object." On the other side, delay occurs due to the propagation delay and transmission delay from the neighboring peer. So the quality of service mainly depends on fast and correct path search. To find the desired video stream by using the mechanism of minimum hop counts towards the storage peer and to avoid the unnecessary query forwarding as well as to minimize the inter server gossiping during the chunk transfer [12, 13], the major routing protocols for wireless ad hoc networks have traditionally focused on finding paths with minimum hop count (MHC). However, such paths can include slow or lossy links, leading to poor throughput [14]. The energy efficient routing algorithm in wireless networks typically selects minimum cost multihop paths. But those energy aware routing algorithms select a path with large number of small distance hops in varied power transmission environment [15]. The quality of service depends on the aggregate stationary bit rate which exceeds the minimum threshold level from the viewer perspective [16]. This paper is structured as follows. Section 1 introduces the problem. The basic, video encryption mechanisms have been discussed in this section, followed with video objects formation. Section 2 presents the chunk of video object transfer over the hybrid architecture. Sections 3 and 4 present the required architecture and simulation environment of the problem with conclusion at the end.

(1) Video Traffic Burst in Network. The repeatedly occurring theme relating to traffic transportation in broad-band network and high-speed network is the traffic "burstiness." It is exhibited by the key services such as compressed video and file transfer. Burstiness occurs in the course of traffic flow, due to the presence of several relatively short interarrival time sequences. The peak rate (R_{peak}) is an important requirement parameter used during the connection setup time. The other major traffic descriptors are the mean burst period "b," the average bit rate "m," and utilization factor "γ" which is defined as $\gamma = m/R_{peak}$. The peak rate (R_{peak}) yields the mean bit rate m and the variance σ^2 of the bit rate. The mean of the burst period "b" is used to describe how bursts occur from sender side. It is used to discriminate between different connection setups for streaming from different sources. During multiplexing, it has the same peak and mean bit rate but displays a different behavior. The multiplexer can be modeled as a single queue of length x and N servers each with fixed streaming rate c [17, 18]. The buffer overflow probability

for finite buffer size is ε. It can be obtained for given x, c, and N. So the connection setup equivalent bandwidth W for the multiplexed connection is the smallest value of c, for which the buffer overflow probability is smaller than ε. The approximate upper bond of the equivalent bandwidth w_i (for single isolated connection) depends upon the parameters (x, R_{peak}, γ, b, and α), where α is the source capacity of streaming. The equivalent bandwidth of the multiplexed connection can be presented as $W = \sum_{i=1}^{N} w_i$. As it is considering the approximated upper bound for w_i, the equivalent capacity is definitely overestimated. To eliminate the constraint, let us consider a stationary estimation derived from a bufferless fluid flow model. The fluid traffic model gives out with individual traffic units. Instead, it views traffic as a steam of fluid, characterized by a flow rate such as bits per second. The traffic count is replaced by a traffic volume. The bufferless fluid flow model for the stationary approximation exhibits the equivalent bandwidth W. W is selected to ensure that the aggregate stationary bit rate B exceeds W only with the probability smaller than ε. In general expression, it can be presented as $\rho(B > W) \leq \varepsilon$, where B can be determined from the stationary distribution of the number of active sources. B can be modeled by the continuous time Markov chain as it potentially captures traffic burstiness, due to the presence of nonzero autocorrelation in the interarrival time sequence [19].

(2) Video Encryption Mechanisms. Video is the collection of still images. The collected set of still images is well orderly sequenced. The compressing technique is used to compress each individual still image of the collected set of images. Encoding technique is used to encode the image independently according to the sequence in the collected set of images. The Joint Photographic Experts Group (JPEG) format is used to compress the still images of the set of images. The sequences of still images are arranged in increasing order independently and individually. The MPEG-4 is the popular coding scheme that encodes the complete frames of video. The MPEG-4 is a collection of coding tools and maintains simple profiles. The most current implementation for temporal scalability is using H.263, MPEG-4, and secular temporal subband coding [20]. The MJPEG format is the motion JPEG video compressed and encoded using JPEG. Each video signal that carries information contains a definite amount of redundancy. So the video sequence contains redundancy. The aim of the video compression is to remove the redundancy from the video signal. Generally, two types of compression technique exist. One type is the lossless compression technique and the other type of technique is lossy compression technique. The lossless compression technique removes the statistical redundancy that is present in the video signal. When the transported video signal at the received end is reconstructed, it presents an identical copy of the original video. The current available technology supports compressing the video signal up to some modest level only. This is one of the greatest handicap legacies for the lossless compression technique, particularly for the storage and transported video signal over the network. This consumes extra space and bandwidth of the underlay network [21–23]. In lossy compression,

we can compress a huge number of video signals, but the reconstructed video signal at the received side is not identical to the original. The lossy compression meets a given bit rate for the storage and can maintain adaptive bit rate during the transmission of the video signal over the network or the internet. Different CODECs run into the storage as well as at the client sites. So, for adaptive bit streaming, lossy compression is a better option for on demand video streaming. The aim of video source coding is bit rate reduction for storage and transmission. The compression is done by removing the different types of redundancy, spatial, temporal, or frequent. Each image is usually divided into many blocks, each of size 8 pixel $\times$ 8 pixels. These 64 pixels are then transformed into frequency-domain representation by using what is called discrete cosine transform (DCT) [24, 25]. The frequency-domain transformation clearly separates out the low-frequency components from high-frequency components. Conceptually, the low-frequency components capture visually important components, whereas the high-frequency components capture visually fewer striking in components. The goal is to represent the low-frequency (or visually more important) coefficients with higher precision or with more bits and the high-frequency (or visually less important) coefficients with lower resolution or with fewer bits. Since the high-frequency coefficients are encoded with fewer bits, some information is lost during compression, and hence this is referred to as "lossy" compression. When inverse DCT (IDCT) is performed on the coefficients to reconstruct the image, it is not exactly the same as the original image but the difference between them is not perceptible to the human eye.

The current enhancements in 2D (two-dimensional) video coding are classified mainly into two categories, nonscalable and scalable, respectively [26]. The nonscalable coding, for example, is H.264/AVC (advanced video coding) and H.265/HEVC (high efficiency video coding). The scalable video coding, for example, is H.264/AVC with SVC (scalable video coding) extension. In nonscalable coding bit rate is not reduced, but in scalable coding bit rate is reduced. Generally, H.264/AVC is using an intracoding concept about the prediction of a block inside a frame. Here the neighboring block within the same frame is considered. H.264/AVC provides more flexibility with the blocks of 4 $\times$ 4 samples and blocks of 8 $\times$ 8 samples for transformation. H.264/AVC is using fundamentally advanced intercoding concept for predicting B-frames from the set of highly eligible candidates of past and future B-frames. H.264/AVC has 10 modes. The modes are eight angular modes, one DC mode, and one planer mode, respectively. The angular prediction interpolates from reference pixels at locations based on the angle. The DC constant value is an average of neighboring pixels (reference samples). Planer is the average of horizontal and vertical prediction. The new key features of H.264/AVC are enhanced motion compression, small block of transform coding, improved deblocking filter, and enhanced coding. H.265/HEVC is the successor to H.264. H.265 is meant to double the compression rates of H.264, allowing for the propagation of 4 K and 8 K content over existing delivery systems. H.265/HEVC used the concepts of frame partitioning "luminance pixels" into coding tree blocks of sample sizes 16 $\times$ 16, 32 $\times$ 32, and 64 $\times$ 64,

respectively. It is flexible and smoothly partitioned into multiple variables sized coding blocks. H.265/HEVC is using updated intracoding procedure for merging of small partition of coding trees. A wide range of intraframe predication is used. H.265/HEVC is massively improving the flexibility stricture of transformation which matches the code tree block structure that is 4 $\times$ 4 up to 32 $\times$ 32. H.265/HEVC improved the error resilience by using video parameter set (VPS). This concept is used for signaling essential syntax information for the decoding. H.265/HEVC has 35 modes. The modes are 33 angular modes, one DC mode, and one planer mode, respectively [26, 27].

(3) Video Object Formation. The DCT coefficients of each 8 $\times$ 8 pixel block are encoded with more bits for highly perceptible low-frequency components and fewer bits for less perceptible high-frequency components. This is achieved in two steps. First step is quantization, which eliminates perceptibly less significant information, and the second step is encoding, which minimizes the number of bits needed for representing the quantized DCT coefficients. Quantization is a technique by which real numbers are mapped into integers within a range, where the integer presents a level or quantum. The mapping is done by rounding a real number up to the nearest higher integer, so some information is lost during this process. At the end of quantization, each 8 $\times$ 8 block will be represented by a set of integers, many of which are zeroes because the high-frequency coefficients are usually small, and they end up being mapped to 0. The goal of encoding is to represent the coefficients using as few bits as possible. This is accomplished in two steps. Run length coding (RLC) is used to do the first level of compression. Variable length coding (VLC) does the next level of compression [12, 20]. After quantization, the majority of high-frequency DCT coefficients become zeroes. Run length coding takes advantage of this by coding the high-frequency DCT coefficients before coding the low-frequency DCT coefficients, so that the consecutive number of zeroes is maximized. This is accomplished by scanning the 8 $\times$ 8 matrices in a diagonal zigzag manner. Run length coding encodes consecutive identical coefficients by using two numbers. The first number is the "run" (the number that occurs consecutively), and the second number is "length" (the number of consecutive occurrences). Thus, if there is N consecutive zeroes, instead of coding each zero separately, RLC will represent the string of N zeroes as $[0, N]$. After RLC, there will be a sequence of numbers and VLC encodes these numbers using a minimum number of bits [20]. The technique is to use the minimum number of bits for the most commonly occurring number and use more bits for less common numbers. Since a variable number of bits are used for coding, it is referred to as variable length coding [21, 22]. In video encoding, the order in which frames are coded is not the same as the order in which they are played. Thus, it is not necessarily true that the reference frame for the future frame is the one just before it in the playing sequence. In fact, the video encoder jumps ahead from the currently displayed frame and encodes a future frame and then jumps back to encode the next frame in display order. Sometimes, the video encoder uses two "reference" frames, the currently

displayed frame and a future encoded frame to encode the next frame in the display sequence. In this case, the future encoded frame is referred to as *P*-frame ("predicted" frame), and the frame encoded using two reference frames is referred to as *B*-frame ("bidirectionally" predictive frame). However, there is a problem for this approach because an error in one of the frames would propagate through the encoding process for ever. To avoid this problem, the video encoders typically encode one video frame (periodically) using still-image techniques and such frames are referred to as "intraframes" or *I*-frames [28]. A sequence of frames from one *I*-frame to another *I*-frame is referred to as a group of pictures (GOP). A GOP is best represented using a two-dimensional matrix. The order of encoding and the order of display are different for the frames in a GOP. It is transported over an IP network just like any other type of data transmission [5]. Typically, videos have three types of frames, *I*-frames, *P*-frames, and *B*-frames, where *I*-frames capture most of the information in a scene followed by *P*-frames and *B*-frames, which capture the "deltas" from the original frame (captured in *I*-frame) resulting from motion. Finally, *I*-, *P*-, and *B*-frames are packetized in the encoded format as a sequence of frames, which itself is video objects. When delivery is requested, the chunk delivery of "video object" is done from the storage server to the neighboring requested peer nodes. The MPEG-4 looks after the collection of video objects (VO) [24]. The video object is an entry that the end user is able to manipulate. It is an area, which can be of any shape and may exit for an arbitrary length of time. The instance in which the video object occurs is called the "Video Object Plane" (VOP). In the traditional view, we can say that the VOP is a single frame and a set of frames forming a VO. The VOP is in irregular shape and occupies only a part of a frame. The separate objects are coded independently with different resolutions and qualities. These coding schemes adopt a linear uniform sampling scheme disregarding the varying semantic importance of different frames or segments. The characteristics of video traffic depend on the quality of service (QoS) of video traffic.

(4) Arrangement of Peer Nodes. The hierarchy is created by distributing peer nodes to the different levels as illustrated in Figure 1. The levels are numbered sequentially with the highest level of the hierarchy being level zero (denoted by L_0). Each level is partitioned into a set of clusters. Each cluster is composed of peer nodes. The size of each cluster varies within k to $3k - 1$, where k is a constant [29]. The cluster is forming with the set of peer nodes. Those are close to each other. Every cluster has one "cluster head." The cluster head also logically belongs to the lower level; that is, a cluster head of level L_i logically belongs to level L_{i-1}. The cluster head has the minimum distance (with respect to hop count) to all other peer nodes in that cluster at the same level. If the size of a set of peer nodes has an upper bond $(2k - 1)$ then during dynamically splitting for cluster formation, the size of the set reaches up to $2k$. This happened, since at least one higher-level cluster head logically belongs to the lower level. So the set splits into two clusters of size k. The data is transported from one level to another level through the cluster head.

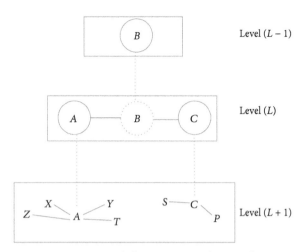

FIGURE 1: Hierarchal arrangement of peer nodes.

By default, the storage server stayed at the level L_0, which logically belongs to every level. The choice of a cluster leader is very important during the joining of new peer node to the system at the specific level in the hierarchy. The new peer node required minimum number of query messages for finding its position. During the video chunk transportation, formed multicast tree is overlaid to the hybrid architecture. If there is N number of peer nodes in the hierarch, the number of level is bounded with $\Theta(\log_k N)$, where $k > 3$ is a constant.

According to Figure 1, A and C are the cluster heads at the level (L). Those cluster heads physically stayed at the level (L), but cluster head is logically part of the level $(L - 1)$. Set of nodes $\{X, Y, Z, T\}$ are directly communicated with the logical cluster head A. Similarly, the set of nodes $\{S, P\}$ are directly communicated with the logical cluster head C for exchanging data and information. This type of hierarchal peer nodes distribution efficiently handles the problem regarding the live streaming of media in large P2P network [30]. The multicast tree construction and efficient clustering of peer nodes based on a hierarchy of bounded cluster size are efficiently improving the performance. The neighbors on the levelwise topology can exchange periodic soft state refreshed without generating high volume of control message. The hierarchal architecture successfully reduces the overburden traffic load to the system. The other important advantages include the peer node departure and smooth cluster head section and cost-effective maintenance of the cluster.

2. Chunk Video Object Transfer over Hybrid Architecture

Figure 2 presents the physical configuration of the overall structure of the video on demand system. Clusters of viewers are symbolically presented by the viewer node. The cache proxy server is connecting viewer nodes to the next level of peer nodes in the multitier architecture. The cache proxy server is installed at the highest level in reverse order in the proposed model of multitier architecture. The proxy cache servers are not directly connected to each other. They are connected to each other via next level peer nodes.

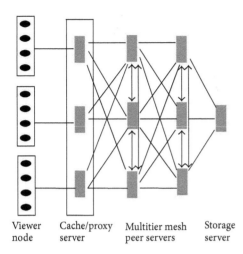

FIGURE 2: Distributed hybrid architecture.

Viewer node · Cache/proxy server · Multitier mesh peer servers · Storage server

FIGURE 2: Distributed hybrid architecture.

All the levels including the lowest level, that is, the video storage server, form the multitier mesh shaped architecture. The work of cache proxy server at the highest level is to import the chunk of video objects from next level peer nodes.

Figure 3 presents the working mechanism of chunk transfer. The architecture is the composition of local and global network. The cache proxy server is the part of the local as well as the global network. $P_1, P_2, P_3, \ldots, P_N$ are the peer nodes belonging to different level in the multitier architecture. P_N node position is fixed for the main video storage. The initial request tries to serve locally from the local cache proxy server.

If the local proxy server cannot serve the chunk video object, then the request is broadcast to the neighboring peer nodes of the next level. In this fashion, the chunk request is forwarded among the peers. If any of the peer nodes possess the chunk video objects, that also rebroadcast the message chunk availability, then chunk video object is transferred according to the buffer map procedure. This is the mesh push mechanism from the sender peer node and mesh pull from the receiver peer. Now the copy of chunk video object is stored at the local cache proxy server before delivery to the viewer node. The preliminary survey of the literature shows that more than 10^6 numbers of user's node can concurrently decode the live video streaming within the range of bits rate 400 to 800 Kbps [31]. Current HDMI H.264 video encoders for live streaming and broadcasting use bit rate 250 Kbps to 10 Mbps. Dynamic page replacement at the cache memory of the proxy server can enhance the performance of the video on demand [32] for the "analysis and implementation of large scale video on demand system" [5]. The literatures [33, 34] show that proper cache memory can reduce 50% to 60% of P2P traffic load. Simultaneous viewers are asynchronous; that is, any viewer can access any part of that video at any instance of time. Due to the playback option in video on demand system, a good number of sequential video objects are always available to the media player buffer of the viewers [35–38]. In general, the viewer assesses that video through the cache proxy server. The video objects are a collection of video frames that feed the media player after sequential arranging

from the received buffer of the viewer. If the complete video is not available to the cache proxy server, the unavailable part or parts of the chunk block or blocks are imported by the "buffer map via mesh pull approach" according to Figure 3. It uses the multichannel cache proxy server from any numbers of peers at any level in the multitier architecture. The similar buffer map concepts are used in the chunk transfer between the peers in the multitier mesh shaped architecture. The previously proposed video on demand architecture can be classified into some major categories.

(i) Closed loop system: the client retrieves the video segments from the server.

(ii) Prefix caching assisted periodic broadcast: it is a combined effect of open loop and closed loop system.

(iii) Client equipped with set-top box: the set-top box stores locally part of some popular video.

(iv) Peer to Peer network used for video on demand system: the video segments are transported through the network according to peer node requirement.

In this paper, the proposed "distributed hybrid architecture" is a combination of P2P and mesh type network architecture. The cost of video object's transfer through this structure successfully reduces both cases of static and dynamic environment.

3. Analytic Architecture

Let $C_{(i)}^{\dagger}$ be the equivalent capacity of network at session i. The minimum required bandwidth to ensure the aggregate stationary bit rate approaches $C_{(i)}^{\dagger}$ with the considerable frame loss probability η. The aggregate stationary bit rate is required to approximate the adaptive encoding run at the client side video playback. Aggregate bit rate maintains the video resolution within a certain standard. In a particular session, n is the numbers of links that are active and simultaneously transfer the chunk of video objects from the peer nodes through the proxy servers in the multitier architecture. If the transferring stream or "chunk contents" are presented by the random vector X, for $i = 1, \ldots, n$, $E(X_i) = \mu_i$ is the mean transferring rate for individual ith viewers, without the loss of generality. We can assume that X_i are the mutually independent random variables. The aggregate content transfer for a particular session is $B = E(\sum_{i=1}^{n} X_i)$ and $B_n = \text{var}(X_1 + X_2 + \cdots + X_n)$; this includes the smooth video objects transmission at interactive session like playback, moves forward, and so forth. So far, nothing is assumed about the behavior of B_n for indefinite values of n. According to the Chebyshev inequality for the small positive numbers ε and η (previously assumed), the least number of active links is k^* to be found for all n, such that

$$n > k^*. \tag{1}$$

Now,

$$P\left\{\left(\left|\frac{X_1 + \cdots + X_n}{n} - \frac{B}{n}\right| < \varepsilon\right)\right\} \geq 1 - \frac{B_n}{n^2 \varepsilon^2}. \tag{2}$$

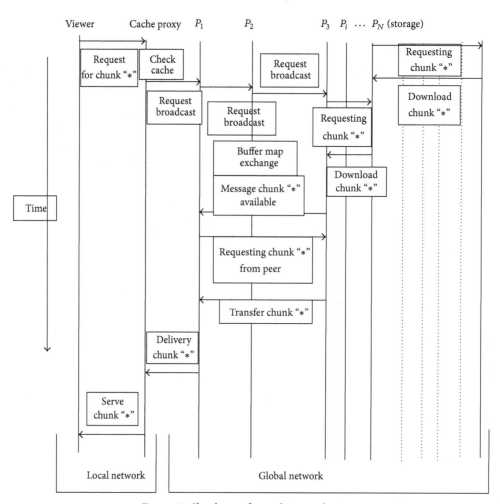

FIGURE 3: Chunk transfer working mechanism.

So $B_n/n^2\varepsilon^2 \prec \eta$ and $\lim_{n\to\infty}(B_n/n^2\varepsilon^2) \to 0$. Here η is the approximate frame loss probability in a session. All the individual and shared individual links use the maximum bandwidth to transmit the chunk content. Clearly, $\sum_{i=1}^{k^*} \max(E(X_i)) \le C_{(i)}^\dagger$. Here $C_{(i)}^\dagger$ is capacity of the network. Since η is the packet loss or bit loss probability, it maintains the aggregate stationary bit rate streaming which remains the same for the short burst period. Without the loss of generality, all the above inequality holds true for the event $(B \succ C_{(i)}^\dagger)$. The probability for the event is

$$\left(B \succ C_{(i)}^\dagger\right). \tag{3}$$

So

$$p\left(B \succ C_{(i)}^\dagger\right) \le \eta. \tag{4}$$

We can consider it as

$$p\left(B \le C_{(i)}^\dagger\right) \le (1-\eta). \tag{5}$$

The distribution of expression (3) can be obtained from the 2-state Markov chain. For every viewer node, there exists at least one active channel, including the case of broadcasting or multicasting of video data objects from the cache proxy server [32, 39]. It contains the full or part of the required video at any level of the pear nodes in multitier architecture. The video content is fully available to the cache proxy server. The proxy server is the part of mesh architecture, which is placed at the maximum level in hierarchy of the multitier architecture at strategic location. The proxy servers are not the peer server, so there are no interlinks between them. The main reason behind it is for the requirement of security and the billing process for commercial purpose also. The billing servers are installed at the level l_1 that is at level one in multitier architecture. Level zero that is l_0 is the position for video storage server. The proxy cache memory is updated or refreshed by the "least frequency frequently used" concepts [32, 40–42]. l_0 is the level for video storage server and height level l_{l+1} is for cache proxy server. If λ is the average fraction of full streaming at a session that each of the supplying peers shares or contributes during that session, clearly $0 \prec \lambda \prec 1$. Let N be the total number of peer nodes including the main storage servers in the multitier architecture. N_c is the upload capacity at level 0 of the mesh type Peer to Peer network. Let $P(l)$ be the sum of the number of peer nodes at the level

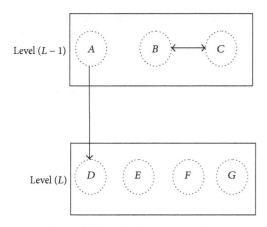

Level (L − 1) A B ↔ C

Level (L) D E F G

FIGURE 4: Dynamic cluster connections.

$(l + 1)$ and $P(0) = N$. Now $N(l)$ is the upload capacity of the peers at the level l. So in a balanced state of traffic flow during the smooth chunk video objects transfer at any level depends on just lower-level peer's nodes of the multitier architecture. In a particular session of synchronous chunk transfer, the upload capacity of the peer nodes at level l is equivalent to the product of the average fraction of full streaming with the upload capacity of the participating peers at the level $(l − 1)$. This is expressed by $N(l) \approx \lambda N(l−1) \Rightarrow N(1) = \lambda N(0) = \lambda N_c$. In real scenario, peer nodes at the higher level (l) get chunk video objects when the lower-level $(l−1)$ participating peers send the video objects for them. The throughput of the system is contributed by the average fraction of full streaming of participating peer nodes. Some portion of the bandwidth is always used for chunk transfer to peers at the same level $(l − 1)$ according to Figure 2. So we get the expression $P(l) = P(l − 1) − N(l − 1)$.

Dynamic cluster connections are presented in Figure 4. We observe that A, B, and C are the peer nodes at the level $(l−1)$ and D, E, F, and G are the peer nodes at the level (l). The dynamic clustering is a logical cluster construction among the peer nodes at every level for the real time requirement at any session. The peer nodes B and C at level $(l − 1)$ exchange the chunk video objects or transfer among themselves. D is the cluster head at level (l) download video chunk from the dynamic cluster head "A" at level $(l − 1)$. Now downloading chunk of video objects from the lower level gives priority over the "chunk video objective" transfers in the same level of multitier architecture in that session. Let us consider that N_l is the number of peer nodes at the level l. To approximate the value N_l by N, the processing is as follows:

$$P(l) = P(l − 1) − N(l − 1) \quad \text{for } 0 < \lambda < 1$$
$$= [P(l − 2) − N(l − 2)] − N(l − 1)$$
$$= P(l − 2) − N(l − 2) − N(l − 1)$$
$$= [P(l − 3) − N(l − 3)] − N(l − 2) − N(l − 1)$$
$$= P(l − 3) − N(l − 3) − N(l − 2) − N(l − 1)$$
$$= \cdots$$

$$= \cdots$$
$$= P(0) − N(0) − N(1) − N(2) − \cdots − N(l − 1)$$
$$= P(0) − N_c − \lambda N_c − \lambda^2 N_c − \cdots − \lambda^{l−1} N_c$$
$$= N − N_c \left(1 + \lambda + \lambda^2 + \cdots + \lambda^{l−1}\right)$$
$$\approx N − N_c \frac{1 − \lambda^l}{1 − \lambda}.$$

$$(6)$$

Finally, N_l is approximate as $N_l \approx N − N_c((1 − \lambda^l)/(1 − \lambda))$.

Let us assume that $p_{k_l}^{(i)}$ is the probability that at least k_l out of N_l number of peer nodes actively participate in the l level of the multitier architecture at ith session. Active means that the peer node has the required portion of encoded video file and remains live during the chunk video object transfer in that session.

So we get the expression

$$p_{k_l}^{(i)} = \sum_{k=k_l+1}^{N_l} \binom{N_l}{k} \rho^k (1 − \rho)^{N_l − k}. \quad (7)$$

So during chunk transfer of video objects, the aggregate bit rates depend upon the active participation of the peer nodes at every level $\{l, l − 1, l − 2, l − 3, \ldots, 0\}$. The distribution of B in the expression ((4) and (5)) can be obtained from the multistate Markov chain. $S_i L_j$ is the sequence of active participation of peer nodes to transfer the chunk of video objects at the session i in the jth level. Since the download capacity at any level depends upon the uploading amount of just the lower level for that session, expression ((4) and (5)) becomes

$$p\left(B \leq C_{(i)}^\dagger\right) = p\left(S_i L_l, S_i L_{l−1}, S_i L_{l−2}, \ldots, S_i L_0\right)$$
$$= p\left(\frac{S_i L_l}{S_i L_{l−1}}\right) p\left(S_i L_{l−1}, S_i L_{l−2}, \ldots, S_i L_0\right)$$
$$= p\left(\frac{S_i L_l}{S_i L_{l−1}}\right) p\left(\frac{S_i L_{l−1}}{S_i L_{l−2}}\right) \cdots p\left(S_i L_0\right) \quad (8)$$
$$= p_{k_l}^{(i)} p_{k_{l−1}}^{(i)} p_{k_{l−2}}^{(i)} \cdots p_{k_0}^{(i)} = \prod_{j=0}^{l} p_{k_{l−j}}^{(i)}.$$

Clearly, $p(S_i L_0) = 1$ for session like session i, by using expression (7), and after reordering the above sequence, we get

$$p\left(B \leq C_{(i)}^\dagger\right) \approx \prod_{j=l}^{1} \sum_{k=k_j+1}^{N_j} \binom{N_j}{k} \rho^k (1 − \rho)^{N_j − k}. \quad (9)$$

According to (5), we get

$$\prod_{j=l}^{1} \sum_{k=k_j+1}^{N_j} \binom{N_j}{k} \rho^k (1 − \rho)^{N_j − k} \leq (1 − \eta). \quad (10)$$

Since N_j is the number of peer nodes at the jth level in multitier architecture, in a session k_m is the least required numbers of actively participating peer nodes at the mth level in mesh architecture during smooth transfer of chunk video objective. According to the expression, (10) holds true and inequality (1) becomes $k_l + k_{l-1} + k_{l-2} + \cdots + k_0 \leq k^*$:

$$\sum_{j=0}^{l} k_{l-j} \leq k^*, \qquad (11)$$

where η is controlled by some threshold that depends on the adaptive bit rate for both sides of sender-receiver CODEC. The CODEC runs at the viewer's end and the content transferring peers or proxy server end. To find the optimized cost for transferring the chunk of the video objects, now the issue comes to efficiently finding the video object chunk storage with minimum hop counts in multitier architecture. To keep the value η at the lower level, the problem is to

minimize the unnecessary searching packet forwarding and inter server gossiping. We propose the heuristic based path search for finding the chunk container of peer nodes for transferring video objects by using Algorithms 1 and 2. The estimated cost function is used to estimate the distance for possible destination of peer nodes in that particular session. The initial information about the higher-level peers is already available to the proxy server in multitier mesh architecture. For finding the peer, the search path is linear. So the cost of the path is optimized, that is, to avoid the unnecessary query forwarding to minimize the inter server gossiping. The path is considered the route to the farthest number in that session. The root is the proxy server. The distance is measured with the hop counts. In reality, more than one peer's node may contain the required chunk of video objects. So the search path will not be always linear. In the path search computation at a session, some extra additional link exists. So we can express it in form of the expression:

$$\text{Min} \quad \{\text{Max } d\,(\text{proxy server}, v) + \text{number of duplicate links exist in } S \mid \text{such that } v \in S, S \text{ is the Collection of churn storage peers.}\}$$

$$\text{Subject to} \quad \prod_{j=1}^{1} \sum_{k=k_j+1}^{N_j} \binom{N_j}{k} \rho^k (1-\rho)^{N_j - k} \leq (1-\eta), \quad 0 < \rho < 1$$

$$(12)$$

$$\sum_{l=0}^{l} k_l \leq k^*,$$

$$k_j < N_j,$$

$$k^* < N.$$

To find the least-cost path that is minimum hop count towards the fastest peer storage is considered. The consisting hashing in the structured overlays for the multitier Peer to Peer network is also being used. The request for the portion of the chunk video object is forwarded through the longest prefix match via Algorithm 2. The consistent hash function [43] is assigned to each node and key by a fixed bit identifier using a base hash function. A node's identifier is chosen by hashing the node IP address, while a key identifier is produced by hashing the key. Here the used term "key" refers to both the original key and its image under the hash functions. Similarly, the term node refers to both the node and its identifier under the hash function. Consistent hashing is assigning key to node. In point to point network, name based consistent hashing maps key onto a node. Both keys and nodes are assigned with an m-bit identifier. For nodes, this identifier is a hash of the node's IP address. For keys, this identifier is a hash of a keyword, such as a file name or query string.

3.1. Proposition and Algorithm

Statement. The hop count between query emitter node for the chunk of video object x_s and query matched x^* node (that node has chunk of video objects) is at most $\|x_s - x^*\| \leq \log_k(n) << (n-1)$ for $n \geq 2$. n is the size of multitier network and k is the base of the prefix for emitter node.

Proof. Let x_s be the query initiative node and let x^* be the query matched node. $(k-1)$ is the size of the adjutancy list for a node that has a base prefix k. When the query emits node the same as the query matched node, that is, proxy server, then inequality (13) holds true for the single hop neighbor, and $n \geq 2$:

$$\|x_s - x^*\| \leq \log_k n. \qquad (13)$$

When the query is forwarded through the intermediate nodes $x_1, x_2, \ldots, x_m$ starting from the emitter node x_s to sink node x^*, the node x_s has the adjustable list size $(l_s - 1)$ with base of the prefix l_s, $x_{(1)}$ has adjustable list size $(l_1 - 1)$ with base of the prefix l_1, and so on; likewise, $x_{(m)}$ has the adjustable list size of $(l_m - 1)$ with the base of the prefix l_m. Query is forwarded by incremental prefix routing. So the path distance is expressed as

$$\|x_s - x^*\| \leq \|x_s - x_{(1)}\| + \|x_{(1)} - x_{(2)}\| + \cdots$$
$$+ \|x_{(k)} - x^*\|. \qquad (14)$$

The number of branches maintained at the node x_s is $(l_s - 1)$, the node $x_{(1)}$ maintains $(l_1 - 1)$, the number of branches, and so on. Now $x_{(m)}$ maintains $(l_m - 1)$, number of branches. As $x_{(1)} \in$ single hop neighbor of x_s, $x_{(i+1)} \in$ single hop neighbor of $x_{(i)}$ and $x^* \in$ single hop neighbor of $x_{(m)}$. It concludes $\|x_s - x_{(1)}\| \approx 1, \|x_{(i)} - x_{(i+1)}\| \approx 1, \ldots, \|x_{(k)} - x^*\| \approx 1$.

Expression (14) becomes $\|x_s - x^*\| < (n-1)$. ☐

```
Input:    x_s // The Query emits node
          x* // The Query sink node
     Initialize
          Buffer1 ← finite size
          Hop_count (every node) ← (−1) // peers at
                                        // every level
     Begin
     Query initiated from x_s // Proxy server
     If {(x_s.node_id = =x*. node_id) && found (query massage)}
          then
          Hop_count = 0
          Return Hop_count
          Output: chunk present in proxy server
          Exit
          End
     else
 for each x ∈ {single hop node from adjutancy list of x_s}
 Compute: Query forward to the longest prefix match node x using Algorithm 2.
 Buffer1 ← push (x)
 while (Bufer1 non empty) do
 {
    pop node (v) from Buffer1
       {
         for each w from N_b(v) // select all the
                         //single hop neighbor w of v
          {
           If  (Hop_count(w) == (−1)) // peer node yet
                              //not received the query
           then
           Hop_count (w) = Hop_count (v) +1;
       {
       If ((node identifier(w)==node identifier(x*))&& match (keyword_identifier))
       then // peer node having the query stream
       return Hop_count(w);
       Output: chunk present
         else w ∈ N_b(x*) // selected w belongs to
                         // single hop neighbor of x*
          {// heuristic search
          return
          Hop_count (w) +1;
          } // end search
    } // end block
    else
    Output: "Search query stream does not exist in this network".
    } // End for each
    } // End Pop
    } // End While
    End begin
    Stop
```

ALGORITHM 1: Heuristic Path Search Algorithm, query initiated from the proxy server.

Algorithms 1 and 2 are developed with the following consideration. The query message is generated from the proxy server. It is bits of a string header of the chunk video objects. There is more than one peer node present in the network. Those possess the required chunk video objects. The aim of the algorithm is to find the fastest least-cost path towards the desired peer node. The query message is routed to desire peer node via key identification.

```
Variable:
Prefix: list
L: Array of Record
LPM, M: Record // LPM is longest prefix match
D, D_l, D': Array of Character
R, i, l, A: integer
Initialize
Prefix ← {set of peer nodes}
L [i].length ← {Prefix length of ith distinct length}
L [i].hash ← {Hash table}
D ← {Storage server address}
B ← {Range of the array}// 32 bits for IPv4, 128
                          // bits for IPv6
M ← {Binary string of size R}
Begin
  A = 0;
    while (R ≠ NULL) do
    {
         i = ⌊ (A + B) / 2 ⌋;
         l = L[i].length; // longest possible length
         D_l = [(Bit String of D) base 2] ≤ l;
         D' = Assign (Most significant bit of D_l);
         // Index position of the binary string associated
         // to D' in hash table.
         M = Search (D', L [i].hash);
         // search hash table for D'
           If (M = = Null) then B= ⌊(A + B)/2⌋ − 1;
           // search in lower half
           else A = ⌊(A + B)/2⌋; // search in upper half
           if (M ∈ LPM) then break; else continue;
    }// end while
  Update: Query forward to (M.address)
  End begin
  Stop
```

ALGORITHM 2: Query forward to longest prefix match

4. Simulation Results and Discussion

The storage server contains the raw file (or coded video). The YUV file is created by decoding the raw file. At first, it is converted to *.m4v file format. Then, we create the mp4 container and simultaneously create the reference videos. The frames are packetized for transport over the network. Here mp4trace command sends the *.mp4 file to the destination peer node through the freely available port except the system port (usually selected ports above 5000) [44]. The transportation of these chunks of video objects, that is, "the sequence of packet frames," is done with RTP/UDP. All this design and implementation of EvalVid-RA, a tool set for rate adaptive VBR (video bit rate) that is added to ns-2, are based on some modification to the EvalVid Version 1.2 tool and the ns-2 interfacing code. The ffmpeg command of EvalVid is used to control rate of some GOP before stabilizing the rate output. The VBR rate controller is set to 600 kbit/s for the individual session. The mesh shaped hybrid multitier architecture, including the cache proxy server, has 10 levels. The higher level l_9 is the cache proxy server and l_0 level

TABLE 1: Simulation parameters.

Parameter	Values/range
Number of levels in multitier	10
Number of peers at each level	4
Raw video frame rate	30/second
Group of picture length	30 frames
Link capacity	400 kbps to 800 kbps
Number of viewers connected to each proxy	20 (Min)
Number of viewers connected to each proxy	40 (Max)

is for the video storage server. Levels l_1 to l_8 possess the peer nodes in mesh shaped multitier. Each level has 4 peers that are interconnected. The peers that belong to the same level exchange buffer information to transfer the chunk video objects. The peers at the higher level are connected to lower-level peers in unicast; that is, the higher-level peers only download the chunk of video objects from the lower level. In the environment, we consider two types of simulation. In type one, the peers maintain dynamic connection. In dynamic connection, every peer has adjacent list size of 4 and 6. These links are selected from the available 11 links to the peer. The 11 links are orientated as 4 links for the unicast downloading from the lower-level peers, 4 links for the unicast uploading for the higher-level peers, and 3 links for the chunk transfer at the same level of peers. In the second type of simulation, we consider the static links 4 and 6 out of the 11 available links to the peer. In the static link, full content of the video is transferred from the storage server or the intermediate peers through the initial fixed setup links for every session. The link capacity maintains 400 kbps to 800 kbps speed. 400 kbp is the link capacity between the viewers to the cache proxy server. The 800 kbps is the link capacity of the storage server to the next higher server (i.e., billing server). The intermediate-level mesh peers maintain the link capacity of 600 kbps. The required parameter values and ranges are summarized in Table 1.

The confidence interval used in this simulation is 90%. For small prototype evaluation, we restricted the number of viewers connected to proxy server and adjacent list size of peer node. The viewers are connected to each proxy server; minimum is 20 and maximum is 40. The number of viewers connected to the proxy server can grow. The sum-up link capacity of the viewers connected to the proxy server is more than the intermediate link capacity.

The simulation result is based on the request initiative from the proxy server, when the viewers submitted his/her requests through the proxy server. In plotting Figures 5–10, we consider the vertical axis as the number of requests sent (cumulative) for the chunk video objects from the cache proxy server. The horizontal axis is the number of hops to the location of those chunk video objects. The request initiative from the cache proxy server is approximately equal to $100999 \approx 10^6 + 10^3 + 10^1$.

Figures 5 and 7 present the simulation result of minimum hop count to the required chunk of the video objects towards the peers or storage server. The peer nodes at ith level,

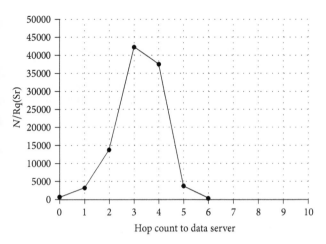

FIGURE 5: Dynamic adjacent list size (4).

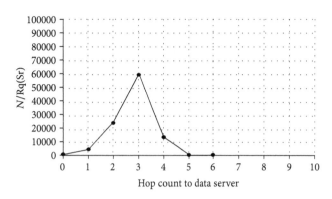

FIGURE 7: Dynamic adjacent list size (6).

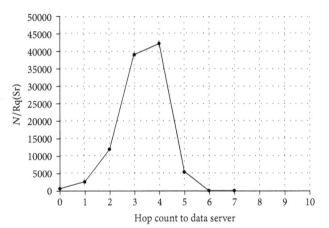

FIGURE 6: Static adjacent list size (4).

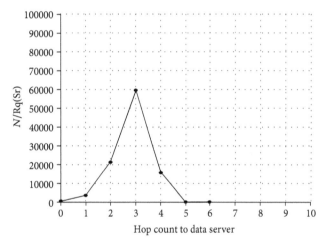

FIGURE 8: Static adjacent list size (6).

for $0 \leq i \leq 9$, maintain dynamic adjacent list sizes 1 to 4 and 1 to 6. Figures 6 and 8 present the simulation result where every peer at every level maintains static adjacent list sizes 4 and 6. To search for destination peers address, we simply start with the longest length hash table and extract the first bits and do a search in the hash table for length entries. If we succeed, we have found the longest prefix match and thus our BMP (best match path); if not, we look at the first length smaller than previous match path (done by the array indexing one position less than the position) and continue the search. The search is forwarded by incremental prefix routing. Keeping $(b - 1)$ hosts at each prefix digit b is the base of the prefix. To minimize the hop count, we consider the number of links at each intermediate node dynamically changing from one to $(b - 1)$. So expression (12) will be always bounded by $\log_b(N)$, and N is the number of "video objects storage" peer nodes. So $\log_b(N)$ is the maximum hop to any destination. The comparative simulation results are presented in Figures 9 and 10. The simulation result shows that 43000 numbers of requests were served from the peer at the hop count 3 for the dynamic adjacent list size 4. We have noticed that 40000 numbers of requests were served from the peer at the hop count 3 for static adjacent list size 4.

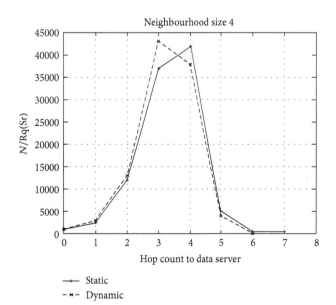

FIGURE 9: Compare dynamic versus static adjacent list size (4).

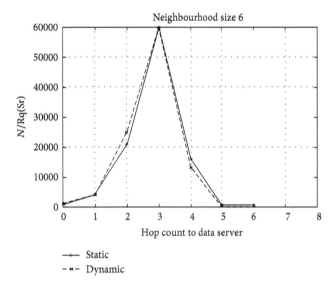

FIGURE 10: Compare dynamic versus static adjacent list size (6).

The chunk size is the same for both the cases. In Figures 9 and 10, we have noticed that the dotted line (dynamic) lies above the nondotted line (static) between the hop count 0 and hop count 3. In the next phase, the nondotted link lies above the dotted line between the hop counts 3 and 7. The longest prefix match with the dynamic adjacent list on the basis of "Heuristic Path Search Algorithm" gives better cost-effective results.

The simulation results with the dynamic adjacent list size 4 and static adjacent list size 4 are presented in Figure 9. The simulation result clearly shows that, in dynamic environment with list adjacent size 4, 35×10^2 numbers of video objects serve from the hop count 1. 130×10^2 numbers of video objects serve from hop count 2. 430×10^2 numbers of video objects serve from hop count 3. 370×10^2 numbers of video objects serve from hop count 4. 40×10^2 numbers of video objects serve from hop count 5. Static environment shows that, with adjacent list size 4, 30×10^2 numbers of video objects serve from hop count 1. 120×10^2 numbers of video objects serve from hop count 2. 360×10^2 numbers of video objects serve from hop count 3. 410×10^2 numbers of video objects serve from hop count 4 and 50×10^2 numbers of video objects serve from hop count 5. Here, we consider a rough estimate to measure the cost of video object transfer by using the metrics, such as "number of video objects serves" and hop counts. Cost is the sum of the "number of video objects serves a_m" multiplied by the "hop counts b_m towards the container that possesses the video objects"; that is, $\sum_{m=1}^{n}(a_m * b_m)$. Here m is the hop count towards the chunk video container peer node, and n is an end of hop counts towards the container. The above expression gives the following cost score. Dynamic environment of simulation produced the score 3265×10^2 according to Figure 9. For static environment of simulation, the produced cost score is 3740×10^2 according to Figure 9. Similarly according to simulation the result is presented

in Figure 10. That cost score in dynamic environment with adjacent list size 4 is 2840×10^2. The cost score in static environment with adjacent list size 6 is 2880×10^2. The cost score directly depends on the number of computations. The performance of the system increases as the score value decreases, during any stage of transfer of chunk video object through the multitier architecture.

5. Conclusions

In this paper, we have shown that the hybrid architecture of Peer to Peer network with mesh type's network enhances the content delivery of video objects. The number of requests generated by the proxy server serves from the distributed chunk video object storage at the various levels of the multitier architecture. The simulation used the static as well as the dynamic growth links at each middle tire containing storage nodes. The result showed the effectiveness of the hybrid architecture over the pure Peer to Peer network. The previous works considered only pure P2P network. The hybrid type's work successfully reduces the cost for the search path; hence it reduces the delay. Another aspect of the work is that it selects the required position of the video objects and supplies it to the desired node in the hybrid multitier architecture, which is the enhancement of previous Peer to Peer type stream data transmission. There is enough scope for further improvement.

Conflict of Interests

The authors Soumen Kanrar and Niranjan Kumar Mandal declare that there is no conflict of interests regarding the publication of the paper.

Acknowledgment

The authors are grateful to Sharmista Das Kanrar from Bishop Westcott, Ranchi, India.

References

[1] H. Jiang, J. Li, Z. Li, and X. Bai, "Effcient large-scale Content Distribution with Combination of CDN and P2P Networks," *International Journal of Hybrid Information Technology*, vol. 2, no. 2, 2009.

[2] C. Liang, Z. Fu, Y. Liu, and C. W. Wu, "Incentivized peer-assisted streaming for on-demand services," *IEEE Transactions on Parallel and Distributed Systems*, vol. 21, no. 9, pp. 1354–1367, 2010.

[3] X. Hei, Y. Liu, and K. Ross, "IPTV over P2P streaming networks: the mesh-pull approach," *IEEE Communications Magazine*, vol. 46, no. 2, pp. 86–92, 2008.

[4] X. Hei, C. Liang, J. Liang, Y. Liu, and K. W. Ross, "A measurement study of a large-scale P2P IPTV system," *IEEE Transactions on Multimedia*, vol. 9, no. 8, pp. 1672–1687, 2007.

[5] S. Kanrar, "Analysis and implementation of the large scale video-on-demand system," *International Journal of Applied Information Systems*, vol. 1, no. 4, 2012.

[6] H. Yin, X. Liu, T. Zhan et al., "Design and deployment of a hybrid CDN-P2P system for live video streaming: experiences with LiveSky," in *Proceedings of the 17th ACM International Conference on Multimedia (MM '09)*, pp. 25–34, ACM, Beijing, China, October 2009.

[7] W.-P. K. Yiu, X. Jin, and S.-H. G. Chan, "VMesh: distributed segment storage for peer-to-peer interactive video streaming," *IEEE Journal on Selected Areas in Communications*, vol. 25, no. 9, pp. 1717–1731, 2007.

[8] ITU-T Study Groups, "Definition of Quality of Experience (QoE)," ITU-T SG12, COM12-LS 62-E, TD 109rev2(PLEN/12), Geneva, Switzerland, January 2007, https://www.itu.int/md/T05-FG.IPTV-IL-0050/en.

[9] N. Zong, "Survey and Gap analysis for HTTP streaming standards and implementations," 2010.

[10] Q. Wu, "Problem statement for HTTP streaming," 2010.

[11] K. D. Singh, Y. Hadjadj-Aoul, and G. Rubino, "Quality of experience estimation for adaptive HTTP/TCP video streaming using H.264/AVC," in *Proceedings of the IEEE Consumer Communications and Networking Conference (CCNC '12)*, pp. 127–131, Las Vegas, Nev, USA, January 2012.

[12] N. Goel, B. Raman, and I. Gupta, "Chaos based joint compression and encryption framework for end-to-end communication systems," *Advances in Multimedia*, vol. 2014, Article ID 910106, 10 pages, 2014.

[13] W. Zeng and S. Lei, "Efficient frequency domain selective scrambling of digital video," *IEEE Transactions on Multimedia*, vol. 5, no. 1, pp. 118–129, 2003.

[14] R. Draves, J. Padhye, and B. Zill, "Comparison of routing metrics for static multi-hop wireless networks," *ACM SIGCOMM Computer Communication Review*, vol. 34, no. 4, pp. 133–144, 2004.

[15] S. Banerjee and A. Misra, "Minimum energy paths for reliable communication in multi-hop wireless networks," in *Proceedings of the 3rd ACM International Symposium on Mobile Ad Hoc Networking & Computing (MobiHoc '02)*, pp. 146–156, ACM, Lausanne, Switzerland, June 2002.

[16] S. Kanrar, N. K. Mandal, and S. D. Kanrar, "Session based storage finding in video on demand system," in *Proceedings of the 3rd International Symposium on Women in Computing and Informatics (WCI '15)*, pp. 131–135, Kochi, India, August 2015.

[17] A. Erramilli, O. Narayan, and W. Willinger, "Experimental queueing analysis with long-range dependent packet traffic," *IEEE/ACM Transactions on Networking*, vol. 4, no. 2, pp. 209–223, 1996.

[18] B. Maglaris, D. Anastassiou, P. Sen, G. Karlsson, and J. D. Robbins, "Performance models of statistical multiplexing in packet video communications," *IEEE Transactions on Communications*, vol. 36, no. 7, pp. 834–844, 1988.

[19] V. S. Frost and B. Melamed, "Traffic modeling for telecommunications networks," *IEEE Communication Magazine*, vol. 32, no. 3, pp. 70–81, 1994.

[20] J. Wen and J. D. Villasenor, "Reversible variable length codes for efficient and robust image and video coding," in *Proceedings of the Data Compression Conference (DCC '98)*, pp. 471–480, IEEE, Snowbird, Utah, USA, April 1998.

[21] F. Liu and H. Koenig, "Puzzle—an efficient, compression independent video encryption algorithm," *Multimedia Tools and Applications*, vol. 73, no. 2, pp. 715–735, 2012.

[22] E. Mallika and K. Sivakumar, "Joint video compression and encryption using secure wavelet transformation and entropy coding," *International Journal of Computer Science and Mobile Computing*, vol. 3, no. 2, pp. 483–489, 2014.

[23] C.-P. Wu and C.-C. J. Kuo, "Design of integrated multimedia compression and encryption systems," *IEEE Transactions on Multimedia*, vol. 7, no. 5, pp. 828–839, 2005.

[24] C. Kim and J.-N. Hwang, "Fast and automatic video object segmentation and tracking for content-based applications," *IEEE Transactions on Circuits and Systems for Video Technology*, vol. 12, no. 2, pp. 122–129, 2002.

[25] K. J. Singh and R. Manimegalai, "A survey on joint compression and encryption techniques for video data," *Journal of Computer Science*, vol. 8, no. 5, pp. 731–736, 2012.

[26] M. M. Hannuksela, D. Rusanovskyy, W. Su et al., "Multiview-video-plus-depth coding based on the advanced video coding standard," *IEEE Transactions on Image Processing*, vol. 22, no. 9, pp. 3449–3458, 2013.

[27] T. Wiegand and G. J. Sullivan, "Overview of the H.264/AVC video coding standard," *IEEE Transactions on Circuits and Systems for Video Technology*, vol. 13, no. 7, pp. 560–576, 2003.

[28] F. H. P. Fitzek and M. Reisslein, "MPEG-4 and H.263 video traces for network performance evaluation," *IEEE Network*, vol. 15, no. 6, pp. 40–54, 2002.

[29] D. A. Tan, K. A. Hua, and T. Do, "ZIGZAG: an efficient peer-to-peer scheme for media streaming," in *Proceedings of the 22nd Annual Joint Conference of the IEEE Computer and Communication (INFOCOM '03)*, vol. 2, pp. 1283–1292, San Francisco, Calif, USA, April 2003.

[30] S. Banerjee, B. Bhattacharjee, and C. Kommareddy, "Scalable application layer multicast," in *Proceedings of the Conference on Applications, Technologies, Architectures, and Protocols for Computer Communications (SIGCOMM '02)*, pp. 205–217, 2002.

[31] Y. Liu, Y. Guo, and C. Liang, "A survey on peer-to-peer video streaming systems," *Peer-to-Peer Networking and Applications*, vol. 1, no. 1, pp. 18–28, 2008.

[32] S. Kanrar and N. K. Mandal, "Dynamic page replacement at the cache memory for the video on demand server," in *Advanced Computing, Networking and Informatics-Volume 2: Wireless Networks and Security Proceedings of the Second International Conference on Advanced Computing, Networking and Informatics (ICACNI-2014)*, vol. 28 of *Smart Innovation, Systems and Technologies*, pp. 461–469, Springer, Berlin, Germany, 2014.

[33] S. Kanrar and N. K. Mandal, "Optimum storage finding in video on demand system," in *Proceedings of the 2nd International Conference on Signal Processing and Integrated Networks (SPIN '15)*, pp. 827–830, IEEE, Noida, India, Feburary 2015.

[34] N. Leibowitz, C. A. Bergman, R. Ben-shaul, and C. A. Shavit, "Are files wrapping network scacheable? Characterizing P2P traffic," in *Proceedings of the 7th International WWW Caching Workshop*, August 2002.

[35] C. Vincenzo, R. Gaeta, R. Loti, and L. Liquori, "Inter connection of large scale unstructured p2p networks: modeling and analysis," in *Analytical and Stochastic Modeling Techniques and Applications*, vol. 7984, pp. 183–197, Springer, 2013.

[36] A. Brocco and I. Baumgart, "A framework for a comprehensive evaluation of ant-inspired peer-to-peer protocols," in *Proceedings of the 20th Euromicro International Conference on Parallel, Distributed and Network-Based Processing (PDP '12)*, pp. 303–310, IEEE, Garching bei München, Germany, February 2012.

[37] J.-S. Li and C.-H. Chao, "An efficient superpeer overlay construction and broadcasting scheme based on perfect difference graph," *IEEE Transactions on Parallel and Distributed Systems*, vol. 21, no. 5, pp. 594–606, 2010.

[38] R. Rodrigues and P. Druschel, "Peer-to-peer systems," *Communications of the ACM*, vol. 53, no. 10, pp. 72–82, 2010.

[39] S. Kanrar, "Performance of distributed video on demand system for multirate traffic," in *Proceedings of the International Conference on Recent Trends in Information Systems (ReTIS '11)*, pp. 52–56, Kolkata, India, December 2011.

[40] S. Kanrar and N. K. Mandal, "Performance enhancement for audio-video proxy server," in *Proceedings of the 3rd International Conference on Frontiers of Intelligent Computing: Theory and Applications (FICTA) 2014*, vol. 327 of *Advances in Intelligent Systems and Computing*, pp. 605–613, Springer, Basel, Switzerland, 2015.

[41] F. Peng, A. Malatras, B. Hirsbrunner, and M. Courant, "Constructing multi-layer overlays for pervasive environments," in *Proceedings of the 8th International Workshop on Mobile P2P Computing (MP2P '12)*, pp. 1–6, March 2012.

[42] S. Tewari and L. Kleinrock, "On fairness, optimal download performance and proportional replication in peer-to-peer networks," in *Proceedings of the 4th International IFIP-TC6 Networking Conference*, Waterloo, Canada, May 2005.

[43] I. Stoica, R. Morris, D. Karger, M. F. Kaashoek, and H. Balakrishnan, "Chord: a scalable peer-to-peer lookup service for internet applications," in *Proceedings of the Conference on Applications, Technologies, Architectures, and Protocols for Computer Communications (SIGCOMM '01)*, pp. 149–160, ACM, San Diego, Calif, USA, August 2001.

[44] B. Tan and L. Massoulie, "Optimal content placement for peer-to-peer video-on-demand systems," *IEEE/ACM Transactions on Networking*, vol. 21, no. 2, pp. 566–579, 2013.

8

A Novel Printable Watermarking Method in Dithering Halftone Images

Hui-Lung Lee and Ling-Hwei Chen

Department of Computer Science, National Chiao Tung University Hsinchu, Hsinchu 300, Taiwan

Correspondence should be addressed to Ling-Hwei Chen; lhchen@cc.nctu.edu.tw

Academic Editor: Martin Reisslein

Halftone images are commonly printed on books, newspapers, and magazines. How to protect the copyright of these printed halftone images becomes an important issue. Digital watermarking provides a solution for copyright protection. In this paper, we will propose a novel printable watermarking method for dithering halftone images. Based on downsampling and the property of a dispersed dithering screen, the method can resist cropping, tampering, and print-and-scan process attacks. In addition, comparing to Guo et al.'s method, the experimental results show that the proposed method provides higher robustness for the above-mentioned attacks and better visual quality in the high-frequency regions of halftone images.

1. Introduction

Digital halftoning is a method to convert continuous-tone images to two-tone ones; it is widely used in printing newspapers, magazines, books, and so forth. When viewed from a proper distance, halftone images resemble the original grayscale images. Today, many digital halftoning methods [1–3] were developed. Error diffusion, ordered dithering, and iteration-based technique are three common types of halftoning methods. Error diffusion [1] is a single-pass sequential algorithm. The past error is diffused back to the unprocessed neighboring pixels. When processing the current pixel, its gray value will add all the past error and compare with a fixed threshold 128 to determine its output. Ordered dithering [2] is applied to a threshold matrix to convert a gray image to a halftone image. It compares the pixel value with the threshold matrix to determine pixel output. Hence, it has better time efficiency. The iteration-based technique [3] is an iterative algorithm; it proceeds by generating an initial halftone image and then iteratively performs a local search on the halftone space by swapping and toggling to minimize the perceived error. It usually generates a better quality images than the error diffusion and the ordered dithering, but it is time consuming.

Many watermarking techniques have been provided for halftone image copyright protection and authentication; they are divided into three categories: error diffusion based [4–11], ordered dithering based [4, 12–18], and iteration-based [19–21] techniques.

For error diffusion based watermark techniques, in 2002, Fu and Au [4] proposed a few data hiding or watermarking methods in halftone images. When the original multitone image is not available, a data hiding smart pair toggling scheme was presented to hide data in halftone images. When the original multitone image is available and the halftoning method is error diffusion, a modified data hiding error diffusion method was provided to hide data in the halftone images by forced self-toggling with its distortion diffused to the surrounding pixels. This method can be applied to the halftone images generated by ordered dithering. Experimental results show that the proposed methods have high data hiding capacity, low computational complexity, good visual quality, and reasonable resistance toward noise. However, it is not robust to any distortions without applying error correction code, and some artifacts are found in the locations of pair toggling. Later, Fu and Au [5] embedded a single watermark or multiwatermarks in the parity domain of a halftone image during halftoning. However, it can only embed 1 bit to indicate whether a watermark or one of two watermarks exists. Thus, this method is improper for copyright authentication. In 2004, Fu and Au [6] proposed an improved method to embed a watermark in the local correlation coefficient between the watermark bits and the halftone image. The local correlation coefficient is computed by the exclusive operation between a security code and halftone image. However, if the security code size is small, the visual quality of the watermarked halftone image would be degraded. In 2006, Pei and Guo [7] proposed a data hiding method in several halftone images or color planes using minimal-error bit searching. It employed the gray code to divide code vectors into two groups, and each group corresponds to a watermark bit 0 or 1. According to the watermark bit embedded, most suitable code vectors with better visual quality are chosen to form the watermarked halftone images. However, the quality degrades significantly when capacity increases up to 50%. In 2007, Li et al. [8] proposed a watermarking method for error diffusion halftone images; the method provides a block-overlapping parity check algorithm to reduce the number of pair toggling required in the Fu and Au's method [4]. Experiments show that the method has better visual quality than Fu and Au's method [4]. To treat Pei and Guo's problem [7], Guo and Liu [9] proposed a data hiding method in several halftone images by using overall minimal-error searching and secret sharing. Moreover, the least-mean-square based scheme is also employed to achieve even better quality and edge enhanced embedded results. However, the homogeneous regions of watermarked images maybe have artifacts.

For ordered dithering based watermark techniques, in 2001, Fu and Au [14] proposed a two-phase watermarking method for ordered dithering images. First, one out of every M pseudorandom locations is selected using threshold selection to embed one data bit. Second, screen modification is applied to the local neighborhood of the selected location to change the ordered dithering screen to achieve the desired data embedding. Some quality measures were proposed to evaluate the visual quality of a dithering image. Simulation results show that the method can hide a large amount of data while maintaining good visual quality. However, it is not robust to the print-and-scan process. In 2001, Hel-Or [13] proposed a method to embed a watermark in printed images. First, based on watermark bits, a dithering screen is created by selecting different dither matrices; then the screen is used to produce a printed image. The method is robust under reconstruction errors. However, it is not robust to cropping and has artifacts.

In 2005, Pei et al. [15] presented a method to embed watermarks into dithered halftone images. The method divides a dithered halftone image into several sub-subimages by the bit and sub-subimage interleaving preprocesses, and each watermark bit is embedded into each pair of sub-subimages. The method has low computational complexity and flexible embedding capacity. But the method requires the knowledge of the original watermark to do copyright authentication. To treat Pei et al.'s problem, in 2008, Guo et al. [12] proposed another watermarking method using the blind paired subimage matching ordered dithering (BPSMOD) technique.

It does not require the knowledge of the original watermark in the watermark extraction. However, the visual quality in the boundary of the embedded dithered image may be degraded.

In 2010, Bulan et al. [16] proposed a data hiding method that embeds bits through clustered-dot orientations during halftoning process. For extracting the embedding data, a moment-based extracting method is used to detect the clustered-dot orientations. The method is only applicable for clustered-dot halftoning methods, and it relies on the ability to accurately control the printing of the halftone image; this may be restrictive in some applications. In 2013, Feng et al. [17] proposed a halftone watermarking algorithm based on particle swarm optimization. It is robust under smearing and cropping attacks. Unfortunately, it needs mean filtering and median filtering to remove noise from the recovered watermark image. This is only suitable for a watermark with a solid black/white object. Thus, the method is unsuitable for a watermark with a random sequence.

For iteration-based watermark techniques, in 2003, Chun and Ha [19] proposed a watermark technique based on iterative halftoning method. In the embedding stage, a pseudorandom number generator is used to locate the embedding locations and force these pixel values at these locations to be 0 or 1 according to the watermark bits. Then, in the error minimizing stage, for each unembedded pixel, check whether toggling the pixel value or swapping the pixel value with neighbor pixels can reduce the perceived halftoning error. In 2012, Guo et al. [20] proposed a DBS-based orientation modulation watermarking method. In this method, the direction of the point spread function is used to represent different watermark values. To extract the watermark bit, the LMS trained filters and naive Bayes classifier are used to classify the angle. In 2015, Guo et al. [21] proposed a halftoning-based multilayer watermarking method. An efficient direct binary search and lookup table method is applied to embed multiple watermarks. Then, the least mean square and native Bayes classifier are used to extract the watermarks. Although all these methods provide excellent image quality, they are time consuming.

In this paper, we focus on ordered dithering halftone images. And a blind watermarking method will be proposed to treat the disadvantages of the above-mentioned dithering based watermarking methods. First, a grayscale image is transformed into a dithering halftone image according to an $n \times n$ dispersed dithering screen (for convenience of illustration, here, we take $n = 4$; see Figure 1); then the halftone image is divided into several subimages through downsampling. For each subimage, to embed watermark bits, it is first divided into several 4×4 blocks. Then, the number of black pixels, p_j, in all blocks corresponding to the position with the jth smallest value T_j (see Figure 1(c), $j = 3$, $T_3 = 56$) in the 4×4 dispersed dithering screen is counted. Finally, we take (p_u, p_v) as a pair to embed a bit based on the sign of $(p_u - p_v)$, where $(u, v) = (0, 4), (1, 5), (2, 6), (3, 7), (8, 15), (9, 14), (10, 12)$, or $(11, 13)$. If the embedding bit is 0 and $p_u < p_v$ or the embedding bit is 1 and $p_u > p_v$, nothing is done. Otherwise, in each block, the pixel at position with the uth smallest value and the pixel at position with the vth smallest value are swapped. Since $|p_u - p_v|$ is usually larger than $|p_u - p_{u+1}|$, this provides higher robustness than Guo et al.'s method [12]

24	232	40	200
152	88	168	104
56	216	8	248
184	120	136	72

(a)

6	238	62	222	10	226	50	210
134	70	190	126	138	74	178	114
38	198	22	254	42	202	26	242
166	102	150	86	170	106	154	90
14	230	54	214	2	234	58	218
142	78	182	118	130	66	186	122
46	206	30	246	34	194	18	250
174	110	158	94	162	98	146	82

(b)

1 $(0,0)$	14 $(0,1)$	2 $(0,2)$	12 $(0,3)$
9 $(1,0)$	5 $(1,1)$	10 $(1,2)$	6 $(1,3)$
3 $(2,0)$	13 $(2,1)$	0 $(2,2)$	15 $(2,3)$
11 $(3,0)$	7 $(3,1)$	8 $(3,2)$	4 $(3,3)$

(c)

1 $(0,0)$	59 $(0,1)$	15 $(0,2)$	55 $(0,3)$	2 $(0,4)$	56 $(0,5)$	12 $(0,6)$	52 $(0,7)$
33 $(1,0)$	17 $(1,1)$	47 $(1,2)$	31 $(1,3)$	34 $(1,4)$	18 $(1,5)$	44 $(1,6)$	28 $(1,7)$
9 $(2,0)$	49 $(2,1)$	5 $(2,2)$	63 $(2,3)$	10 $(2,4)$	50 $(2,5)$	6 $(2,6)$	60 $(2,7)$
41 $(3,0)$	25 $(3,1)$	37 $(3,2)$	21 $(3,3)$	42 $(3,4)$	26 $(3,5)$	38 $(3,6)$	22 $(3,7)$
3 $(4,0)$	57 $(4,1)$	13 $(4,2)$	53 $(4,3)$	0 $(4,4)$	58 $(4,5)$	14 $(4,6)$	54 $(4,7)$
35 $(5,0)$	19 $(5,1)$	45 $(5,2)$	29 $(5,3)$	32 $(5,4)$	16 $(5,5)$	46 $(5,6)$	30 $(5,7)$
11 $(6,0)$	51 $(6,1)$	7 $(6,2)$	61 $(6,3)$	8 $(6,4)$	48 $(6,5)$	4 $(6,6)$	62 $(6,7)$
43 $(7,0)$	27 $(7,1)$	39 $(7,2)$	23 $(7,3)$	40 $(7,4)$	24 $(7,5)$	36 $(7,6)$	20 $(7,7)$

(d)

FIGURE 1: An example of dispersed dithering screens. (a) A 4×4 dispersed dithering screen. (b) An 8×8 dispersed dithering screen. (c) The order and position of each pixel in (a). (d) The order and position of each pixel in (b).

for the print-and-scan process. In addition, since the number of black pixels in each block is not changed, the proposed method also provides higher visual quality in the edge boundary than Guo et al.'s method [12]. Furthermore, the downsampling technique is presented to provide higher robustness than Guo et al.'s method for cropping and tampering. The rest of the paper is organized as follows. Section 2 outlines Guo et al.'s [12, 15] methods. Section 3 describes the proposed method. Section 4 shows the experimental results and comparisons. Section 5 draws conclusions.

2. A Brief Description for Guo et al.'s Methods

As mentioned previously, Guo et al. [12] proposed a watermarking method using BPSMOD in dithering halftone images. At first, a dispersed dithering method is adopted to convert a grayscale image into a dithering halftone image. Then, the bit-interleaving algorithm proposed by Pei et al. [15] is used to arrange the dithering halftone image. After that, the BPSMOD is applied to the arranged image to embed watermark bits. To raise the embedding capacity, a sub-subimage

FIGURE 2: An example of bit-interleaving algorithm [12]. (a) Lena image. (b) Dithering halftone image of (b) using Figure 1(a). (c) Bit-interleaving result of (b). (d) Dithering halftone image divided into 16 subimages. (e) The result of applying bit-interleaving to each subimage in (d).

interleaving algorithm [12, 15] is adopted. The details are described in the following subsections.

2.1. Bit-Interleaving Algorithm in a Dithering Halftone Image.
As mentioned above, in Guo et al.'s method [12], an $n \times n$ dispersed dithering screen (DS) [1] is first applied to a $P \times Q$ grayscale image I to result in a dithering halftone image H according to the following equation:

$$H(i, j) = \begin{cases} 0, & x(i, j) < DS \ (i \bmod n, j \bmod n), \\ 255, & \text{otherwise,} \end{cases} \quad (1)$$

where $x(i, j)$ and $H(i, j)$ are the gray levels of pixel (i, j) in I and H, respectively. $DS(i, j)$ is the value of the position (i, j) in the dispersed dithering screen. Figure 2(a) shows a 128×128 grayscale image. Figure 2(b) is the resulting dithering halftone image by applying Figure 1(a) to Figure 2(a).

After obtaining the dithering halftone image, all pixels corresponding to the same screen value are then grouped into a subimage; this will result in $n \times n$ subimages, each of which has $P/n \times Q/n$ pixels. Finally, according to the screen values, all subimages will be sorted in ascending order of the screen

values and arranged from left to right and bottom to top to result in a binary image RH. Let RH_j be the jth subimage, where $j = 0, 1, \ldots, (n \times n) - 1$, and the bottom-left subimage is RH_0. The above process is called bit-interleaving [12, 15]. Figure 2(c) shows the bit-interleaving result of Figure 2(b), and it contains 16 subimages, and the bottom-left subimage corresponds to screen value 8.

2.2. BPSMOD.
In BPSMOD, based on RH, subimages RH_j and RH_{j+1} are considered a pair (RH_j, RH_{j+1}), where $j = 2m$ and $m = 0, 1, \ldots, (n \times n)/2 - 1$. Since the screen value used to form RH_j is smaller than that used to form RH_{j+1}, RH_j will usually have less black pixels than RH_{j+1}. However, RH_j sometimes has black pixels more than (equal to) RH_{j+1}; this kind of pairs is called nonincreased black pixel pair (NIP). Before embedding, if a pair (RH_j, RH_{j+1}) is a NIP, it will be modified by increasing black pixels of RH_{j+1} or decreasing black pixels of RH_j to make the modified RH_j have less black pixels than the modified RH_{j+1}. Then, in embedding, each pair (RH_j, RH_{j+1}) will embed 1 bit. If watermark bit being embedded is 1, RH_j and RH_{j+1} will be swapped. Otherwise, nothing is done.

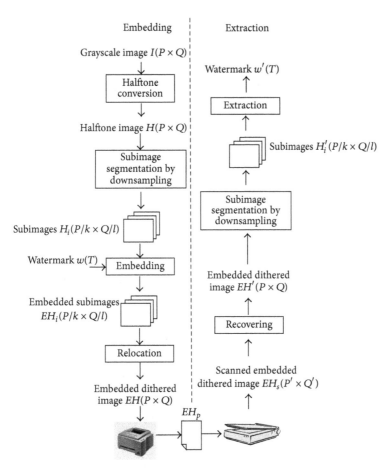

FIGURE 3: The block diagram of the proposed method.

Since there are $(n \times n)/2$ pairs of subimages in RH and each pair of subimages embeds a bit, the embedding capacity is $(n \times n)/2$. To increase the embedding capacity, Guo et al. [12] first divides the original halftone image H into $k \times l$ subimages H_is. Then, the above-mentioned bit-interleaving method is applied to each H_i to get $n \times n$ sub-subimages $SH_{i,j}$'s to embed $(n \times n)/2$ bits. Hence, the capacity is increased to $(nk \times nl)/2$. Figure 2(d) shows the result of dividing Figure 2(c) into 16 subimages. Figure 2(e) shows the result of applying bit-interleaving to each subimage in Figure 2(d).

Table 1 shows the numbers of black pixels in the sub-subimage pairs $(SH_{0,j}, SH_{0,j+1})$ of the subimage H_0 in the bottom-left of Figure 2(e), where $j = 2m$ and $m = 0, 1, \ldots, 7$. In Table 1, the difference of the numbers of black pixels between $SH_{0,j}$ and $SH_{0,j+1}$ is 0, for $j = 4, 8, 12$. These sub-subimage pairs are NIPs. To eliminate these NIPs, at least one white pixel is chosen and changed into a black pixel in $SH_{0,5}$, $SH_{0,9}$, and $SH_{0,13}$, respectively. This may make the visual quality degraded. Furthermore, from Table 1, we find that the average difference of numbers of black pixels in the eight sub-subimage pairs is 5.25. The low difference of black pixel numbers between $SH_{0,j}$ and $SH_{0,j+1}$ could lead to the sign of the difference being altered, when the embedded dithered image is processed by print-and-scan process. This will make the extracted watermark bit wrong. Here, we will propose a method to treat these disadvantages.

TABLE 1: The black pixel numbers of eight sub-subimage pairs in the bottom-left subimage of Figure 2(d).

j	# Black pixels		The difference of black pixel numbers between $SH_{0,j}$ and $SH_{0,j+1}$
	$SH_{0,j}$	$SH_{0,j+1}$	
0	0	2	2
2	23	33	10
4	0	0	0
6	18	37	19
8	0	0	0
10	3	6	3
12	0	0	0
14	1	9	8

3. The Proposed Method

The proposed method contains two parts: embedding and extraction. Figure 3 shows the block diagram of the proposed method. In the embedding part, first, a grayscale image I is converted into a halftone image H. Secondly, H is segmented into $k \times l$ subimages H_i through downsampling. Thirdly, watermark bits are embedded into each subimage. Fourthly, all pixels in the embedded subimages EH_i are relocated to their original positions to form the embedded dithered image

EH. Finally, *EH* can be printed on a paper. In the extraction, after transmission, the printed embedded dithered image EH_p is scanned by a scanner, and then a scanned embedded dithered image EH_s is produced. Since the print-and-scan process could cause distortion, a recovering algorithm proposed by Guo et al. [12] is used to correct the distortion in EH_s. After that, the output EH' will be segmented into several subimages through downsampling. Finally, the watermark w' can be extracted from each subimage.

In this section, we will first introduce the proposed embedding algorithm. Then, the provided extracting algorithm is described.

3.1. Embedding Algorithm. The embedding algorithm contains four stages: halftone conversion, subimage segmentation, embedding, and relocation. They are described in the following.

3.1.1. Halftone Conversion. An $n \times n$ dispersed dithering screen (DS) [1] is first applied to a $P \times Q$ grayscale image I to result in a dithering halftone image H according to (1).

3.1.2. Subimage Segmentation. Suppose that a watermark w with T bits will be embedded. In the subimage segmentation stage, H is segmented into $k \times l$ subimages through downsampling, where $k \times l \geq \lceil T/(n \times n)/2 \rceil$ and each subimage has $P/k \times Q/l$ pixels. First, H is divided into $P/kn \times Q/ln$ blocks, each of which has $kn \times ln$ pixels. Then, each block is further divided into $k \times l$ subblocks, each of which has $n \times n$ pixels. Let $A_{i,j}$ be the jth subblock in block i, where $i = 0, 1, \ldots, ((P \times Q)/(kn \times ln) - 1)$ and $j = 0, 1, \ldots, (kl - 1)$, respectively. Finally, through downsampling, all jth subblocks ($A_{i,j}$, $i = 0, 1, \ldots, ((P \times Q)/(kn \times ln) - 1)$) are grouped into a subimage H_j. For the convenience of explanation, all H_js are arranged into an image.

Figure 4(a) shows an image divided into 3×3 blocks with $P = Q = 48$, $k = l = 4$, and $n = 4$, each of which is further divided into 4×4 subblocks. Figure 4(b) shows the subimage segmentation result of Figure 4(a). Figure 4(c) shows the segmentation result of Figure 2(b) with $T = 120$, $k = 4$, $l = 4$, and $k \times l = 16 > 120/((4 \times 4)/2) = 15$. The rectangles in Figure 4(c) denote the 16 subimages.

3.1.3. Embedding. In the embedding stage, an $n \times n$ dispersed dithering screen with $n = 2^k$ and $k \in N$ is used. The $n \times n$ dispersed dithering screen is first divided into 2×2 dispersed dithering screens. Secondly, in each 2×2 dispersed dithering screen, two elements with thresholds more than 128 are grouped as a pair, and the other two elements with thresholds less than 128 are grouped as a pair. Hence, we can obtain $(n \times n)/2$ pairs.

Thirdly, sort all values in the $n \times n$ dispersed dithering screen and give each value an order; then each pair is represented by its corresponding order. For example, in Figure 1(b) with $n = 8$, the four elements in the top-left 2×2 dispersed dithering screen marked by a red rectangle have thresholds 6, 238, 134, and 70. The two elements with thresholds 6 and 70 are grouped as a pair, and 134 and 238 are grouped as another

TABLE 2: The black pixel numbers in eight pairs of the top-left subimage in Figure 4(c).

Pairs	The number of black pixels	
	p_u	p_v
(p_0, p_4)	0	18
(p_1, p_5)	0	32
(p_2, p_6)	10	35
(p_3, p_7)	16	44
(p_8, p_{15})	53	64
(p_9, p_{14})	54	64
(p_{10}, p_{12})	58	64
(p_{11}, p_{13})	60	64

pair. After sorting the values in the dispersed dithering screen in Figure 1(b), the corresponding order of each element is shown in Figure 1(d). The two pairs are represented by their corresponding orders as $(1, 17)$ and $(33, 59)$.

Fourthly, let ODS_j be the position with order j in the dispersed dithering screen DS, where $j = 0, \ldots, (n \times n) - 1$. Figure 1(c) shows the order and position of each pixel in the 4×4 dispersed dithering screen shown in Figure 1(a); in this figure, $ODS_0 = (2, 2)$, $ODS_{15} = (2, 3)$. Fifthly, each subimage H_i is divided into blocks with size $n \times n$, and all pixels at position ODS_j of all blocks are grouped into a sub-subimage $SH_{i,j}$.

Sixthly, the number, p_j, of black pixels at $SH_{i,j}$ is counted. Then, we take (p_u, p_v) as a pair, when $n = 4$, $(u, v) = (0, 4), (1, 5), (2, 6), (3, 7), (8, 15), (9, 14), (10, 12)$, or $(11, 13)$. Note that, for each of above-mentioned pair (p_u, p_v) with $n = 4$, the difference, $d_{(u,v)}$, of values of ODS_u and ODS_v in the dispersed dithering screen DS is not less than 32. However, for each pair (p_i, p_{i+1}) used by Guo et al., the difference, $d_{(i,i+1)}$, of values of ODS_i and ODS_{i+1} in the dispersed dithering screen DS is equal to 16. This will make each pair (p_u, p_v) used in the proposed method have larger $|p_u - p_v|$ than $|p_i - p_{i+1}|$ used in Guo et al.'s method. One example is given in Table 2. Table 2 shows the black pixel numbers of each pair (p_u, p_v) in the top-left subimage of Figure 4(c); the average difference of numbers of black pixels in the eight pairs is 16.75, which is greater than 5.25 in Guo et al.'s method (see Table 1). This means that the proposed method will provide higher robustness than Guo et al.'s method for the print-and-scan process.

Finally, one bit is embedded into each pair (p_u, p_v). If the embedding bit is 0 and $p_u < p_v$ or the embedding bit is 1 and $p_u > p_v$, nothing is done. Otherwise, in each block, the pixel at position ODS_u and the pixel at position ODS_v are swapped. Note that if $p_u = p_v$, no bit will be embedded into the pair. This kind of pairs is called equivalent black pixel pair (EBP).

3.1.4. Relocation. After embedding, all pixels are relocated to their original positions to form the embedded dithered image *EH*. Then *EH* can be printed on a paper to form a printed embedded dithered image EH_p. Note that the embedding capacity is $k \times l \times (n \times n)/2$ bits.

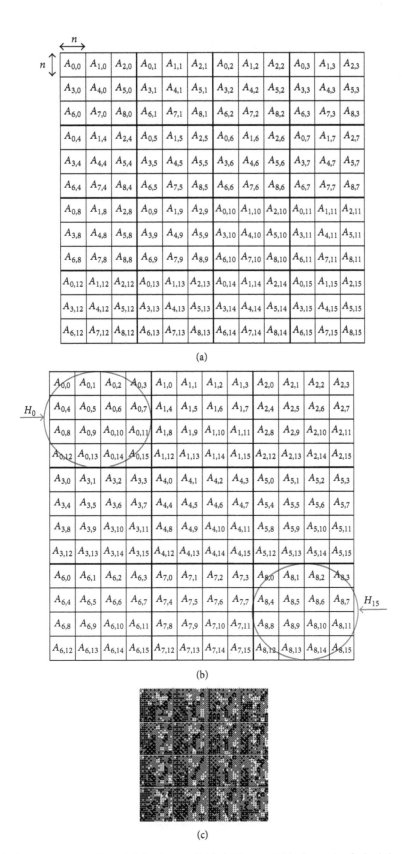

FIGURE 4: An example of subimage segmentation. (a) An image divided into 3 × 3 blocks, each of which has 4 × 4 subblocks. (b) The segmentation result of (a). (c) The segmentation result of Figure 2(b).

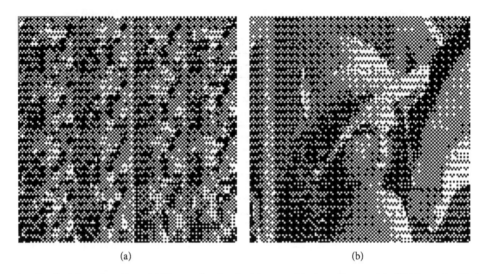

(a)   (b)

FIGURE 5: An example of embedding algorithm. (a) The result of embedding 120 bits into Figure 4(c). (b) The embedded dithered image by relocating (a).

Figure 5(a) shows the result of embedding 120 watermark bits into Figure 4(c). The rectangle marked in Figure 5(a) denotes the first subimage with 8 watermark bits 10101010 embedded. Figure 5(b) shows the embedded dithered image resulting from relocating Figure 5(a).

3.2. Recovering Algorithm for Print-and-Scan Process.
When we receive the paper with the printed embedded dithered image EH_p, a scanner is used to capture EH_p and produce a scanned image EH_s. The scanned image EH_s usually has geometrical distortion and dot gain effect due to the scanner and printer properties. Dot gain is a phenomenon in printing which causes the size of a dot to be increased or decreased slightly. Here, we adopt the recovering algorithm proposed by Guo et al. [12] to get the embedded dithered image EH'.

3.3. Watermark Extraction Algorithm.
The watermark extraction contains two steps: subimage segmentation and extraction. To extract the embedded watermark, EH' will be segmented into several subimages through downsampling mentioned in the embedding algorithm. For each subimage H_i', we divide it into blocks with size $n \times n$ and then count the number, p_j, of black pixels at position ODS_j of all blocks. Then, (p_u, p_v) is taken as a pair, when $n = 4$, $(u, v) = (0, 4), (1, 5), (2, 6), (3, 7), (8, 15), (9, 14), (10, 12)$, or $(11, 13)$. Finally, for each pair (p_u, p_v), a watermark bit is extracted and considered to be 0 if $p_u < p_v$ and 1 if $p_u > p_v$. Otherwise, no watermark bit is embedded if $p_u = p_v$.

4. Experimental Results and Comparisons

Eight 512×512 test images used in [12, 15] are shown in Figure 6 and also used in our experiments. Figure 7 shows the visual quality comparison of different methods when $n = 4$. The regions marked by cycles in Figures 7(e)–7(h) are high-frequency ones of Figures 7(a)–7(d), respectively. Compared to Figure 7(e), we can see that Figure 7(h) is similar to

Figure 7(e), but the boundary area in Figure 7(f) is smeared and unclear. This means that the proposed method provides higher visual quality in high-frequency areas than Guo et al.'s method [12]. Besides, we can see that Figure 7(c) has salt-and-pepper noises. Hence, the proposed method provides better visual quality than Hagit's method [13].

Figure 8 shows the visual quality comparison of different methods when $n = 8$. Compared to Figure 8(e), we can see that Figure 8(h) is similar to Figure 8(e), but the boundary area in Figure 8(f) is smeared and unclear. Compared to Figures 7(f) and 8(f), we can see that Figure 8(f) is more smeared and unclear than Figure 7(f). Besides, we can see that Figure 8(c) has more salt-and-pepper noises. Hence, the proposed method provides better visual quality than Hagit's method [13].

Next, two objective methods [7, 14] are used to measure the halftone image quality. One is the Pei-Guo-PSNR proposed by Pei and Guo [7]; it is adopted to measure the quality of a halftone image and is evaluated as follows:

Pei-Guo-PSNR

$$= \frac{P \times Q}{\sum_{i=1}^{P} \sum_{j=1}^{Q} \left[x_{i,j} - \sum_{(m,n) \in R} \sum w_{m,n} b_{i+m, j+n} \right]^2}, \quad (2)$$

where $w_{m,n}$ is an $r \times r$ least-mean square filter and can be obtained by a training process [7], $R = \{(m, n) \mid -(r - 1)/2 \le m, n \le (r - 1)/2\}$, x is the original grayscale image, and b is the corresponding halftone image. Here, a 7×7 least-mean square (LMS) filter [7] (see Figure 9) is adopted to measure the quality of halftone images. Table 3 shows the quality comparisons of various methods using Pei-Guo-PSNR; a random bit stream is adopted as a watermark. From this table, we can see that the proposed methods and Guo et al.'s method provide similar qualities when $n = 4$. But the proposed method provides better qualities than Hagit's method. When $n = 8$, the proposed method provides better qualities than other methods. Because Pei-Guo-PSNR is basically the PSNR of

TABLE 3: Quality comparisons of various algorithms using Pei-Guo-PSNR [12].

Algorithm	Original		Hagit's method [13]		Guo et al.'s method [12]		Proposed method	
				Average Pei-Guo-PSNR				
Screen size	$n = 4$	$n = 8$	$n = 4$	$n = 8$	$n = 4$	$n = 8$	$n = 4$	$n = 8$
Embedded bits 0	31.56	31.19	N/A	N/A	N/A	N/A	N/A	N/A
32	N/A	N/A	26.83	27.55	29.21	26.29	28.65	29.14
128	N/A	N/A	26.80	27.52	29.17	26.55	28.58	28.82
512	N/A	N/A	26.87	27.38	28.91	26.31	28.49	28.92

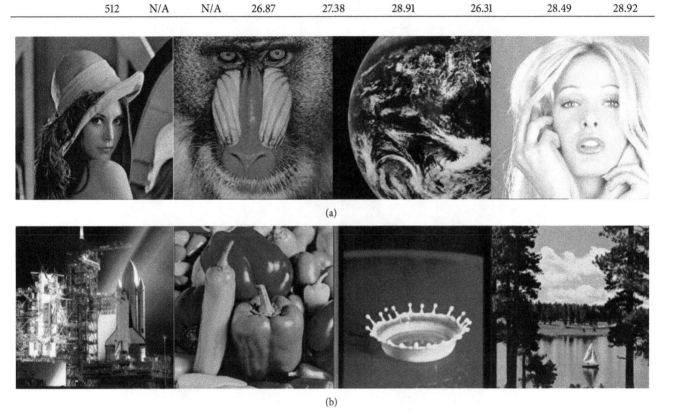

FIGURE 6: Thumbnail of eight test images. (a) Lena, Mandrill, Earth, and Tiffany. (b) Shuttle, Peppers, Milk, and Lake.

the original grayscale image and a low-pass version of the halftone image, it measures effectively the distortions to the low-frequency image content [14]. But Pei-Guo-PSNR is improper for measuring the high-frequency image content.

Fu and Au [14] proposed another measure to treat the above-mentioned disadvantage. Let x be the original grayscale image; let EH be the embedded halftone image. Fu and Au [14] define two special classes of elements in EH as follows:

Class 1. Black pixel in bright region ($EH(m, n) = 0$, $x(m, n) \geq 128$).

Class 2. White pixel in dark region ($EH(m, n) = 255$, $x(m, n) \leq 127$).

Based on these two classes, Fu and Au [14] define four scores as follows:

$$S_1 = \sum_{i=0}^{4} N_i,$$

$$S_2 = \sum_{i=0}^{4} (i + 1) N_i,$$

$$S_3 = \frac{S_2}{S_1},$$

$$S_4 = \sum_{i=2}^{4} N_i,$$

$$(3)$$

where N_i is the total number of Class 1 and Class 2 elements in EH having i neighbors with the same pixel values in the 4-neighborhood. N_0 corresponds to the number of isolated Class 1 or Class 2 elements. S_3 and S_4 can be used to measure the visual disturbing of "salt-and-pepper" clusters formed by neighboring pixels [14]. Thus, we adopt scores S_3 and S_4 to measure the quality of a halftone image. Algorithms with smaller scores of S_3 and S_4 are better. Table 4 shows the quality comparisons of various methods based on scores S_3 and S_4.

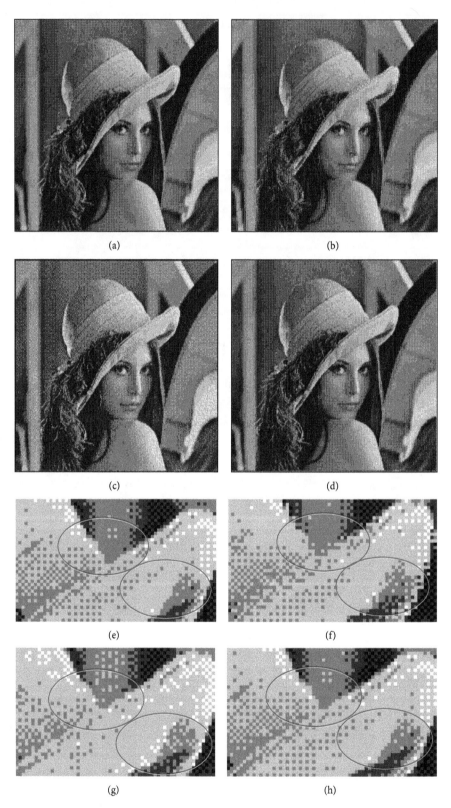

FIGURE 7: Visual quality comparison with 128 embedding bits when $n = 4$. (a) Original dithered image. (b) Embedded dithered image using Guo et al.'s method [12]. (c) Embedded dithered image using Hagit's method [13]. (d) Embedded dithered image using the proposed method. (e) Enlarged partial image of (a). (f) Enlarged partial image of (b). (g) Enlarged partial image of (c). (h) Enlarged partial image of (d).

FIGURE 8: Visual quality comparison with 128 embedding bits when $n = 8$. (a) Original dithered image. (b) Embedded dithered image using Guo et al.'s method [12]. (c) Embedded dithered image using Hagit's method [13]. (d) Embedded dithered image using the proposed method. (e) Enlarged partial image of (a). (f) Enlarged partial image of (b). (g) Enlarged partial image of (c). (h) Enlarged partial image of (d).

From this table, we can see that the proposed method has smaller scores of S_3 and S_4; thus, it is better than other methods.

From the above experiments, we can see that the image quality of Guo et al.'s method becomes worse when the dispersed dithering screen size increases. The reason is that if the dispersed dithering screen size increases, the NIP problem in Guo et al.'s method becomes more serious. Many black pixels will be added to eliminate these NIPs in Guo et al.'s method. Hence, the number of black pixels in some subimages will be changed. In addition, the pixel swapping distance of Guo et al.'s method also increases if the dispersed dithering screen size increases. Hence, the boundary of Guo et al.'s method will become more smeared and unclear and its image

TABLE 4: Quality comparisons of various algorithms based on scores S_3 and S_4 [14].

Algorithm		Hagit's method [13]		Guo et al.'s method [12]		Proposed method	
				Average S_3			
Screen size		$n = 4$	$n = 8$	$n = 4$	$n = 8$	$n = 4$	$n = 8$
	32	2.49	2.23	1.61	1.69	1.61	1.18
Embedded bits	128	2.64	2.32	1.67	1.52	1.67	1.18
	512	2.58	2.32	1.68	1.61	1.68	1.18
				Average S_4			
Screen size		$n = 4$	$n = 8$	$n = 4$	$n = 8$	$n = 4$	$n = 8$
	32	17459	11164	1372	2583	829	899
Embedded bits	128	17528	11738	1503	1833	824	815
	512	17328	11382	1660	2240	799	854

TABLE 5: Quality comparisons of various algorithms with 64×64 watermark bits embedded in Figure 8(a).

Algorithm	Guo et al.'s method [12]	Proposed method	Feng et al.'s method [17]
Pei-Guo-PSNR	28.68	30.17	15.15
S_3	1.43	1.07	3.86
S_4	1847	201	54592

−0.001	0.006	0.013	0.015	0.013	0.006	−0.001
0.003	0.007	0.022	0.0.29	0.022	0.009	0.002
0.010	0.025	0.051	0.067	0.051	0.024	0.009
0.007	0.030	0.064	0.091	0.064	0.031	0.007
0.007	0.020	0.042	0.054	0.041	0.019	0.006
0.003	0.011	0.024	0.030	0.023	0.009	0.003
−0.004	0.002	0.008	0.006	0.007	0.002	−0.004

FIGURE 9: Coefficients of 7×7 LMS filter.

quality is degraded. However, the proposed method does not have this problem. Hence, the boundary is still clear when the dispersed dithering screen size increases.

Since Feng et al.'s method [17] can only embed $P/8 \times Q/8$ watermark bits, we compare the qualities of the embedded halftone images using Feng et al.'s method [17] and others only for $P/8 \times Q/8$ watermark bits embedded. Table 5 shows the comparison results for the 512×512 halftone image shown in Figure 8(a). From this table, we can see that the proposed method provides better qualities than other methods.

To justify the selection of (u, v) pair, we use three different kinds of selection for (u, v) pairs. The first selection is used by Guo et al.'s method with $v - u = 1$; all (u, v) pairs are $(0, 1)$,

$(2, 3)$, $(4, 5)$, $(6, 7)$, $(8, 9)$, $(10, 11)$, $(12, 13)$, and $(14, 15)$. The second selection follows the rule $2 \leq v - u \leq 5$; all (u, v) pairs are $(0, 4)$, $(1, 5)$, $(2, 6)$, $(3, 7)$, $(8, 15)$, $(9, 14)$, $(10, 12)$, and $(11, 13)$. The third selection follows the rule $6 \leq v - u \leq 11$; all (u, v) pairs are $(0, 8)$, $(1, 9)$, $(2, 10)$, $(3, 11)$, $(4, 15)$, $(5, 14)$, $(6, 12)$, and $(7, 13)$. From the dispersed dithering screens shown in Figure 1, we can see that when $(v - u)$ is larger, $T_v - T_u$ is larger; this will make $|p_u - p_v|$ larger. When $|p_u - p_v|$ is larger, then it can provide a higher robustness for the print-and-scan process. But the quality will be degraded. Thus, the second selection will provide higher robustness and better quality. To prove this point, we have done some experiments based on these three kinds of selection by embedding 128 watermark bits into a 512×512 image.

Table 6 shows quality comparisons of three different kinds of pair selections using Pei-Guo-PSNR, scores S_3 and S_4. From this table, we can see that these pair selections provide similar qualities in Pei-Guo-PSNR. But, in S_3 and S_4, the second selection used in the proposed method has the best result, and the third selection has the worst result. Table 7 shows the black pixel numbers in eight pairs of the top-left subimage for various pair selections. The average difference on numbers of black pixels in the eight pairs for the second selection used in the proposed method is 223.5, the third selection is 238.5, and the first selection used in Guo et al.'s method is 62.75. This means that Guo et al.'s method provides less robustness than the other pair selections, and the third selection will provide similar robustness to the second pair selection for the print-and-scan process. However, the image quality using the third pair selection is worse than those of two pair selections. Therefore, under the consideration of image quality and robustness, the second selection used in the proposed method is better.

Furthermore, in the experiments of Guo et al. [12], based on a 4×4 dispersed dithering screen, the average percentages of NIPs with 8, 32, 128, and 512 bits embedded into each of

TABLE 6: Quality comparisons of three different kinds of pair selections using Pei-Guo-PSNR [12] and scores S_3 and S_4 [14].

Selection	The 1st selection used in Guo et al. [12] with $v - u = 1$			The 2nd selection used in the proposed method with $2 \le v - u \le 5$			The 3rd selection with $6 \le v - u \le 11$		
					Quality				
Images	Pei-Guo-PSNR	S_3	S_4	Pei-Guo-PSNR	S_3	S_4	Pei-Guo-PSNR	S_3	S_4
Lena	30.78	1.37	480	29.24	1.06	204	28.26	2.26	12967
Mandrill	27.30	2.24	3201	27.32	1.59	2758	26.54	2.36	16866
Earth	27.06	2.07	2772	28.17	1.28	1233	28.45	2.09	6841
Tiffany	31.06	1.12	189	29.06	1.03	159	28.82	1.70	1981
Shuttle	27.66	1.90	2134	28.08	1.20	871	28.12	2.18	10062
Peppers	30.34	1.46	755	29.00	1.08	381	28.25	2.18	10525
Milk	31.04	1.32	529	29.63	1.02	129	28.65	2.17	10080
Lake	28.15	1.88	1967	28.15	1.13	857	28.34	1.95	5753
Average	29.17	1.67	1503.4	28.58	1.17	824	28.18	2.11	9384.4

TABLE 7: The black pixel numbers of the eight pairs in the top-left subimage for different kinds of selections.

	Selection				
The 1st selection used in Guo et al. [12] with $v - u = 1$		The 2nd selection used in the proposed method with $2 \leq v - u \leq 5$		The 3rd selection with $6 \leq v - u \leq 11$	
Pairs (u, v)	The number of black pixels	Pairs (u, v)	The number of black pixels	Pairs (u, v)	The number of black pixels
	p_u $\quad$ p_v		p_u $\quad$ p_v		p_u $\quad$ p_v
$(0, 1)$	322 $\quad$ 352	$(0, 4)$	389 $\quad$ 641	$(0, 8)$	389 $\quad$ 734
$(2, 3)$	320 $\quad$ 354	$(1, 5)$	391 $\quad$ 725	$(1, 9)$	391 $\quad$ 826
$(4, 5)$	386 $\quad$ 540	$(2, 6)$	364 $\quad$ 757	$(2, 10)$	364 $\quad$ 884
$(6, 7)$	545 $\quad$ 547	$(3, 7)$	421 $\quad$ 712	$(3, 11)$	421 $\quad$ 873
$(8, 9)$	611 $\quad$ 758	$(8, 15)$	734 $\quad$ 672	$(4, 15)$	641 $\quad$ 672
$(10, 11)$	801 $\quad$ 668	$(9, 14)$	826 $\quad$ 675	$(5, 14)$	725 $\quad$ 675
$(12, 13)$	672 $\quad$ 674	$(10, 12)$	884 $\quad$ 711	$(6, 12)$	757 $\quad$ 711
$(14, 15)$	672 $\quad$ 672	$(11, 13)$	873 $\quad$ 741	$(7, 13)$	712 $\quad$ 741

TABLE 8: Numbers of equivalent black pixel pairs in eight test images using the proposed method.

Number of subimages		1	4	16	64	128	256
Total number of pairs		8	32	128	512	1024	2048
Number of EBPs	Lena	0	0	0	0	0	0
	Mandrill	0	0	0	0	0	0
	Earth	0	0	0	0	0	0
	Tiffany	0	2	22	146	373	830
	Shuttle	0	0	0	0	0	0
	Peppers	0	0	0	0	0	0
	Milk	0	0	0	0	0	0
	Lake	0	0	0	0	0	0

eight test images shown in Figure 6 are 12.5%, 15.62%, 27.32%, and 45%, respectively. Guo et al. modify the number of black pixels in these NIPs before embedding watermark. This may lower visual quality. On the contrary, in the proposed method, we do not modify any pair before data embedding.

As to the embedding capacity, since the data embedding depends on the difference of black pixel numbers of each pair, if the difference is zero, the pair cannot be used for data embedding in the proposed method. This will reduce the embedding capacity. Fortunately, from our experimental results, we found that the situation rarely appears in most images. Table 8 shows the numbers of equivalent black pixel pairs (EBP) in eight dithered test images. From this table, we can see that most images have zero EBP, except "Tiffany" image. The reason is that most pixels in "Tiffany" image have gray values >90, and the gray values of pixels in a local area are nearly constant. For example, for pair (p_1, p_5), the corresponding values in DS are $(24, 88)$ (see Figure 1); thus, each pixel in $SH_{i,1}$ and $SH_{i,5}$ for each i will be a white point. This will make $(p_1, p_5) = (0, 0)$ and make it an EBP.

In the next experiment, we demonstrate the robustness of the proposed method and Guo et al.'s method by cropping and tampering attacks. To measure the integrity of the extracted watermark, the correct decoding rate (CDR) is defined as follows:

$$CDR = \frac{\text{Lev\_Dist}\left(w, w'\right)}{T} \times 100\%, \quad (4)$$

where Lev_Dist(), w, and w' denote the Levenshtein distance [22], original watermark, and extracted watermark, respectively. The Levenshtein distance is a string metric for estimating the least number of edit operations that is necessary to modify one string to obtain another string. In Figures 10 and 11, a 32×32 watermark shown in Figure 10(a) is embedded into the halftone image in Figure 11(b) using the proposed method and Guo et al.'s method, respectively, and the results are shown in Figures 10(b) and 11(a), respectively. Figures 10(c) and 11(b) show the embedded dithered images cropped by 1/4 portion. Figures 10(d) and 11(c) show the embedded dithered images tampered with several words. Note that when the number of embedding bits >8, the dithered image is first divided into t subimages, and the watermark bits are also divided into t parts. Each part is embedded into one subimage. The resulting subimages using the proposed method and Guo et al.'s method are shown in Figures 10(e), 10(f), 11(d), and 11(e). From Figure 10(e), we can see that each subimage using the proposed method is also cropped by 1/4 portion; the reason is that each subimage is obtained by block downsampling (see Figure 4). The cropping will make 1/4 portion of all pixel pairs (u, v) lost. Since a watermark bit is embedded through the sign of $(p_u - p_v)$, 1/4 portion of pairs (u, v) lost will not affect the sign of $(p_u - p_v)$. Thus, the watermark can be extracted correctly (see Figure 10(g)). Figure 10(h) shows the watermark extracted from Figure 10(d) and it can also be extracted correctly. On the contrary, in Figure 11(d), we can see that some subimages using Guo et al.'s method are totally removed; this will make the watermark parts embedded in these subimages lost (see Figure 11(f)). Figures 11(f) and 11(g) show the watermarks extracted from Figures 11(b) and 11(c), respectively. Table 9 shows the average correct decoding rates of cropping 1/3, 1/4, and 1/2 portions, respectively. Note that in this experiment, each of the eight images is cropped at three different locations for

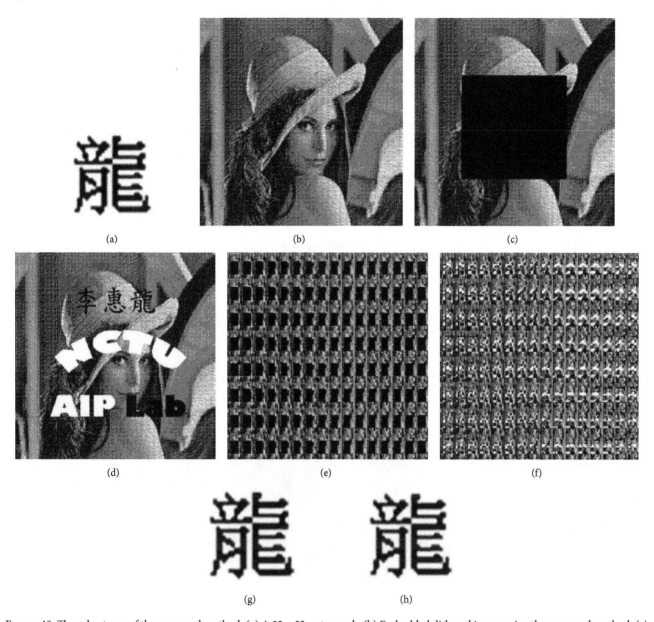

FIGURE 10: The robustness of the proposed method. (a) A 32×32 watermark. (b) Embedded dithered image using the proposed method. (c) Embedded dithered image cropped by 1/4 portion. (d) Embedded dithered image with tampering. (e) Downsampled subimages of (c). (f) Downsampled subimages of (d). (g) The watermark extracted from (c). (h) The watermark extracted from (d).

each cropping portion; thus there are 72 ($3 \times 3 \times 8$) cropped images. From this table, we can see that the proposed method is more robust than Guo et al.'s method and Feng et al.'s method [17].

To measure the robustness of the proposed method and Guo et al.'s method [12] under print-and-scan attack, for each of eight test images, we first embed 8, 32, 128, and 512 bits into its corresponding halftone image; then each embedded halftone image is printed at 150 dpi. After printing, each printed image is scanned at 150, 450, and 750 dpi, respectively, and then the embedded watermark from each scanned image is extracted. Table 10 shows the average correct decoding rate with eight test images as shown in Figure 6. From this table, we can see that the average correct decoding rates of

the proposed method are higher than those of Guo et al.'s method. This means that the proposed method provides more robustness than Guo et al.'s method under print-and-scan attack.

5. Conclusions

In this paper, a robust watermarking method has been proposed for dithered halftone images. Before embedding, a dithered halftone image is divided into subimages through downsampling; this step provides robustness to cropping and tampering. In the embedding step, each pair (p_u, p_v) is taken to embed a watermark bit with $(u, v) = (0, 4), (1, 5), (2, 6), (3, 7), (8, 15), (9, 14), (10, 12),$ or $(11, 13)$; however, in

TABLE 9: Average correct decoding rates of different cropping size.

Cropping size	Guo et al.'s method [12] Watermark size 32 × 32	64 × 64	Proposed method Watermark size 32 × 32	64 × 64	Feng et al.'s method [17] 64 × 64
1/2	50.00%	50.00%	93.98%	91.87%	67.20%
1/3	66.50%	66.55%	94.20%	94.77%	78.25%
1/4	75.00%	75.00%	95.24%	96.05%	83.64%

TABLE 10: Average correct decoding rates of all scanned embedded images with different scanning resolutions.

Algorithm Scanning resolution		Guo et al.'s method [12] Average correct decoding rate 150	450	750	Proposed method 150	450	750
Embedded bits	32	65%	72%	70%	77%	85%	84%
	128	60%	70%	75%	78%	82%	86%
	512	57%	65%	72%	78%	83%	86%

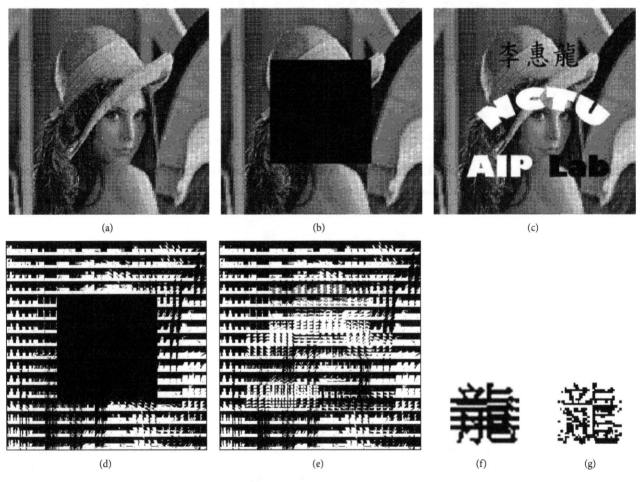

FIGURE 11: The robustness of Guo et al.'s method [12]. (a) Embedded dithered image using Guo et al.'s method. (b) Embedded dithered image cropped by 1/4 portion. (c) Embedded dithered image with tampering. (d) The result of applying bit-interleaving to each subimage of (b). (e) The result of applying bit-interleaving to each subimage of (c). (f) The watermark extracted from (b). (g) The watermark extracted from (c).

Guo et al.'s method, the pair (p_i, p_{i+1}) is taken to embed a watermark bit. Since the average of $|p_u - p_v|$ is larger than the average of $|p_i - p_{i+1}|$, this makes the proposed method provide higher correct decoding rate than Guo et al.'s method after print-and-scan process. Experimental results show that the proposed method actually provides higher robustness than Guo et al.'s method in cropping, tampering, and print-and-scan process. In addition, experimental results also show that the proposed method provides higher visual quality in the high-frequency areas than Guo et al.'s method.

Competing Interests

The authors declare that there are no competing interests regarding the publication of this paper.

Acknowledgments

This work was supported in part by the Ministry of Science and Technology of Taiwan under Contract MOST 103-2221-E-009-121-MY2.

References

[1] R. W. Floyd and L. Steinberg, "An adaptive algorithm for spatial grey scale," in *Proceedings of the SID International Symposium, Digest of Technical Papers*, pp. 36–37, 1975.

[2] B. E. Bayers, "An optimum method for two level renditions of continuous tone pictures," in *Proceedings of the IEEE International Conference Communication*, pp. 2611–2615, June 1973.

[3] J. P. Allebach, R. Eschbach, and G. G. Marcu, "DBS: retrospective and future directions," in *Color Imaging: Device-Independent Color, Color Hardcopy, and Graphic Arts VI*, Proceedings of SPIE, pp. 358–376, San Jose, Calif, USA, January 2001.

[4] M. S. Fu and O. C. Au, "Data hiding watermarking for halftone images," *IEEE Transactions on Image Processing*, vol. 11, no. 4, pp. 477–484, 2002.

[5] M. S. Fu and O. C. Au, "A robust public watermark for halftone images," in *Proceedings of the IEEE International Symposium on Circuits and Systems*, pp. III/639–III/642, May 2002.

[6] M. S. Fu and O. C. Au, "Correlation-based watermarking for halftone images," in *Proceedings of the International Symposium on Circuits and Systems (ISCAS '04)*, vol. 2, pp. II-21–II-24, Vancouver, Canada, May 2004.

[7] S.-C. Pei and J.-M. Guo, "High-capacity data hiding in halftone images using minimal-error bit searching and least-mean square filter," *IEEE Transactions on Image Processing*, vol. 15, no. 6, pp. 1665–1679, 2006.

[8] R. Y. M. Li, O. C. Au, C. K. M. Yuk, S.-K. Yip, and S.-Y. Lam, "Halftone image data hiding with block-overlapping parity check," in *Proceedings of the IEEE International Conference on Acoustics, Speech and Signal Processing (ICASSP '07)*, vol. 2, pp. II-193–II-196, Honolulu, Hawaii, USA, April 2007.

[9] J.-M. Guo and Y.-F. Liu, "Halftone-image security improving using overall minimal-error searching," *IEEE Transactions on Image Processing*, vol. 20, no. 10, pp. 2800–2812, 2011.

[10] Y. F. Guo, O. C. Au, and K. Tang, "Watermark embedding for multiscale error diffused halftone images by adopting visual cryptography," *International Journal of Digital Crime and Forensics*, vol. 7, no. 1, pp. 51–68, 2015.

[11] Y. F. Guo, O. C. Au, J. T. Zhou, K. Tang, and X. P. Fan, "Halftone image watermarking via optimization," *Signal Processing: Image Communication*, vol. 41, pp. 85–100, 2016.

[12] J.-M. Guo, S.-C. Pei, and H. Lee, "Paired subimage matching watermarking method on ordered dither images and its high-quality progressive coding," *IEEE Transactions on Multimedia*, vol. 10, no. 1, pp. 16–30, 2008.

[13] H. Z. Hel-Or, "Watermarking and copyright labelling of printed images," *Journal of Electronic Imaging*, vol. 10, no. 3, pp. 794–803, 2001.

[14] M. S. Fu and O. C. Au, "Data hiding in ordered dithered halftone images," *Circuits, Systems, and Signal Processing*, vol. 20, no. 2, pp. 209–232, 2001.

[15] S.-C. Pei, J.-M. Guo, and H. Lee, "Novel robust watermarking technique in dithering halftone images," *IEEE Signal Processing Letters*, vol. 12, no. 4, pp. 333–336, 2005.

[16] O. Bulan, G. Sharma, and V. Monga, "Orientation modulation for data Hiding in clustered-dot halftone prints," *IEEE Transactions on Image Processing*, vol. 19, no. 8, pp. 2070–2084, 2010.

[17] L. Feng, D. Cong, H. Shu, and B. Liu, "Adaptive halftone watermarking algorithm based on particle swarm optimization," *Journal of Multimedia*, vol. 8, no. 3, pp. 183–190, 2013.

[18] C.-H. Son and H. S. Choo, "Watermark detection from clustered halftone dots via learned dictionary," *Signal Processing*, vol. 102, pp. 77–84, 2014.

[19] I. G. Chun and S. Ha, "A watermarking method for halftone images based on iterative halftoning method," in *E-Commerce and Web Technologies*, vol. 2738 of *Lecture Notes in Computer Science*, pp. 165–175, Springer, Berlin, Germany, 2003.

[20] J.-M. Guo, C.-C. Su, Y.-F. Liu, H. Lee, and J.-D. Lee, "Oriented modulation for watermarking in direct binary search halftone images," *IEEE Transactions on Image Processing*, vol. 21, no. 9, pp. 4117–4127, 2012.

[21] J.-M. Guo, G.-H. Lai, K. Wong, and L.-C. Chang, "Progressive halftone watermarking using multilayer table lookup strategy," *IEEE Transactions on Image Processing*, vol. 24, no. 7, pp. 2009–2024, 2015.

[22] V. I. Levenshtein, "Binary codes capable of correcting deletions, insertions, and reversals," *Soviet Physics—Doklady*, vol. 10, no. 8, pp. 707–710, 1966.

9

Classification of Error-Diffused Halftone Images Based on Spectral Regression Kernel Discriminant Analysis

Zhigao Zeng,[1,2] **Zhiqiang Wen,**[1] **Shengqiu Yi,**[1] **Sanyou Zeng,**[3] **Yanhui Zhu,**[1] **Qiang Liu,**[1] **and Qi Tong**[1]

[1]*College of Computer and Communication, Hunan University of Technology, Hunan 412007, China*
[2]*Intelligent Information Perception and Processing Technology, Hunan Province Key Laboratory, Hunan 412007, China*
[3]*Department of Computer Science, China University of Geosciences, Wuhan, Hubei 430074, China*

Correspondence should be addressed to Zhigao Zeng; zzgzzg99@163.com

Academic Editor: Stefanos Kollias

This paper proposes a novel algorithm to solve the challenging problem of classifying error-diffused halftone images. We firstly design the class feature matrices, after extracting the image patches according to their statistics characteristics, to classify the error-diffused halftone images. Then, the spectral regression kernel discriminant analysis is used for feature dimension reduction. The error-diffused halftone images are finally classified using an idea similar to the nearest centroids classifier. As demonstrated by the experimental results, our method is fast and can achieve a high classification accuracy rate with an added benefit of robustness in tackling noise.

1. Introduction

As a popular image processing technology, digital halftoning [1] has found wide applications in converting a continuous tone image into a binary halftone image for a better display on binary devices, such as printers and computer screens. Usually, binary halftone images can only be obtained in the process of printing, image scanning, and fax, from which the original continuous tone images need to be reconstructed [2, 3], using an inverse halftoning algorithm [4], for image processing, for example, image classification, image compression, image enhancement, and image zooming. However, it is difficult for inverse halftoning algorithms to obtain the optimal reconstruction quality due to unknown halftoning patterns in practical applications. Furthermore, a basic drawback of the existing inverse halftone algorithms is that they do not distinguish the types of halftone images or can only coarsely divide halftone images into two major categories of error-diffused halftone images and orderly dithered halftone images. This inability of exploiting a prior knowledge on the halftone images largely weakens the flexibility, adaptability, and effectiveness of the inverse halftoning techniques,

making the study on the classification of halftone images imperative for not only optimizing the existing inverse halftoning schemes, but also guiding the establishment of adaptive schemes on halftone image compression, halftone image watermarking, and so forth.

Motivated by observing the significance of classifying halftone images, several halftone image classification methods have been proposed. In 1998, Chang and Yu [5] classified halftone images into four types using an enhanced one-dimensional correlation function and a backpropagation (BP) neural network, for which the data sets in the experiments are limited to the halftone images produced by clustered-dot ordered dithering, dispersed-dot ordered dithering, constrained average, and error diffusion. Kong et al. [6, 7] used an enhanced one-dimensional correlation function and a gray level cooccurrence matrix to extract features from halftone images, based on which the halftone images are divided into nine categories using a decision tree algorithm. Liu et al. [8] combined support region and least mean square (LMS) algorithm to divide halftone images into four categories. Subsequently, they [9] used LMS to extract features from Fourier spectrum in nine categories of halftone images and classify these halftone images using naive Bayes. Although these methods work well in classifying some specific halftone images, their performance largely decreases when classifying error-diffused halftone images produced by Floyd-Steinberg filter, Stucki filter, Sierra filter, Burkers filter, Jarvis filter, and Stevenson filter, respectively. They are described as follows.

Different Error Diffusion Filters. Consider the following:

(a) Floyd-Steinberg filter:

$$\left(\frac{1}{16}\right) \begin{array}{ccc} & \bullet & 7 \\ 3 & 5 & 1 \end{array} \tag{1}$$

(b) Sierra filter:

$$\left(\frac{1}{32}\right) \begin{array}{ccccc} & & \bullet & 5 & 3 \\ 2 & 4 & 5 & 4 & 2 \\ 0 & 2 & 3 & 2 & 0 \end{array} \tag{2}$$

(c) Burkers filter:

$$\left(\frac{1}{32}\right) \begin{array}{ccccc} & & \bullet & 8 & 4 \\ 2 & 4 & 8 & 4 & 2 \end{array} \tag{3}$$

(d) Jarvis filter:

$$\left(\frac{1}{48}\right) \begin{array}{ccccc} & & \bullet & 7 & 5 \\ 3 & 5 & 7 & 5 & 3 \\ 1 & 3 & 5 & 3 & 1 \end{array} \tag{4}$$

(e) Stevenson filter:

$$\left(\frac{1}{200}\right) \begin{array}{ccccc} & & \bullet & & 32 \\ 12 & & 26 & & 30 & & 16 \\ & 12 & & 26 & & 12 \\ 5 & & 12 & & 12 & & 5 \end{array} \tag{5}$$

The Error Diffusion of Stucki

(a) Error kernel of Stucki filter is

$$\left(\frac{1}{42}\right) \begin{array}{ccccc} & & \bullet & 8 & 4 \\ 2 & 4 & 8 & 4 & 2 \\ 1 & 2 & 4 & 2 & 1 \end{array} \tag{6}$$

(b) Matrix of coefficients template is

$$\begin{array}{|c|c|c|c|c|} \hline 0 & 0 & \underline{0} & 8 & 4 \\ \hline 2 & 4 & 8 & 4 & 2 \\ \hline 1 & 2 & 4 & 2 & 1 \\ \hline \end{array} \tag{7}$$

(c) O denotes the pixel being processed; A, B, C, and D indicate the four neighborhood pixels:

$$\left(\frac{1}{42}\right) \begin{array}{|c|c|c|c|c|} \hline 0 & 0 & \underline{0} & 8 & 4 \\ \hline 2 & 4 & 8 & 4 & 2 \\ \hline 1 & 2 & 4 & 2 & 1 \\ \hline \end{array} \tag{8}$$

based on different error diffusion kernels, as summarized in [10–12]. Moreover, these literatures did not consider all types of error diffusion halftone images. For example, only three error diffusion filters are included in [6, 7, 9] and only one is involved in [5, 8]. The idea of halftoning for the six error diffusion filters is quite similar, with the only difference lying in the templates used (shown in different error diffusion filters and the error diffusion of Stucki described above; the templates are shown at the right-hand side in each equation). It is difficult to classify the error-diffused halftone images because of the almost inconspicuous differences among various halftone features extracted from, using these six error diffusion filters, the error-diffused halftone images. However, as a scalable algorithm, the error diffusion has gradually become one of the most popular techniques, due to its ability to provide a solution of good quality at a reasonable cost [13]. This asks for an urgent requirement to study the classification mechanism for various error diffusion algorithms, with the hope to promote the existing inverse halftone techniques widely used in different application fields of graphics processing.

This paper proposes a new algorithm to classify error-diffused halftone images. We first extract the feature matrices of pixel pairs from the error-diffused halftone image patches, according to statistical characteristics of these patches. The class feature matrices are then subsequently obtained, using a gradient descent method, based on the feature matrices of pixel pairs [14]. After applying the spectral regression kernel discriminant analysis to realize the dimension reduction in the class feature matrices, we finally classify the error-diffused halftone images using the idea similar to the nearest centroids classifier [15, 16].

The structure of this paper is as follows. Section 2 presents the method of kernel discriminant analysis. Section 3 describes how to extract the feature extraction of pixel pairs from the error-diffused halftone images. Section 4 describes the proposed classification method for the error-diffused halftone image based on the spectral regression kernel discriminant analysis. Section 5 shows the experimental results. Some concluding remarks and possible future research directions are given in Section 6.

2. An Efficient Kernel Discriminant Analysis Method

It is well known that linear discriminant analysis (LDA) [17, 18] is effective in solving classification problems, but it fails for nonlinear problems. To deal with this limitation, the approach called kernel discriminant analysis (KDA) [19] has been proposed.

2.1. Overview of Kernel Discriminant Analysis. Suppose that we are given a sample set $\{x_1, x_2, \ldots, x_m\}$ of the error-diffused halftone images with $x_1, x_2, \ldots, x_m$ belonging to different class C_i ($i = 1, 2, \ldots, K$), respectively. Using a nonlinear mapping function ϕ, the samples of the halftone images in the input space R^n can be projected to a high-dimensional separable feature space f; namely, $R^n \rightarrow f$, $x \rightarrow \phi(x)$. After extracting features, the error-diffused halftone images will be classified along the projection direction along which the within-class scatter is minimal and the between-class scatter is maximal. For a proper ϕ, an inner product described as $\langle \cdot, \cdot \rangle$ can be defined on f to form a reproducing kernel Hilbert space. That is to say, $\langle \phi(x_i), \phi(x_j) \rangle = \kappa(x_i, x_j)$, where $\kappa(\cdot, \cdot)$ is a positive semidefinite kernel function. In the feature space f, let S_b^ϕ be the between-class scatter matrix, let S_w^ϕ be the within-class scatter matrix, and let S_t^ϕ be the total scatter matrix:

$$S_b^\phi = \sum_{k=1}^{c} m_k \left(\mu_\phi^k - \mu_\phi \right) \left(\mu_\phi^k - \mu_\phi \right)^T,$$

$$S_w^\phi = \sum_{k=1}^{c} \left(\sum_{i=1}^{m_k} \left(\phi\left(x_i^k\right) - \mu_\phi^k \right) \left(\phi\left(x_i^k\right) - \mu_\phi^k \right)^T \right), \quad (9)$$

$$S_t^\phi = S_b^\phi + S_w^\phi = \sum_{i=1}^{m} \left(\phi\left(x_i\right) - \mu_\phi \right) \left(\phi\left(x_i\right) - \mu_\phi \right)^T,$$

where m_k is the number of the samples in the kth class, $\phi(x_i^k)$ is the ith sample of the kth class in the feature space f, $\mu_\phi^k = (1/m_k) \sum_{i=1}^{N_i} \phi(x_i^k)$ is the centroid of the kth class, and $\mu_\phi = (1/N) \sum_{k=1}^{c} \sum_{i=1}^{m_k} \phi(x_i^k)$ is the global centroid. In the feature space, the aim of the discriminant analysis is to seek the best projection direction, namely, the projective function v to maximize the following objective function:

$$v_{\text{opt}} = \arg \max \frac{v^T S_b^\phi v}{v^T S_w^\phi v}. \quad (10)$$

Equation (10) can be solved by the eigenproblem $S_b^\phi v = \lambda S_t^\phi v$. According to the theory of reproducing kernel Hilbert space, we know that the eigenvectors are linear combinations of $\phi(x_i)$ in the feature space f: there exist weight coefficients a_i ($i = 1, 2, \ldots, m$) such that $v^\phi = \sum_{i=1}^{m} a_i \phi(x_i)$. Let $a = [a_1, a_2, \ldots, a_m]^T$; then it can be proved that (10) can be rewritten as follows:

$$a_{\text{opt}} = \arg \max \frac{a^T KWKa}{a^T KKa}. \quad (11)$$

The optimization problem of (11) is equal to the eigenproblem

$$KWKa = \lambda KKa, \quad (12)$$

where K is the kernel matrix and $K_{ij} = \kappa(x_i, x_j)$; W is the weight matrix defined as follows:

$$w_{ij} = \begin{cases} \dfrac{1}{m_k}, & \text{if } x_i, x_j \text{ belong to the } k\text{th class,} \\ 0, & \text{others.} \end{cases} \quad (13)$$

For sample x, the projective function in the feature space f can be described as

$$f^*(x) = \langle v, \phi(x) \rangle = \sum_{i=1}^{m} a_i \langle \phi(x_i), \phi(x) \rangle$$

$$= \sum_{i=1}^{m} a_i \kappa(x_i, x) = a^T \kappa(\cdot, x). \quad (14)$$

2.2. Kernel Discriminant Analysis via Spectral Regression. To efficiently solve the eigenproblem of the kernel discriminant analysis in (12), the following theorem will be used.

Theorem 1. *Let y be the eigenvector of the eigenproblem $Wy = \lambda y$ with eigenvalue λ. If $K\alpha = y$, then α is the eigenvector of eigenproblem (12) with the same eigenvalue λ.*

According to Theorem 1, the projective function of the kernel discriminant analysis can be obtained according to the following two steps.

Step 1. Obtain y by solving the eigenproblem in (12).

Step 2. Search eigenvector α which satisfies $K\alpha = y$, where K is the positive semidefinite kernel matrix.

As we know, if K is nonsingular, then, for any given y, there exists a unique $\alpha = K^{-1} y$ satisfying the linear equation described in Step 2. If K is singular, then, the linear equation may have infinite solutions or have no solution. In this case, we can approximate α by solving the following equation:

$$(K + \delta I) \alpha = y, \quad (15)$$

where $\delta \geq 0$ is a regularization parameter and I is the identity matrix. Combined with the projective function described in (14), we can easily verify that the solution $\alpha^* = (K + \delta I)^{-1} y$ given by (15) is the optimal solution of the following regularized regression problem:

$$\alpha^* = \min_{f \in F} \sum_{i=1}^{m} \left(f(x_i) - y_i \right)^2 + \delta \| f \|_K^2, \quad (16)$$

where y_i is the ith element of y and F is the reproducing kernel Hilbert space induced from the Mercer kernel K with $\| \cdot \|_K$ being the corresponding norm. Due to the essential combination of the spectral analysis and regression techniques in the above two-step approach, the method is named as spectral regression (SR) kernel discriminant analysis.

3. Feature Extraction of the Error-Diffused Halftone Images

Since its introduction in 1976, the error diffusion algorithm has attracted widespread attention in the field of printing applications. It deals with pixels of halftone images using, instead of point processing algorithms, the neighborhood processing algorithms. Now we will extract the features of the error-diffused halftone images which are produced using the six popular error diffusion filters mentioned in Section 1.

3.1. Statistic Characteristics of the Error-Diffused Halftone Images. Assume that $f_g(x, y)$ is the gray value of the pixel located at position (x, y) in the original image and $F(x, y)$ is the value of the pixel located at position (x, y) in the error-diffused halftone image. For the original image, all the pixels are firstly normalized to the range $[0, 1]$. Then, the pixels of the normalized image are converted to the error-diffused image F line by line; that is to say, if $f_g(x, y) \geq T_0$, $F(x, y)$, which is the value of the pixel located at position (x, y) in error-diffused image F, is 1; otherwise, $F(x, y)$ is 0, where T_0 is the threshold value. The error between $F(x, y)$ and T_0 is diffused ahead to some subsequent pixels not necessary to deal with. Therefore, for some subsequent pixels, the comparison will be implemented between T_0 and the value which is the sum of $f_g(x, y)$ and the diffusion error e. A template matrix can be built using the error diffusion modes and the error diffusion coefficients, as shown in the error diffusion of Stucki described above, for example, (a) the error diffusion filter and (b) the error diffusion coefficients which represent the proportion of the diffusion errors. If the coefficient is zero, then the corresponding pixel does not receive any diffusion errors. According to the error diffusion of Stucki described above, pixel A suffers from more diffusion errors than pixel B; that is to say, O-A has a larger probability to become 1-0 pixel pair than O-B. The reasons are as follows. Suppose that the pixel value of O is $0 \leq p_O \leq 1$, and pixel O has been processed by the thresholding method according to the following equation:

$$q_O = \begin{cases} 1, & p_O \geq T_0, \\ 0, & \text{else.} \end{cases} \tag{17}$$

In general, threshold T_0 is set as 0.5. According to the template shown in the error diffusion of Stucki described above, we can know that the diffusion error is $e = q_O - p_O$, the new value of pixel A is $p_A = f(x_A + y_A) + 8e/42$, and the new value of pixel B is $p_B = f(x_B + y_B) + e/42$, where $f_g(x_A + y_A)$ and $f_g(x_B + y_B)$ are the original values of pixels A and B, respectively.

Since the value of each pixel in the error-diffused halftone image can only be 0 or 1, there are 4 kinds of pixel pairs in the halftone image: 0-1, 0-0, 1-0, and 1-1. Pixel pairs 0-1 and 1-0 are collectively known as 1-0 pixel pairs because of their exchange ability. Therefore, there are only three kinds of pixel pairs essentially: 0-0, 1-0, and 1-1. In this paper, three statistical matrices are used to store the number of different pixel pairs with different neighboring distances and different directions, which are of size $L \times L$ and are referred to as M_{00}, M_{10}, and

M_{11}, respectively (L is an odd number satisfying $L = 2R + 1$ and R is the maximum neighboring distance). Suppose that the center entry of the statistical matrix template covers pixel O of the error-diffused halftone image with the size $W * H$, and other entries overlap other neighborhood pixels $F(u, v)$. Then, we can compute three statistics on 1-0, 1-1, and 0-0 pixel pairs within the scope of this statistics matrix template. If the position (i, j) of pixel O changes continually, the matrices M_{00}, M_{10}, and M_{11} with zero being the initial values can be updated according to

$$M_{11}(x, y) = M_{11}(x, y) + 1$$

$$\text{if } F(i, j) = 1, \ F(u, v) = 1,$$

$$M_{00}(x, y) = M_{00}(x, y) + 1$$

$$\text{if } F(i, j) = 0, \ F(u, v) = 0, \tag{18}$$

$$M_{10}(x, y) = M_{00}(x, y) + 1$$

$$\text{if } F(i, j) = 1, \ F(u, v) = 0 \text{ or } F(i, j) = 0, \ F(u, v) = 1,$$

where $u = i - R + x - 1, v = j - R + y - 1, 1 \leq i, u \leq W, 1 \leq j, v \leq H, 1 \leq x \leq L$, and $1 \leq y \leq L$. After normalization, the three statistic matrices can be ultimately obtained as the statistical feature descriptor of the error-diffused halftone images.

3.2. Process of Statistical Feature Extraction of Halftone Images. According to the analysis described above, the process of statistical feature extraction of the error-diffused halftone images can be represented as follows.

Step 1. Input the error-diffused halftone image F, and divide F into several blocks B_i ($i = 1, 2, \ldots, H$) with the same size $K \times K$.

Step 2. Initialize the statistical feature matrix M (including M_{00}, M_{10}, M_{11}) as the zero matrix, and let $i = 1$.

Step 3. Obtain the statistical matrix M_i of block B_i according to (18), and update M using the equation $M = M + M_i$.

Step 4. Set $i = i + 1$. If $i \leq H$, then return to Step 3. Otherwise, go to Step 5.

Step 5. Normalize M such that it satisfies $\sum_{x=1}^{L} \sum_{x=1}^{L} M(x, y) = 1$ and $M(x, y) \geq 0$, where K satisfies $K \geq \min(T_i)$ and T_i ($1 \leq i \leq 6$) represents the size of the template matrix of the ith error diffusion filter.

According to the process described above, we know that the statistical features of the error-diffused halftone image F are extracted based on the method that divides F into image patches, which is significantly different with other feature extraction methods based on image patches. For example, in [20], the brightness and contrast of the image patches are normalized by Z-score transformation, and whitening (also called "sphering") is used to rescale the normalized data to remove the correlations between nearby pixels (i.e., low-frequency variations in the images) because these correlations tend to be very strong even after brightness and contrast normalization. However, in this paper, features of the patches are extracted based on counting statistical measures of different pixel pairs (0/0, 1/0, and 1/1) within a moving statistical matrix template and are optimized using the method described in Section 3.3.

3.3. Extraction of the Class Feature Matrix. The statistics matrices $M_{00}^i, M_{10}^i, M_{11}^i$ $(i = 1, 2, \ldots, N)$, after being extracted, can be used as the input of other algorithms, such as support vector machines and neural networks. However, the curse of dimensionality could occur, due to the high dimension of M_{00}, M_{10}, M_{11}, making the classification effect possibly not significant. Thereby, six class feature matrices $G_1, G_2, \ldots, G_6$ are designed in this paper for the error-diffused halftone images produced by the six error diffusion filters mentioned above. Then, a gradient descent method can be used to optimize these class feature matrices.

$N = 6 \times n$ error-diffused halftone images can be derived from n original images using the six error diffusion filters, respectively. Then, N statistics matrices M_i $(M_{00}^i, M_{10}^i, M_{11}^i)$ $(i = 1, 2, \ldots, N)$ can be extracted as the samples from N error-diffused halftone images using the algorithm mentioned in Section 3.2. Subsequently, we label these matrices as $\text{label}(M_1), \text{label}(M_2), \ldots, \text{label}(M_N)$ to denote the types of the error diffusion filters used to produce the error-diffused halftone image. Given the ith sample M_i as the input, the target out vector $t_i = [t_{i1}, \ldots, t_{i6}]$ $(i = 1, \ldots, N)$, and the class feature matrices $G_1, G_2, \ldots, G_6$, the square error e_i between the actual output and the target output can be derived according to

$$e_i = \sum_{j=1}^{6} \left(t_{ij} - M_i \bullet G_j \right)^2, \tag{19}$$

where

$$t_{ij} = \begin{cases} 1 & \text{if } j = \text{label}(M_i), \ j = 1, 2, \ldots, 6 \\ 0 & \text{else}. \end{cases} \tag{20}$$

The derivatives of $G_j(x, y)$ in (19) can be explicitly calculated as

$$\frac{\partial e_i}{\partial G_j(x, y)} = -2 \left(v_{ij} - M_i \bullet G_j \right) M_i(x, y), \tag{21}$$

where $1 \leq x \leq L, 1 \leq y \leq L$, and $\bullet$ is the dot product of matrices defined, for any matrices A and B with the same size $C \times D$, as

$$A \bullet B = \sum_{u=1}^{C} \sum_{v=1}^{D} A(u, v) \times B(u, v). \tag{22}$$

The dot product of matrices satisfies the commutative law and associative law; that is to say, $A \bullet B = B \bullet A$ and $(A \bullet B) \bullet C =$

$A \bullet (B \bullet C)$. Then, the iteration equation (23) can be obtained using the gradient descent method:

$$\begin{aligned} G_j^{k+1}(x, y) &= G_j^k(x, y) - \eta \frac{\partial e_i}{\partial G_j^k(x, y)} \\ &= G_j^k(x, y) \\ &\quad + 2\eta \left(v_{ij} - M_i \bullet G_j \right) M_i(x, y), \end{aligned} \tag{23}$$

where η is the learning factor and k means the kth iteration. The purpose of learning is to seek the optimal matrices G_j $(j = 1, 2, \ldots, 6)$ by minimizing the total square error $e = \sum_{i=1}^{N} e_i$, and the process of seeking the optimal matrices G_j can be described as follows.

Step 1. Initialize parameters: initialize the numbers of iterations *inner* and *outer*, the iteration variables $t = 0$ and $i = 1$, the nonnegative thresholds ε_1 and ε_2 used to indicate the end of iterations, the learning factor η, the total number of samples N, and the class feature matrices G_j $(j = 1, 2, \ldots, 6)$.

Step 2. Input the statistics matrices M_i $(i = 1, 2, \ldots, N)$, and let $G_j^0 = G_j$ $(j = 1, \ldots, 6)$ and $k = 0$. The following three substeps are executed.

(1) According to (23), G_j^{k+1} $(j = 1, \ldots, 6)$ can be computed.

(2) Compute e_i^{k+1} and $\Delta e_i^{k+1} = |e_i^{k+1} - e_i^k|$.

(3) If $k >$ inner or $\Delta e_i^{k+1} < \varepsilon_1$, then set $e_i = e_i^{k+1}$ and go to Step 3; otherwise, set $k = k + 1$ and return to (10).

Step 3. Set $G_j = G_j^{k+1}$ $(j = 1, \ldots, 6)$. If $i = N$, then go to Step 4. Otherwise, set $i = i + 1$, and go to Step 2.

Step 4. Compute the total error $e^t = \sum_{i=1}^{N} e_i$. If $|e^t - e^{t-1}| < \varepsilon_2$ or $t = $ *outer*, then end the algorithm. Otherwise, set $t = t + 1$ and go to Step 2.

4. Classification of Error-Diffused Halftone Images Using Nearest Centroids Classifier

This section describes the details on classifying error-diffused halftone images using the spectral regression kernel discriminant analysis as follows.

Step 1. Input N error-diffused halftone images produced by six error-diffused filters, and extract the statistical feature matrices M_i, including $M_{00}^i, M_{10}^i, M_{11}^i, i = 1, 2, \ldots, N$, using the method presented in Section 3.2.

Step 2. According to the steps described in Section 3.3, all the statistical feature matrices M_i $(M_{00}^i, M_{10}^i, M_{11}^i$ and $i = 1, 2, \ldots, N)$ are converted to the class feature matrices G_i, including $G_{00}^i, G_{10}^i, G_{11}^i$ and $i = 1, 2, \ldots, N$, correspondingly. Then, convert $G_{00}^i, G_{10}^i, G_{11}^i$ $(i = 1, 2, \ldots, N)$ into one-dimensional matrices by columns, respectively.

Step 3. All the one-dimensional class feature matrices $G_{00}^i, G_{10}^i, G_{11}^i$ ($i = 1, 2, \ldots, N$) are used to construct the samples feature matrices F_{00}, F_{10}, F_{11} of size $N \times M$ ($M = L \times L$), respectively.

Step 4. A label matrix *information* of the size $1 \times N$ is built to record the type to which the error-diffused halftone images belong.

Step 5. The first m features $G_{00}^1, G_{00}^2, \ldots, G_{00}^m$ of the samples feature matrices F_{00} are taken as the training samples (the first m features of F_{10}, F_{11}, or F_{all} which is the composition of F_{00}, F_{10}, and F_{11} also can be used as the training samples). Reduce the dimension of these training samples using the spectral regression discriminant analysis. The process of dimension reducing can be described by three substeps as follows.

(1) Produce orthogonal vectors. Let

$$y_k = \left[\underbrace{0, 0, \ldots, 0}_{\sum_{i=1}^{k-1} m_i}, \underbrace{1, 1, \ldots, 1}_{m_k}, \underbrace{0, 0, \ldots, 0}_{\sum_{i=k+1}^{c} m_i} \right]^T \tag{24}$$

$$k = 1, 2, \ldots, c$$

and $y_0 = [1, 1, \ldots, 1]^T$ be the matrix with all elements being 1. Let y_0 be the first vector of the weight matrix W, and use Gram-Schmidt process to orthogonalize the other eigenvectors. Remove the vector y_0, leaving $c - 1$ eigenvectors of W denoted as follows:

$$\{\bar{y}_k\}_{k=1}^{c-1}, \quad \left(\bar{y}_i^T y_0 = 0, \ \bar{y}_i^T \bar{y}_j = 0, \ i \neq j \right). \tag{25}$$

(2) Add an element of 1 to the end of each input data (G_{00}^i ($i = 1, 2, \ldots, m$)), and obtain $c - 1$ vectors $\{\bar{a}_k\}_{k=1}^{c-1} \in \mathfrak{R}^{n+1}$, where $\bar{a}_k$ is the solution of the following regular least squares problem:

$$\bar{a}_k = \arg \min \left(\sum_{i=1}^{m} \left(\bar{a}^T G_{00}^i - \bar{y}_i^k \right)^2 + \alpha \|\bar{a}\|^2 \right). \tag{26}$$

Here $\bar{y}_i^k$ is the ith element of eigenvectors $\{\bar{y}_k\}_{k=1}^{c-1}$ and α is the contraction parameter.

(3) Let $A = [\bar{a}_1, \ldots, \bar{a}_{c-1}]$ be the transformation matrix with the size $(M + 1) \times (c - 1)$. Perform dimension reduction on the sample features $G_{00}^1, G_{00}^2, \ldots, G_{00}^m$, by mapping them to $(c - 1)$ dimensional subspace as follows:

$$x \longrightarrow z = A^T \begin{bmatrix} x \\ 1 \end{bmatrix}. \tag{27}$$

Step 6. Compute the mean values of samples in different classes according to following equation:

$$\text{aver}_i = \frac{\sum_{s=1}^{m_i} G_{00}^s}{m_i} \quad (i = 1, 2, \ldots, 6), \tag{28}$$

where m_i is the number of samples in the ith class; $\sum_{i=1}^{6} m_i = m$. Let aver$_i$ be the class-centroid of the ith class.

Step 7. The remaining $N - m$ samples are taken as the testing samples, and the dimension reduction is implemented for them using the method described in Step 5.

Step 8. Compute the square of the distance $|G_{00}^s - \text{aver}_i|^2$ ($s = m + 1, m + 2, \ldots, N$ and $i = 1, 2, \ldots, 6$) between each testing sample G_{00}^s and different class-centroid aver$_i$, according to the nearest centroids classifier; the sample G_{00}^s is assigned to the class i if $i = \arg \min |G_{00}^s - \text{aver}_i|^2$.

In Step 8, the weak classifier (i.e., the nearest centroid classifier) is used to classify error-diffused halftone images, because this classifier is simple and easy to implement. Simultaneously, in order to prove that these class feature matrices, which are extracted according to the method mentioned in Section 3 and handled by the algorithm of the spectral regression discriminant analysis, are well suited for the classification of error-diffused halftone images, this weak classifier is used in this paper instead of a strong classifier [20], such as support vector machine classifiers and deep neural network classifiers.

5. Experimental Analysis and Results

We implement various experiments to verify the efficiency of our methods in classifying error-diffused halftone images. The computer processor is Intel(R) Pentium(R) CPU G2030 @3.00 GHz, the memory of the computer is 2.0 GB, the operating system is Windows 7, and the experimental simulation software is matlab R2012a. In our experiments, all the original images are downloaded from http://decsai.ugr.es/cvg/dbimagenes/ and http://msp.ee.ntust.edu.tw/. About 4000 original images have been downloaded and they are converted into 24000 error-diffused halftone images produced by six different error-diffused filters.

5.1. Classification Accuracy Rate of the Error-Diffused Halftone Images

5.1.1. Effect of the Number of the Samples.
This subsection analyzes the effect of the number on the feature samples on classification. When $L = 11$, and feature matrices F_{00}, F_{10}, F_{11}, F_{all} are taken as the input data, respectively, the accuracy rate of classification under different conditions is shown in Tables 1 and 2. Table 1 shows the classification accuracy rates under different number of training samples, when the total number of samples is 12000. Table 2 shows the classification accuracy rates under different number of training samples, when the total number of samples is 24000. The digits in the first line of each table are the size of the training samples.

According to Tables 1 and 2, the classification accuracy rates under 12000 samples are higher than that under 24000 samples. Moreover, the classification accuracy rates improve with the increase of the proportion of the training samples when the number of the training samples is lower than the 80% of sample size. And it achieves the highest classification accuracy rates when the number of the training samples is

TABLE 1: Classification accuracy rates (%) (12000 samples).

	2000	3000	4000	5000	6000	7000	8000	9000	10000
F_{00}	97.750	97.500	99.050	99.150	99.150	99.150	99.100	98.950	98.900
F_{10}	99.950	99.950	100.00	100.00	100.00	100.00	100.00	100.00	100.00
F_{11}	99.500	99.250	99.350	99.400	99.200	99.350	99.300	99.300	99.450
F_{all}	99.100	99.100	99.450	99.500	99.650	99.650	99.650	99.650	99.600

TABLE 2: Classification accuracy rates (%) (24000 samples).

	14000	15000	16000	17000	18000	19000	20000	21000	22000
F_{00}	95.810	95.878	95.413	95.286	94.933	98.580	98.100	98.267	98.650
F_{10}	97.600	97.378	97.150	96.957	96.450	99.680	99.600	99.533	99.300
F_{11}	96.420	96.256	95.925	95.614	95.000	99.040	98.825	98.700	98.400
F_{all}	97.230	97.100	96.888	96.686	96.233	99.680	99.600	99.533	99.350

TABLE 3: Classification accuracy rates obtained by different algorithms (%).

F_{00} + SR	F_{10} + SR	F_{11} + SR	F_{all} + SR	ECF + BP	LMS + Bayes	G_{10} + ML	G_{11} + ML
98.40	99.53	98.74	99.54	90.04	90.38	98.32	96.15

TABLE 4: The training and testing time under different sample sizes (in seconds).

		14000	15000	16000	17000	18000	19000	20000	21000	22000
F_{00}	Training time	65.208	78.317	94.660	110.47	129.32	150.18	178.94	205.11	513.54
	Testing time	6.3742	6.2583	5.8530	5.5251	4.8792	4.4947	3.7872	3.0375	4.3393
F_{10}	Training time	65.851	78.796	95.113	110.70	130.97	150.76	173.98	198.95	240.10
	Testing time	6.3674	6.0804	5.7496	5.503	4.9287	4.3261	3.6775	3.0353	2.9631
F_{11}	Training time	65.662	79.936	95.173	110.69	130.33	150.63	174.41	198.34	239.96
	Testing time	6.5226	6.1817	5.7826	5.3778	4.8531	4.5513	3.7137	2.9735	3.0597
F_{all}	Training time	68.902	82.554	99.189	115.27	135.34	156.71	179.94	204.85	288.36
	Testing time	10.200	9.8393	9.3112	8.7212	8.016	6.902	5.8556	4.9363	3.6921

about 80% of the sample size. In addition, from Tables 1 and 2, we can also see that F_{00}, F_{10}, F_{11} can be used as the input data alone. Simultaneously, they can also be combined into the input data F_{all}, based on which the classification accuracy rates would be high.

5.1.2. Comparison of Classification Accuracy Rate. To analyze the effectiveness of our classification algorithm, the mean values of classification accuracy rate of the four data sets on the right-hand side of each row in Table 2 are computed. The algorithm SR outperforms other baselines in achieving higher classification accuracy rates, when compared with LMS + Bayes (the method composed of least mean square and Bayes method), ECF + BP (the method based on the enhanced correlation function and BP neural network), and ML (the maximum likelihood method). According to Table 3, the mean values of classification accuracy rates obtained using SR and different features F_{00}, F_{10}, F_{11}, and F_{all}, respectively, are higher than the mean values obtained by other algorithms mentioned above.

5.2. Effect of the Size of Statistical Feature Template on Classification Accuracies. Here, different features F_{00}, F_{10}, F_{11} of the 24000 error-diffused halftone images are used to test the effect of the size of statistical feature template. F_{00}, F_{10}, F_{11} are constructed using the corresponding class feature matrices G_{00}, G_{10}, G_{11} with deferent size $L \times L$ ($L = 5, 7, 9, 11, 13, 15, 17, 19, 21, 23, 25$). Figure 1 shows that the classification accuracy rate achieves the highest value when $L = 11$, no matter which feature is selected for experiments.

5.3. Time-Consumption of the Classification. Now, the experiments are implemented to test the time-consumption of the error-diffused halftone image classification under the condition that the total number of samples is 24000 and $L = 11$. It is well known that the time-consumption of the classification includes the training time and the testing time. From Table 4, we can know that the training time increases with the increase of the number of training samples; on the contrary, the testing time decreases with the increase of the number of training samples.

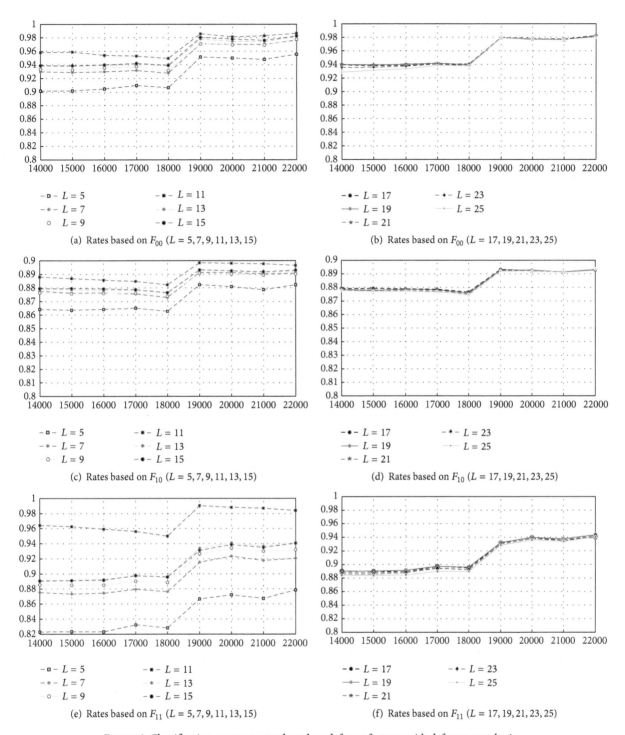

(a) Rates based on F_{00} ($L = 5, 7, 9, 11, 13, 15$)

(b) Rates based on F_{00} ($L = 17, 19, 21, 23, 25$)

(c) Rates based on F_{10} ($L = 5, 7, 9, 11, 13, 15$)

(d) Rates based on F_{10} ($L = 17, 19, 21, 23, 25$)

(e) Rates based on F_{11} ($L = 5, 7, 9, 11, 13, 15$)

(f) Rates based on F_{11} ($L = 17, 19, 21, 23, 25$)

FIGURE 1: Classification accuracy rates based on deferent features with deferent sample size.

To compare the time-consumption of the classification method proposed in this paper with other algorithms, such as the backpropagation (BP) neural network, radial basis function (RBF) neural network, and support vector machine (SVM), all the experiments are implemented using F_{10}, which is divided into two parts: 12000 training samples and 12000 testing samples ($L = 11$). From the digits listed in Table 5,

we can know that SR achieves the minimal summation of the training and testing time.

In addition, Table 5 implies that the time-consumption of classifiers based on neural networks, such as the classifier based on RBF or BP, are much more than that of other algorithms, especially SR. This is because these neural network algorithms essentially use gradient descent methods to

TABLE 5: Time-consumption of different algorithms (in second).

	ML	RBF	BP	SVM	SR
Training time	110.42	76.390	2966.7	49.297	43.9337
Testing time	1.2000	276.00	3.6000	62.400	6.3161

TABLE 6: Classification accuracy rates under different variances (%).

Variance	14000	15000	16000	17000	18000	19000	20000	21000	22000
0.01	95.570	95.422	95.425	95.529	95.217	98.440	98.200	98.033	97.950
0.10	95.370	95.233	95.188	95.157	94.867	98.200	98.000	97.767	98.000
0.50	94.580	94.522	94.600	94.671	94.567	98.320	98.225	98.033	98.550
1.00	93.060	93.067	93.013	93.343	93.200	96.980	97.175	96.800	97.350

TABLE 7: Classification accuracy rates using other algorithms under different variances.

Variance	ECF + BP	LMS + Bayes	ML	Variance	ECF + BP	LMS + Bayes	ML
0.01	89.5000	88.7577	97.9981	0.50	79.7333	40.2682	82.9169
0.10	88.1333	78.4264	96.8315	1.00	61.5000	33.8547	64.3861

optimize the associated nonconvex problems, which are well known to converge very slowly. However, the classifier based on SR performs the classification task through computing the square of the distance between each testing sample and different class-centroids directly. Hence, the time-consumption of it is very cheap.

5.4. The Experiment of Noise Attack Resistance. In the process of actual operation, the error-defused halftone images are often polluted by noise before the inverse transform. In order to test the ability of SR to resist the attack of noise, different Gaussian noises with mean 0 and different variances are embedded into the error-defused halftone images. Then classification experiments have been done using the algorithm proposed in this paper and the experimental results are listed in Table 6. According to Table 6, the accuracy rates decrease with the increase of the variances. As compared with the accuracy rates listed in Table 7 achieved by other algorithms, such as ECF + BP, LMS + Bayes, and ML, we find that our classification method has obvious advantages in resisting the noise.

6. Conclusion

This paper proposes a novel algorithm to solve the challenging problem of classifying the error-diffused halftone images. We firstly design the class feature matrices, after extracting the image patches according to their statistical characteristics, to classify the error-diffused halftone images. Then, the spectral regression kernel discriminant analysis is used for feature dimension reduction. The error-diffused halftone images are finally classified using an idea similar to the nearest centroids classifier. As demonstrated by the experimental results, our method is fast and can achieve a high classification accuracy rate with an added benefit of robustness in tackling noise. A very interesting direction is to solve the disturbance, possibly introduced by other attacks

such as image scaling and rotation, in the process of error-diffused halftone image classification.

Competing Interests

The authors declare that they have no competing interests.

Acknowledgments

This work is supported in part by the National Natural Science Foundation of China (Grants nos. 61170102, 61271140), the Scientific Research Fund of Hunan Provincial Education Department, China (Grant no. 15A049), the Education Department Fund of Hunan Province in China (Grants nos. 15C0402, 15C0395, and 13C036), and the Science and Technology Planning Project of Hunan Province in China (Grant no. 2015GK3024).

References

[1] Y.-M. Kwon, M.-G. Kim, and J.-L. Kim, "Multiscale rank-based ordered dither algorithm for digital halftoning," *Information Systems*, vol. 48, pp. 241–247, 2015.

[2] Y. Jiang and M. Wang, "Image fusion using multiscale edge-preserving decomposition based on weighted least squares filter," *IET Image Processing*, vol. 8, no. 3, pp. 183–190, 2014.

[3] Z. Zhao, L. Cheng, and G. Cheng, "Neighbourhood weighted fuzzy c-means clustering algorithm for image segmentation," *IET Image Processing*, vol. 8, no. 3, pp. 150–161, 2014.

[4] Z.-Q. Wen, Y.-L. Lu, Z.-G. Zeng, W.-Q. Zhu, and J.-H. Ai, "Optimizing template for lookup-table inverse halftoning using elitist genetic algorithm," *IEEE Signal Processing Letters*, vol. 22, no. 1, pp. 71–75, 2015.

[5] P. C. Chang and C. S. Yu, "Neural net classification and LMS reconstruction to halftone images," in *Visual Communications and Image Processing '98*, vol. 3309 of *Proceedings of SPIE*, pp. 592–602, The International Society for Optical Engineering, January 1998.

[6] Y. Kong, P. Zeng, and Y. Zhang, "Classification and recognition algorithm for the halftone image," *Journal of Xidian University*, vol. 38, no. 5, pp. 62–69, 2011 (Chinese).

[7] Y. Kong, *A study of inverse halftoning and quality assessment schemes [Ph.D. thesis]*, School of Computer Science and Technology, Xidian University, Xian, China, 2008.

[8] Y.-F. Liu, J.-M. Guo, and J.-D. Lee, "Inverse halftoning based on the Bayesian theorem," *IEEE Transactions on Image Processing*, vol. 20, no. 4, pp. 1077–1084, 2011.

[9] Y.-F. Liu, J.-M. Guo, and J.-D. Lee, "Halftone image classification using LMS algorithm and naive Bayes," *IEEE Transactions on Image Processing*, vol. 20, no. 10, pp. 2837–2847, 2011.

[10] D. L. Lau and G. R. Arce, *Modern Digital Halftoning*, CRC Press, Boca Raton, Fla, USA, 2nd edition, 2008.

[11] *Image Dithering: Eleven Algorithms and Source Code*, http://www.tannerhelland.com/4660/dithering-elevenalgorithms-source-code/.

[12] R. A. Ulichney, "Dithering with blue noise," *Proceedings of the IEEE*, vol. 76, no. 1, pp. 56–79, 1988.

[13] Y.-H. Fung and Y.-H. Chan, "Embedding halftones of different resolutions in a full-scale halftone," *IEEE Signal Processing Letters*, vol. 13, no. 3, pp. 153–156, 2006.

[14] Z.-Q. Wen, Y.-X. Hu, and W.-Q. Zhu, "A novel classification method of halftone image via statistics matrices," *IEEE Transactions on Image Processing*, vol. 23, no. 11, pp. 4724–4736, 2014.

[15] D. Cai, X. He, and J. Han, "Efficient kernel discriminant analysis via spectral regression," in *Proceedings of the 7th IEEE International Conference on Data Mining (ICDM '07)*, pp. 427–432, Omaha, Neb, USA, October 2007.

[16] D. Cai, X. He, and J. Han, "Speed up kernel discriminant analysis," *The International Journal on Very Large Data Bases*, vol. 20, no. 1, pp. 21–33, 2011.

[17] M. Zhao, Z. Zhang, T. W. S. Chow, and B. Li, "A general soft label based Linear Discriminant Analysis for semi-supervised dimensionality reduction," *Neural Networks*, vol. 55, pp. 83–97, 2014.

[18] M. Zhao, Z. Zhang, T. W. S. Chow, and B. Li, "Soft label based Linear Discriminant Analysis for image recognition and retrieval," *Computer Vision & Image Understanding*, vol. 121, no. 1, pp. 86–99, 2014.

[19] L. Zhang and F.-C. Tian, "A new kernel discriminant analysis framework for electronic nose recognition," *Analytica Chimica Acta*, vol. 816, pp. 8–17, 2014.

[20] B. Gu, V. S. Sheng, K. Y. Tay, W. Romano, and S. Li, "Incremental support vector learning for ordinal regression," *IEEE Transactions on Neural Networks and Learning Systems*, vol. 26, no. 7, pp. 1403–1416, 2015.

10

Deep Learning for Person Reidentification Using Support Vector Machines

Mengyu Xu, Zhenmin Tang, Yazhou Yao, Lingxiang Yao, Huafeng Liu, and Jingsong Xu

Nanjing University of Science and Technology, Nanjing 210094, China

Correspondence should be addressed to Mengyu Xu; mengyxu@hotmail.com

Academic Editor: Chong Wah Ngo

Due to the variations of viewpoint, pose, and illumination, a given individual may appear considerably different across different camera views. Tracking individuals across camera networks with no overlapping fields is still a challenging problem. Previous works mainly focus on feature representation and metric learning individually which tend to have a suboptimal solution. To address this issue, in this work, we propose a novel framework to do the feature representation learning and metric learning jointly. Different from previous works, we represent the pairs of pedestrian images as new resized input and use linear Support Vector Machine to replace softmax activation function for similarity learning. Particularly, dropout and data augmentation techniques are also employed in this model to prevent the network from overfitting. Extensive experiments on two publically available datasets VIPeR and CUHK01 demonstrate the effectiveness of our proposed approach.

1. Introduction

With the advances in computer version [1–4], machine learning [5–8], and deep neural networks [9, 10], we enter into an era that it is possible to build a real world identification system. Person reidentification (Re-ID) problem aims to recognize individuals across cameras at different locations and time from a distributed multicamera surveillance system in large public spaces [11]. Given a probe image captured from one camera, a person reidentification surveillance system attempts to identify the person from a gallery of candidate images taken from a different camera. The same person can be observed differently in cross-view cameras (see Figure 1). So it is quite difficult to find a kind of feature which is reliable and distinct and directly adapt to changes and misalignment in cross-view condition. Because of these challenge issues, researches in person reidentification still mainly focus on people appearance features, with the acceptable assumption that people will not change their clothing during the whole monitoring period.

Existing methods on this research topic have primarily focused on two aspects. The first aspect is to extract robust and discriminative feature descriptors to identify persons. It has been indicated that three important cues for person reidentification are color information, texture descriptors, and interest points; some of these features are learned from datasets and others are designed by hand. Low-level features such as biologically inspired features (BIF) [12], color histograms and variants [13–17], local binary patterns (LBP) [13, 14, 17, 18], Gabor features [14], and interest points (color SIFT [19, 20] and SURF [21]) were proposed to represent appearance features of different people from nonoverlapping cameras. Some other works have also investigated combinations of multiple visual features, including [13, 14, 16]. The second aspect is to develop metric learning methods to learn discriminative models. The idea of metric learning is to design classifiers to enforce features from the same person to be closer than those from different individuals. Usually used metric learning methods such as Large Margin Nearest Neighbour (LMNN) [16], Logistic Discriminant Metric Learning (LDML) [22], KISSME [18], and Marginal Fisher Analysis (MFA) [16] performed well in solving challenging issues. These approaches typically extract handcrafted features and subsequently learn the metrics. However, these methods optimize feature extraction and metric learning separately or sequentially which leads to suboptimal solutions easily.

In recent years, with the wide use of convolutional neural networks (CNN) in the tasks of object recognition,

(a) CUHK01   (b) VIPeR

FIGURE 1: Samples of pedestrian observed from CUHK01 and VIPeR datasets. The same person's appearance change in different camera views.

tracking [23], classification [24], and face recognition [25], it has been proved to have a strong automatic learning ability. However, CNN has little progress in person reidentification. In this paper, inspired by the outstanding performance on person reidentification and facial expression recognition in [26, 27], we introduce a deep learning architecture with joint representation learning and linear SVM top layer of CNN to measure the similarity of the comparing image pairs. We randomly select two pedestrian images and horizontally join them as a new resized input image. Joint representation learning method which refers to [26] reduces the complexity of the network rather than two input branches used in Siamese network. We replace the standard softmax layer with L2-SVM to measure the distance of pedestrians in different cameras and estimate whether the inputs of the two pedestrians are the same or not. Compared with softmax function for predicting class labels, we use linear SVM to measure the distance to the decision boundary that is more suitable for the person reidentification which is solved as ranking-like comparison issue. Since L1-SVM is not differentiable, we introduce L2-SVM which is differentiable during function optimization and more stable in numerical computation. Pretrained and dropout techniques are also used in the model to prevent the overfitting problem and boost the performance of person reidentification. The major contributions of this paper are twofold:

(i) We present a deep learning network combined joint representation learning with linear SVM to increase discriminative power of CNN network.

(ii) Extensive experiments are conducted on two benchmark datasets to validate the effectiveness of our architecture and achieve the best results.

2. Related Work

The typical workflow of existing person reidentification system is shown in Figure 2. It indicates that most of them focus on two main components: feature representation and metric learning. The aim of feature representation is to develop discriminate and robust appearance of the same pedestrian across different camera views.

Global features are divided into two categories: color based and texture based features. HSV [28] and LAB [29]

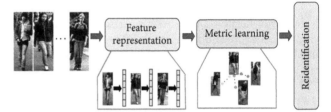

FIGURE 2: The general procedure of person reidentification.

color histograms are normal color based features. LBP histogram [30] and Gabor filter [14] are used to describe the textures of images. Recently, based on these traditional color and texture features, some more distinct and reliable feature representations for pedestrians have been proposed. Bazzani et al. [31] proposed to use a global mean color histogram and recurrent local patterns through local epitomic analysis to represent a person which is called the histogram plus epitome (HPE). Farenzena et al. [28] proposed to combine weighted HSV histogram of two separated human bodies with salient texture and stable color region as famous symmetry-driven method (SDALF) approach. Yang et al. [32] developed the semantic Salient Color Names based Color Descriptor (SCNCD) employing color naming. Local maximal occurrence (LOMO) features [33] and Scale Invariant Local Ternary Pattern (SILTP) histograms are used to analyse the horizontal occurrence of local features and maximize the occurrence to describe the mean information of pixel features. However, handcrafted features are difficult to achieve the balance between discriminative power and robustness which are highly susceptible to cross-view variations caused by illumination, occlusions, background clutter, and view orientation variations.

Besides feature representation, metric learning is also widely applied for person reidentification. Metric learning is formulated to learn the optimal similarity from features of training images which have strong interclass differences and intraclass similarities. Xiong et al. [34] proposed regularized PCCA (rPCCA), kernel LFDA (kLFDA), and Marginal Fisher Analysis (MFA) when the data space is undersampled. Chopra et al. proposed an algorithm to learn a similarity metric from data [35]. Zheng et al. [36] introduced the

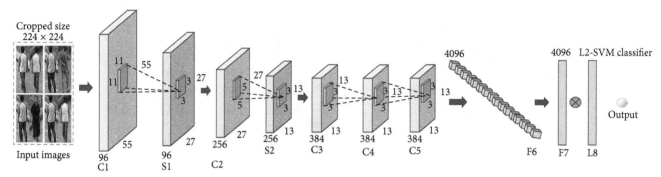

FIGURE 3: The framework of our proposed model. Both of positive and negative pairs are randomly selected as input images. The first to fifth layers are convolution layers and subsampling layers with Relu activation. Sixth and seventh layers are fully connected layers with 4096 neural units. The top layer is linear L2-SVM layer instead of traditional softmax layer to measure the similarity of input images.

Probabilistic Relative Distance Comparison (PRDC) model which aims to maximize the probability of a pair of right match having a smaller distance than that of a wrong match pair and optimizes the relative distance comparison. Prosser et al. [37] reformulated the person reidentification problem as a ranking problem and proposed the Ensemble RankSVM model learning a subspace where the potential true match is given highest ranking rather than any direct distance measure.

Recently, deep learning has become one of the state-of-the-art recognition algorithms, especially that CNN has shown great potential in computer vision tasks. Li et al. [38] propose a new filter pairing neural network (FPNN) that jointly optimizes feature learning, misalignment, occlusions, classification, photometric transforms, and geometric transforms to learn filter pairs encoding photometric transforms. Different from FPNN learning the joint representation of two images, Yi et al. [39] proposed Deep Metric Learning (DML) model inspired by a Siamese neural network that combines the separate modules together, learning the color feature, texture feature, and metric in a unified framework. Matsukawa and Suzuki [40] conducted a fine-tuning of CNN features on a pedestrian attribute dataset to bridge the gap of ImageNet classification and person reidentification and proposed a loss function for classifying combination attributes to increase discriminative power of CNN features. Ahmed et al. [41] presented a deep convolutional architecture with cross-input neighbourhood differences layer and subsequent layer that capture local relationships between the two input images based on mid-level features from each input image and summarized these differences.

3. Algorithm

In the person reidentification task, it usually needs to measure the similarity between gallery set and probe set. CNN is exactly proved to outperform on classification problems rather than comparison problems. Directly using CNN in person reidentification is not suitable and it is hard to leverage its power. In this section, we describe the proposed architecture of CNN specifically. Details of layers and the strategies we used in network training are introduced in the following subsections.

3.1. Joint Representation Learning. The standard pipeline of person reidentification includes feature extracting from input images and metric learning for those features across images. As mentioned above, optimizing feature representation and metric learning separately or sequentially easily leads to suboptimal solutions. Different from this ordinary framework of learning metric over handcrafted features, we develop to use joint representation learning on input images in our network which is similar to deep rank CNN proposed by Chen et al. [26].

Motived by human assessment, it is used to assess two images whether they belong to the same person by comparing their depicted appearance separately. For instance, pictures A, B, and C are three quite similar but different pedestrian images. Setting picture C as probe image, the discriminative region between A and C is a handbag that appeared in C. Compared with B, pedestrian A wears dress, while B wears pants. As we compare different pedestrian images separately, some value information will be ignored or hidden when appearance features are extracted independently. In our proposed model, jointly representing two input pedestrian images and generating discriminative information will instead separately input images with two branches.

3.2. Architecture. Our deep learning network (see Figure 3) is composed of five convolutional layers (C1, C2, C3, C4, and C5) to extract features, three subsampling layers (S1, S2, and S5), and two fully connected layers (F6, F7). One branch is used as the input of network instead of two branches used in [27]. Different from the architecture of network proposed in [26], the top layer of our network ($L8$) is linear SVM instead of ranking layer which is more discriminative for different pedestrians, and we also optimize the gradient backpropagating learning problem in linear SVM. Randomly given two pedestrian images I and J observed from two cross-view cameras with three color channels (RGB) and sized $H_i \times W_i$ ($H_i = 2W_i$), then we join them horizontally. Since pedestrian images are not square-shaped and all of them are quite small, both of the images are resized to 12×256 in the experiment, and the new joint image is square with size of 256×256; then a 224×224 random crop is presented as the input to the whole network in order to get center areas

TABLE 1: The layer parameters of our network. The output dimension in the table is given by height × width × width. All convolution and fully connected layers use Relu activation function.

Name	Output dim	Filter size	Stride
C1	$55 \times 55 \times 96$	11×11	4
S1	$27 \times 27 \times 96$	3×3	2
C2	$27 \times 27 \times 256$	5×5	1
S2	$13 \times 13 \times 256$	3×3	2
C3	$13 \times 13 \times 384$	3×3	1
C4	$13 \times 13 \times 384$	3×3	1
C5	$13 \times 13 \times 256$	3×3	1
S5	$6 \times 6 \times 256$	3×3	2
F6	—	4096	—
F7	—	4096	—
L8	2	—	—

of images we focus on. Processed by this method, the aspect of images remains nearly unchanged and it avoids a large number of parameters contained in Siamese network. The processed images are represented as x_i, $i = 1, 2, \ldots, N$.

The first convolutional layer (C1) is convolved with 96 different filters (see Table 1) of size 11×11 with a stride of 4 in each horizontal and vertical directions. Then the 96 various 55×55 feature maps are passed through the Relu layer and subsampling layer (S1) with size of 3×3 to reduce the maps into 27×27 size. The Batch Normalization (BN) layer is employed before each of the Relu layers which allows the network to use much higher learning rates and less focus on initialization of weights and biases. The feature maps are more robust to illumination and variations. If we use K filters and each filter is in size of $m \times m \times C$, the output consists of C' channels of height H_i' and width W_i'. The convolution operation is expressed as function x_i^l:

$$x_i^l = \sigma \left(b_i^{(l)} + \sum_j k_{ij}^{(l)} * x_j^{(l-1)} \right), \tag{1}$$

where $x_i^{(l)}$ and $x_j^{(l-1)}$ represent the ith output channel at the lth layer and the jth input channel at the $(l - 1)$th layer; $k_{ij}^{(l)}$ denotes convolutional kernel between the ith and jth feature map. The function $\sigma(\cdot)$ is the Relu neuron activation function of the network and represented as $\sigma(x) = \max(x, 0)$. The max-pooling operation is formulated as

$$x_{(i,j)}^{(l)} = \max_{\forall (p,q) \in \Omega_{(i,j)}} x_{(p,q)}^{(l)}, \tag{2}$$

where $\Omega_{(i,j)}$ represents the pooling region with index (i, j).

The second convolutional layer (C2) takes the outputs of S1 as input with filters of size 5×5 and gives 256 different 27×27 feature maps. The third and fourth convolutional layers (C3 and C4) are both with filters of size 3×3 and give 384 different 13×13 feature maps. With the same size of filters in C3 and C4, the fifth convolutional layer (C5) provides 256 different 13×13 feature maps. The two subsampling layers (S2 and S5) repeat the same pooling options as S1. The sixth

and seventh fully connected layers (F6 and F7) connect with $6 \times 6 \times 256$ neurons from S5 layer and reduce to 4096 nodes and form compact and robust features. The fully connected layers are expressed as

$$x^{(l)} = w^{(l)} \cdot x^{(l-1)} + b^{(l)}. \tag{3}$$

Instead of traditional softmax layer used in multiple classifications, we use L2-SVM objective for learning the lower level parameters in the top layer (L8) of the whole network to find the max margin of true match ($+1$) and false match (-1) over training sample pairs.

3.3. Linear SVM versus Softmax

3.3.1. Softmax. Softmax is usually used in deep learning technique at top layer of the network. It is a generalization of logistic regression to the case in multiclass classification. The class labels are formulated as $y^{(i)} \in \{1, \ldots, K\}$, where K is the number of classes. Let h_k be the activation in penultimate layer and let W_k be the weight connecting between penultimate layer and softmax layer. The input to softmax is represented as

$$a_i = \sum_k h_k W_{ki}. \tag{4}$$

The probability is defined as

$$p_i = \frac{\exp(a_i)}{\sum_j^{10} \exp(a_j)}. \tag{5}$$

So the predicted class label $\hat{i}$ would be

$$\hat{i} = \arg \max_i p_i. \tag{6}$$

3.3.2. Linear Support Vector. Softmax is usually used as activation function which is focused on classification and less suitable for ranking-like comparison issue of person reidentification. So in this paper, we proposed to use L2-SVM objection training CNN instead of softmax layer. In linear Support Vector Machines (SVM), corresponding data and labels are represented as (x_n, y_n), $x_n \in \mathbb{R}^D$, $t_n \in \{-1, +1\}$, $n = 1, \ldots, N$, and the linear SVM is defined as the following constrained optimization:

$$\min_w \frac{1}{2} w^T w + C \sum_{n=1}^N \max \left(1 - w^T x_n t_n, 0 \right). \tag{7}$$

Equation (7) is known as typical L1-SVM, and a differentiable representation is known as L2-SVM, given as follows:

$$l(w) = \min_w \frac{1}{2} w^T w + C \sum_{n=1}^N \max \left(1 - w^T x_n t_n, 0 \right)^2. \tag{8}$$

L2-SVM is differentiable during optimization and imposes a bigger loss for points which violate the margin. Equation (9) shows the predicted class labels of probe sets

$$\arg \max_t \left(w^T x \right) t. \tag{9}$$

We use the L2-SVM as objective function in our deep network and backpropagate the gradients from linear SVM layer to learn parameters of network. Therefore, the partial derivative of weight w is formulated as

$$\frac{\partial l(w)}{\partial w} = w - 2Cx_n t_n \left(\max \left(1 - w^T x_n t_n, 0 \right) \right). \quad (10)$$

The penultimate activation h is given as

$$\frac{\partial l(w)}{\partial h} = -2Ct_n w \left(\max \left(1 - w^T h_n t_n, 0 \right) \right). \quad (11)$$

In this way, a joint representation based L2-SVM neural network is obtained and the following section will show its performance on two public datasets.

3.4. Training Strategies Used in CNN

Dropout. During the training, random dropping units which are along with their connection from the neural network is an efficient technique to prevent overfitting and approximately combine exponentially different network architectures efficiently. The dropout technique is usually performed during supervised training and the network is likely forced to learn an averaging model. In this paper, we use dropout in the two fully connected layers (F6, F7) and randomly drop out 50% neurons of these two layers.

Data Augmentation and Data Balancing. Data augmentation is a widely used trick in deep learning. Since neural networks need to be trained on a huge number of training images to achieve satisfactory performance, the public datasets used in person reidentification usually contain limited images. In the training set, the positive pairs (the matched sample pairs) are generally fewer than negative pairs (nonmatched sample pairs). So in the experiment, doing data augmentation is better to boost the performance when training the deep network. In the training set, we randomly crop the input images into 224×224 patches and horizontally flip them around the y-axis. These augmented data will be used as new input of our network. To achieve data balancing, we online sample the same number of positive pairs and negative pairs with a $1:1$ positive-negative ratio in each minibatch size of 32 images at the very beginning of the training process. As the whole network achieves a reasonably good configuration after the initial training, the positive-negative ratio will gradually reach $1:5$ to alleviate overfitting.

Stochastic Gradient Descent. Our model is trained using minibatch stochastic gradient descent (SGD) for faster backpropagation and smoother convergence. In each iteration of the training phase, 32 images of a minibatch are the input of the network. We use the SGD with a momentum of 0.9, the learning rate of $\gamma = 10^{-4}$, and weight decay of 0.0005. Note that for every 10000 iterations the learning rate will decrease by $\gamma_{new} = 0.1 * \gamma$.

Pretraining and Fine-Tuning. The network proposed in this paper is a great depth network, so a great number of labeled

TABLE 2: Comparison of state-of-the-art results of feature representation reported with VIPeR database. The cumulative matching scores (%) at ranks 1, 5, 10, and 20 are listed.

Method	VIPeR ($p = 316$)			
	Top 1	Top 5	Top 10	Top 20
ELF6	8.73	18.76	23.75	31.75
gBiCov	9.87	27.64	36.75	48.96
HSV_Lab_LBP	12.47	26.95	33.37	44.16
Ours	*34.15*	*67.86*	*80.95*	*90.63*

TABLE 3: Comparison of state-of-the-art results of feature representation reported with CUHK01 database. The cumulative matching scores (%) at ranks 1, 5, 10, and 20 are listed.

Method	CUHK01 ($p = 485$)			
	Top 1	Top 5	Top 10	Top 20
ELF18	5.37	13.45	17.28	23.45
gBiCov	7.25	13.75	18.64	24.26
LOMO	10.80	23.20	27.35	36.12
Ours	*50.01*	*64.75*	*73.85*	*84.96*

TABLE 4: Comparison of state-of-the-art results of metric learning reported with VIPeR database. The cumulative matching scores (%) at ranks 1, 5, 10, and 20 are listed.

Method	VIPeR ($p = 316$)			
	Top 1	Top 5	Top 10	Top 20
LMNN	6.23	19.65	32.63	52.25
ITML	12.4	27.5	39.7	55.2
Euclidean	14.46	28.75	39.14	50.10
RDC	15.7	32.5	53.9	70.1
KISSME	25.78	56.24	70.14	82.92
Ours	*34.15*	*67.86*	*80.95*	*90.63*

images are needed to train the whole network. Before training on VIPeR and CUHK01 datasets, we use CUHK02 datasets to learn a pretrained model. When we test on different datasets, we fine-tune a few top layers of pretrained model with a small learning rate.

4. Experiments

Our proposed network is implemented by Theano deep learning framework. The network is trained in NVIDIA TITAN X. We evaluate the proposed method on several famous person reidentification datasets carried out to compare with state-of-the-art approaches. The results are shown in Cumulative Matching Characteristic (CMC) curve. The cumulative matching scores are also shown in Tables 2–9.

4.1. Datasets and Evaluation Protocol

Datasets. We evaluate our method on two public datasets: VIPeR dataset and CUHK01 dataset. The deep learning model is pretrained on CUHK02 dataset. VIPeR dataset is a relatively small and quite challenging dataset in person

TABLE 5: Comparison of state-of-the-art results of metric learning reported with CUHK01 database. The cumulative matching scores (%) at ranks 1, 5, 10, and 20 are listed.

Method	CUHK01 ($p = 485$)			
	Top 1	Top 5	Top 10	Top 20
Euclidean	10.52	28.07	39.94	55.07
LMNN	13.45	31.33	42.52	54.11
ITML	16.0	28.5	45.3	60.1
KISSME	29.40	57.67	72.43	86.07
Ours	*50.01*	*64.75*	*73.85*	*84.96*

TABLE 6: Comparison of some other state-of-the-art results reported with VIPeR database. The cumulative matching scores (%) at ranks 1, 5, 10, and 20 are listed.

Method	VIPeR ($p = 316$)			
	Top 1	Top 5	Top 10	Top 20
L2-norm	10.89	22.37	32.34	45.19
L1-norm	12.15	26.01	32.09	34.72
aPRDC	16.14	37.72	50.98	65.95
RankSVM	14.00	37.00	51.00	67.00
SSCDL	25.60	54.15	68.10	83.60
eSCD	26.31	46.61	58.86	72.77
PCCA	19.62	51.55	68.23	82.92
rPCCA	21.96	54.78	70.95	85.29
SVMML	30.07	63.17	77.44	88.08
MFA	32.24	65.99	79.66	90.64
KLFDA	32.33	65.78	79.72	90.95
Ours	*34.15*	*67.86*	*80.95*	*90.63*

TABLE 7: Comparison of some other state-of-the-art results reported with CUHK01 database. The cumulative matching scores (%) at ranks 1, 5, 10, and 20 are listed.

Method	CUHK01 ($p = 485$)			
	Top 1	Top 5	Top 10	Top 20
L2-norm	5.6	16.0	22.9	30.6
SDALF	9.90	22.57	30.33	41.03
L1-norm	10.8	15.5	37.6	35.6
SVMML	30.23	55.58	67.49	78.92
KLFDA	32.76	59.01	69.63	79.18
MFA	38.09	56.34	64.59	72.62
Ours	*50.01*	*64.75*	*73.85*	*84.96*

TABLE 8: Comparison of CNN-based algorithms results reported with VIPeR database. The cumulative matching scores (%) at ranks 1, 5, 10, and 20 are listed.

Method	VIPeR ($p = 316$)			
	Top 1	Top 5	Top 10	Top 20
Deep_CNN	12.5	21.2	26.3	39.7
ImageNet + XQDA	19.7	44.5	58.1	72.9
DML	28.23	59.27	73.45	86.39
Ours	*34.15*	*67.86*	*80.95*	*90.63*

TABLE 9: Comparison of CNN-based algorithms results reported with CUHK01 database. The cumulative matching scores (%) at ranks 1, 5, 10, and 20 are listed.

Method	CUHK01 ($p = 485$)			
	Top 1	Top 5	Top 10	Top 20
FPNN	27.87	58.20	73.46	86.31
ImageNet + XQDA	28.5	52.3	63.6	74.9
FFN + XQDA	32.4	55.9	66.5	76.6
Ours	*50.01*	*64.75*	*73.85*	*84.96*

reidentification. It has 632 pedestrian pairs captured by two camera views in outdoor environment. Each pair contains two images of the same person seen from different viewpoints, including Cam A and Cam B. Images in Cam A are mainly from 0 to 90 degrees while images in Cam B are from 90 to 180 degrees. All images are normalized to 128×48.

The CUHK01 dataset is a larger dataset than VIPeR which contains 972 persons captured from two cross-views with 3884 images in a campus environment. Camera view A and camera view B include two images for the same person and view A captures the frontal or back view of the individuals while view B captures the profile view. All images are scaled to 160×60 pixels. The CUHK02 dataset contains five pairs of views (P1-P2). Images from P2-P2 were used to learn a pretrained model.

Evaluation Protocol. In each experiment on different datasets, we randomly divide each dataset into gallery set and probe set. The gallery set is composed of two kinds of image pairs: positive pairs and negative pairs. The positive pairs are created by the same people from different camera views, and the negative pairs are created by two separate people. Specifically, for VIPeR dataset, we set the number of individuals in the gallery/probe sets split to 316/316. For CUHK01 dataset, we use 485 pedestrians for training and 486 for testing. We compare our method with some state-of-the-art methods on VIPeR and CUHK01 datasets. The whole procedure is repeated ten times, and the average of Cumulative Matching Characteristic (CMC) curves are used to evaluate the performance of different approaches.

4.2. Comparison with Feature Representation

4.2.1. Experiments on VIPeR Dataset. In this experiment, we pretrained the network model with CUHK02 dataset and randomly divide the 632 pairs of images into half for training and half for testing. We compare our proposed approach with the following three available and typical person reidentification features: Ensemble of Local Features (ELF) [42], gBiCov [12], and HSV with Lab and LBP feature proposed in [18]. In the experiment, we used ELF6 implemented in [42].

We compared our proposed method with these three different kinds of features, results of CMC curves, and top-ranked matching rates shown in Figure 4(a) and Table 2. From Figure 4(a), it can be observed that our approach gives the best result. Comparing to the three baseline methods, the performance of our approach gains is over 20% at rank-1.

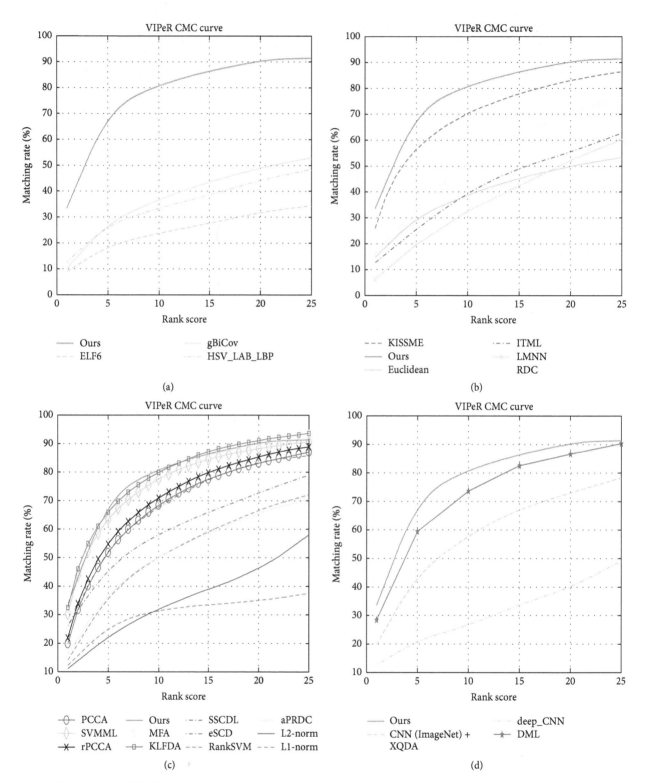

FIGURE 4: CMC curves on VIPeR data set. (a) Performance comparison with feature representation algorithms; (b) performance comparison with metric learning algorithms; (c) performance comparison with other state-of-the-art algorithms; (d) performance comparison with other CNN-based algorithms.

Such trend grows as the rank number increases. As shown in Table 2, our proposed method achieves a 34.15% rank-1 matching rate outperforming the ELF6 with 8.73%, gBiCov with 9.87%, and HSV_Lab_LBP with 12.47%. In our method, the feature learning is directly performed on the input images avoiding missing the critical information during the feature extracting by using handcrafted features. It confirms that utilizing deep convolutional neural network for learning feature representation and similarity measurement is an effective solution for solving people reidentification tasks.

4.2.2. Experiments on CUHK01 Dataset.

Same as the pretrained strategy for CUHK02 dataset used on VIPeR dataset, we chose the following approaches as baselines: ELF18 [42], gBiCov [12], and Local Maximal Occurrence (LOMO) representation [33]. The ELF18 feature is the same as ELF6 which is computed from eighteen equally divided horizontal stripes histograms rather than six.

The comparison results are shown in Figure 5(a) and Table 3. It is observed that our method outperforms the three feature representation methods by a large margin which is over 40% at all ranks and again validates its effectiveness. It is notable that our method achieves 50.01% rank-1 matching rate, outperforming the gBiCov which achieved a 7.25% rank-1 matching rate, by a more significant sizeable margin than VIPeR. The main reason for its superior performance on CUHK01 is that there are less positive pairs in VIPeR dataset even though we have used data augmentation strategy. It still lacks training data to train a robust network. Compared with VIPeR, CUHK01 is larger in scale and has more training data to feed into the deep network to learn a data-driven optimal framework.

4.3. Comparison with Metric Learning Algorithms

4.3.1. Experiments on VIPeR Dataset.

We evaluated the proposed algorithm and several metric learning algorithms, including ITML [43], Euclidean [38], LMNN [16], KISSME [18], and RDC [44]. The results of Cumulative Matching Characteristic (CMC) curves are shown in Figure 4(b). It can be seen that our proposed method is better than the compared metric learning algorithms. To present the quantized comparison results more clearly, we summarize the performance comparison at several top ranks in Table 4. Note that our approach achieves a 34.15% rank-1 matching rate, outperforming the performance of KISSME nearly 10% at all ranks. The main reason for its superior performance is that our proposed framework is capable of joint representation learning and SVM rather than requiring two-step separate optimization.

4.3.2. Experiments on CUHK01 Dataset.

We compare our proposed method with the same methods which have been validated on the VIPeR dataset. Figure 5(b) plots the CMC curves and Table 5 shows the ranking results of all methods on the CUHK01. It can be seen that our method outperforms state-of-the-art methods with a rank-1 recognition rate of 50.01% (versus 29.40% by the next best method). Notice that the second best method on this dataset is KISSME. Our method performs best over 1, 5, and 10, whereas KISSME is better at rank-20 and rank-25. Even though KISSME got better performance on rank-20 and rank-25, our proposed method still performs well.

4.4. Comparison with Other State-of-the-Art Algorithms

4.4.1. Experiments on VIPeR Dataset.

We compare the performance of our algorithm with the following approaches:

KLFDA [34], PCCA [45], rPCCA [34], SVMML [46], MFA [16], SSCDL [47], eSCD [29], RankSVM [37], aPRDC [48], L1-norm [49], and L2-norm. Figure 4(c) and Table 6 show the CMC curves and the matching rate comparing our method with state-of-the-art methods. It is obvious that our method gives the best result among these algorithms which achieves 34.15% rank-1 matching rate, outperforming the result of KLFDA with 32.33%. The other better performing method on the VIPeR dataset is MFA which achieved 32.24% rank-1 matching rate. Our method performs best over ranks 1, 5, and 10, whereas KLFDA and MFA perform better over ranks 15, 20, and 25. The experiment results suggest that even though our model suffers from a severe lack of training data, it still achieves state-of-the-art performance on the highly challenging VIPeR dataset.

4.4.2. Experiments on CUHK01 Dataset.

We compare our method with several state-of-the-art approaches on CUHK01 dataset, such as KLFDA [34], SVMML [46], MFA [16], SDALF [29], L1-norm [49], and L2-norm. As shown in Figure 5(c) and Table 7, our method achieves more significant outperformance than KLFDA and MFA in all ranks on the CUHK01 dataset rather than VIPeR. It suggests that the large train dataset will improve the learning ability of CNN network.

Experiment results on both VIPeR and CUHK01 datasets clearly indicate that our proposed CNN method outperforms these feature representation and metric learning algorithms, particularly when sufficient training data are provided. In our proposed method, feature learning is directly performed on the input images. Joint input branch of the lower level layers designed in the framework transforms the input images gradually into the higher-level representation with more refined features without dramatic feature reduction. The linear SVM classifier layer effectively measures the similarity of representations among the people appearances.

4.5. Comparison with CNN-Based Algorithms.

In this section, we compare our method with five types of deep learning based person reidentification algorithms: FPNN [38], ImageNet + XQDA [40], FFN + XQDA [40], Deep_CNN [50], and DML [39]. ImageNet + XQDA algorithm is the combination of ImageNet feature and XQDA metric learning. We compare our method with it on both of VIPeR and CUHK01 datasets. FPNN and FFN + XQDA network model were trained on large-scale CUHK dataset because the other existing datasets are too small to train deep networks. Therefore, we compare our method with these two networks on CUHK01 and with DML on VIPeR dataset. It is notable that the train setting on CUHK01 of FPNN conducted in a different setting, with 871 pedestrians chosen for training and 100 for testing. Figures 4(d) and 5(d) and Tables 8 and 9 show the result of our experiments, and our method still achieves the best performance among these CNN-based approaches. The matching rate of our method on rank-1 outperforms ImageNet + XQDA more than 10% on both of VIPeR and CUHK01 datasets, far surpassing that of FPNN and Deep_CNN, which were only 27.87% and 12.5% separately.

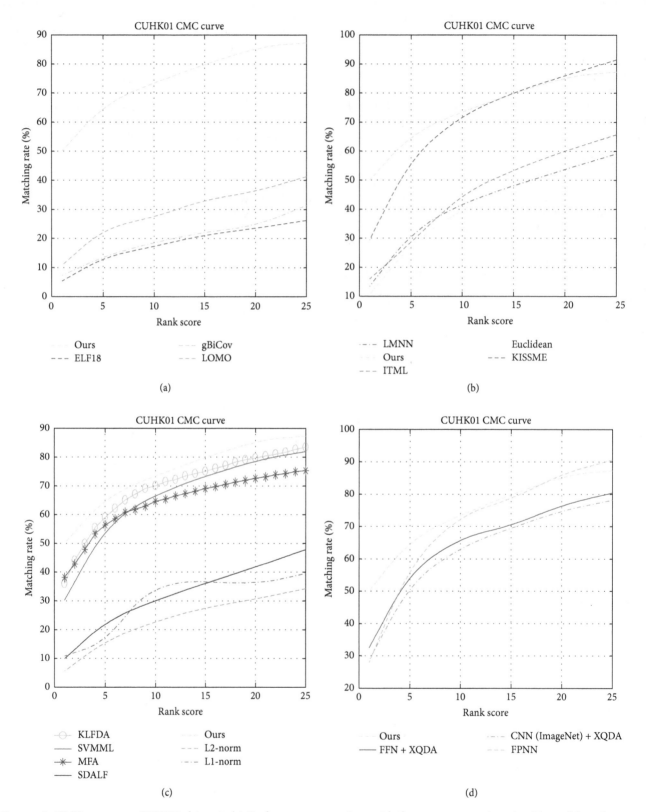

FIGURE 5: CMC curves on CUHK01 data set. (a) Performance comparison with feature representation algorithms; (b) performance comparison with metric learning algorithms; (c) performance comparison with other state-of-the-art algorithms; (d) performance comparison with other CNN-based algorithms.

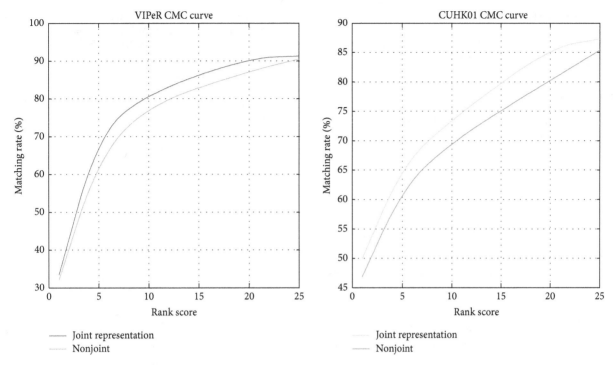

FIGURE 6: Performance comparison with two branches input method using CMC curves on VIPeR and CUHK01 datasets.

4.6. Superiority of Joint Representation Learning. Many previous works on deep learning of person reidentification share the common input framework that they extract features from two images separately. As mentioned above, joint representation learning is easier to avoid features ignored and hidden when they are extracted independently. To validate the effectiveness of our proposed framework, we compare it with two branches on VIPeR dataset and CUHK01 dataset. The CMC curves in Figure 6 show that joint representation learning method consistently surpasses methods which have two branches, thereby demonstrating the good performance of our method depending on joint representation learning.

4.7. Superiority of Linear SVM Layer. In this paper, we introduce linear SVM to replace the traditional softmax activation function to measure the similarity of the comparing pair. We also perform experiments to evaluate the contribution of our linear SVM layer. We employ a softmax layer to replace the last linear SVM layer with the other layers left unchanged. In this way, the deep network is used to assess whether two input images belonged to the same person. The experiments are conducted on the CUHK01 dataset. The results in Figure 7 show that the linear SVM layer is more suitable for person reidentification problem than softmax layer.

5. Conclusion

In this paper, we present an effective linear Support Vector Machines network based on joint representation for person reidentification. The proposed model introduces L2-SVM to replace traditional softmax layer to deal with rank-like comparison problem. Instead of using the Siamese network to train a pair of input images, we use joint representation learning strategy to avoid designing new network architecture with two entrances. Extensive experiments on two challenging person reidentification datasets (VIPeR and CUHK01) demonstrate the effectiveness of our proposed approach. In the future, we intend to adapt our method on video sequence data and promote the efficiency of reidentification.

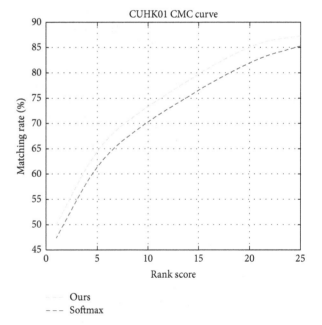

FIGURE 7: Performance comparison with softmax layer using CMC curves on CUHK01 datasets.

Conflicts of Interest

The authors declare that there are no conflicts of interest regarding the publication of this paper.

Acknowledgments

This work was supported by the Unmanned Equipment Intelligent Control Support Software System (Grant no. 2015ZX01041101).

References

[1] F. Shen, C. Shen, X. Zhou, Y. Yang, and H. T. Shen, "Face image classification by pooling raw features," *Pattern Recognition*, vol. 54, pp. 94–103, 2014.

[2] F. Shen, C. Shen, A. van den Hengel, and Z. Tang, "Approximate least trimmed sum of squares fitting and applications in image analysis," *IEEE Transactions on Image Processing*, vol. 22, no. 5, pp. 1836–1847, 2013.

[3] Y. Yao, J. Zhang, F. Shen, X. Hua, J. Xu, and Z. Tang, "Exploiting Web Images for Dataset Construction: A Domain Robust Approach," *IEEE Transactions on Multimedia*, vol. 19, no. 8, pp. 1771–1784, 2017.

[4] Y. Yao, J. Zhang, F. Shen, X. Hua, J. Xu, and Z. Tang, "A new web-supervised method for image dataset constructions," *Neurocomputing*, vol. 236, pp. 23–31, 2017.

[5] F. Shen, X. Zhou, Y. Yang, J. Song, H. T. Shen, and D. Tao, "A fast optimization method for general binary code learning," *IEEE Transactions on Image Processing*, vol. 25, no. 12, pp. 5610–5621, 2016.

[6] F. Shen, C. Shen, Q. Shi, A. van den Hengel, Z. Tang, and H. T. Shen, "Hashing on nonlinear manifolds," *IEEE Transactions on Image Processing*, vol. 24, no. 6, pp. 1839–1851, 2015.

[7] Y. Yao, X.-S. Hua, F. Shen, J. Zhang, and Z. Tang, "A domain robust approach for image dataset construction," in *Proceedings of the 24th ACM Multimedia Conference, MM 2016*, pp. 212–216, gbr, October 2016.

[8] Y. Yao, J. Zhang, F. Shen, X. Hua, J. Xu, and Z. Tang, "Automatic image dataset construction with multiple textual metadata," in *Proceedings of the 2016 IEEE International Conference on Multimedia and Expo, ICME 2016*, usa, July 2016.

[9] D. Cheng, Y. Gong, S. Zhou, J. Wang, and N. Zheng, "Person re-identification by multi-channel parts-based cnn with improved triplet loss function," *Computer Vision and Pattern Recognition*, pp. 1335–1344, 2016.

[10] L. Ren, J. Lu, J. Feng, and J. Zhou, "Multi-modal uniform deep learning for RGB-D person re-identification," *Pattern Recognition*, vol. 72, pp. 446–457, 2017.

[11] S. Gong, M. Cristani, S. Yan, and C. C. Loy, "Person Re-identification," *Advances in Computer Vision and Pattern Recognition*, 2014.

[12] B. Ma, Y. Su, and F. Jurie, "Covariance descriptor based on bio-inspired features for person re-identification and face verification," *Image and Vision Computing*, vol. 32, no. 6-7, pp. 379–390, 2014.

[13] S. Khamis, C.-H. Kuo, V. K. Singh, V. D. Shet, and L. S. Davis, "Joint learning for attribute-consistent person re-identification," *Lecture Notes in Computer Science (including subseries Lecture Notes in Artificial Intelligence and Lecture Notes in Bioinformatics)*, vol. 8927, pp. 134–146, 2015.

[14] W. Li and X. Wang, "Locally aligned feature transforms across views," in *Proceedings of the 26th IEEE Conference on Computer Vision and Pattern Recognition, CVPR 2013*, pp. 3594–3601, usa, June 2013.

[15] B. Ma, Y. Su, and F. Jurie, "BiCov: A novel image representation for person re-identification and face verification," in *Proceedings of the 2012 23rd British Machine Vision Conference, BMVC 2012*, gbr, September 2012.

[16] K. Q. Weinberger, J. Blitzer, and L. K. Saul, "Distance metric learning for large margin nearest neighbor classification," *Advances in Neural Information Processing Systems*, pp. 1473–1480.

[17] R. Zhao, W. Ouyang, and X. Wang, "Person re-identification by salience matching," in *Proceedings of the 2013 14th IEEE International Conference on Computer Vision, ICCV 2013*, pp. 2528–2535, aus, December 2013.

[18] M. Kostinger, M. Hirzer, P. Wohlhart, P. M. Roth, and H. Bischof, "Large scale metric learning from equivalence constraints," in *Proceedings of the IEEE Conference on Computer Vision and Pattern Recognition (CVPR '12)*, pp. 2288–2295, IEEE, Providence, RI, USA, June 2012.

[19] K. Jüngling, C. Bodensteiner, and M. Arens, "Person re-identification in multi-camera networks," in *Proceedings of the 2011 IEEE Computer Society Conference on Computer Vision and Pattern Recognition Workshops, CVPRW 2011*, usa, June 2011.

[20] W.-S. Zheng, S. Gong, and T. Xiang, "Associating groups of people," in *Proceedings of the 2009 20th British Machine Vision Conference, BMVC 2009*, gbr, September 2009.

[21] N. Gheissari, T. B. Sebastian, P. H. Tu, J. Rittscher, and R. Hartley, "Person reidentification using spatiotemporal appearance," in *Proceedings of the 2006 IEEE Computer Society Conference on Computer Vision and Pattern Recognition, CVPR 2006*, pp. 1528–1535, usa, June 2006.

[22] M. Guillaumin, J. Verbeek, and C. Schmid, "Is that you? Metric learning approaches for face identification," in *Proceedings of the 12th International Conference on Computer Vision (ICCV '09)*, pp. 498–505, Kyoto, Japan, October 2009.

[23] R. Girshick, J. Donahue, T. Darrell, and J. Malik, "Rich feature hierarchies for accurate object detection and semantic segmentation," in *Proceedings of the 27th IEEE Conference on Computer Vision and Pattern Recognition (CVPR '14)*, pp. 580–587, Columbus, Ohio, USA, June 2014.

[24] A. Krizhevsky, I. Sutskever, and G. E. Hinton, "Imagenet classification with deep convolutional neural networks," in *Proceedings of the 26th Annual Conference on Neural Information Processing Systems (NIPS '12)*, pp. 1097–1105, Lake Tahoe, Nev, USA, December 2012.

[25] Y. Sun, Y. Chen, X. Wang, and X. Tang, "Deep learning face representation by joint identification-verification," in *Proceedings of the 28th Annual Conference on Neural Information Processing Systems 2014, NIPS 2014*, pp. 1988–1996, can, December 2014.

[26] S.-Z. Chen, C.-C. Guo, and J.-H. Lai, "Deep ranking for person re-identification via joint representation learning," *IEEE Transactions on Image Processing*, vol. 25, no. 5, pp. 2353–2367, 2016.

[27] Y. Tang, *Deep Learning Using Support Vector Machines*, CoRR, 2013.

[28] M. Farenzena, L. Bazzani, A. Perina, V. Murino, and M. Cristani, "Person re-identification by symmetry-driven accumulation of local features," in *Proceedings of the IEEE Conference on Computer Vision and Pattern Recognition (CVPR '10)*, pp. 2360–2367, IEEE, San Francisco, Calif, USA, June 2010.

[29] R. Zhao, W. Ouyang, and X. Wang, "Unsupervised salience learning for person re-identification," in *Proceedings of the 26th IEEE Conference on Computer Vision and Pattern Recognition (CVPR '13)*, pp. 3586–3593, IEEE, Portland, Ore, USA, June 2013.

[30] T. Ojala, M. Pietikäinen, and T. Mäenpää, "Multiresolution gray-scale and rotation invariant texture classification with local binary patterns," *IEEE Transactions on Pattern Analysis and Machine Intelligence*, vol. 24, no. 7, pp. 971–987, 2002.

[31] L. Bazzani, M. Cristani, A. Perina, and V. Murino, "Multiple-shot person re-identification by chromatic and epitomic analyses," *Pattern Recognition Letters*, vol. 33, no. 7, pp. 898–903, 2012.

[32] Y. Yang, J. Yang, J. Yan, S. Liao, D. Yi, and S. Z. Li, "Salient color names for person re-identification," *Lecture Notes in Computer Science (including subseries Lecture Notes in Artificial Intelligence and Lecture Notes in Bioinformatics)*, vol. 8689, no. 1, pp. 536–551, 2014.

[33] S. Liao, Y. Hu, X. Zhu, and S. Z. Li, "Person re-identification by Local Maximal Occurrence representation and metric learning," in *Proceedings of the IEEE Conference on Computer Vision and Pattern Recognition, CVPR 2015*, pp. 2197–2206, usa, June 2015.

[34] F. Xiong, M. Gou, O. Camps, and M. Sznaier, "Person re-identification using kernel-based metric learning methods," *Lecture Notes in Computer Science (including subseries Lecture Notes in Artificial Intelligence and Lecture Notes in Bioinformatics)*, vol. 8695, no. 7, pp. 1–16, 2014.

[35] S. Chopra, R. Hadsell, and Y. LeCun, "Learning a similarity metric discriminatively, with application to face verification," in *Proceedings of the IEEE Computer Society Conference on Computer Vision and Pattern Recognition (CVPR '05)*, pp. 539–546, IEEE, Washington, DC, USA, June 2005.

[36] W. S. Zheng, S. Gong, and T. Xiang, "Person re-identification by probabilistic relative distance comparison," in *Proceedings of the IEEE Conference on Computer Vision and Pattern Recognition (CVPR '11)*, pp. 649–656, June 2011.

[37] B. Prosser, W.-S. Zheng, S. Gong, and T. Xiang, "Person re-identification by support vector ranking," in *Proceedings of the 2010 21st British Machine Vision Conference, BMVC 2010*, gbr, September 2010.

[38] W. Li, R. Zhao, T. Xiao, and X. Wang, "DeepReID: Deep filter pairing neural network for person re-identification," in *Proceedings of the 27th IEEE Conference on Computer Vision and Pattern Recognition, CVPR 2014*, pp. 152–159, usa, June 2014.

[39] D. Yi, Z. Lei, S. Liao, and S. Z. Li, "Deep metric learning for person re-identification," in *Proceedings of the 22nd International Conference on Pattern Recognition, ICPR 2014*, pp. 34–39, swe, August 2014.

[40] T. Matsukawa and E. Suzuki, "Person re-identification using CNN features learned from combination of attributes," in *Proceedings of the 2016 23rd International Conference on Pattern Recognition (ICPR)*, pp. 2428–2433, Cancun, December 2016.

[41] E. Ahmed, M. Jones, and T. K. Marks, "An improved deep learning architecture for person re-identification," in *Proceedings of the IEEE Conference on Computer Vision and Pattern Recognition, CVPR 2015*, pp. 3908–3916, usa, June 2015.

[42] D. Gray and H. Tao, "Viewpoint invariant pedestrian recognition with an ensemble of localized features," in *Computer Vision—ECCV 2008: 10th European Conference on Computer Vision, Marseille, France, October 12–18, 2008, Proceedings, Part I*, vol. 5302 of *Lecture Notes in Computer Science*, pp. 262–275, Springer, Berlin, Germany, 2008.

[43] J. V. Davis, B. Kulis, P. Jain, S. Sra, and I. S. Dhillon, "Information-theoretic metric learning," in *Proceedings of the 24th International Conference on Machine Learning (ICML '07)*, pp. 209–216, June 2007.

[44] W.-S. Zheng, S. Gong, and T. Xiang, "Reidentification by relative distance comparison," *IEEE Transactions on Pattern Analysis and Machine Intelligence*, vol. 35, no. 3, pp. 653–668, 2013.

[45] A. Mignon and F. Jurie, "PCCA: a new approach for distance learning from sparse pairwise constraints," in *Proceedings of the IEEE Conference on Computer Vision and Pattern Recognition (CVPR '12)*, pp. 2666–2672, June 2012.

[46] Z. Li, S. Chang, F. Liang, T. S. Huang, L. Cao, and J. R. Smith, "Learning locally-adaptive decision functions for person verification," in *Proceedings of the 26th IEEE Conference on Computer Vision and Pattern Recognition, CVPR 2013*, pp. 3610–3617, usa, June 2013.

[47] X. Liu, M. Song, D. Tao, X. Zhou, C. Chen, and J. Bu, "Semi-supervised coupled dictionary learning for person re-identification," in *Proceedings of the 27th IEEE Conference on Computer Vision and Pattern Recognition, CVPR 2014*, pp. 3550–3557, usa, June 2014.

[48] C. Liu, S. Gong, C. C. Loy, and X. Lin, "Person re-identification: what features are important?" in *Computer Vision—ECCV 2012. Workshops and Demonstrations: Florence, Italy, October 7–13, 2012, Proceedings, Part I*, vol. 7583 of *Lecture Notes in Computer Science*, pp. 391–401, Springer, Berlin, Germany, 2012.

[49] X. Wang, G. Doretto, T. Sebastian, J. Rittscher, and P. Tu, "Shape and appearance context modeling," in *Proceedings of the 2007 IEEE 11th International Conference on Computer Vision, ICCV*, bra, October 2007.

[50] G. Zhang, J. Kato, Y. Wang, and K. Mase, "People re-identification using deep convolutional neural network," in *Proceedings of the 9th International Conference on Computer Vision Theory and Applications, VISAPP 2014*, pp. 216–223, prt, January 2014.

11

A No-Reference Modular Video Quality Prediction Model for H.265/HEVC and VP9 Codecs on a Mobile Device

Debajyoti Pal and Vajirasak Vanijja

IP Communications Laboratory, School of Information Technology, King Mongkut's University of Technology Thonburi, Bangkok 10140, Thailand

Correspondence should be addressed to Debajyoti Pal; debajyoti.pal@gmail.com

Academic Editor: Constantine Kotropoulos

We propose a modular no-reference video quality prediction model for videos that are encoded with H.265/HEVC and VP9 codecs and viewed on mobile devices. The impairments which can affect video transmission are classified into two broad types depending upon which layer of the TCP/IP model they originated from. Impairments from the network layer are called the network QoS factors, while those from the application layer are called the application/payload QoS factors. Initially we treat the network and application QoS factors separately and find out the 1:1 relationship between the respective QoS factors and the corresponding perceived video quality or QoE. The mapping from the QoS to the QoE domain is based upon a decision variable that gives an optimal performance. Next, across each group we choose multiple QoS factors and find out the QoE for such multifactor impaired videos by using an additive, multiplicative, and regressive approach. We refer to these as the integrated network and application QoE, respectively. At the end, we use a multiple regression approach to combine the network and application QoE for building the final model. We also use an Artificial Neural Network approach for building the model and compare its performance with the regressive approach.

1. Introduction

There has been a rapid advance in various video services and their applications, like video telephony, High Definition (HD) and Ultra High Definition (UHD) television, Internet protocol television (IPTV), and mobile multimedia streaming in recent years. Thus, quality assessment of videos that are being streamed and watched online has become an area of active research. As per a report published in [1], video streaming over the Internet is becoming increasingly popular on devices having small form factor screens (4 inches to 6 inches). Most of the mobile phones as of today have a screen resolution of at least 1280 × 720 pixels (HD) or 1920 × 1080 pixels (Full HD). Some phones even have a higher screen resolution of 2556 × 1440 (2K resolution) pixels. Price of the mobile phones has also fallen to a great extent which makes them a perfect candidate for watching videos on the go. Advancements in mobile hardware coupled with decreasing costs have resulted in a greater demand for high resolution video content that

could be watched anytime. A report published in [2] confirms this fact stating that presently video traffic constitutes more than 55% of the overall Internet traffic. In order to mitigate the problem of increased load on the existing network infrastructure, sophisticated video compression techniques have been developed that provide an excellent viewing quality without consuming a large network bandwidth during the streaming sessions. H.265/HEVC (High Efficiency Video Coding) developed by the International Telecommunication Union's (ITU) Video Coding Expert Group (VCEG) and VP9 by Google Inc. are prime examples of such modern codecs. Both of them provide an excellent quality to compression ratio.

Quality of Service (QoS) has been defined by ITU as *"a characteristic of a telecommunications service that bear on its ability to satisfy stated and implied needs of the users of the service"* [3]. On the contrary, the concept of Quality of Experience (QoE) is multidimensional that is influenced by a number of systems, users, and other contextual factors

[4]. For the purpose of successful QoE management by the Internet service providers (ISPs), it is extremely important to understand the relationships between QoE and the underlying network and application-layer QoS parameters. In fact, QoS parameters are the most important business relevant parameters for the ISPs [5]. Therefore, in order to measure the user satisfaction, there is a need for mapping from the QoS to the QoE domain.

In this paper, a video quality prediction model has been presented for videos encoded with H.265/HEVC and VP9 codecs and viewed on mobile devices that are connected to a Wireless Local Area Network (WLAN-802.11 ac standard). We have considered only the infrastructure mode. A total of seven QoS parameters are considered (four representing the network QoS and the remaining three used for application QoS). Large scale subjective tests are carried out for the purpose of model building. Packet loss, jitter, throughput, and auto resolution scaling are the network QoS factors taken into consideration, while bit rate, frame rate, and video resolution are the application QoS factors taken into account. In order to introduce a modularity concept, the video model has been built in three stages. In stages one and two the video quality model for the network and application QoS factors is built separately one after another independent of each other. In stage three, the video models from stage one and stage two are combined together to obtain the final comprehensive model. This modular approach provides more flexibility since it treats the network and application video models independently. This modular feature should be particularly useful to the ISPs because if any change or modification in the model is required afterwards; then they can work on only those specific factors without having to disturb the remaining ones. Detailed methodology has been provided in a later section.

Rest of the paper is organized as follows. In Section 2, related literature review is done. Section 3 presents the detailed methodology for building the video model. Section 4 illustrates the subjective tests that have been conducted along with the relevant data analysis. Sections 5 and 6 present the video model for network and application QoS factors, respectively, while Section 7 presents the final integrated video model. Section 8 introduces the Artificial Neural Network (ANN) approach for model building along with the relevant statistics. Finally, in Section 9, we provide the conclusion and the scope for future work.

2. Literature Review

In this section, we present a brief review of all the relevant works.

2.1. Video Service Quality Estimation Methods. There are two main techniques for video quality assessment: subjective and objective methods. A concise report on both techniques is provided in the following paragraphs.

Till date, subjective tests are considered to be the most accurate video quality assessment method. Typically, in a subjective test, users are gathered together in a room to view some video samples. Then they are asked to rate those samples (typically on a scale of 1 to 5), where 1 denotes the worst and

5 the best quality. The rating which is given by the users is commonly referred to as the Mean Opinion Score (MOS), also known as the QoE. ITU has several recommendations where the procedure for conducting subjective tests has been laid down in detail. Different techniques are available for conducting the subjective tests depending upon the application requirement. Absolute Category Rating (ACR), Absolute Category Rating with Hidden Reference (ACR-HR), Degradation Category Rating (DCR), and Pair Comparison (PC) are some of the most frequently employed techniques. Both ACR and ACR-HR are examples of single stimulus method where only one video sequence is shown at a time. DCR and PC are examples of double stimulus methods where both the original and the degraded video sequences are shown to the users in pair. Further detail about these techniques can be obtained from relevant ITU recommendations [6–8]. The recommendations suggest using video sequences having duration of at least 10 seconds. However, the effect of using videos lesser or greater than 10 seconds on the subjective quality assessment has not been accounted for [9]. Papers [10, 11] provide a detailed comparison among the different subjective techniques. Although subjective methods are very accurate, they are time consuming and very expensive to be carried out. Hence, there is a necessity of objective approach.

Objective techniques are based upon certain algorithms or mathematical formulae that try to predict the perceived video quality by a human observer. An objective approach can be of intrusive or nonintrusive type. Intrusive methods are also known as Full Reference (FR) techniques, because the evaluation process requires both the original and degraded video sequences to be present. Peak Signal to Noise Ratio (PSNR), Structural Similarity Index (SSIM), and Video Quality Metric (VQM) are examples of such a scheme [12–15]. There is another variation to the intrusive method where only a subset of the original video sequence is presented to the user for the purpose of quality evaluation. This is referred to as the Reduced Reference (RR) method [16]. Nonintrusive methods do not require the presence of any original video sequence; hence, they are also called no-reference (NR) methods. The models presented in [17–19] represent such a technique. For a video streaming scenario, a NR model is more preferable since it involves minimum overhead as it does not require the presence of the original video sequence. Further detail about these methods can be obtained from [20].

There is a third technique that is increasingly becoming popular in recent years. It involves a combination of the subjective and objective approach as mentioned above. The very recently published ITU-T Recommendation P.1203 is an example of such an approach [21].

2.2. Studies of Correlation between QoS and QoE. Due to the high cost of the subjective tests and relatively low accuracy of the objective algorithms, researchers have tried to estimate the QoE from various QoS factors. ITU-T Recommendation P.861 estimates the listening quality from various voice transmission factors and establishes a nonlinear relationship between the two [22]. Similar work has been done by authors in [23], where they discuss in detail how the human satisfaction of HTTP service (web browsing) is affected by two network QoS parameters, namely, network bandwidth and latency. A nonlinear relationship between the QoS and QoE for web user satisfaction has been proposed by the authors. However, both the works consider only the network QoS parameters and it needs to be seen if the same type of relationship hold true for video traffic also.

A generic formula in which QoE and QoS parameters are connected through an exponential relationship called the IQX hypothesis is presented by the authors in [24]. The IQX hypothesis is tested for two different services: voice over IP (VoIP) and web browsing for different values of packet loss, jitter, and reordering conditions. However, the validity of IQX hypothesis for other interactive and streaming applications like video is a matter of further investigation. Similarly, the authors in [25] explain the relationship between QoE and QoS in terms of the Weber-Fechner Law (WFL) that is an important principle in psychophysics. The testing environment is limited to a VoIP system and a mobile broadband application scenario involving web browsing, e-mails, and downloads only. Both IQX hypothesis and WFL have been tested for VoIP application and web services only and they are found to be just the inverse of each other. With respect to video streaming, other factors like video resolution, type of the codec used for compression, nature of the video content, and so on are very important towards determining the video QoE. However, they cannot be taken into account by the IQX hypothesis or WFL since they explain only the network QoS factors.

An adaptive QoE measurement scheme for IPTV services has been presented in paper [26]. The authors propose a Video Intelligent Probe (VIP) that integrates the analysis of video processing and network parameters together. The assessment is based upon the quality of images contained in the video signal, packet loss, and the packet arrival time. Similar work has been done by authors in [27] for an IPTV service where the effects of delay, jitter, packet loss rate, error rate, bandwidth, and signal success rate are considered. Both these works primarily take into consideration network QoS factors and they are targeted towards watching videos on a big screen like television. However, there is a considerable difference in the viewing experience on a television and small form factor mobile devices [28, 29].

Authors in [30] evaluate the video quality on a mobile platform considering the impact of spatial resolution, temporal resolution, and the quantization step size. All the videos that are considered have a resolution of 4 CIF (704 × 576) only. QoE modeling for VP9 and H.265 encoded videos on mobile devices have been investigated by the authors in [31]. Although application QoS factors like bit rate and video resolution have been taken into consideration, they do not include any network QoS factors. Also, the effect of frame rate has not been taken into account. A content based video quality prediction model over wireless local area networks that combine both application and network level parameters has been proposed in [32]. Bit rate and frame rate are the application QoS factors considered, whereas only the effect of packet loss has been taken into account as the network QoS factor across a variety of video content. Similar models have also been proposed in [33–36].

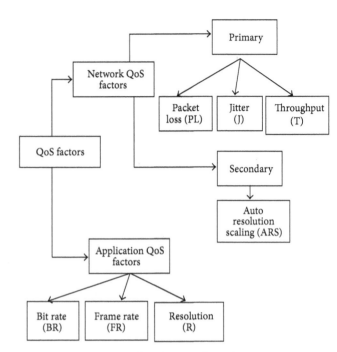

FIGURE 1: Classification of QoS factors.

A Dynamic Adaptive Streaming over HTTP (DASH) based multiview video streaming system that can minimize the view-switching delay by employing proper buffer control, parallel streaming, and server push schemes has been presented by authors in [37]. Similar HTTP based video streaming for long-term evolution (LTE) cellular networks has been proposed in [38]. Authors in [39–41] try to predict the video QoE for a DASH based video streaming scenario. Papers [42–44] provide an excellent survey on the QoE estimation techniques in place for a video streaming scenario in general.

From this section, we conclude that a lot of research has been done on the quality estimation of videos. The factors taken into consideration belong either to the application layer or the network layer of the TCP/IP protocol suite. Some authors who have considered an effect of both use low resolution videos encoded with older generation codecs like MPEG-2 and H.264/AVC. Also, very little work has been done with respect to video quality estimation on mobile devices. Considering the tremendous and ever increasing popularity of online video streaming services, it is the need of the hour to develop a comprehensive quality prediction model which takes into account factors from both the network and application layers for videos that have been encoded with the current generation H.265/HEVC and VP9 codecs on a mobile device.

3. Methodology

3.1. Problem Statement. In a video streaming service, there are several factors that affect the visual quality as perceived by the end users. These QoS factors can be grouped under the category of network and application QoS factors. Figure 1 gives a detailed classification of the factors that we have

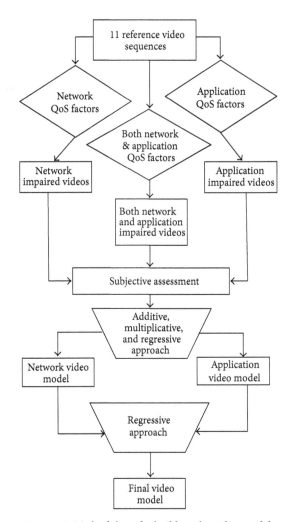

FIGURE 2: Methodology for building the video model.

considered in this paper. Therefore, for our case, the network layer perceptual QoS/video model will be a function of

$$\frac{\text{Perceptual QoS}}{\text{QoE}_{\text{Network}}} = f\left(\text{PL}, \text{J}, \text{T}, \text{ARS}\right). \tag{1}$$

Similarly, in the application layer, it will be a function of

$$\frac{\text{Perceptual QoS}}{\text{QoE}_{\text{Application}}} = f\left(\text{BR}, \text{FR}, \text{R}\right). \tag{2}$$

As both $\text{QoE}_{\text{Network}}$ and $\text{QoE}_{\text{Application}}$ have the same scale (equivalent to the MOS scale of 1 to 5), hence, the overall/final video model can be expressed as

$$\text{QoE}_{\text{Overall}} = f\left(\text{QoE}_{\text{Network}}, \text{QoE}_{\text{Application}}\right). \tag{3}$$

Equations (1) and (2) are absolutely independent of each other, while (3) integrates (1) and (2) together. This is the reason that our proposed model is modular in nature. Depending upon the requirement either $\text{QoE}_{\text{Network}}$, $\text{QoE}_{\text{Application}}$, or $\text{QoE}_{\text{Overall}}$ can be obtained. Figure 2 depicts the overall methodology that is followed for building the video model.

11 reference videos are chosen from the SVT High Definition Multiformat Test Set database maintained by the Video Quality Experts Group (VQEG) [45]. These reference videos are then subjected to various types of network and application level impairments. The degraded video sequences are then shown to the users who rate them on a scale of 1 to 5. The results from the subjective test are used for creating the objective model.

We begin by mapping the individual network and application QoS factors to their corresponding QoE. Various types of fitting functions are considered, but we choose the optimal one based upon a decision variable (DV) that is discussed in a later part of the paper. After this, we find the perceived video quality due to multiple impairment factors, that is, multiple network and application QoS factors, and refer to them as $\text{QoE}_{\text{Network}}$ and $\text{QoE}_{\text{Application}}$, respectively. This is done in three steps as discussed below:

(1) In step 1, we use a weighted sum (additive) approach to find the network and application QoE by using the Analytic Hierarchy Process (AHP) algorithm and refer to them as $\text{QoE}_{\text{Add}_{(\text{Network})}}$ and $\text{QoE}_{\text{Add}_{(\text{Application})}}$, respectively. However, due to a drawback in this approach next we use a multiplicative technique.

(2) In step 2, we use a multiplicative approach to find the network and application QoE and refer to them as $\text{QoE}_{\text{Mul}_{(\text{Network})}}$ and $\text{QoE}_{\text{Mul}_{(\text{Application})}}$, respectively.

(3) In step 3, we take into account the interaction of the additive and multiplicative approaches to find the final network and application QoE denoted by $\text{QoE}_{\text{Network}}$ and $\text{QoE}_{\text{Application}}$, respectively.

The final video model $\text{QoE}_{\text{Video-Model}}$ is found out from $\text{QoE}_{\text{Network}}$ and $\text{QoE}_{\text{Application}}$ by using a multiple regression approach. Due to the widespread use of different machine learning algorithms we also find $\text{QoE}_{\text{Video-Model}}$ using an Artificial Neural Network (ANN) approach and compare the results across the two methods.

Next we discuss in detail the various QoS factors that have been considered in this paper.

3.2. Network QoS Factors. Here we provide the detail of the considered network QoS factors.

(1) Packet Loss (PL). IP packets may be discarded during their transit over the network or dropped at any intermediate nodes due to network congestion or buffer overflow. Here, we consider a random packet loss pattern as it has a significant detrimental effect on the video stream quality as compared to other types of packet losses [46]. The different packet loss levels that we have considered have been taken from the recommended range of values as suggested by ITU-T via their recommendation ITU-T Y.1541 [47] and presented in Table 4.

(2) Jitter (J). It is defined as the variable delay in receiving packets at the receiver end. It can occur due to network congestion, improper queuing, or several other factors.

(3) Throughput (T). It refers to the amount of data that is successfully transferred from one place to another in a given

time period. Its influence towards the video QoE has been well accepted by the research community.

(4) Auto Resolution Scaling (ARS). In an adaptive video streaming scenario, the videos are encoded at multiple discreet bitrates, that is, at different resolutions. For example, the most commonly used video resolution by YouTube is at 144p, 240p, 360p, 480p, 720p, or 1080p. Depending upon the available network bandwidth and other factors, a particular bitrate stream is broken into multiple segments or chunks, with each segment lasting between 2 and 10 seconds. For the sake of this research, the resolution combinations that we choose are (360p + 480p), (720p + 360p), (720p + 480p), (360p + 1080p), and (1080p + 720p). The duration of the video sequences that we use in our experiment are 10 seconds each. Considering the fact that the duration of each fragmented segment should be between 2 and 10 seconds in case of a resolution switch, we take into account only two resolution switches for a particular video playback. Higher number of resolution switches have not been considered keeping in mind the total length of the original video sequences. For the purpose of data analysis, we express the ARS factor as the ratio of a particular resolution combination to the minimum resolution combination of the videos that is used. For example, the ARS factor for (720p + 360p) combination is $(1280 \times 720 + 640 \times 360)/(640 \times 360 + 854 \times 480) = 1.8$. Similarly, for (360p + 480p), (720p + 480p), (360p + 1080p), and (1080p + 720p), the ARS factors are 1, 2.1, 3.6, and 4.7, respectively.

Now we explain how the secondary ARS factor is related to the primary ones. Auto resolution scaling is a type of adaptive bitrate streaming technique that is used by the video content providers with an aim to improve the viewing QoE. The video content provider stores the same video contents in multiple resolutions and then depending on various network factors like the available network bandwidth, extent of jitter, and the overall network loading conditions select a particular resolution for showing them to the users. Automatic switching to lower or higher resolutions than what is currently being played happens depending upon the network conditions and factors like amount of playout buffer left, video rendering capability of the viewer's device, and so on. Hence, the ARS factor that we have considered is a consequence of the primary ones.

3.3. Application QoS Factors. Bitrate, frame rate, and resolution of the source videos are the application QoS factors that are considered. The videos that are used in the experiment vary over a wide range of video content. The bitrate factor is different from the throughput one (although they are measured using the same units). Bitrate is a codec related feature, while throughput is a network property that refers to the available bandwidth at any point of time.

The perceived video quality depends on the type of video content to a great extent which has been discussed by authors in [32, 48–50]. To define the different types of video contents we have considered the Spatial Information (SI) and Temporal Information (TI) of the source videos. SI gives an indication of the amount of spatial details that each frame has

and it has a higher value for more spatially complex scenes. The SI value for every video frame has been calculated by filtering each one of them using the Sobel filter followed by computing the standard deviation. The maximum value in the frame represents the SI content of the scene. Similarly, TI values give an indication of the amount of temporal changes in a particular video sequence. It has a higher value for sequences having greater amount of motion. Equations (4) and (5) show the calculation of the SI and TI values, respectively,

$$\text{SI} = \max_{\text{time}} \left\{ \text{std}_{\text{space}} \left[\text{Sobel} \left(F_n \right) \right] \right\}, \tag{4}$$

$$\text{TI} = \max_{\text{time}} \left\{ \text{std}_{\text{space}} \left[F_n \left(i, j \right) - F_{n-1} \left(i, j \right) \right] \right\}, \tag{5}$$

where F_n is the video frame at time n, $\text{std}_{\text{space}}$ is the standard deviation across all the pixels for each filtered frame, and $\max_{\text{time}}$ is the corresponding maximum value in the considered time interval. The SI and TI values are multiplied in order to arrive at the overall content complexity of any video sequence.

The Sobel filter is implemented by convolving two 3×3 kernels over the video frame and taking the square root of the sum of the squares of the results of these convolutions. For $y = \text{Sobel}(x)$, if $x(i, j)$ denotes the pixels of the input image at the ith row and jth column, then the result of the first convolution denoted by $Gv(i, j)$ is given by

$$\begin{aligned}
Gv \left(i, j \right) = {}&-1 \times x \left(i - 1, j - 1 \right) - 2 \times x \left(i - 1, j \right) - 1 \\
&\times x \left(i - 1, j + 1 \right) + 0 \times x \left(i, j - 1 \right) + 0 \\
&\times x \left(i, j \right) + 0 \times x \left(i, j + 1 \right) + 1 \\
&\times x \left(i + 1, j - 1 \right) + 2 \times x \left(i + 1, j \right) + 1 \\
&\times x \left(i + 1, j + 1 \right).
\end{aligned} \tag{6}$$

Similarly, $Gh(i, j)$ which is the result of the second convolution is given by

$$\begin{aligned}
Gh \left(i, j \right) = {}&-1 \times x \left(i - 1, j - 1 \right) + 0 \times x \left(i - 1, j \right) + 1 \\
&\times x \left(i - 1, j + 1 \right) - 2 \times x \left(i, j - 1 \right) + 0 \\
&\times x \left(i, j \right) + 2 \times x \left(i, j + 1 \right) - 1 \\
&\times x \left(i + 1, j - 1 \right) + 0 \times x \left(i + 1, j \right) + 1 \\
&\times x \left(i + 1, j + 1 \right).
\end{aligned} \tag{7}$$

Hence, the output from the Sobel filter image at the ith row and jth column is given by

$$y \left(i, j \right) = \sqrt{\left[Gv \left(i, j \right) \right]^2 + \left[Gh \left(i, j \right) \right]^2}. \tag{8}$$

The calculations are performed for all $2 \le i \le N - 1$ and $2 \le j \le M - 1$, where N denotes the number of rows and M the number of columns.

Figure 3 shows the SI and TI values for the eleven video sequences that have been used in this paper.

TABLE 1: Video sequences used.

Seq. number	Seq. name	Frame rate	Resolution	Chroma format	Content complexity
(1)	Harbor	60 fps	1920×1080	4.2.0	1014
(2)	Ice	60 fps	1920×1080	4.2.0	756
(3)	DucksTakeOff	50 fps	1920×1080	4.2.0	2728
(4)	ParkJoy	50 fps	1920×1080	4.2.0	2450
(5)	Crew	60 fps	1920×1080	4.2.0	1053
(6)	CrowdRun	50 fps	1920×1080	4.2.0	2688
(7)	Akiyo	30 fps	1920×1080	4.2.0	255
(8)	Soccer	60 fps	1920×1080	4.2.0	2704
(9)	Foreman	30 fps	1920×1080	4.2.0	1140
(10)	Football	30 fps	1920×1080	4.2.0	2760
(11)	News	30 fps	1920×1080	4.2.0	1470

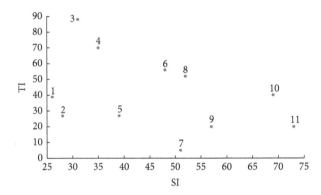

FIGURE 3: Calculated SI and TI values of chosen video sequences.

TABLE 2: Encoder configuration for H.265/HEVC codec.

Parameter	Details
Encoder version	HM 16.6
Profile	Main
Reference frames	4
R/D optimization	Enabled
GOP	8
Coding unit size/depth	64/4
Fast encoding	Enabled
Rate control	Disabled
Internal bit depth	8

For each video sequence, we have taken four different resolutions (VGA, qHD, HD, and Full HD). The resolution factor R that is considered is totally different from the ARS factor discussed previously. R refers solely to the resolution of the videos that have not been subjected to any sort of network impairments. However, the ARS factor has been introduced as a network QoS factor in order to take into consideration the effects of adaptive bitrate streaming. For the sake of data analysis, we express the resolution of a particular video sample denoted by R_{Video} in a ratio format given by

$$R_{\text{Video}} = \frac{R_{\text{Original}}}{R_{\text{Minimum}}}, \tag{9}$$

where R_{Original} refers to the actual resolution of the video under consideration and R_{Minimum} refers to its corresponding minimum resolution. For example, the resolution value for any Full HD content will be $(1920 \times 1080)/(640 \times 480) = 6.75$. Similarly, the resolution value for any VGA content will be $(640 \times 480)/(640 \times 480) = 1$. Thus, a video having a higher R_{Video} value will be at a higher resolution. Next, we discuss the experiment that has been carried out in detail and the subsequent data analysis.

4. Experiment Details

First, we present the video sequences that have been used in this research.

4.1. Video Selection. The publicly available video database of VQEG has been used for selecting our reference videos. A total of 11 sequences are taken; the details of which are shown in Table 1. All the sequences are roughly of 10-second duration each and in native YUV 4.2.0 format. The raw videos are encoded using the H.265 and VP9 codecs. Tables 2 and 3 show the encoder configuration used for both the codecs, respectively.

Figures 4(a)–4(k) show the snapshot of the videos that are considered.

4.2. Simulation Test-Bed. The simulation test-bed has been shown in Figure 5. We have created 2 sending nodes, namely, a constant bitrate (CBR) background traffic source node and a streaming server that contains all the video sequences we use encoded with the H.265 and VP9 codecs. The bitrate of the CBR has been fixed at 2 Mbps in order to simulate a realistic scenario. Both these sending nodes are connected to router A over the Internet across a 20 Mbps link. Router A is in turn connected to router B over a variable link. Router B is again connected to a wireless access point at 20 Mbps which further transmits this traffic to a mobile node at transmission speeds of up to 600 Mbps typically found in 802.11ac WLANs. No packets are dropped in the wired portion of the video delivery path. The maximum transmitted packet size is 1024 bytes. We use a random pattern for packet loss that takes six values at (0.1, 0.5, 1, 3, 5, and 10%). The effect of jitter

TABLE 3: Encoder configuration for VP9 codec.

Parameter	Details
Encoder version	Ffmpeg 3.1.3
Encoding quality	Best
Number of passes	2
Bit rate control mode	Variable bit rate (VBR defined by target bit rate)
Constrained quality (CQ) level	Same as quantization Parameter QP
Initial, optimal, and maximum buffer level	4000 ms, 5000 ms, 6000 ms
GOP size	Auto
GOP length (intraperiod)	320
Internal bit depth	8

TABLE 4: Simulation parameters.

Parameter	Value
Packet loss (%)	0.1, 0.5, 1, 3, 5, 10
Jitter (ms)	1, 2, 3, 4, 5
Throughput (Kbps)	500, 1000, 2000, 3000, 5000
Autoresolution scaling	1, 1.8, 2.1, 3.6, 4.7
Bitrate (Kbps)	500, 1000, 2000, 4000, 8000
Frame rate (fps)	10, 15, 25, 30, 50/60
Resolution	1, 1.69, 3, 6.75

TABLE 5: Viewing conditions.

Parameter	Setting
Viewing distance from screen	76 cm
Peak luminance of the screen	890 nits
Background room illumination	180 nits
Ratio of brightness of background to peak brightness of screen	0.20

has been added by introducing a fixed delay of 100 ms plus five variable delays corresponding to (1, 2, 3, 4, and 5 ms). The network throughput is varied by changing the bandwidth of the variable link between routers A and B and has been fixed at (500, 1000, 2000, 4000, and 8000 Kbps). As previously mentioned, range of all the values considered is based upon the ITU and ETSI recommendations provided in [47, 51, 52]. Values of all the parameters used in the experiment are provided in Table 4. For videos that have been impaired by a single ARS factor only or any particular application QoS factor, the simulation test-bed has not been used. In order to simulate the ARS factor, a particular video is segmented, with each segment being played back at two different resolutions. For example, in case of a video having 300 frames in total, the first 150 frames are played back at a particular resolution and the remaining 150 frames are played back at a different resolution.

The experiment has been conducted with Evalvid framework [53] and network simulator toolkit NS2 [54]. Integrating NS2 with the Evalvid platform gives us a lot of flexibility in choosing the parameters.

Next, the subjective evaluation process has been described in detail.

4.3. Subjective Evaluation. 59 participants are involved in the subjective test and they are mixed in gender. Figure 6 shows the percentage breakdown of the participants' age. Before recruiting the participants, an Ishihara color vision test has been conducted on them in order to ensure that none of them suffer from color blindness [55]. The test has been conducted in a controlled laboratory environment. It took 16 weeks to complete the entire subjective test. Table 5 gives the details

of the viewing conditions under which the test has been performed.

The subjects had to evaluate 462 video sequences that have been impaired by exactly 1 network QoS factor. The total number of network impairment conditions is 21 (6 for PL + 5 for J + 5 for T and 5 for ARS). Considering the 11 video sequences across 2 codecs (21 impaired conditions × 11 video sequences × 2 codecs), we arrive at the number 462. In order to assess the quality of videos impaired by multiple network QoS factors, we limit the number of test sequences to 176. Since carrying out a subjective test consumes considerable amount of time and effort; hence, it was not feasible to include all possible values of the different impairment combinations while presenting the test video sequences. Instead, we choose 176 specific combinations, the details of which have been shown in Table 6.

32 video sequences are impaired by all the network QoS factors, while for all the other remaining conditions, we use 16 sequences for each one. For both the single and multifactor impaired videos, exactly half the number of samples is used for model building and the rest for validation.

Similarly, for creating the application video model, we have 308 video sequences impaired by exactly 1 application QoS factor. Five different BR and FR levels, respectively, along with 4 different resolution values across 2 codecs and 11 sequences give a total of 308 combinations. For creating the multifactor impaired videos, as explained previously we have used a subset of the total possible combination. In particular, 140 sequences are used, the details of which are provided in Table 7. As before, the 140 sequences are split evenly for the purpose of model creation and validation.

The final model is created by combining all the network and application QoS factors together. Thus, we have a total of 7 different factors. Since it is not possible to let the users

FIGURE 4: Snapshot of used video sequences: (a) Harbor, (b) Ice, (c) DucksTakeOff, (d) ParkJoy, (e) Crew, (f) CrowdRun, (g) Akiyo, (h) Soccer, (i) Foreman, (j) Football, and (k) News.

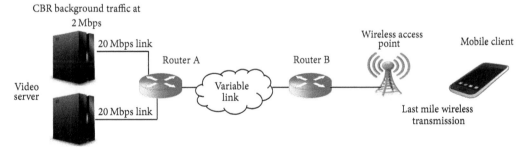

FIGURE 5: Simulation test-bed.

watch such a huge number of videos, we limit the number of impaired videos to 156. Table 8 shows the relevant details. For this case, while creating the video sequences, care has been taken to include the effect of both the network and application QoS factors for every condition. 78 sequences are being used for model creation and the rest for validation.

All the videos are presented on a Samsung Galaxy Note 5 for the purpose of evaluation. We chose this device as it has hardware level decoding capability for the H.265 and VP9 codecs. Hardware level decoding has certain advantages over software decoding. Sometimes software decoding results in a jittery/distorted playback for certain format of videos

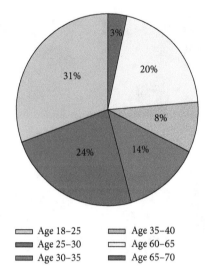

Age 18–25   Age 35–40
Age 25–30   Age 60–65
Age 30–35   Age 65–70

FIGURE 6: Breakdown of participants' ages.

TABLE 6: Impairment choice for 176 video sequences (network QoS).

Impairment combination	Total number of impairments	Number of impaired video sequences
(PL + J)	2	16
(J + T)	2	16
(T + ARS)	2	16
(PL + T)	2	16
(PL + ARS)	2	16
(J + ARS)	2	16
(PL + J + T)	3	16
(PL + J + ARS)	3	16
(J + T + ARS)	3	16
(PL + J + T + ARS)	4	32

TABLE 7: Impairment choice for 140 video sequences (application QoS).

Impairment combination	Total number of impairments	Number of impaired video sequences
(BR + FR)	2	20
(BR + R)	2	20
(FR + R)	2	20
(BR + FR + R)	3	80

TABLE 8: Sequence detail for creating final video model.

Impairment combination	Total number of impairments	Number of impaired video sequences
(PL + J + BR + FR)	4	28
(J + T + BR + FR + R)	5	30
(PL + J + T+ ARS + BR + FR)	6	20

encoded specially with newer codecs. Hardware acceleration is very useful for such cases. In case of hardware acceleration

manufacturers specifically implement multimedia chipsets as a part of the motherboard to assist with the video decoding process, whereas software decoders only use the CPU to play videos. Hence, the choice is between something specific (hardware decoders) versus something generic (software decoders). This is the exact reason why we choose Samsung Galaxy Note 5 as it has a dedicated decoder chip for H.265 and VP9 codecs.

Single stimulus ACR technique as outlined in ITU-T Recommendation P.910 has been used for designing the experiment. The total number of test videos that the participants have to watch is quiet large (1242 sequences). Approximately, each subject needs about 4 hours of time in order to complete the entire assessment procedure. We divided the entire test duration into 9 different subsessions. Five sessions were completed on the first day and the remaining 4 on the next day for each subject. Each session lasted for about 30 minutes followed by a 15-minute break in order to remove any sort of tiredness and fatigue that may arise due to the extended viewing period. The videos were presented to the subjects in a random order.

Next, we discuss the data processing method used.

4.4. Outlier Detection and Score Estimation. In case of the subjects whose scores deviate to a certain extent from the mean score, outlier detection has to be carried out in order to remove the subject bias. Roughly, the score distribution should be normal which we find out using β_2 test (by calculating the kurtosis coefficient of the function, i.e., the ratio of the fourth-order moment to the square of the second-order moment). For a particular test video sequence k, we calculate the mean $(\overline{x}_k)$, standard deviation (S_k), and the kurtosis coefficient (β_{2k}) as

$$\beta_{2k} = \frac{m_4}{m_2^2},$$

$$\text{with } m_x = \frac{\sum_{i=1}^{N} (x_{ik} - \overline{x}_k)^x}{N}, \tag{10}$$

where N is total number of subjects and x_{ik} is score given by ith user for kth test video

For each observer i we find P_i and Q_i as given below.

If $2 \leq \beta_{2k} \leq 4$, then:

$$\text{if } (x_{ik} \geq \overline{x}_k + 2s_k), P_i = P_i + 1$$
$$\text{if } (x_{ik} \leq \overline{x}_k - 2s_k), Q_i = Q_i + 1$$

Else:

$$\text{if } (x_{ik} \geq \overline{x}_k + \sqrt{20}s_k), P_i = P_i + 1$$
$$\text{if } (x_{ik} \leq \overline{x}_k - \sqrt{20}s_k), Q_i = Q_i + 1.$$

Following the above procedure, any subject i will be removed from the analysis if $(P_i - Q_i)/N > 0.05$ and $(P_i - Q_i)/(P_i + Q_i) < 0.3$. Consequently, the ratings from 4 subjects for the packet loss factor, 5 subjects for the jitter factor, 7 subjects for the ARS factor, and 3 subjects for the frame rate factor have been removed from further analysis. Based upon the user rating the QoE or MOS is calculated as

$$\frac{\text{QoE}_k}{\text{MOS}_k} = \frac{1}{N}\sum_{i=1}^{N} x_{ik},\tag{11}$$

where N is number of subjects and x_{ik} is score given by the ith user for kth video

Next, we present the network video model.

5. Network Video Model

To build the network video model first we consider the effect of single network QoS factors on the user QoE. Thereafter, we find the joint effect of all the network QoS factors considered.

5.1. Mapping for Individual QoS Factors to User QoE. We do a nonlinear curve-fitting on the subjective dataset to arrive at the relationships between the QoS factors and their corresponding QoE. An optimal fitting is chosen based upon a decision variable (DV) that is introduced here. The overall goodness-of-fit statistics is generally expressed in terms of the sum of squared error (SSE), root mean square error (RMSE), R^2 change, or the adjusted $- R^2$ change values. For SSE and RMSE, values closer to 0 indicate that the model has a smaller random error component and that the fit will be more useful for prediction. Similarly, R^2 and adjusted $- R^2$ values close to 1 indicate that a greater proportion of variance is accounted for by the model. R^2 and adjusted $- R^2$ are given as

$$R^2 = \frac{\text{SSR}}{\text{SST}} = 1 - \frac{\text{SSE}}{\text{SST}},$$

$$\text{Adjusted}R^2 = 1 - \left(\frac{n-1}{n-p}\right)\frac{\text{SSE}}{\text{SST}},\tag{12}$$

where SST is sum of squared total, n is number of observations, and p is number of regression coefficients including the intercept. Based upon the above discussion, we propose the variable DV as

$$\text{DV} = \frac{\left(R^2 \times \text{Adjusted}R^2\right)}{(\text{SSE} \times \text{RMSE})}.\tag{13}$$

Equation (13) suggests that a higher value of DV is always desirable. We considered various types of fitting models and choose the one which is optimized to get the highest value of DV possible. The goodness-of-fit statistics for each individual mapping has been shown in Table 9.

Equations (14)–(17) give the mapping from QoS to QoE domain for packet loss, jitter, throughput, and auto resolution scaling factor, respectively.

$$\text{QoE}_{\text{PL}} = a \times \exp^{(b \times \text{PL})} + c \times \exp^{(d \times \text{PL})},\tag{14}$$

$$\text{QoE}_{\text{J}} = a \times \exp^{(b \times \text{J})} + c \times \exp^{(d \times \text{J})},\tag{15}$$

$$\text{QoE}_{\text{T}} = a \times \log(\text{T}) + b,\tag{16}$$

$$\text{QoE}_{\text{ARS}} = a \times \exp^{(-b \times \text{ARS})} + c,\tag{17}$$

TABLE 9: Model fitting statistics for network factors.

Parameter	Codec	SSE	RMSE	R^2	AdjustedR^2	DV
PL	H.265	0.011	0.076	0.998	0.996	1132.51
J	H.265	0.002	0.049	0.999	0.997	8328.25
T	H.265	0.091	0.175	0.985	0.980	60.13
ARS	H.265	0.016	0.04	0.985	0.981	1509.82
P	VP9	0.006	0.059	0.999	0.997	2407.75
J	VP9	0.013	0.022	0.999	0.996	3479.03
T	VP9	0.161	0.282	0.962	0.960	20.34
ARS	VP9	0.092	0.097	0.958	0.936	100.48

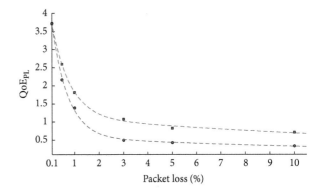

FIGURE 7: Relationship between PL (%) and QoE_{PL} (from subjective test).

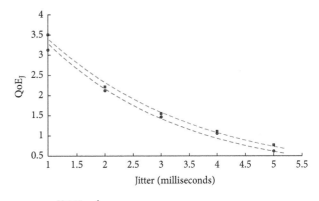

FIGURE 8: Relationship between jitter (ms) and QoE_{J} (from subjective test).

where $a, b, c,$ and d are the coefficients that are found out from curve-fitting and presented in Table 10.

Figures 7–10 show the relationship between the QoS and the corresponding QoE/MOS.

Generally we observe that, for all the factors, videos encoded with VP9 codec have a slightly better QoE as compared to the H.265 codec.

The PCC (Pearson Correlation Coefficient) has also been calculated for the set of equations obtained above for the individual factors. This has been shown in Table 11. Results

TABLE 10: Coefficient values for network factors.

Parameter	a H.265/VP9 (95% CI)	b H.265/VP9 (95% CI)	c H.265/VP9 (95% CI)	d H.265/VP9 (95% CI)
PL	3.66/2.96	−1.56/−1.38	0.57/1.13	−0.06/−0.05
J	4.51/11.62	−0.37/−3.39	-2×10^{-16}/4.4	6.73/−0.35
T	−1.39/−1.65	−7.44/−9.40	—	—
ARS	3.47/3.38	-4.4×10^{-8}/-3.7×10^{-7}	8.6×10^{-16}/0.69	—

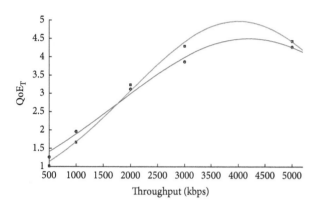

FIGURE 9: Relationship between throughput (Kbps) and $\mathrm{QoE_T}$ (from subjective test).

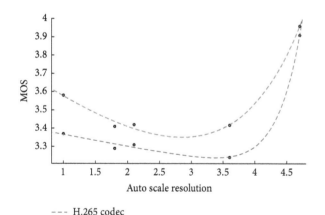

FIGURE 10: Relationship between auto resolution scaling and $\mathrm{QoE_{ARS}}$ (from subjective test).

TABLE 11: Correlational analysis of the different network QoS factors.

Parameter	PCC
PL	0.952
J	0.978
T	0.874
ARS	0.924

show that the QoE values which the equations predict have a high degree of correlation with the actual subjective scores.

Next we present the integrated QoE measurement technique from the individual QoS factors.

5.2. Integrated QoE Measurement for Network Factors. An additive and multiplicative approach is used for finding out the integrated QoE. The final network video model is obtained by carrying out a regression across both the approaches.

In an additive form, the QoE is generally represented as

$$\mathrm{QoE}\,(x_1, x_2) = w_1 \mathrm{QoE}_{x_1} + w_2 \mathrm{QoE}_{x_2}, \qquad (18)$$

where w_1 and w_2 are the weights that need to be found out for QoS factors x_1 and x_2, respectively. Not all the network QoS factors considered here have the same impact on the perceived video quality. The factor which affects more should be given a higher weight as compared to the factor which is lesser important. Before going for the additive approach, in order to explicitly find out the effect of the different network QoS parameters on the QoE, we perform ANOVA (Analysis of Variance) on the subjective dataset that has the score collected from the 176 video sequences which have been impaired by all the network factors. Table 12 shows the result from the ANOVA analysis.

Small p value ($p \leq 0.01$) suggests that all the parameters that are considered are significant. Based upon the magnitude of the p values we can make further claim that jitter impacts the MOS results the most followed by packet loss and auto resolution scaling. Throughput has the least influence. This observation is extremely important in assigning proper weights to the different factors in the additive approach.

For assigning the weights, Analytic Hierarchy Process (AHP) algorithm has been used [56, 57]. It is a well-known structured technique that is often used in multicriteria decision making systems. As the first step we obtain the criteria comparison matrix that has been shown in Table 13.

The next step is to build the normalized matrix from which we can get the weight of every factor considered. This normalized matrix has been shown in Table 14.

Thus, for the case of the network QoE in additive form (18) reduces to

$$\mathrm{QoE}_{\mathrm{Add_{(Network)}}} = 0.26\mathrm{PL} + 0.55\mathrm{J} + 0.07\mathrm{T} + 0.12\mathrm{ARS}. \qquad (19)$$

From (19), it is evident that the weight associated with the jitter factor is maximum, while it is minimum for the throughput factor. The QoE which is calculated by the additive method has a disadvantage that is now explained.

A video that has been distorted by two QoS metrics should not have a better QoE than the video which has been distorted by only one of the two QoS metrics. For example, we refer to Table 15 that shows a sample calculation.

TABLE 12: Four-way ANOVA on MOS collected from 176 video sequences.

Parameter	Sum of squares	Degrees of freedom	Mean squares	F-statistic	p value
PL	15.74	5	3.15	37.38	1.91×10^{-4}
J	8.50	4	2.12	114.56	4.2×10^{-5}
T	15.69	4	3.92	109.57	4.7×10^{-3}
ARS	1.43	4	0.36	59.70	2.08×10^{-4}

TABLE 13: Criteria comparison matrix for network factors.

Factors	PL	J	T	ARS
PL	1	0.333	5	3
J	3	1	7	5
T	0.2	0.143	1	0.333
ARS	0.333	0.2	3	1
Intermediate loading	4.533	1.676	16	9.333

TABLE 14: Normalized matrix for weight calculation.

Factors	PL	J	T	ARS
PL	0.22	0.19	0.31	0.32
J	0.66	0.59	0.43	0.53
T	0.04	0.08	0.06	0.03
ARS	0.07	0.12	0.18	0.10
Weight contribution	0.26	0.55	0.07	0.12

TABLE 15: Sample calculation of $QoE_{Add_{(Network)}}$.

Network factor	QoS value	QoE	Additive QoE
PL	1%	1.31	0.35
J	5 ms	0.62	0.34
T	2000 Kbps	3.10	0.22
ARS	1	4.07	0.49
$QoE_{Add_{(Network)}}$			1.4

TABLE 16: Sample calculation of $QoE_{Mul_{(Network)}}$.

Network factor	QoS value	QoE	Multiplicative QoE
PL	1%	1.31	0.26
J	5 ms	0.62	0.12
T	2000 Kbps	3.10	0.62
ARS	1	4.07	0.81
$QoE_{Add_{(Network)}}$			0.08

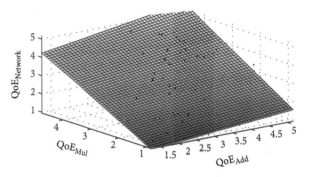

FIGURE 11: Network video model.

The QoE value for each network factor is calculated from the individual QoS to QoE mapping functions that we presented previously in (14)–(17). The additive contribution of each QoE factor is calculated by multiplying each individual network QoS factor by its weight. Finally, $QoE_{Add_{(Network)}}$ is obtained by adding the contribution of the corresponding impairment terms. For this particular case, the range of the QoE values for the individual factors varies from 0.62 to 4.07. The additive QoE value obtained is 1.4, which is within this range. However, it contradicts the fact that the QoE should not be greater than 0.62 (which is the minimum QoE obtained). Thus, clearly there is an anomaly while calculating the QoE using the additive approach.

Hence, we consider an alternative multiplicative approach. As the subjects give their opinion on a scale of 1 to 5, we present the QoE equation in multiplicative form by

$$QoE_{Mul_{(Network)}} = 5 \times \left(\frac{PL}{5}\right) \times \left(\frac{J}{5}\right) \times \left(\frac{T}{5}\right) \times \left(\frac{ARS}{5}\right). \quad (20)$$

Each individual QoS factor has been weighed on a scale of 5, while evaluating its contribution towards the final multiplicative QoE. Table 16 shows a sample calculation using (20). For the purpose of illustration, same set of QoS values have been taken for both the approaches. The $QoE_{Mul_{(Network)}}$ value obtained is 0.08 (lesser than the minimum QoE value of 0.62 corresponding to jitter).

Comparison of the QoE values obtained from both the approaches for the same set of network QoS conditions reveal that the additive approach tends to overpredict the actual viewing quality, while the multiplicative approach tends to underpredict the same. Hence, for building the final network video model $QoE_{Network}$, we use a regression based approach that combines the additive and multiplicative techniques just presented.

The regressive model is built based upon (19) and (20) along with the results of the subjective dataset that have 88 video sequences impaired by multiple network QoS factors. Equation (21) represents the network video model which is further shown in Figure 11.

$$QoE_{Network}$$
$$= 0.14 QoE_{Add_{(Network)}} + 0.81 QoE_{Mul_{(Network)}} \quad (21)$$
$$+ 0.04 \left(QoE_{Add_{(Network)}} \times QoE_{Mul_{(Network)}} \right).$$

TABLE 17: Modeling accuracy of each stage.

Model stages	R^2	Adjusted R^2
Additive	0.654	0.649
Multiplicative	0.889	0.888
Regression	0.913	0.912

TABLE 18: Coefficient values for application factors.

Parameter	a	b	c	d
BR	0.36/0.34	0.86/1.05	—	—
FR	10.27/7.1	−0.01/−0.02	−8.40/−5.1	−0.03/−0.02
R	3.47/3.51	5.15/5.98	8.64/12.2	—

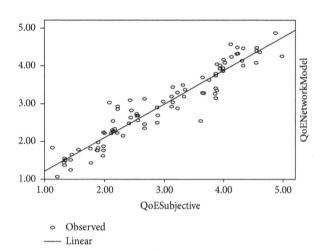

FIGURE 12: Accuracy of network video model.

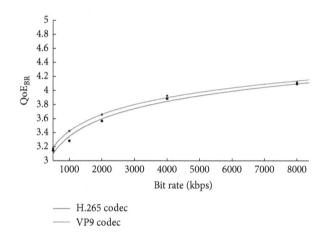

FIGURE 13: Relationship between bit rate (Kbps) and QoE_{BR} (from subjective test).

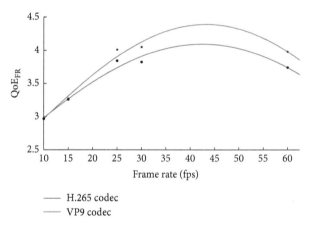

FIGURE 14: Relationship between frame rate (fps) and QoE_{FR} (from subjective test).

Equation (21) suggests that for the network video model the contribution of the multiplicative part is more as compared to the additive one. Accuracy of the network model is shown in Figure 12, while Table 17 reports the accuracy of each stage in the model building phase. While creating Figure 12, we have used the unseen subjective data that has not been used for the purpose of model building. We note that at each stage there is a gradual increase in the modeling accuracy.

Next, we present the application video model.

6. Application Video Model

A similar approach like the network video model is followed to build the application video model. First, the effects of the individual application QoS factors to the viewing quality are examined followed by an integrated application QoE estimation using the same three techniques previously presented.

6.1. Mapping for Individual Application QoS Factors to User QoE. Equations (22)–(24) show the variation of QoE with respect to bitrate, frame rate, and resolution of the impaired videos, respectively. All the mappings have been done with respect to the decision variable that has already been introduced in the previous section of the paper.

$$QoE_{BR} = a \times \log (BR) + b, \qquad (22)$$

$$QoE_{FR} = a \times \exp (b \times FR) + c \times \exp (d \times FR), \qquad (23)$$

$$QoE_R = a \times \exp \left(-\left(\frac{R-b}{c} \right)^2 \right). \qquad (24)$$

The relevant coefficients are found out from the experiment and presented in Table 18. The corresponding graphs have been shown in Figures 13–15. For all the factors VP9 codec offers a better viewing experience. Figure 14 suggests that for every video sequence there is an optimal frame rate beyond which the viewing quality does not improve and enters a saturation stage. Similarly, the effect of resolution on the perceived quality follows a Gaussian distribution as evident from (24) and Figure 15. We attribute this observation to the limitations of the human visual system and the size of the screen on which the video is being watched. In case of our experiment, the videos are viewed on a mobile device. The results clearly indicate that, for small sized screens, there will not be any substantial improvement in the viewing quality by increasing the resolution of the videos.

TABLE 19: Model fitting statistics for application factors.

Parameter	Codec	SSE	RMSE	R^2	Adjusted R^2	DV
BR	H.265	0.009	0.055	0.985	0.981	1952.01
FR	H.265	0.018	0.095	0.972	0.964	547.96
R	H.265	0.002	0.014	0.991	0.989	35003.5
BR	VP9	0.001	0.020	0.998	0.997	49750.3
FR	VP9	0.019	0.097	0.981	0.962	512.06
R	VP9	0.00004	0.006	0.999	0.992	4.1×10^6

TABLE 20: Correlational analysis of the different application QoS factors.

Parameter	PCC
BR	0.916
FR	0.941
R	0.987

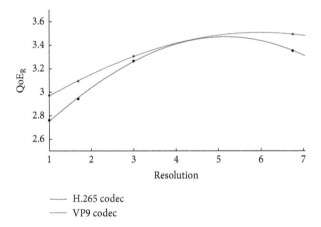

FIGURE 15: Relationship between resolution and QoE_R (from subjective test).

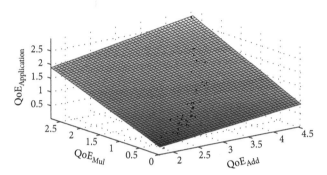

· MOSSubjectiveApplication versus QoEAdditionApplication, QoEMultiplicativeApplication

FIGURE 16: The application video model.

The model fitting statistics for the individual application factors are shown in Table 19. PCC coefficients presented in Table 20 show a relatively high correlation between the subjective scores and the calculated MOS.

Next, we present the integrated approach towards finding the application level QoE.

6.2. Integrated QoE Measurement for Application Factors.
The application video model is also built in three stages comprising the additive, multiplicative, and the regressive approach, respectively. As before, an ANOVA analysis is carried out in the beginning over the subjective dataset containing 140 videos that have been impaired by all the application QoS factors. The result of this analysis is used to choose the relative importance of the factors and assign proper weights to them based upon the AHP algorithm. The ANOVA report has been presented in Table 21. The viewing quality is most impacted by frame rate followed by bitrate and resolution, respectively.

The additive form for the application factors has been shown in (25). Intermediate criteria comparison matrix and the final normalized weight matrix that are obtained from the AHP algorithm are presented in Tables 22 and 23, respectively.

$$QoE_{Add_{(Application)}} = 0.26BR + 0.63FR + 0.11R. \quad (25)$$

The additive approach suffers from the same type of anomaly that has already been discussed in the previous section. Hence, we present the multiplicative form in

$$QoE_{Mul_{(Application)}} = 5 \times \left(\frac{BR}{5}\right) \times \left(\frac{FR}{5}\right) \times \left(\frac{R}{5}\right). \quad (26)$$

As before, the additive approach tends to overpredict the viewing quality, whereas the multiplicative approach tends to underpredict the same. Therefore, a regression based model is presented in (27) that integrates both the approaches for finding the final video quality due to the application factors. The regression model is build based on (25) and (26) along with the subjective score obtained from the 70 video sequences that have been impaired by all the concerned application QoS factors.

$$QoE_{Application}$$
$$= 0.19QoE_{Add_{(Application)}} + 0.49QoE_{Mul_{(Application)}} \quad (27)$$
$$+ 0.042\left(QoE_{Add_{(Application)}} \times QoE_{Mul_{(Application)}}\right).$$

The application video model and its accuracy are shown in Figures 16 and 17, respectively. Table 24 presents the modeling accuracy across all the three stages.

Next, we find the final integrated video model by combining the network and application video models just presented.

TABLE 21: Three-way ANOVA on MOS collected from 140 video sequences.

Parameter	Sum of squares	Degrees of freedom	Mean squares	F-statistic	p value
BR	112.458	4	28.114	44.661	1.4×10^{-4}
FR	277.677	5	55.535	118.872	5.2×10^{-5}
R	14.039	3	4.680	6.448	0.003

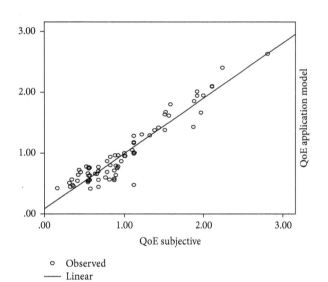

FIGURE 17: Accuracy of application video model.

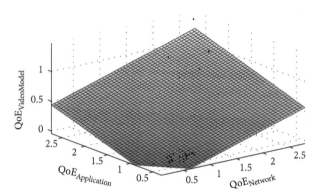

FIGURE 18: Final integrated video model.

TABLE 22: Criteria comparison matrix for application factors.

Factors	BR	FR	R
BR	1	0.33	3
FR	3	1	5
R	0.33	0.20	1
Intermediate loading	4.33	1.53	9

TABLE 23: Normalized weight matrix for application factors.

Factors	BR	FR	R
BR	0.23	0.22	0.33
FR	0.69	0.65	0.55
R	0.08	0.13	0.11
Weight contribution	0.26	0.63	0.11

TABLE 24: Modeling accuracy of each stage.

Model stages	R^2	Adjusted R^2
Additive	0.848	0.846
Multiplicative	0.904	0.903
Regression	0.912	0.910

7. Final Integrated Video Model

Till now, separate models have been built for the network and application QoS factors. With an aim to build a cross-layer model, we now combine these two models into one single entity.

For creating the final video model 78 video sequences are taken. All these video sequences are impaired by multiple network and application QoS factors considered here. Details about the video sequences are provided in Table 8. Based on the MOS scores obtained across these 78 sequences and (21) and (27); a regression approach is used to build the final video model. A stepwise method of variable entering scheme is used. During any step if we obtain a nonsignificant result, then the corresponding parameter is removed. Equation (28) represents the final video model and Figure 18 depicts the same. The coefficients of each of the contributing factors suggest that while calculating the overall video quality, the effect of the network QoE is more than the effect due to the

$$QoE_{Video-Model} = 0.38 QoE_{Network} + 0.23 QoE_{Application} - 0.19 \tag{28}$$

application QoE. R^2, adjusted R^2, and PCC values of 0.953, 0.952, and 0.976, respectively, are obtained for our final model. The modeling accuracy has been shown in Figure 19. For finding out the final model accuracy, we have used the remaining 78 sequences from the subjective dataset that have not been used for the purpose of model building.

Next, we present the same video model using an Artificial Neural Network (ANN) based approach.

8. ANN Based Video Model

Till now we have used a regression based technique for building the video quality prediction model. The model is able to predict the perceived video quality with reasonable accuracy. However, recently due to the widespread use of different machine learning techniques for analysis of data, we decided to use an Artificial Neural Network approach for building the same model limited to the same parameters

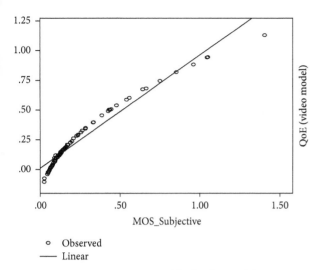

FIGURE 19: Accuracy of final video model.

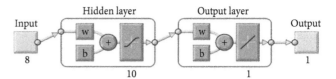

FIGURE 20: System architecture of the neural network.

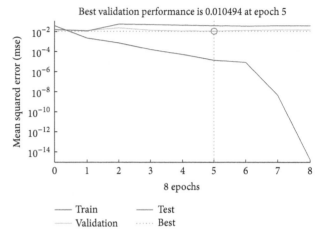

FIGURE 21: MSE variation across all sets.

TABLE 25: Weight and bias value for input layer.

PL	J	T	ARS	BR	FR	R	Codec	Bias
0.769	0.073	0.644	−0.35	0.540	−0.20	−0.53	0.228	−2.18
0.099	0.342	1.006	0.182	0.933	0.682	1.657	0.101	1.44
1.085	0.183	0.256	0.383	−0.80	−0.10	−0.01	−0.28	−1.57
1.117	0.293	0.194	0.232	1.037	0.478	0.786	0.828	−1.13
−0.90	−0.31	0.238	0.900	−0.44	−0.24	0.847	−0.36	1.13
0.775	0.508	0.893	0.537	0.880	1.801	0.644	0.025	−0.23
0.106	0.351	0.694	−0.97	1.182	−0.53	0.566	0.002	−0.28
0.505	1.085	0.276	0.462	1.710	0.161	1.542	0.094	0.34
0.169	1.144	0.094	1.648	−0.59	1.476	0.571	−0.04	0.21
0.329	0.742	0.133	0.085	0.515	0.324	0.473	1.206	0.42

TABLE 26: Weight and bias value for hidden layer.

Weight										Bias
0.53	1.26	−0.3	−0.1	00.2	1.22	0.73	0.19	0.14	1.01	−0.8

that we have considered before and evaluate the performance of both. The same subjective data consisting of 78 impaired video sequences that we have used previously is taken in this case also.

Video quality estimation using different types of neural networks has been attempted by several researchers in the past. Probabilistic Neural Networks (PNN), Backpropagation Neural Network (BPNN), Adaptive Neurofuzzy Inference System (ANFIS), and Random Neural Networks (RNN) are some of the techniques commonly used. However, as pointed out in the literature review section, video quality assessment on mobile devices has been done with low resolution videos and using only the H.264 and MPEG-2/4 video codecs. In order to estimate the video quality from subjective metrics like MOS feedforward type ANNs are most commonly used [58–61]. This is the reason why we decided to use an ANN technique for this paper keeping in mind the current research gaps and trying to overcome those.

The ANN which we have used in our work is a multilayer perceptron model having one hidden layer. Considering the number of inputs that we have, that is, 7, going for more hidden layers would have increased the overall complexity of the system unnecessarily and also resulted in overfitting problems. Hence, we opted for the one hidden layer architecture. Training of the neural network has been done using the Levenberg-Marquardt (LM) algorithm by issuing the trainlm command in MATLAB. The trainlm command is a network training function that updates the weight and biases of the different nodes according to the LM optimization technique. It is considered to be one of the fastest back propagation algorithms and is highly recommended as a first-choice supervised algorithm, although it consumes more computer memory as compared to other algorithms. For the hidden layer, we have used a hyperbolic tangent sigmoid transfer function by issuing the tansig command. For the output layer, a pure linear transfer function is used by giving the purelin command. The neural network has the same 7 parameters that we have discussed previously as input, plus one extra factor for the type of codec used. As the output, we have the score that predicts the quality of the video.

We use a 70 : 30 split ratio for the input data as training, testing, and validation sets. To find the configuration of the network that achieves the best performance, several rounds of tests are conducted by varying the number of neurons in the hidden layer and observing the output. Since we have 8 inputs and 1 output, hence we varied the number of hidden neurons from 4 to 15. Optimal performance was observed with 10 hidden nodes. The system architecture showing the best configuration has been given in Figure 20. In the figure, the symbols w and b stand for the weight and bias factors for each node, respectively. The value of w and b for our configuration set for both input and hidden layer has been provided in Tables 25 and 26, respectively.

The performance of our model across the training, testing, and validation sets has been shown in Figure 21. The best

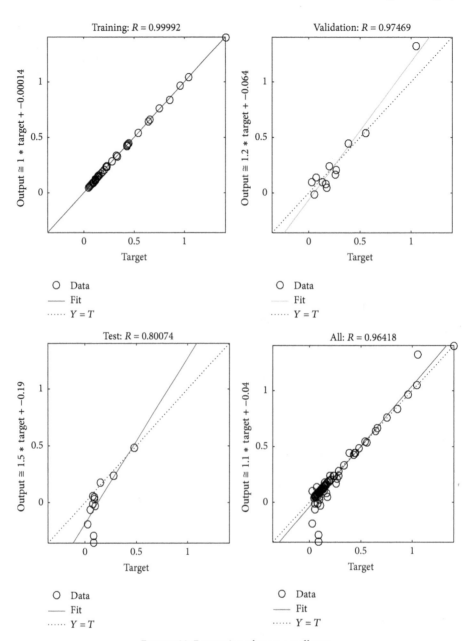

FIGURE 22: Regression plot across all sets.

validation performance is obtained at epoch 5 and marked in the figure. Also, we find that as the model learns during the training phase, the mean squared error (MSE) across all the three sets decreases and then becomes almost constant. Figure 22 shows the regression plot across all the 3 sets. The overall R^2 value for all the video sequences is 0.964 which is pretty high. The PCC value obtained is 0.984 at a significance level of less than 0.01. Compared to the regressive approach, the ANN model gives a slightly better performance.

9. Conclusion and Future Work

In this paper, we have proposed a no-reference video quality prediction model for relevant network and application QoS factors for a video streaming scenario. Our proposed model is a cross layered one as it takes into account factors from multiple layers of the TCP/IP protocol stack. At the same time, it has the unique characteristic of being a modular one. Depending upon the requirement, the model can be tuned for predicting the quality due to the network and application factors or a combination of both. At each stage, proper subjective tests have been done for the purpose of model building and validation. The ANN approach provides slightly better prediction accuracy as compared to the regression based approach.

All the videos that are used have Full HD resolution and encoded using the latest generation H.265/HEVC and VP9 codecs. Even though these codecs are capable of compressing videos at much higher resolutions up to 4K, we did not consider them in this paper due to the limited availability of the 4K video contents. With more improved network speed and widespread availability of 4K video content, we plan to investigate the effect of higher resolutions in future work. Also, all the video sequences that were used had roughly 10 seconds duration. The effect of longer video sequences has not been investigated in this research, which would be considered in the future.

Conflicts of Interest

The authors declare that there are no conflicts of interest regarding the publication of this paper.

References

[1] *2013 Video Index-TV is no longer a single screen in your Living Room*, Ooyala Corp, USA, 2013.

[2] *Cisco Global Mobile Data Traffic Forecast Update Report 2014–2019*, Cisco Corp, USA, 2016.

[3] "Definitions of Terms related to Quality of Service," ITU-T Recommendation E.800, September, 2008.

[4] P. Le Callet, S. Möller, and A. Perkis, *Qualinet White Paper on Definitions of Quality of Experience- 2012*, Lausanne, Switzerland, 2012.

[5] T. Hoßfeld, R. Schatz, M. Varela, and C. Timmerer, "Challenges of QoE management for cloud applications," *IEEE Communications Magazine*, vol. 50, no. 4, pp. 28–36, 2012.

[6] "Subjective Video Quality Assessment Methods for Multimedia Applications," ITU-T Recommendation P.910, June 200.

[7] "Methodology for the Subjective Assessment of the Quality of Television Pictures," ITU-T Recommendation BT.500, January 2012.

[8] "Methods for Subjective Determination of Transmission Quality," ITU-T Recommendation P.800, August 1996.

[9] F. M. Moss, K. Wang, F. Zhang, R. Baddeley, and D. R. Bull, "On the optimal presentation duration for subjective video quality assessment," *IEEE Transactions on Circuits and Systems for Video Technology*, vol. PP, no. 99, 2015.

[10] M. Pinson and S. Wolf, "Comparing subjective video quality testing methodologies," in *Proceedings of the Visual Communications and Image Processing 2003*, pp. 573–582, Switzerland, July 2003.

[11] D. M. Rouse, R. Pépion, P. Le Callet, and S. S. Hemami, "Trade-offs in subjective testing methods for image and video quality assessment," in *Proceedings of the Human Vision and Electronic Imaging XV*, USA, January 2010.

[12] "Reference Algorithm for Computing Peak Signal to Noise Ratio of a Processed Video Sequence with Compensation for Constant Spatial Shifts, Constant Temporal Shift, and Constant Luminance Gain and Offset," TU-T Recommendation J.340, June 2010.

[13] Z. Wang, A. C. Bovik, H. R. Sheikh, and E. P. Simoncelli, "Image quality assessment: from error visibility to structural similarity," *IEEE Transactions on Image Processing*, vol. 13, no. 4, pp. 600–612, 2004.

[14] "Objective Perceptual Video Quality Measurement Techniques for Digital Cable Television in the Presence of a Full Reference," ITU-T Recommendation J.144, March 2001.

[15] "Objective Perceptual Video Quality Measurement Techniques for Standard Definition Digital Broadcast Television in the Presence of a Full Reference," ITU-R Recommendation BT.1683, June 2004.

[16] S. Kanumuri, P. C. Cosman, A. R. Reibman, and V. A. Vaishampayan, "Modeling Packet-Loss Visibility in MPEG-2 Video," *IEEE Transactions on Multimedia*, vol. 8, no. 2, pp. 341–355, 2006.

[17] J. Søgaard, S. Forchhammer, and J. Korhonen, "No-Reference Video Quality Assessment Using Codec Analysis," *IEEE Transactions on Circuits and Systems for Video Technology*, vol. 25, no. 10, pp. 1637–1650, 2015.

[18] M. Shahid, A. Rossholm, B. Lövström, and H.-J. Zepernick, "No-reference image and video quality assessment: a classification and review of recent approaches," *Eurasip Journal on Image and Video Processing*, vol. 2014, no. 1, article no. 40, 2014.

[19] "Opinion Model for Video Telephony Applications," *ITU-T Recommendation G.1070*, July 2012.

[20] M. Mu, P. Romaniak, A. Mauthe, M. Leszczuk, L. Janowski, and E. Cerqueira, "Framework for the integrated video quality assessment," *Multimedia Tools and Applications*, vol. 61, no. 3, pp. 787–817, 2012.

[21] "Parametric Bit-stream based Quality Assessment of Progressive Download and Adaptive Audio-visual Streaming Services over Reliable Transport," ITU-T Recommendation P.1203, January 2017, ITU-T Recommendation P.1203.

[22] "Objective Quality Measurement of Telephone Band (300-3400 Hz) Speech Codec," ITU-T Recommendation P.861, August 1996.

[23] S. Khirman and P. Henricksen, "Relationship between Quality of Service and Quality of Experience for Public Internet Services," in *Proceedings of the 3rd Workshop on Passive and Active Measurement*, pp. 23–28, March 2002.

[24] M. Fiedler, T. Hossfeld, and P. Tran-Gia, "A generic quantitative relationship between quality of experience and quality of service," *IEEE Network*, vol. 24, no. 2, pp. 36–41, 2010.

[25] P. Reichl, S. Egger, R. Schatz, and A. D'Alconzo, "The logarithmic nature of QoE and the role of the Weber-Fechner law in QoE assessment," in *Proceedings of the IEEE International Conference on Communications (ICC '10)*, pp. 1–5, Cape Town, South Africa, May 2010.

[26] J. A. Lozano, A. Castro, B. Fuentes, J. M. González, and Á. Rodríguez, "Adaptive QoE measurement on Video streaming IP services," in *Proceedings of the 7th International Conference on Network and Service Management*, pp. 1–4, Paris, fra, 2011.

[27] H. J. Kim and S. G. Choi, "QoE assessment model for multimedia streaming services using QoS parameters," *Multimedia Tools and Applications*, pp. 1–13, 2013.

[28] W. Song, D. Tjondronegoro, and M. Docherty, "Exploration and optimization of user experience in viewing videos on a mobile phone," *International Journal of Software Engineering and Knowledge Engineering*, vol. 20, no. 8, pp. 1045–1075, 2010.

[29] H. Knoche, J. D. McCarthy, and M. A. Sasse, "Can small be beautiful? assessing image resolution requirements for mobile TV," in *Proceedings of the 13th ACM International Conference on Multimedia, MM 2005*, pp. 829–838, Singapore, November 2005.

[30] Y.-F. Ou, Y. Xue, Z. Ma, and Y. Wang, "A perceptual video quality model for mobile platform considering impact of spatial, temporal, and amplitude resolutions," in *Proceedings of the 2011 IEEE 10th IVMSP Workshop: Perception and Visual Signal Analysis, IVMSP 2011*, pp. 117–122, usa, June 2011.

[31] W. Song, Y. Xiao, D. Tjondronegoro, and A. Liotta, "QoE modelling for VP9 and H.265 videos on mobile devices," in *Proceedings of the 23rd ACM International Conference on Multimedia, MM 2015*, pp. 501–510, Australia, October 2015.

[32] A. Khan, L. Sun, and E. Ifeachor, "Content clustering based video quality prediction model for MPEG4 video streaming over wireless networks," in *Proceedings of the 2009 IEEE International Conference on Communications, ICC 2009*, Germany, June 2009.

[33] H. Koumaras, A. Kourtis, C.-H. Lin, and C.-K. Shieh, "A theoretical framework for end-to-end video quality prediction of MPEG-based sequences," in *Proceedings of the 3rd International Conference on Networking and Services, ICNS 2007*, Greece, June 2007.

[34] Z. Duanmu, A. Rehman, K. Zeng, and Z. Wang, "Quality-of-experience prediction for streaming video," in *Proceedings of the 2016 IEEE International Conference on Multimedia and Expo, ICME 2016*, USA, July 2016.

[35] P. Calyam, E. Ekici, C.-G. Lee, M. Haffner, and N. Howes, "A "GAP-model" based framework for online VVoIP QoE measurement," *Journal of Communications and Networks*, vol. 9, no. 4, pp. 446–455, 2007.

[36] A. Khan, L. Sun, and E. Ifeachor, "Learning models for video quality prediction over wireless local area network and universal mobile telecommunication system networks," *IET Communications*, vol. 4, no. 12, pp. 1389–1403, 2010.

[37] D. Yun and K. Chung, "DASH-based Multi-view Video Streaming System," *IEEE Transactions on Circuits and Systems for Video Technology*, pp. 1-1.

[38] S. Colonnese, F. Cuomo, T. Melodia, and I. Rubin, "A Cross-Layer Bandwidth Allocation Scheme for HTTP-Based Video Streaming in LTE Cellular Networks," *IEEE Communications Letters*, vol. 21, no. 2, pp. 386–389, 2017.

[39] K. Jia, Y. Guo, Y. Chen, and Y. Zhao, "Measuring and Predicting Quality of Experience of DASH-based Video Streaming over LTE," in *Proceedings of the 19th International Symposium on Wireless Personal Multimedia Communications (WPMC)*, pp. 102–107, Shenzhen, China, 2016.

[40] T. Maki, M. Varela, and D. Ammar, "A Layered Model for Quality Estimation of HTTP Video from QoS Measurements," in *Proceedings of the 11th International Conference on Signal-Image Technology and Internet-Based Systems, SITIS 2015*, pp. 591–598, tha, November 2015.

[41] J. Jiang, V. Sekar, and H. Zhang, "Improving fairness, efficiency, and stability in HTTP-based adaptive video streaming with festive," *IEEE/ACM Transactions on Networking*, vol. 22, no. 1, pp. 326–340, 2014.

[42] Y. Chen, K. Wu, and Q. Zhang, "From QoS to QoE: A tutorial on video quality assessment," *IEEE Communications Surveys & Tutorials*, vol. 17, no. 2, pp. 1126–1165, 2015.

[43] M. Seufert, S. Egger, M. Slanina, T. Zinner, T. Hoßfeld, and P. Tran-Gia, "A survey on quality of experience of HTTP adaptive streaming," *IEEE Communications Surveys & Tutorials*, vol. 17, no. 1, pp. 469–492, 2015.

[44] P. Juluri, T. Venkatesh, and D. Medhi, "Measurement of quality of experience of video-on-demand services: a survey," *IEEE Communications Surveys & Tutorials*, 2015.

[45] "VQEG Standard Database maintained," http://www.its.bldrdoc.gov/vqeg/downloads.aspx.

[46] J. Nightingale, Q. Wang, C. Grecos, and S. Goma, "The impact of network impairment on quality of experience (QoE) in H.265/HEVC video streaming," *IEEE Transactions on Consumer Electronics*, vol. 60, no. 2, pp. 242–250, 2014.

[47] "Network Performance Objectives for IP-based Services," TU-T Recommendation Y.1541, December 2011.

[48] K. Gu, J. Zhou, J.-F. Qiao, G. Zhai, W. Lin, and A. C. Bovik, "No-reference quality assessment of screen content pictures," *IEEE Transactions on Image Processing*, vol. 26, no. 8, pp. 4005–4018, 2017.

[49] H. Malekmohamadi, W. A. C. Fernando, and A. M. Kondoz, "Content-based subjective quality prediction in stereoscopic videos with machine learning," *IEEE Electronics Letters*, vol. 48, no. 21, pp. 1344–1346, 2012.

[50] T. Ghalut, H. Larijani, and A. Shahrabi, "Content-based video quality prediction using random neural networks for video streaming over LTE networks," in *Proceedings of the 15th IEEE International Conference on Computer and Information Technology, CIT 2015, 14th IEEE International Conference on Ubiquitous Computing and Communications, IUCC 2015, 13th IEEE International Conference on Dependable, Autonomic and Secure Computing, DASC 2015 and 13th IEEE International Conference on Pervasive Intelligence and Computing, PICom 2015*, pp. 1626–1631, gbr, October 2015.

[51] "Framework and Methodologies for the Determination and Application of QoS Parameters," ITU-T Recommendation E.802, February 2007.

[52] "Speech and Multimedia Transmission Quality (STQ); End-to-End Jitter Transmission Planning Requirements for Real Time Services in an NGN Context," ETSI TR 103 210 v.1.1.1 (2013-10) Recommendation, 2013.

[53] J. Klaue, B. Rathke, and A. Wolisz, "Evalvid–a framework for video transmission and quality evaluation," in *Computer Performance Evaluation. Modelling Techniques and Tools*, vol. 2794 of *Lecture Notes in Computer Science*, pp. 255–272, Springer, New York, NY, USA, 2003.

[54] "NS2," http://www.isi.edu/nsnam/ns/.

[55] L. H. Hardy, G. Rand, and M. C. Rittler, "Tests for the Detection and Analysis of Color-Blindness III The Rabkin Test," *Journal of the Optical Society of America*, vol. 35, no. 7, p. 481, 1945.

[56] T. L. Saaty, *The Analytic Hierarchy Process*, McGraw-Hill, New York, NY, USA, 1980.

[57] F. Zahedi, "The analytic hierarchy process-a survey of the method and its applications," *Interfaces*, vol. 16, no. 4, pp. 96–108, 1986.

[58] X. Zhang, L. Wu, Y. Fang, and H. Jiang, "A study of FR video quality assessment of real time video stream," *International Journal of Advanced Computer Science and Applications*, vol. 3, no. 6, 2012.

[59] P. Reichl, S. Egger, S. Moller et al., "Towards a comprehensive framework for QOE and user behavior modelling," in *Proceedings of the 17th International Workshop on Quality of Multimedia Experience (QoMEX '15)*, pp. 1–6, IEEE, Pylos-Nestoras, Greece, May 2015.

[60] L. Pierucci and D. Micheli, "A Neural Network for Quality of Experience Estimation in Mobile Communications," *IEEE MultiMedia*, vol. 23, no. 4, pp. 42–49, 2016.

[61] E. Danish, M. Alreshoodi, A. Fernando, B. Alzahrani, and S. Alharthi, "Cross-layer QoE prediction for mobile video based on random neural networks," in *Proceedings of the IEEE International Conference on Consumer Electronics, ICCE 2016*, pp. 227–228, USA, January 2016.

12

Deep Binary Representation for Efficient Image Retrieval

Xuchao Lu,[1] Li Song,[1,2] Rong Xie,[1,2] Xiaokang Yang,[1,2] and Wenjun Zhang[1,2]

[1]*Institute of Image Communication and Network Engineering, Shanghai Jiao Tong University, Shanghai, China*
[2]*Future Medianet Innovation Center, Shanghai, China*

Correspondence should be addressed to Li Song; song_li@sjtu.edu.cn

Academic Editor: XiangLong Liu

With the fast growing number of images uploaded every day, efficient content-based image retrieval becomes important. Hashing method, which means representing images in binary codes and using Hamming distance to judge similarity, is widely accepted for its advantage in storage and searching speed. A good binary representation method for images is the determining factor of image retrieval. In this paper, we propose a new deep hashing method for efficient image retrieval. We propose an algorithm to calculate the target hash code which indicates the relationship between images of different contents. Then the target hash code is fed to the deep network for training. Two variants of deep network, DBR and DBR-v3, are proposed for different size and scale of image database. After training, our deep network can produce hash codes with large Hamming distance for images of different contents. Experiments on standard image retrieval benchmarks show that our method outperforms other state-of-the-art methods including unsupervised, supervised, and deep hashing methods.

1. Introduction

Millions of images are uploaded and stored on the Internet every second with the rapid development of storage technique. Given a query image, how to efficiently locate a certain number of content similar images from a large database is a big challenge. Speed and accuracy need to be carefully balanced. This kind of task is content-based image retrieval (CBIR) [1–4], a technique for retrieving images by automatically derived features such as colour, texture, and shape. There are also some applications of CBIR like free-hand sketch-based image retrieval [5] whose query images are abstract and ambiguous sketches. In CBIR, derived features are not easy to store. Searching from millions and even billions of images is very time-consuming.

The binary representation of images is an emerging approach to deal with both storage and searching speed of CBIR task. This method is called hashing method, and it works in three steps. First, use a hash function to map database images (gallery images) into binary codes and store them on the storage device; the typical length is 48 bits. Then calculate the Hamming distance between the binary code of query image and stored binary codes. The images

with smallest Hamming distance to the query image indicate similar content and should be retrieved. Some examples of proposed hashing methods are in [6–11].

The critical part of hashing method is the features it uses to derive the hash code. The process of all hashing method includes feature extracting; the quality of feature directly affects the retrieval accuracy. Recently, convolutional neural network (CNN) has proved its remarkable performance in tasks highly depending on feature extracting, like image classification [12], natural language processing [13], and video analysis [14]. CNN based methods outperform previous leading ones in these areas, which shows that CNN can learn robust features representing the semantic information of images. A very natural idea is to use deep learning for learning compact binary hash codes. Following semantic hashing [15], deep hashing methods using CNN show high performance in content-based image retrieval.

In this paper, we propose a new supervised deep hashing method for learning compact hash code to perform content-based image retrieval; we call it deep binary representation (DBR). This paper is an extended version of the work [16]. Our method is an end-to-end learning framework with three main steps. The first step is to generate optimal target hash code from pointwise label information. The second step is to learn image features and hash function simultaneously through the training process of carefully designed deep network. The third step is to map image pixels to compact binary codes through a hash function and perform image retrieval. Compared to other deep hashing methods, our method has the following merits.

(1) Our deep hash network is trained with calculated target hash code. The target hash code is optimal that Hamming distance between different labels is maximized. Methods like [17] derive hash codes from a middle layer of the deep network. Our method produces hash codes from the output layer. This method is more direct and shows better performance.

(2) Our training process is pointwise; one training sample consists of one image and one target hash code. Compared to pairwise [18] and triplet methods [19, 20] whose training process needs two images or three images as one training sample, the training time is largely shortened. Our training process is a linear time algorithm, not exponential time algorithm for methods mentioned above.

(3) Our method reaches state-of-the-art performance on both small image datasets like CIFAR-10 and relatively large datasets like ImageNet. For large image datasets, we further propose an architecture based on inception-v3 net [21]; we call it DBR-v3. DBR-v3 achieves state-of-the-art performance on image retrieval of ImageNet dataset. When we apply DBR-v3 to CIFAR-10, a 15 percent performance improvement is achieved.

2. Overview of Hashing Methods

Hashing methods include data-independent methods [22] and data-dependent methods [10, 23–26]. Methods of the first category are proposed in earlier days. The most representative ones are locality-sensitive hashing (LSH) [22] and the variants of it. The hash function is not related to training data. Instead, they do random projections to map images into a feature space. The second category learns the hash function from the training data. Because of the extra information, data-dependent methods outperform data-independent ones.

Data-dependent methods can be further divided into unsupervised methods and supervised methods. Unsupervised methods include spectral hashing (SH) [23] and iterative quantization (ITQ) [26]. These methods learn hash functions from unlabelled training sets. To deal with the more complicated image database, supervised methods are proposed to learn a better hash function from label information of training images. For example, supervised hashing with kernels (KSH) [24] requires a limited amount of supervised information and achieves high-quality hashing. Minimal loss hashing (MLH) [25] is based on structured prediction with latent variables and a hinge-like loss function. And binary reconstructive embedding (BRE) [10] develops an algorithm for learning hash functions based on explicitly minimizing the reconstruction error between the original distances and the Hamming distances. Asymmetric inner-product binary coding (AIBC) [27] is a special hashing method based on asymmetric hash functions. AIBC learns two different

hash functions for query images and dataset images. It can be applied to both unsupervised datasets and supervised datasets.

Hashing methods mentioned above use hand-crafted features which are not powerful enough for more complicated semantic similarity. Moreover, the feature extracting procedure is independent of hash function learning. Recently, CNN based hashing methods called deep hashing methods are proposed to issue these problems. CNN can learn more representative features over hand-crafted features. Furthermore, most deep hashing methods perform feature learning and hash function learning simultaneously and show great improvement compared to previous methods. Several deep hashing methods have been proposed and proved to have better accuracy in content-based image retrieval. For example, CNNH [18] proposes a two-stage deep hashing method. It simultaneously learns features and hash functions based on learned approximate hash codes. Deep pairwise-supervised hashing (DPSH) [28] performs learning based on pairwise labels. Reference [29] poses hash learning as a problem of regularized similarity learning and simultaneously learns hash function and image features through triplet samples. Our approach proposed in this paper outperforms the above methods.

3. Proposed Method

Our method aims to find a hash function solving the content-based image retrieval task. Given N training images $X = \{x_1, x_2, \ldots, x_N\}$ belonging to K categories, x_i is in the form of raw RGB values. Label information is noted as $L = \{l_1, l_2, \ldots, l_N\}, l_i \in \{1, 2, \ldots, K\}$. Our goal is to learn a function $H(x)$ mapping input images to compact binary codes $b_i = H(x_i)$ and $b_i \in \{0, 1\}^C$, where C stands for the hash length. The hash function $H(x)$ satisfies the following:

(1) b_i and b_j are similar in the Hamming space when $l_i = l_j$.

(2) b_i and b_j are far away in the Hamming space when $l_i \neq l_j$.

Figure 1 shows the whole flowchart of our system and Figure 2 shows the proposed network. A target hash code generation component is proposed to generate optimal hash code for training based on code length and category number. Our framework contains a CNN model as the main component. Normally the last layer of CNN is a Softmax classification layer. We replace it with a hash layer of C nodes. Since the output layer of CNN model has been changed, we need new output information to replace the labels. The hash function $H(x)$ is the trained model concatenated with a revised sgn function. Finally, we use the trained hash function to perform content-based image retrieval.

3.1. Target Hash Code Generation

3.1.1. Normal Situation. Target hash code is the mathematically optimal code set with K codewords; the Hamming distance between each codeword is maximized. We use target hash code together with raw images as the training sample to train the whole network. We hope to get a network which accepts the raw image as input and can map it to binary

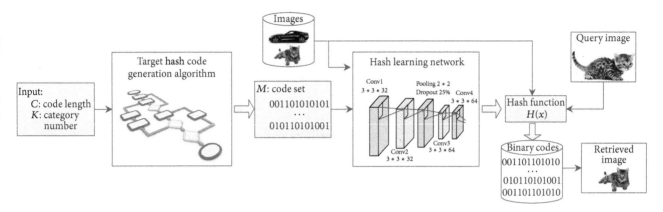

FIGURE 1: The process flow of our work. First, we use our proposed target hash code generation algorithm to generate optimal hash code set. Next, we use hash code set and training images to train the hash learning CNN network, which is regarded as the hash function. Finally, we use the hash function to perform content-based image retrieval.

codes close to the target hash code. The trained network, which is used as hash function $H(x)$, produces binary codes satisfying the goal. Learning the relationship between images with different labels is not our purpose. Instead, our purpose is to teach the network how to map image to a binary code. That is why we calculate the target hash codes and feed it to the network, not letting the network learn from original labels. This is the major difference between our method and others. Furthermore, the target hash code generation component makes our learning a pointwise manner. We require no pairwise inputs like [18], and the training speed is much faster. Our target hash code's function is similar to the prototype code in adaptive binary quantization (ABQ) [30]. The difference is that, in ABQ, the binary code of any data point is represented by its nearest prototype. The output binary code of the hash function lies in the prototype code set. In our method, the target hash code is only used for training. Hash function can produce binary codes not in target hash code set.

To fit the target hash code length, we replace the last layer of original CNN classification model with a fully connected layer called hash layer which has C nodes. How to generate the target hash code for images in K different labels is the main focus of this part. The following is the detailed problem description and main algorithm.

Since the training images are in K categories, our target is to find a binary code set with K codewords. The minimum Hamming distance between any two codewords should be as large as possible. In a more specific way, given binary code length C and codeword number K, we want to find a code set $M = \{m_1, m_2, \ldots, m_K\}$, $m_i \in \{0, 1\}^C$, whose minimum Hamming distance is maximized. This optimization problem can first be divided into smaller jobs: given code length C and minimum Hamming distance H, find a code set with more than K code words. After that, repeat this process with larger H until no code set can be found. The last solvable H is the maximized minimum Hamming distance. The whole process is described in Algorithm 1. Please note that this optimization problem is a complicated problem with no fixed result. For different C and H, the scale of code set may not be a certain

TABLE 1: Target 12-bit hash code set for a 10-category dataset.

Label	Decimal code	Target hash code
0	504	000111111000
1	1611	011001001011
2	1652	011001110100
3	1932	011110001100
4	1971	011110110011
5	2709	101010010101
6	2730	101010101010
7	2898	101101010010
8	2925	101101101101
9	3294	110011011110

number [31]. We have proved that our algorithm is able to at least find a second optimal solution in our experiment cases. Consider a 24-bit code set for a 12-category dataset, the best solution is a code set whose minimum Hamming distance is 13 bits. Our algorithm will find one with the minimum Hamming distance of 12 bits.

For instance, given code length $C = 12$ for a dataset with $K = 10$ categories, with our algorithm, the minimum Hamming distance $H = 6$ results in a code set M with 16 codewords. We further try $H = 7$ and it results in a set with 4 codewords, which fails to meet our need. Then we randomly choose 10 codewords from the former set $M(C = 12, H = 6)$ and the target hash code is constructed as Table 1 shows.

3.1.2. Semantically Uneven Situation. In some situations, the semantic relation between different labels is not evenly distributed. For example, image samples in a dataset are divided into 3 different categories and their labels are $L = \{l_1, l_2, l_3\} = \{cat, dog, car\}$. The images belonging to labels l_1 and l_2 are of different categories but quite similar. However, images of label l_3 are really far away from l_2 and l_3. When we input a cat as a query image, we hope to retrieve dogs before cars. The target hash code needs to be redesigned; an evenly distributed Hamming distance between each label is

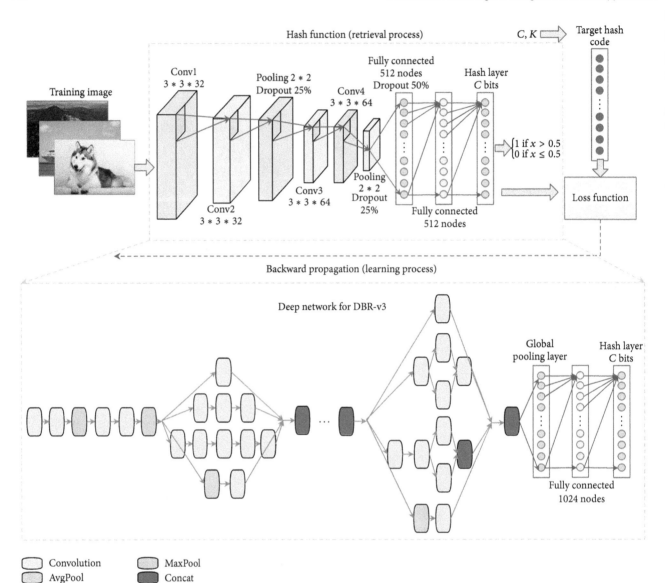

FIGURE 2: The CNN network of our proposal. The upper part is the DBR network, and the lower one is the DBR-v3 network based on inception-v3 net. First, target hash code set is generated based on hash length C and image category number K. Then deep network is trained with raw images and target hash code. Finally, image retrieval is processed with the hash function, which is the trained network concatenated with a sgn function.

not reasonable. In this example, we need a target hash code set $M = \{m_1, m_2, m_3\}$ with small Hamming distance between m_1 and m_2. In this {cat, dog, car} example, target hash code set $M = \{11001, 11010, 00000\}$ is a reasonable one since the Hamming distance between cat and dog is 2 and others are 3.

To generate such target hash code set, we need further information called semantic relation matrix S. S is a $K \times K$ matrix. Each element $s_{i,j}$ in S shows the semantic relation between label l_i and label l_j. So $s_{i,j}$ always equals $s_{j,i}$ and $s_{i,i} = 0$. A negative number means closer relation than average, for example, cat and dog. A positive number means more dissimilar relation than other labels. Zero value means the normal relation between two labels and most values should be zero. For the {cat, dog, car} example, S will be a 3×3 matrix. $s_{1,2}$ and $s_{2,1}$ are −1 and all other values are

0. To generate this kind of uneven semantic target hash code, we need a slight revise to Algorithm 1. The whole process is shown in Algorithm 2. The only difference is in line (5). When comparing the Hamming distance between the generating code and already generated code, we need to add the corresponding s of these two codes defined in semantic relation matrix S. In Algorithm 2, s means the value in S of the currently compared codes. For example, if we are generating the fifth code and comparing it to the first code in current code set, s is the value of $s_{5,1}$.

For instance, given code length $C = 12$ for a dataset with $K = 10$ categories, the semantic relation matrix S is defined as follows. Labels l_1, l_2, l_3 are very similar and their Hamming distance should be closer, so $s_{1,2} = s_{1,3} = s_{2,3} = -2$. Labels l_8, l_9, l_{10} are very dissimilar and their Hamming distance should

---

Input: binary code length C, number of categories K
Output: code set $\{m_1, m_2, \ldots, m_K\}$, $m_i \in \{0, 1\}^C$ satisfies $\min(\text{Hamming}(m_i, m_j)) \geq H$
(1) codeset.add(0)
(2) **for** $(i = 1, 2, \ldots, 2^C - 1)$ **do**
(3)   flag=0
(4)   **for** j = codeset[0], codeset[1], ... **do**
(5)   **if** $\text{Hamming}(i, j) < H$ **then**
(6)   flag=1
(7)   break
(8)   **if** flag==0 **then**
(9)   codeset.add(i)
(10) **return** codeset
Repeat: Perform the algorithm with $H = 1, 2, 3, \ldots$ until the length of code set is larger than K. Choose K codewords from the code set with largest H, that will be the target hash code set.

ALGORITHM 1: Optimal hash code generation.

Input: binary code length C, number of categories K, semantic relation matrix S. s means the corresponding value in S of the currently being compared two codes.
Output: code set $\{m_1, m_2, \ldots, m_K\}$, $m_i \in \{0, 1\}^C$ satisfies $\min(\text{Hamming}(m_i, m_j)) \geq H$
(1) codeset.add(0)
(2) **for** $(i = 1, 2, \ldots, 2^C - 1)$ **do**
(3)   flag=0
(4)   **for** j = codeset[0], codeset[1], ... **do**
(5)   **if** $\text{Hamming}(i, j) < H + s$ **then**
(6)   flag=1
(7)   break
(8)   **if** flag==0 **then**
(9)   codeset.add(i)
(10) **return** codeset
Repeat: Perform the algorithm with $H = 1, 2, 3, \ldots$ until the length of code set is larger than K. Choose K codewords from the code set with largest H, that will be the target hash code set.

ALGORITHM 2: Uneven semantic optimal hash code generation.

---

be larger, so $s_{8,9} = s_{8,10} = s_{9,10} = 2$. All other values are zero. The target hash code is constructed as Table 2 shows. The first three codes have Hamming distance 4 and the last three codes have Hamming distance 8. All other codes have the minimum Hamming distance 6. This code set satisfied the semantic relation between different labels. To the best of our knowledge, there is no dataset that includes numerical defined semantic relation between different labels. We state our algorithm here to give a solution to such semantically uneven label situation.

3.2. Learning Hash Function. With the label information $L = \{l_1, l_2, \ldots, l_N\}$ and target hash code set $M = \{m_1, m_2, \ldots, m_K\}$, we can construct our new training set T with N training samples; x_i is raw RGB value of training images and m_{l_i} is the target hash code for x_i:

$$T = \left\{ \left(x_1, m_{l_1}\right), \left(x_2, m_{l_2}\right), \ldots, \left(x_N, m_{l_N}\right) \right\}. \tag{1}$$

After preparing the training samples, we build a deep network to learn to map images to hash codes. For small image datasets with the size of around $30 * 30$ pixels, we

TABLE 2: Semantically uneven target 12-bit hash code set for a 10-category dataset: Hamming distances between codes 0, 1, and 2 are small and those between codes 7, 8, and 9 are large.

Label	Decimal code	Target hash code
0	0	000000000000
1	15	000000001111
2	51	000000110011
3	252	000011111100
4	853	001101010101
5	874	001101101010
6	1430	010110010110
7	1449	010110101001
8	2714	101010011010
9	3174	110001100110

present DBR network based on relatively shallow convolutional neural networks. For large image datasets with image size of $299 * 299$, we build our network called DBR-v3 based on inception-v3 [21].

3.2.1. Deep Network for Small Images. For small image deep network, we call our method deep binary representation (DBR). We take CIFAR-10 training as an example. We adopt a widely used simple CNN model for CIFAR-10 for fast retrieval. CNN has the powerful ability to learn image features through the concatenation of convolution layer and fully connected layer. As shown in Figure 2, we use 32, 32, 64, 64 3×3 convolution kernels for the convolution layers. 2×2 max pooling and 25% dropout are added after 2nd and 4th convolution layer. Following convolution layers are two fully connected layers with 512 nodes and a 50% dropout after the first one. All these layers are activated with ReLU function for adding nonlinearity. The hash layer is a fully connected layer with C nodes, depending on the length of target hash code. For larger C, the network can be trained to learn more features from the input image and lead to better performance. Each node implies a hidden feature of the input image. Sigmoid function ranges in $(0, 1)$ and for most cases lies in $(0, 0.1) \cup (0.9, 1)$. It is very suitable for indexing the output to binary codes.

Target hash code includes all the information needed to learn features from images, so loss function need not be specially designed; simple mean squared error (MSE) loss function works well. For training optimizer, we choose Adadelta [32] for its good balance of speed and convergence point. Without huge modifications on the CNN model, our proposed model can learn a robust hash function fast in hundreds of training epochs.

3.2.2. Deep Network for Large Images. For input images with relatively large size like $299 * 299$ pixels or similar size, we call our method DBR-v3. We build our deep network based on inception-v3 [21]. Inception net-v3 is a very deep convolutional neural network with more than 20 layers evolving from inception v1 [33]. This network achieves 21.2% top-1 and 5.6% top-5 error in ILSVRC for single frame evaluation with a computational cost of 5 billion multiply-adds per inference and with using less than 25 million parameters. We adopt the ImageNet pretrained inception-v3 model as our basic model and perform our revise and training.

We make some changes to the inception-v3 to make it fit our hash function. After the final global pooling layer, we add one fully connected layer with 1024 nodes activated with ReLU function. Following this layer is the hash layer, a fully connected layer with C nodes. The weights of newly added layers are randomly initialized and others are pretrained weights of original inception-v3. The training is a two-step process. First, we train the whole network for several epochs. After the top layers are well trained, we freeze the bottom layers and fine-tune the top 2 inception-blocks for several epochs. The loss function and training optimizer are also MSE and Adadelta [32].

This network accepts input images of $299 * 299$ pixels. For small image datasets, we use the upsampling algorithm to make images fit the network. This can make further performance improvement compared to original shallow network in Section 3.2.1. This performance improvement comes from two aspects, the power of pretrained weights and deeper networks.

3.3. Image Retrieval. After training, we combine all the components together to perform image retrieval. Our trained network accepts an input image x in raw pixels and gives an output $y \in (0, 1)^C$. To convert output y to binary hash codes $h \in \{0, 1\}^C$, we redefine the sgn function:

$$\text{sgn} = \begin{cases} 1 & \text{if } x > 0.5 \\ 0 & \text{if } x \leq 0.5. \end{cases} \tag{2}$$

Finally, we get our hash function:

$$H(x) = \text{sgn}(y) = h, \tag{3}$$

where y is the output of our proposed model.

For image retrieval, we regard training images as the image database and test images as query images. Image retrieval process searches top A most similar images from the database. Three steps are performed to do the image retrieval.

Step 1. Map N training images to hash codes $H_{db} = \{H(x_1), H(x_2), \ldots, H(x_N)\} = \{h_1, h_2, \ldots, h_N\}$.

Step 2. For each query image x_q, first calculate $h_q = H(x_q)$ and then retrieve A images by the rank of the Hamming distance (h_q, x_i); smaller Hamming distance ranks higher.

Step 3. Compare the similarities of retrieved images and the query image. Then evaluate the performance in MAP according to the result.

4. Experiments

In this part, we state our experiment settings and results. We calculate the MAP (mean average precision) of the image retrieval on different datasets and list it in Table 3. We apply our DBR method on MNIST and CIFAR-10, and DBR-v3 method on ImageNet. Furthermore, we upsample the images in CIFAR-10 and apply DBR-v3 to it. For each method, we list the time each network costs to train and to calculate the hash code of one image. The running time is listed in Table 6. We choose not to calculate the time of retrieving one image. The reason is that once the hash length is determined, the time to retrieve images according to the hash code is the same for all hashing methods. What matters is the time to map one image to the hash code. Please note that some results are missing because they are not available in corresponding paper and these methods are not totally open-source.

4.1. Results on MNIST. The MNIST dataset [34] consists of 70000 28×28 grey-scale images belonging to 10 categories of handwritten Arabic numerals from 0 to 9.

For MNIST, we use 32 convolution kernels of size 3×3 for each one of the two convolution layers. 2×2 max pooling and 25% dropout are added after the 2nd convolution layer. Following convolution layers are two fully connected layers with 128 nodes and a 50% dropout after the first fully connected layer. The last layer is the hash layer and the number of nodes is adjustable with hash length. The model

TABLE 3: MAP of image retrieval on MNIST, CIFAR10, and ImageNet dataset with 4 different bit lengths. We use 1000 query images and calculate the MAP within top 5000 returned neighbors in MNIST and CIFAR10 dataset. We use images from 100 random categories in ImageNet dataset and all validation images of these categories are used as query sets.

Method	MNIST (MAP)				CIFAR-10 (MAP)				ImageNet (MAP)			
	12 bits	24 bits	32 bits	48 bits	12 bits	24 bits	32 bits	48 bits	16 bits	32 bits	48 bits	64 bits
DBR-v3	—	—	—	—	0.826	0.837	0.842	0.847	0.733	0.761	0.768	0.769
DBR	0.980	0.984	0.984	0.990	0.612	0.648	0.658	0.680	—	—	—	—
HashNet	—	—	—	—	—	—	—	—	0.442	0.606	0.663	0.684
DHN	—	—	—	—	0.555	0.594	0.603	0.621	0.311	0.472	0.542	0.573
DNNH	—	—	—	—	0.552	0.566	0.558	0.581	0.290	0.461	0.530	0.565
CNNH+	0.969	0.975	0.971	0.975	0.465	0.521	0.521	0.532	—	—	—	—
CNNH	0.957	0.963	0.956	0.960	0.439	0.511	0.509	0.522	0.281	0.450	0.525	0.554
KSH	0.872	0.891	0.897	0.900	0.303	0.337	0.346	0.356	0.160	0.298	0.342	0.394
ITQ-CCA	0.659	0.694	0.714	0.726	0.264	0.282	0.288	0.295	0.266	0.436	0.548	0.576
MLH	0.472	0.666	0.652	0.654	0.182	0.195	0.207	0.211	—	—	—	—
BRE	0.515	0.593	0.613	0.634	0.159	0.181	0.193	0.196	0.063	0.253	0.330	0.358
SH	0.265	0.267	0.259	0.250	0.131	0.135	0.133	0.130	0.207	0.328	0.395	0.419
ITQ	0.388	0.436	0.422	0.429	0.162	0.169	0.172	0.175	0.326	0.462	0.517	0.552
LSH	0.187	0.209	0.235	0.243	0.121	0.126	0.120	0.120	0.101	0.235	0.312	0.360

training uses Adadelta optimizer with mean squared error loss function.

Our proposed method is compared with state-of-the-art hashing methods including data-independent method LSH [22], two unsupervised methods SH [23] and ITQ [26], four supervised methods KSH [24], MLH [25], BRE [10], and ITQ-CCA [26], and CNN based deep hashing method CNNH [18] and its variant CNNH+ [18].

We follow the experiment configurations of [18] and derive results from the same resource. We randomly select 100 images per class and total 1000 images as test query images. For the unsupervised methods, we use all the rest images as the training set. And for supervised methods including CNNH, CNNH+, and ours, we select 5000 images (500 images per class) as the training set. The whole training process lasts around 120 s for 100 epochs training on a GTX1060 6 GB graphic processing unit. It costs around 80 us to map one MNIST image to its hash code.

To evaluate the performance of retrieval, we use mean average precision (MAP). For each query image, we calculate the average precision of retrieved images. MAP is the mean value of these average precisions. Please note that, for each query image, the correctness of high ranking retrieved image counts more. The MAP result of our test is shown in Table 3; the DBR column is our method. We can find that our method outperforms other methods in grey-scale image retrieval.

4.2. Results on CIFAR-10.

CIFAR-10 [35] dataset consists of 60000 32 × 32 images belonging to 10 categories including airplane, automobile, and bird. The layer information of CIFAR-10 implementation is stated in Section 3.2.

Other than the methods we compared in Section 4.1, we compare our method with two more CNN based deep hash methods DHN [36] and DNNH [20]. And we also follow their experiment configuration. We randomly select 100 images per class as query set. For the unsupervised methods, we use

all the rest images as the training set. For supervised methods, 5000 images (500 images per class) are randomly selected as the training set. The whole training process lasts around 600 s for 300 epochs training on a GTX1060 6 GB graphic processing unit. It costs around 160 us to map one CIFAR-10 image to its hash code. Two images are considered to be similar if they have the same label. The top 12 retrieved images of two query images are shown in Figure 3 as an illustration.

Furthermore, we upsample images in CIFAR-10 to the size of 299 * 299 and apply DBR-v3 network to it. We train the whole network for 50 epochs and perform the fine-tuning for 20 epochs. The total training time is 37 s * 50 + 51 s * 20 = 2870 s on a GTX1060 6 GB graphic processing unit. For DBR-v3, it costs around 3 ms to map one CIFAR-10 image to its hash code.

The MAP results are in Table 3; the result of our method is shown in columns DBR and DBR-v3. We can see that our method is better than other methods including unsupervised methods, supervised methods, and deep methods with feature learning. DBR-v3 has a big advantage over DBR. This is because the network is a lot deeper and pretrained with ImageNet. However, the training time and hash code calculating time sacrifice a lot.

We also conduct experiments on semantically uneven situations. For ten categories in CIFAR-10 dataset, we suppose that the automobile and the truck are semantically similar. We set the value of $s_{truck,automobile} = -2$ and all other values in semantic relation matrix $s_{ij} = 0$. When the query image is an automobile, we can observe that trucks will be retrieved with higher rank compared to categories other than the automobile. At the same time, Table 4 shows that the overall MAP result remains at the same level. This experiment indicates that our target hash code can have the same semantic relation between different categories.

Following [28], we further do the comparison to some deep hashing methods with different experiment settings

Query image   Top 12 retrieved images

FIGURE 3: Top 12 retrieved images of two query image samples. The dataset is CIFAR-10 and hash length is 24 bits. As shown in the figure, the precision of high-rank retrieved images is very high.

TABLE 4: MAP of image retrieval on CIFAR-10 dataset with 4 different bit lengths. We use 1000 query images and calculate the MAP within top 5000 returned neighbors. The first line is the result of semantically even situation and the second is semantically uneven situation.

Method	CIFAR-10 (MAP)			
	16 bits	24 bits	32 bits	48 bits
DBR-even	0.612	0.648	0.658	0.680
DBR-uneven	0.608	0.647	0.658	0.683

TABLE 5: MAP of image retrieval on CIFAR-10 dataset with 4 different bit lengths. We use 10000 query images and calculate the MAP within top 50000 returned neighbors.

Method	CIFAR-10 (MAP)			
	16 bits	24 bits	32 bits	48 bits
DBR	0.822	0.821	0.833	0.862
DPSH	0.763	0.781	0.795	0.807
DRSCH	0.615	0.622	0.629	0.631
DSCH	0.609	0.613	0.617	0.620
DSRH	0.608	0.611	0.617	0.618

including DSCH, DRSCH [29], DSRH [19], and DPSH [28]; the results are directly derived from [28]. More specifically, we use 10000 test images as query set and 50000 images as the training set. The total training time is 1.5 hours for 300 epochs on a GTX1060 6 GB graphic processing unit. The MAP values are calculated according to top 50000 returned neighbours and are shown in Table 5. We can find out that our method still leads the MAP results.

4.3. Results on ImageNet. ImageNet is an image database with more than 1.2 million images in training set and more than 50 thousand images in the validation set. Each image is in one of the 1000 categories. The image size varies, and the common size is hundreds by hundreds of pixels. ImageNet is currently the largest image database for various tasks. And experiments on ImageNet show the ability to deal with large-scale high-definition images.

The network details including loss function and training optimizes are stated in Section 3.2.2. For a fair comparison, we follow the experiment settings in [37]. We randomly select 100 categories; all the images of these categories in the training set are used as training images. All the images of these categories in the validation set are used as query images. We train the whole network for 50 epochs and fine-tune the top 2 inception-blocks and hash layer for 20 epochs. The total training time is about 18 hours on a GTX1060 6 GB graphic processing unit. It costs around 3 ms to map one ImageNet image its hash code.

Our proposed method is compared to state-of-the-art hashing methods including HashNet [37] and most methods mentioned in Section 4.1. The data is derived directly from [37] and the test set is the same.

To evaluate the performance of retrieval, we use mean average precision (MAP), and the result is shown in Table 3.

TABLE 6: The running time of each experiment. Training time means the time to train the hash function. Hash time means the time to map one image to hash code.

Dataset	Method	Epoch	Training time	Hash time
MNIST	DBR	100	120 s	80 us
CIFAR10	DBR	300	600 s	160 us
CIFAR10	DBR-v3	50 + 20	2870 s	3 ms
ImageNet	DBR-v3	50 + 20	18 h	3 ms

The result shows that our method has a great advantage over other methods. This indicates that our DBR-v3 method can solve large-scale image retrieval for high-definition images.

5. Conclusion

In this paper, we present a novel end-to-end hash learning network for content-based image retrieval. We design the optimal target hash code for each label to feed the network with the relation between different labels. Since the target hash codes between different labels have maximized Hamming distance, the deep network can map different-category images to hash codes with significant distance. For similar images, the network tends to produce exact same hash code. The deep network is based on convolutional neural network. We design two variants of our method: (1) DBR for small images: this network trains fast and it calculates fast; with powerful clusters online training is even possible. (2) DBR-v3 based on inception-v3 net: it benefits from the powerful learning ability of inception net and performs very good on high-definition image retrieval. Finally, we do experiments on standard image retrieval benchmarks. The results show that our method outperforms the previous works.

Conflicts of Interest

The authors declare that there are no conflicts of interest regarding the publication of this article.

Acknowledgments

This work is supported by NSFC (61671296, 61521062, and U1611461) and the National Key Research and Development Program of China (BZ0300013).

References

[1] J. Eakins and G. Margaret, "Content-based image retrieval," 1999.

[2] A. W. M. Smeulders, M. Worring, S. Santini, A. Gupta, and R. Jain, "Content-based image retrieval at the end of the early years," *IEEE Transactions on Pattern Analysis and Machine Intelligence*, vol. 22, no. 12, pp. 1349–1380, 2000.

[3] Y. Liu, D. Zhang, G. Lu, and W.-Y. Ma, "A survey of content-based image retrieval with high-level semantics," *Pattern Recognition*, vol. 40, no. 1, pp. 262–282, 2007.

[4] J. Wan, D. Wang, S. C. H. Hoi et al., "Deep learning for content-based image retrieval: A comprehensive study," in *Proceedings of the 2014 ACM Conference on Multimedia, MM 2014*, pp. 157–166, usa, November 2014.

[5] L. Liu, S. Fumin, S. Yuming, L. Xianglong, and S. Ling, *Deep sketch hashing: Fast free-hand sketch-based image retrieval*, 2017, https://arxiv.org/abs/1703.05605.

[6] A. Torralba, R. Fergus, and Y. Weiss, "Small codes and large image databases for recognition," in *Proceedings of the IEEE Computer Society Conference on Computer Vision and Pattern Recognition (CVPR '08)*, pp. 1–8, 2008.

[7] N. Mohammad and M. D. Blei, "Minimal loss hashing for compact binary codes," in *Proceedings of the 28th international conference on machine learning (ICML-11)*, pp. 353–360, 2011.

[8] B. Kulis and K. Grauman, "Kernelized locality-sensitive hashing for scalable image search," in *Proceedings of the Proceeding of the 12th International Conference on Computer Vision (ICCV '09)*, pp. 2130–2137, Kyoto, Japan, October 2009.

[9] Y. Gong and S. Lazebnik, "Comparing data-dependent and data-independent embeddings for classification and ranking of Internet images," in *Proceedings of the 2011 IEEE Conference on Computer Vision and Pattern Recognition, CVPR 2011*, pp. 2633–2640, usa, June 2011.

[10] B. Kulis and T. Darrell, "Learning to hash with binary reconstructive embeddings," in *NIPS*, pp. 1042–1050.

[11] J. Wang, S. Kumar, and S.-F. Chang, "Semi-supervised hashing for scalable image retrieval," in *Proceedings of the IEEE Computer Society Conference on Computer Vision and Pattern Recognition (CVPR '10)*, pp. 3424–3431, IEEE, San Francisco, Calif, USA, June 2010.

[12] D. Ciregan, U. Meier, and J. Schmidhuber, "Multi-column deep neural networks for image classification," in *Proceedings of the IEEE Conference on Computer Vision and Pattern Recognition (CVPR '12)*, pp. 3642–3649, June 2012.

[13] R. Collobert and J. Weston, "A unified architecture for natural language processing: deep neural networks with multitask learning," in *Proceedings of the 25th International Conference on Machine Learning*, pp. 160–167, ACM, July 2008.

[14] A. Karpathy, G. Toderici, S. Shetty, T. Leung, R. Sukthankar, and F.-F. Li, "Large-scale video classification with convolutional neural networks," in *Proceedings of the 27th IEEE Conference on Computer Vision and Pattern Recognition, (CVPR '14)*, pp. 1725–1732, Columbus, OH, USA, June 2014.

[15] R. Salakhutdinov and G. Hinton, "Semantic hashing," *International Journal of Approximate Reasoning*, vol. 50, no. 7, pp. 969–978, 2009.

[16] X. Lu, L. Song, R. Xie, X. Yang, and W. Zhang, "Deep hash learning for efficient image retrieval," in *Proceedings of the IEEE International Conference on Multimedia & Expo Workshops (ICMEW)*, pp. 579–584, Hong Kong, July 2017.

[17] K. Lin, H.-F. Yang, J.-H. Hsiao, and C.-S. Chen, "Deep learning of binary hash codes for fast image retrieval," in *Proceedings of*

the IEEE Conference on Computer Vision and Pattern Recognition Workshops, CVPRW 2015, pp. 27–35, usa, June 2015.

[18] R. Xia, Y. Pan, H. Lai, C. Liu, and S. Yan, "Supervised hashing for image retrieval via image representation learning," *AAAI Conference on Artificial Intelligence,* pp. 2156–2162, 2014.

[19] F. Zhao, Y. Huang, L. Wang, and T. Tan, "Deep semantic ranking based hashing for multi-label image retrieval," in *Proceedings of IEEE Conference on Computer Vision and Pattern Recognition, CVPR 2015,* pp. 1556–1564, June 2015.

[20] H. Lai, Y. Pan, Y. Liu, and S. Yan, "Simultaneous feature learning and hash coding with deep neural networks," in *Proceedings of IEEE Conference on Computer Vision and Pattern Recognition, CVPR',* pp. 3270–3278, June 2015.

[21] C. Szegedy, V. Vanhoucke, S. Ioffe, J. Shlens, and Z. Wojna, "Rethinking the inception architecture for computer vision," in *Proceedings of the 2016 IEEE Conference on Computer Vision and Pattern Recognition, CVPR 2016,* pp. 2818–2826, July 2016.

[22] M. Datar, N. Immorlica, P. Indyk, and V. S. Mirrokni, "Locality-sensitive hashing scheme based on p-stable distributions," in *Proceedings of the 20th Annual Symposium on Computational Geometry (SCG '04),* pp. 253–262, ACM, June 2004.

[23] Y. Weiss, A. Torralba, and R. Fergus, "Spectral hashing," in *Proceedings of the 22nd Annual Conference on Neural Information Processing Systems (NIPS '08),* pp. 1753–1760, Vancouver, Canada, December 2008.

[24] W. Liu, J. Wang, R. Ji, Y.-G. Jiang, and S.-F. Chang, "Supervised hashing with kernels," in *Proceedings of the IEEE Conference on Computer Vision and Pattern Recognition (CVPR '12),* pp. 2074–2081, Providence, RI, USA, June 2012.

[25] M. Norouzi and D. J. Fleet, "Minimal loss hashing for compact binary codes," in *Proceedings of the 28th International Conference on Machine Learning, ICML 2011,* pp. 353–360, usa, July 2011.

[26] Y. Gong, S. Lazebnik, A. Gordo, and F. Perronnin, "Iterative quantization: A procrustean approach to learning binary codes for large-scale image retrieval," *IEEE Transactions on Pattern Analysis and Machine Intelligence,* vol. 35, no. 12, pp. 2916–2929, 2013.

[27] F. Shen, Y. Yang, L. Liu, W. Liu, D. Tao, and H. T. Shen, "Asymmetric Binary Coding for Image Search," *IEEE Transactions on Multimedia,* vol. 19, no. 9, pp. 2022–2032, 2017.

[28] L. Wu-Jun, W. Sheng, and K. Wang-Cheng, *Feature learning based deep supervised hashing with pairwise labels,* 2015, https://arxiv.org/abs/1511.03855.

[29] R. Zhang, L. Lin, R. Zhang, W. Zuo, and L. Zhang, "Bit-scalable deep hashing with regularized similarity learning for image retrieval and person re-identification," *IEEE Transactions on Image Processing,* vol. 24, no. 12, pp. 4766–4779, 2015.

[30] X. Liu, Z. Li, C. Deng, and D. Tao, "Distributed adaptive binary quantization for fast nearest neighbor search," *IEEE Transactions on Image Processing,* vol. 26, no. 11, pp. 5324–5336, 2017.

[31] M. Plotkin, "Binary codes with specified minimum distance," *IRE Transactions on Information Theory,* vol. 6, no. 4, pp. 445–450, 1960.

[32] D. M. Zeiler, "Adadelta: an adaptive learning rate method," https://arxiv.org/abs/1212.5701.

[33] C. Szegedy, W. Liu, Y. Jia et al., "Going deeper with convolutions," in *Proceedings of the IEEE Conference on Computer Vision and Pattern Recognition (CVPR '15),* pp. 1–9, Boston, Mass, USA, June 2015.

[34] Y. LeCun, C. Cortes, and C. J. C. Burges, *The mnist database of handwritten digits,* 1994.

[35] A. Krizhevsky, N. Vinod, and H. Geoffrey, "The cifar-10 dataset," 2014.

[36] H. Zhu, M. Long, J. Wang, and Y. Cao, "Deep hashing network for efficient similarity retrieval," in *Proceedings of the 30th AAAI Conference on Artificial Intelligence, AAAI 2016,* pp. 2415–2421, usa, February 2016.

[37] C. Zhangjie, L. Mingsheng, W. Jianmin, and S. P. Yu, *Hashnet: Deep Learning to Hash by Continuation,* 2017, https://arxiv.org/abs/1702.00758.

13

SDP-Based Quality Adaptation and Performance Prediction in Adaptive Streaming of VBR Videos

Thoa Nguyen,[1] Thang Vu,[1] Nam Pham Ngoc,[1] and Truong Cong Thang[2]

[1]*Hanoi University of Science and Technology, Hanoi, Vietnam*
[2]*The University of Aizu, Aizuwakamatsu, Japan*

Correspondence should be addressed to Thoa Nguyen; thoa.nguyenthikim@hust.edu.vn

Academic Editor: Mei-Ling Shyu

Recently, various adaptation methods have been proposed to cope with throughput fluctuations in HTTP adaptive streaming (HAS). However, these methods have mostly focused on constant bitrate (CBR) videos. Moreover, most of them are qualitative in the sense that performance metrics could only be obtained after a streaming session. In this paper, we propose a new adaptation method for streaming variable bitrate (VBR) videos using stochastic dynamic programming (SDP). With this approach, the system should have a probabilistic characterization along with the definition of a cost function that is minimized by a control strategy. Our solution is based on a new statistical model where the future streaming performance is directly related to the past bandwidth statistics. We develop mathematical models to predict and develop simulation models to measure the average performance of the adaptation policy. The experimental results show that the prediction models can provide accurate performance prediction which is useful in planning adaptation policy and that our proposed adaptation method outperforms the existing ones in terms of average quality and average quality switch.

1. Introduction

Nowadays, video services are increasingly popular on the Internet. According to a recent study and forecast [1], global Internet video traffic will be 80% of the entire consumer Internet traffic in 2019. Besides, HTTP protocol has become a cost-effective solution for video streaming thanks to the abundance of Web platforms and broadband connections [2, 3]. Furthermore, for interoperability of HTTP streaming in the industry, ISO/IEC MPEG has developed "Dynamic Adaptive Streaming over HTTP" (DASH) [4] as the first standard for video streaming over HTTP.

DASH requires a video to be available in multiple bitrates and split into small segments each containing a few seconds of playtime. Based on the current network conditions and terminal capacity, the client can adaptively decide a suitable data rate so that stalling is avoided and the available bandwidth is best possibly utilized. If the video is encoded in only one bitrate, either the bitrate is smaller than the available bandwidth resulting in a smooth playback but sparing resources which could be utilized for a better video quality, or the video bitrate is higher than the available bandwidth leading to video stalling. Thus, DASH enables service providers to improve resource utilization and quality of experience (QoE).

So far, existing studies have proposed simple heuristics for adapting video at the client. These heuristics can be divided into two types, buffer-based methods and throughput-based methods. The purpose of buffer-based methods is to maintain the stability of the buffer within a certain range to ensure continuous video playback. However, when the bandwidth is drastically reduced, the buffer-based methods may cause sudden change of bitrate [5–8]. Meanwhile, throughput-based methods adaptively decide version based on the estimated throughput. These methods are generally able to react quickly to the throughput variations; the streaming quality, however, may be unstable [9].

Recently, several Markov decision-based methods have been proposed to optimize decision making for the streaming client under time-varying network conditions. However, these existing methods mostly focus on constant bitrate (CBR) videos. The authors in [10] are the first to propose an adaptation algorithm in which stochastic dynamic programming (SDP) is employed to find optimal decision policies when streaming VBR videos. The segment requests are ruled by the policies which map a control parameter to every possible state of the system; however, it is limited to videos with weak bitrate fluctuations. To the extent of the authors' knowledge, in the context of adaptive streaming, there have not been any adaptive streaming methods that could (1) support variable bitrate (VBR) videos with strong bitrate fluctuations and (2) predict the streaming performance with different streaming settings in order to select the optimal one.

In this paper, we tackle these challenges by proposing an adaptation method using stochastic dynamic programming. Firstly, we discretize a system including data throughput, buffer level, and bitrate of a VBR video to form the system states. Secondly, we define a cost function that takes into account parameters that affect the subjective perceptual quality of users. In the cost function, the weights are assigned to the difference between data throughput and the bitrate of the next segment, the variance of the buffer from its optimal value, and the quality switch of the video. Finally, we construct an infinite horizon problem (IHP) and solve it to find the optimal policies for all system states. The role of a policy is mapping the control parameter (i.e., the version of the video) to every possible state of the system. This paper is an extended work of our preliminary study in [11]. The extension in this work is multifold. First, we predicted the CDF of the requested versions in a streaming session, so the maximum version could be decided for the streaming session. Second, we predicted CDF of the buffer levels to know the variance of the buffer level under the fluctuations of the network. Finally, we also evaluated the proposed method in the online context, where the statistics of bandwidth is updated periodically. Besides, we compared the performance prediction results with measurement ones in in both offline and online contexts.

A policy is optimal when it minimizes an average cost. Based on the obtained policies and the constructed system model, we develop mathematical models that could predict the streaming performance for the new streaming session including average video version, average version switch per segment, average buffer, and average underflow probability. Experiments are conducted to verify the mathematical models by comparing the predicted performance obtained from the models and the measured performance. The proposed method is evaluated in two contexts (1) offline context using statistics of a history bandwidth trace and (2) online context using bandwidth statistics of previous video segments.

The paper is organized as follows. Section 2 briefly reviews related work. Section 3 describes the system and the modeling of the system in detail. Section 4 presents the formulation of the IHP which is solved by SDP. The performance prediction is given in Section 5. Section 6 presents the experimental results and discussions. Finally, Section 7 concludes our work.

2. Related Work

In recent years, many heuristic adaptation methods for adaptive streaming have been developed (e.g., [5–9, 14]). An extensive evaluation of typical adaptation methods has been carried out in [15]. Though these methods prove to be effective in their specific settings, they cannot tell quantitatively the streaming performance with different system settings. Furthermore, most of them focus on CBR videos.

For streaming VBR video, several adaptation methods have been proposed based on the sensibility of the receiver's buffer [6, 16]. Dubin et al. [16] propose an adaptation logic that supports its bandwidth estimation decisions based on the client buffer redundancy. This method considers the fluctuations of mobile network without emphasizing the characteristics of bitrate fluctuation of VBR videos, which leads to the lack of smoothness. In [6], a partial-linear trend prediction model is developed to estimate the trend of client buffer level variation. The client will continue to have the current version for the next segment when the estimated buffer level has no significant change. The drawback of this method is the sudden version switch when the actual buffer level drops dramatically. In [14], the authors propose an adaptive logic for VBR videos based on bitrate estimation. The method demonstrates an effective adaptation behavior as it keeps the buffer at a stable and high level; however, it is still qualitative and has no mechanism to balance the streaming performance.

Several recent studies have proposed mathematical model based adaptation methods in streaming video [17–21]. A mathematical model is proposed in [17] to calculate the underflow probability of VBR streaming under VBR channel based on initial delay and maximum buffer. However, this work only considered VBR videos with one version and constant play-out curve without developing any adaptive logic. Meanwhile, Kang et al. [18] present a no-reference, content-based QoE estimation model for video streaming service over wireless networks using neural networks. Nonetheless, neural networks are computationally complex and require large training data and long training time. Besides, Xiang et al. [19] propose a rate adaptation method using the Markov Decision Process to obtain an optimal streaming strategy for VBR videos. Nevertheless, their proposal is not able to adapt to the real bandwidth changes and has no performance prediction. The prediction of streaming performance was first proposed for streaming CBR videos in [20] and VBR videos in [21] by Liu et al. In their studies, a video session is divided into subsessions. With a given target rebuffering probability, the video bitrate/the average video bitrate for each streaming subsession is predicted when streaming CBR videos/VBR videos, respectively. The results show that the average actual rebuffering probability achieved by these methods is reasonably close to the target. However, they have not done any assessments in terms of video quality and video quality switch, so the QoE can be affected.

Recently, SDP has been known as an effective technique for solving optimization problems in video streaming [10, 22, 23]. For instance, the authors in [22] apply SDP to find the optimal policy for choosing sending rates when streaming

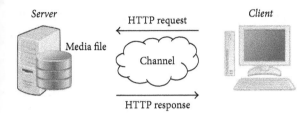

FIGURE 1: General DASH system.

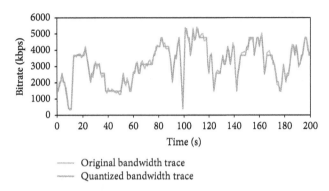

— Original bandwidth trace
— Quantized bandwidth trace

FIGURE 2: A bandwidth trace obtained from a mobile network [12].

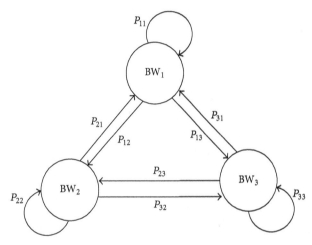

FIGURE 3: General 3-state Markov-chain bandwidth model.

on-demand scalable VBR videos over wireless network. Nevertheless, they have not considered the effect of channel-state aware adaptation. Meanwhile, García et al. [10] construct an infinite horizon problem and apply SDP to solve it specifically for HTTP adaptive streaming. They propose a channel model in which transitions are only possible to adjacent states, with equal probabilities, which is only suitable for the stable bandwidth, with little fluctuation. In addition, by observing the histograms of segment size encoded with VBR, the authors assume that segment size (which is proportional to segment bitrate) can be modeled through a discrete Gaussian distribution. Then, the probability distribution of segment sizes is used to calculate transition probabilities. However, the probability distribution of segment sizes is not taken into account in the cost function. Instead, the average bitrate representing the bitrate for each version is used. This is only reasonable when the deviations of segment sizes (i.e., segment bitrates) are small. In another study, Xing et al. [23] use SDP to find the optimization for Advance Video Coding content when streaming through several wireless connections at the same time. They offer a cost function in terms of QoE, but the computational complexity of their model is significantly caused by eight system variables in each state.

The SDP-based method proposed for HTTP streaming in this paper is *different from the previous studies in several points*. First, our method considers an actual time-varying bandwidth of mobile networks. Second, the drastic bitrate fluctuations of actual VBR videos are effectively supported. Third, we develop mathematic models to predict the performance of a streaming subsession, which helps to select the maximum allowed version parameter in advance.

3. System Modeling

3.1. System Overview. Figure 1 shows the functional diagram of a general DASH system consisting of a server and a client. The server holds the media files with different quality versions. Each version is further divided into small segments. The client has the information about the characteristics and locations of media segments and can request any of them during a streaming session. For the next segment, the client makes a decision of what video version to request based on current status of client buffer and data throughput to provide the best streaming experience possible. In this paper, the segment selection policy for the client aims at maintaining the client buffer at a reasonable level while balancing between average version (i.e., average quality) and average version switch (i.e., quality variations).

In order to apply SDP, our system is modeled as a discrete-time stochastic one. Specifically, the timeline is divided into time stages. At each stage k, the system is represented by a state variable s_k. When the next segment is completely downloaded at stage $k + 1$, the system moves to the state s_{k+1}. As the system transits to the next state, a certain cost occurs. Besides, the channel, the buffer, and the media are discretized as explained in the following subsection.

3.2. Channel, Buffer, and Media Model. In our work, we discretize the bandwidth range into W levels. The bandwidth trace before and after discretization is shown in Figure 2 with $W = 10$. With this level of quantization, the quantized bandwidth covers the original bandwidth well. We then create W different bandwidth states BW_i ($1 \leq i \leq W$) from these W bandwidth levels. The value of each bandwidth state is the average of the maximum value and minimum value of the corresponding bandwidth level. To represent the transition from one bandwidth state to another on a bandwidth state space, we use the Markov chain model which has been used widely in previous studies [10, 24, 25].

Figure 3 presents a general Markov-chain model which consists of three bandwidth states. Each state is represented by one data throughput value. There is a transition probability when the bandwidth moves from one state to another after

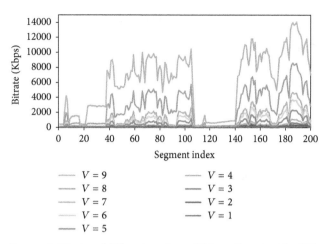

FIGURE 4: Bitrates of different versions of Tokyo Olympic video [13].

each time step. Thus, by simply extracting the statistics from the bandwidth history, the transition probability between all bandwidth states is generated.

Similar to the bandwidth trace, we divide the buffer into B levels from 0 to B_s, with B_s being the buffer size. In addition, we denote the video version by V and represent the version with lowest quality as $V = 1$ and the highest quality as $V = V$max assuming that the video has Vmax different versions. The bitrates of different versions of a VBR video are shown in Figure 4.

Because the segment bitrate of a VBR video version fluctuates very strongly, we divide the bitrate of each version into I intervals (from interval 1 to interval I), each of which is represented by its average bitrate value. For example, if a version that has the highest bitrate of 5000 kbps is divided into 10 bitrate intervals, the interval 1 will range from 0 to 500 kbps and its representative bitrate will be 250 kbps.

We assume that all versions at a bitrate interval represent a separate video flow. If the current segment bitrate belongs to one interval, the next segment bitrate will also belong to that interval regardless of segment version. With this assumption, we generate I different policy sets for I bitrate intervals. When a segment is completely downloaded, the client measures its bitrate to find the bitrate interval it belongs to. Then, the client will determine the policy set corresponding to that bitrate interval.

4. Problem Formulation and Solution

4.1. System State. With the system being discretized above, we observe the system state variable $s_k(b_k, \mathrm{bw}_k, v_k)$ when a video segment is completely downloaded at stage k. Here, b_k is the buffer level representing the number of segments available in the buffer, bw_k is the bandwidth whose value belongs to $\{\mathrm{BW}_i\}$, and v_k is the version index of the downloaded segment. The case where $b_k = 1$ corresponds to the buffer underflow event. In each state s_k, the system may choose any action a. For our system, an action is basically a decision about the version for the next segment. As there are $V_{\max}$ versions to choose from, we have totally $V_{\max}$ possible actions.

The system then randomly moves into a new state s_{k+1} at the next time step, resulting in a corresponding cost $C(s_k, s_{k+1}, a)$. With each bitrate interval i ($1 \leq i \leq I$), we have a system state set $\mathbf{s}_i$ and a policy set $\boldsymbol{\mu}_i$. Let N be the number of states in $\mathbf{s}_i$, and we have

$$N = B * W * V_{\max}. \tag{1}$$

4.2. Transition Probabilities. Since the system is stochastic, which means the system outcome of each action a is not deterministic, the state transition probability between every two states that depends on action a must be constructed. We denote the probability that state s_k will lead to state s_{k+1} given action a as follows:

$$P(s_k, s_{k+1}, a) = \Pr\{s_{k+1} \mid s_k, a\}. \tag{2}$$

Due to the independence among $(b_k, \mathrm{bw}_k, v_k)$, we have

$$\Pr\{s_{k+1} \mid s_k, a\} = \Pr\{b_{k+1} \mid b_k, \mathrm{bw}_k, v_k, a\}$$
$$\cdot \Pr\{\mathrm{bw}_{k+1} \mid \mathrm{bw}_k\} \Pr\{v_{k+1} \mid a\}. \tag{3}$$

In the right hand side of (3), the first term can be calculated as follows:

$$\Pr\{b_{k+1} \mid b_k, \mathrm{bw}_k, v_k, a\} = \begin{cases} 1, & b_{k+1} = b_a \\ 0, & \text{otherwise,} \end{cases} \tag{4}$$

where b_a is the next buffer level estimated based on the current system status and action a. We calculate b_a as follows:

$$b_a = b_k + 1 - \left[\frac{r_a}{\mathrm{bw}_{k+1}}\right], \tag{5}$$

where r_a is the bitrate of the target version.

When the throughput significantly drops, meaning a very low value of bw_{k+1}, b_a could be lower than zero. However, at the beginning of a new stage, there is one segment being downloaded resulting in at least one segment being always in the buffer. Therefore, (5) can be modified as follows:

$$b_a = \max\left\{b_k + 1 - \left[\frac{r_a}{\mathrm{bw}_{k+1}}\right], 1\right\}. \tag{6}$$

The second term is easily obtained from the bandwidth model. And the third term can be simply calculated by

$$\Pr\{v_{k+1} \mid a\} = \begin{cases} 1, & v_{k+1} = a \\ 0, & \text{otherwise.} \end{cases} \tag{7}$$

Thus, expression (3) can be simplified as follows:

$$\Pr\{s_{k+1} \mid s_k, a\}$$
$$= \begin{cases} \Pr\{\mathrm{bw}_{k+1} \mid \mathrm{bw}_k\}, & b_{k+1} = b_a, v_{k+1} = a \\ 0, & \text{otherwise.} \end{cases} \tag{8}$$

Input: number of states N,
          probability function P,
          cost function C
Output: optimal policy for each state μ_{s_k}
$j = 0$ // j is the iteration index
$\mu_{s_k}^j = 0,\ \forall s_k \in \mathbf{s}\ //\mu_{s_k}^j$ is policy of state s_k at jth iteration
repeat
     $j = j + 1$
     Policy evaluation: compute $\lambda^j, h^j(s_k)$ using the below
$N + 1$ equations:

$$h^j(s_N) = 0$$

$$\lambda^j + h^j(s_k) = C\left(s_k, s_{k+1}, \mu_{s_k}^j\right) + \sum_{r=1}^{N} P\left(s_k, s_r, \mu_{s_r}^j\right) h^j(s_r),$$

$$\forall s_k \in \mathbf{s}$$

     Policy improvement: find for all s_k

$$\mu_{s_k}^{j+1} = \arg\min_a [C(s_k, s_{k+1}, a) + \sum_{r=1}^{N} P(s_k, s_r, a) h^j(s_r)],$$

until $\lambda^{j+1} = \lambda^j$ and $h^{j+1}(s_k) = h^j(s_k),\ \forall s_k \in \mathbf{s}$

ALGORITHM 1: Finding the policy set for one interval.

4.3. Cost Function. In this section, a cost function is defined to punish the situations that may cause a decrease in users' QoE. We focus on three objective parameters that affect strongly the subjective perception of the users which are quality level, video stalling, and quality switch. First, the cost function should favor the selected bitrate to be close to the current bandwidth, so it punishes the difference Δr between the current bandwidth and the bitrate of the next segment selected by action a, with

$$\Delta r = |\mathrm{bw}_k - r_a|. \tag{9}$$

Second, to prevent video stalling, the buffer level should never be underflow. We define an optimal buffer level b_{opt} that is a desired value the client should try to keep during a streaming session. When the buffer level is close to b_{opt}, the buffer underflow is avoided. Therefore, the cost function penalizes the deviation Δb of the current buffer level from the optimal buffer level, where

$$\Delta b = |b_k - b_{\mathrm{opt}}|. \tag{10}$$

Third, in order to reduce the quality switches, the cost function should contain the difference Δq between the selected quality and the last one. To punish a QoE reduction because of high quality variations, we define Δq as follows:

$$\Delta q = (a - v_k)^2. \tag{11}$$

Let α, β, γ be the trade-off parameters of three objects, namely, quality level, video stalling, and quality switch, respectively. The cost incurred when the system changes from state s_k to state s_{k+1} given action a can be calculated by

$$C(s_k, s_{k+1}, a) = \alpha \Delta r + \beta \Delta b + \gamma \Delta q. \tag{12}$$

4.4. Optimization Solution. As the system is discrete and the number of states is large, we can formulate an infinite horizon

problem. For every state s_k, the most appropriate action a, called policy for state s_k, has to be decided so that the mean cost per state is minimum. As mentioned above, our system has I system state sets corresponding to I bitrate intervals, so we have to find I corresponding policy sets. For simplicity, we only present the optimization solution for a general bitrate interval with the system state set $\mathbf{s}$ and a corresponding policy set μ. Finding optimal solutions for all bitrate intervals will be done similarly. Mathematically, we have to minimize C_A which is the average cost per state obtained after downloading L video segments. C_A is calculated as follows:

$$C_A = \lim_{L \to \infty} \frac{1}{L} \sum_{l=1}^{L} P(s_k, s_{k+1}, a) C_l(s_k, s_{k+1}, a), \tag{13}$$

with $C_l(s_k, s_{k+1}, a)$ being the cost incurred after downloading the lth segment. Here, L is the number of state transitions and is also the number of video segments in the session. Based on the standard policy iteration algorithm (PIA) [26], we solve the IHP problem by using an algorithm as presented in Algorithm 1.

Applying PIA of SDP for I bitrate intervals, we would generate I policy sets which serve like a look-up table mapping each state to an optimal action. Thus, the client is able to decide an appropriate version for the next segment based on the current system condition.

Let $C_{\mathrm{prob}}, C_{\mathrm{cost}}$ be the computational complexity of the calculation of transition probability and the cost from one state to the remaining states, respectively. Let C_{PIA} be the computational complexity of Algorithm 1. The complexity of our model is $C = C_{\mathrm{prob}} + C_{\mathrm{cost}} + C_{\mathrm{PIA}}$. For each interval, each action, and each state, we consider the cost and the transition probability to $N - 1$ remaining states. So the complexity of the calculation of transition probability and the cost is described as follows:

$$C_{\mathrm{prob}} = C_{\mathrm{cost}} = O\left(IV_{\mathrm{max}}N^2\right). \tag{14}$$

Based on [27], we have

$$C_{\text{PIA}} = O\left(IV_{\max}^N\right). \tag{15}$$

Therefore, the complexity of our model is

$$C = O\left(2IV_{\max}N^2 + IV_{\max}^N\right). \tag{16}$$

5. Performance Prediction

After Section 4, we achieve I policy sets corresponding to I intervals of a video bitrate. In this section, we use the Markov chain model to predict the streaming performance for a session. Similar to Section 4.4, this section only presents the performance prediction for a general bitrate interval with a system state set $\mathbf{s}$ and a corresponding policy set $\boldsymbol{\mu}$. Predicting performance for all bitrate intervals will be done similarly. After carrying out the calculation for all I bitrate intervals, we take the average values as the final results.

The key is to determine the average state probability $\mathbf{p}_a = [p_{a1}, p_{a2}, \ldots, p_{aN}]$ with p_{an} $(1 \leq n \leq N)$ being the average probability that the system is at the nth state throughout the streaming session. The probability $\mathbf{p}_a$ is the average value of state probabilities after downloading l segments $\mathbf{p}_l = [p_{l1}, p_{l2}, \ldots, p_{lN}]$, $(1 \leq l \leq L)$. Here, p_{ln} $(1 \leq n \leq N)$ is the probability that the system is at the nth state after downloading l segments. From the Markov chain theory, the state probability after downloading $l + 1$ segments can be computed as the product of the state probability after downloading l segments and a transition matrix $\mathbf{p}_{l+1} = \mathbf{p}_l \mathbf{P}_{\text{TS}}$. Assuming that the initial probability p_0 is known. The transition matrix $\mathbf{P}_{\text{TS}}$ is a $N \times N$ matrix which represents the transition probability from state s_k to state s_{k+1}. $\mathbf{P}_{\text{TS}}$ is defined as follows:

$$\mathbf{P}_{\text{TS}} = P\left(s_k, s_{k+1}\right) = \Pr\left\{s_{k+1} \mid s_k, a \in \boldsymbol{\mu}\right\}. \tag{17}$$

The average state probability $\mathbf{p}_a$ is calculated as follows.

$$\mathbf{p}_a = \frac{\sum_{l=1}^{L} \mathbf{p}_l \mathbf{P}_{\text{TS}}}{L}. \tag{18}$$

Currently, most of the adaptation algorithms developed for HTTP streaming are qualitative in the sense that the performance metrics could only be obtained after the streaming session. In this study, the predicted streaming performance could be calculated based on the average state probability and the information inside every state. Specifically, we mainly focus on the following aspects: bitrate prediction, quality switch prediction, and buffer prediction.

5.1. Quality Prediction. The video quality that the users perceive is presented through the selected version. The higher the version is selected, the better the video quality is perceived by the users. Furthermore, setting the maximum version for the streaming session also affects the perceptual quality of the users. Obviously, a very low value of the maximum version may result in a poor perceptual quality while a very high value may increase the chance of buffer underflow. In this section, we predict the quality performance of the streaming

session based on the average version A_v that is calculated using (19) and the cumulative distribution function (CDF) of the versions $f(v)$ $(v \in [1; V\max])$ that is shown in (20). Based on the predicted probability of the versions throughout a streaming session, the maximum version could be decided for the session

$$A_v = \frac{\sum_{n=1}^{N} v_n p_{an}}{N}, \tag{19}$$

$$f(v) = \frac{\sum_{n=1}^{N} v_n p_{an}}{N} \mid v = v_n. \tag{20}$$

5.2. Quality Switch Prediction. Quality switch is an important factor affecting the perception of the users. The users often expect a smooth playback with the minimum number of quality switches and small switch amplitude from one segment to the next. We can predict the average version switch per segment A_{sw} as follows:

$$A_{sw} = \frac{\sum_{n=1}^{N} |a_n - v_n| p_{an}}{N}, \quad a_n \in \boldsymbol{\mu}. \tag{21}$$

5.3. Buffer Prediction. Video stalling is one of the important objective parameters that affect the subjective perception of the users. Stalling occurs when the play-out buffer underruns. To prevent this event, the buffer must be maintained within a safe range. In this session, we evaluate the buffer performance through the average buffer level A_b, the CDF of the buffer level $\hat{f}(b)$ $(b \in [1; B\max])$, and the buffer underflow probability $\Pr_{\text{und}}$ (i.e., when the system stays at buffer level 1) which are described as follows:

$$A_b = \frac{\sum_{n=1}^{N} b_n p_{an}}{N},$$

$$\hat{f}(b) = \frac{\sum_{n=1}^{N} b_n p_{an}}{N} \mid b_n < b, \tag{22}$$

$$\Pr_{\text{und}} = \frac{\sum_{n=1}^{N} p_{an}}{N} \mid b_n = 1.$$

A_b represents the safety of the buffer. If A_b is small, the buffer level is often in low levels, which may cause playback interruption when the current bandwidth drops dramatically. $\hat{f}(b)$ reflects the variance of the buffer level under the fluctuations of the network. $\Pr_{\text{und}}$ shows the probability that the playback would be interrupted in the streaming session.

6. Experimental Results

In order to evaluate the proposed system model and performance prediction accuracy, in this section, we perform a number of experiments in both offline and online contexts and compare the performance predicted results with the measurement ones. We also compare our proposed method with two existing ones, namely, the SDP method presented [10] which could obtain the best performance among the SDP methods and the bitrate estimation based method presented [14], which is the best among the qualitative methods.

6.1. Experiment Setup.

6.1. Experiment Setup. For the simulation, our test-bed consists of a client running Java 8.0 which implements the adaptation and a server running Apache2 which holds the media segments. The client runs on a Window 7 computer with an Intel i5-1.7 GHz CPU and 4 GB memory and the server runs on Ubuntu 12.04LTS (with default TCP CUBIC) with 1 G RAM. The channel bandwidth is simulated using DummyNet [28]. We use the Tokyo Olympic video from [6]. For the video, $V\text{max} = 9$, and, for the bandwidth, $W = 10$. Since we measure the buffer size and compute the buffer cost in the segment duration unit, we implement our adaptation method with one setting of the segment duration. In our experiments, we select a segment duration of 2 seconds, which is similar to those of [7, 8, 10]. The impacts of segment durations on adaptation performance have been considered in some recent studies [29, 30]. Further evaluation of different segment durations with a fixed buffer size (in seconds) will be reserved for our future work. Maximum buffer level is set to 5 segments (i.e., 10 seconds) and optimal buffer level is set to 4 segments (i.e., 8 seconds).

In our method, a streaming provider can adjust the balance between the requirements for high quality level, preventing video stalling, and reducing quality switches by changing the trade-off parameters α, γ, and β. Since selecting an optimal combination of trade-off parameters of the cost function involves solving a hard optimization problem, it will be investigated in our future work. In this paper, we select qualitatively the trade-off parameters of cost function as follows. Initially, we fix β and select the other two parameters. Since we want to prioritize requirement of smooth quality switch, γ is selected so that the contribution of the quality switch cost Δq is higher than that of buffer cost Δb. With parameter α, because the bitrate cost Δr can be up to thousands, parameter α should be small to reduce the contribution of the bitrate cost to the overall cost C. Based on our experience, good empirical values on parameters α, β, and γ are 0.003, 4, and 20, respectively.

6.2. Experimental Results.

6.2. Experimental Results. In the first part of the experiment, we evaluate the accuracy of performance prediction in offline context using a given bandwidth trace obtained from a mobile network [12]. In this context, the number of video segments L is 300.

Figures 5 and 6 show the predicted performance using the formulas presented in Section 5 and the measured performance obtained from the experiments when the maximum allowed version is set to 7, 8, and 9. These figures point out that the prediction results are close to the measurement ones. We can see from Figure 5 that when the maximum version increases the average version as well as the average version switch also increases. Figure 6 shows that, in both prediction and measurement cases, when the maximum version is 7, the underflow probability is almost zero and increases very slowly when the maximum allowed version increases. This analysis implies that setting the maximum version to 8 is reasonable in terms of balancing between average video quality and quality switch; meanwhile setting the maximum version to 7 ensures a very stable streaming experience.

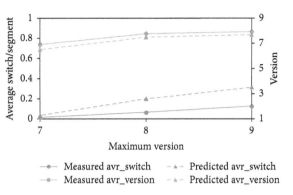

FIGURE 5: Predicted performance and measured performance in terms of average version and average version switch per segment in offline context using a given bandwidth trace.

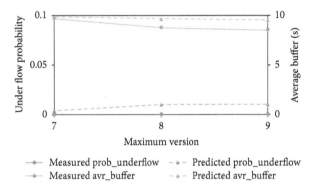

FIGURE 6: Predicted performance and measured performance in terms of average buffer and underflow probability in offline context using a given bandwidth trace.

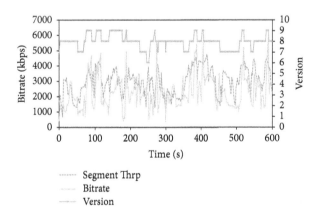

FIGURE 7: Experimental results of proposed method in offline context using a given bandwidth trace with $V\text{max} = 9$.

Figures 7, 8, and 9 show the bitrate and version switch behavior of the proposed method in the three cases of maximum version. It can be seen very clearly from these figures that when the maximum version is reduced, the number of version switches (or quality changes) decreases.

Table 1 shows more detailed statistics of the experimental results in three cases of maximum version. It can be drawn

TABLE 1: Compare predicted performance and measured performance in offline context using a given bandwidth trace.

Statistics	$V_{max} = 9$		$V_{max} = 8$		$V_{max} = 7$	
	Predicted	Measured	Predicted	Measured	Predicted	Measured
$A_b(s)$	9.48	8.52	9.59	8.77	9.8	9.68
A_q	7.64	7.88	7.45	7.73	6.48	6.87
A_{sw}	0.30	0.18	0.14	0.09	0.03	0.02
$Pr_{undflow}$	0.01	0.00	0.006	0.00	0.00	0.00

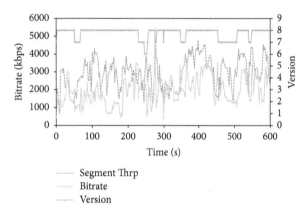

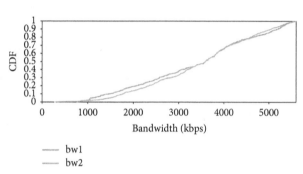

FIGURE 10: The cumulative distribution function of bw1 and bw2.

FIGURE 8: Experimental results of proposed method in offline context using a given bandwidth trace with Vmax = 8.

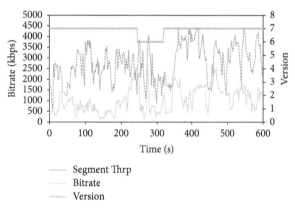

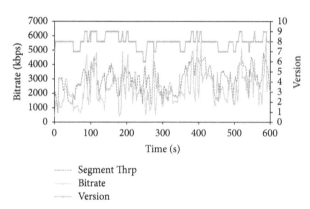

FIGURE 11: Experimental results of proposed method in offline context using a history bandwidth trace with Vmax = 9.

FIGURE 9: Experimental results of proposed method in offline context using a given bandwidth trace with Vmax = 7.

from the table that there is no significant difference between the predicted performance and the measured performance.

In the second part of the experiment, we use two history bandwidth traces recorded from two previous streaming sessions of the client. The CDFs of both bandwidths are shown in Figure 10.

Bandwidth bw_1 is used for calculating the statistical models and bw_2 is used in the simulation for measuring performance parameters. Figures 11, 12, and 13 show the bitrate and version switch behavior of the proposed method in the three cases of maximum version. The detailed results are listed in Table 2. Based on these figures and table, we affirm once again that the mathematical performance prediction model agrees well with the measurement.

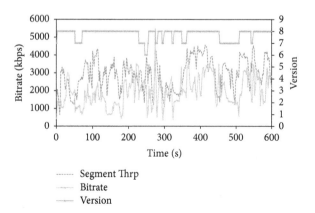

FIGURE 12: Experimental results of proposed method in offline context using a history bandwidth trace with Vmax = 8.

TABLE 2: Compare predicted performance and measured performance in offline context using a history bandwidth trace for statistics.

Statistics	$V_{max} = 9$		$V_{max} = 8$		$V_{max} = 7$	
	Predicted	Measured	Predicted	Measured	Predicted	Measured
$A_b(s)$	9.52	8.44	9.61	8.85	9.69	9.65
A_q	7.48	7.92	7.27	7.71	6.80	6.98
A_{sw}	0.31	0.19	0.18	0.11	0.08	0.05
$Pr_{undflow}$	0.00	0.00	0.00	0.00	0.00	0.00

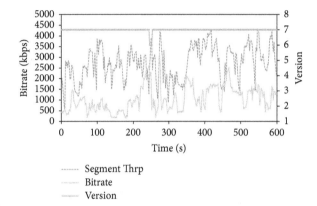

----- Segment Thrp
----- Bitrate
----- Version

FIGURE 13: Experimental results of proposed method in offline context using a history bandwidth trace with Vmax = 7.

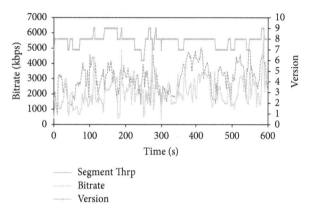

······ Segment Thrp
----- Bitrate
······ Version

FIGURE 14: Experimental results of the proposed method in online context with Vmax = 9.

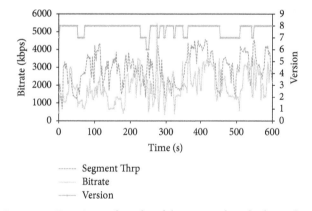

······ Segment Thrp
----- Bitrate
----- Version

FIGURE 15: Experimental results of the proposed method in online context with Vmax = 8.

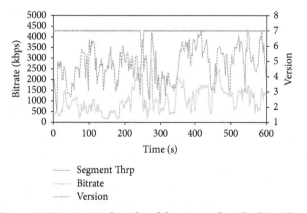

······ Segment Thrp
----- Bitrate
------ Version

FIGURE 16: Experimental results of the proposed method in online context with Vmax = 7.

In the third part of the experiment, we consider the online context in which the prediction of the future bandwidth is based on the statistical parameters of all previous segments. Specifically, we divide an entire session into chunks, each of which has L video segments. We treat each chunk individually as a mini streaming session. Assuming that, initially we have enough statistical data to predict the performance of the first chunk. The prediction of the subsequent chunks will be done based on the previous chunks. At the beginning of each chunk, the bandwidth statistics are updated leading to a recomputation of the policy set and the performance. In the experiment, we set L to 100 video segments. It can be observed from our experiments that it took only several seconds to (re)compute the whole model. Therefore, the computational overhead is about 3%, which is appropriate for the online context. Figures 14, 15, and 16 show the adaptation, bitrate, and version switch behavior of the proposed method in the three cases of maximum version. The predicted performance and the measured performance in the online context in the three cases are presented in detail in Tables 3, 4, and 5. It is very clear that, in the online context, the predicted performance is also very close to the measured performance.

Next, we compare our proposed method with the SDP method [10] and the bitrate estimation based method [14] using the same simulation settings as in the first part of our experiment. The experimental results obtained by simulating the SDP method [10] and bitrate estimation based method [14] are shown in Figures 17 and 18, respectively. We can see that both methods provide very fluctuating version switches. The detailed statistics of these adaptation methods with the maximum version set to 9 and our proposed method with the

TABLE 3: Compare predicted performance and measured performance in online context with $V_{max} = 9$.

Statistics	Chunk 1		Chunk 2		Chunk 3	
	Predicted	Measured	Predicted	Measured	Predicted	Measured
$A_b(s)$	9.31	8.96	8.92	8.45	9.36	8.86
A_q	7.69	8.04	7.89	7.68	7.83	7.72
A_{sw}	0.05	0.09	0.04	0.07	0.02	0.05
$Pr_{undflow}$	0.00	0.00	0.00	0.00	0.00	0.00

TABLE 4: Compare predicted performance and measured performance in online context with $V_{max} = 8$.

Statistics	Chunk 1		Chunk 2		Chunk 3	
	Predicted	Measured	Predicted	Measured	Predicted	Measured
$A_b(s)$	9.53	9.01	9.42	8.63	9.42	8.96
A_q	7.56	7.86	7.65	7.63	7.65	7.67
A_{sw}	0.00	0.03	0.01	0.03	0.02	0.04
$Pr_{undflow}$	0.00	0.00	0.00	0.00	0.00	0.00

TABLE 5: Compare predicted performance and measured performance in online context with $V_{max} = 7$.

Statistics	Chunk 1		Chunk 2		Chunk 3	
	Predicted	Measured	Predicted	Measured	Predicted	Measured
$A_b(s)$	9.77	9.93	9.77	9.52	9.83	9.59
A_q	6.92	7.00	6.92	6.95	6.92	7.00
A_{sw}	0.00	0.00	0.00	0.02	0.00	0.00
$Pr_{undflow}$	0.00	0.00	0.00	0.00	0.00	0.00

TABLE 6: Statistics of different adaptation methods in offline context.

Statistics	SDP method $V_{max} = 9$	Bitrate estimation method $V_{max} = 9$	Proposed method $V_{max} = 9$	Proposed method $V_{max} = 8$	Proposed method $V_{max} = 7$
$A_b(s)$	8.62	8.85	8.52	8.77	9.68
A_q	7.40	7.85	7.88	7.73	6.87
A_{sw}	0.76	0.43	0.18	0.09	0.02
$Pr_{undflow}$	0.00	0.00	0.00	0.00	0.00

maximum version set to 7, 8, and 9 are shown in Table 6. It can be seen that the performance of the bitrate estimation method is less effective than our method in terms of average version and average version switch. Regarding the SDP method, it is evident that the performance of this method is the worst among all (with low average version and highest average switch per segment). This can be expected because this method was not originally designed for real VBR videos.

The buffer level curves of the three methods in offline context are shown in Figure 19. We can see that all buffer curves imply streaming sessions without any freezes for users. Among these, the SDP method and the proposed method with $V_{max} = 9$ provide the most unstable buffers, while the bitrate estimation based method and the proposed method with $V_{max} = 7$ provide the most stable buffers. It can be observed from Figures 17 and 18 and Table 6 that the SDP method and bitrate estimation based method result in very fluctuating version curves, and the proposed method with

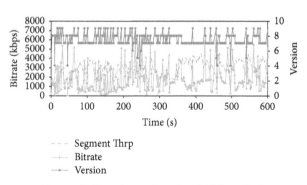

--- Segment Thrp
—·— Bitrate
—•— Version

FIGURE 17: Experimental results of SDP method.

$V_{max} = 7$ obtains the lowest average quality. Therefore, from Table 6 and Figure 19 we can see that the proposed method in offline context with $V_{max} = 8$ or 9 can provide the best performance.

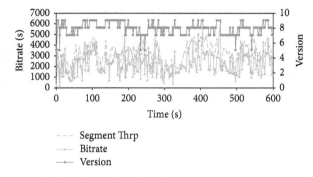

FIGURE 18: Experimental results of bitrate estimation based method.

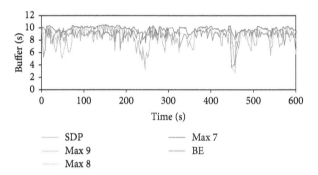

FIGURE 19: Buffer level curves of SDP method, bitrate estimation based method, and the proposed method (Max9, Max8, and Max7) in offline context.

7. Conclusion

In this paper, we have proposed an adaptation method for HTTP streaming based on stochastic dynamic programming. The system model was targeted at real bandwidth trace with strong bitrate fluctuation of VBR videos. Furthermore, we have developed a model to predict the system performance with the aim of choosing the best setting based on the performance requirements. The experimental results have shown that our method can effectively adapt VBR videos and perform accurate performance prediction which is useful in planning adaptation policy.

Conflicts of Interest

The authors declare that there are no conflicts of interest regarding the publication of this paper.

References

[1] Cisco Systems, Inc., "Networking index: Forecast and methodology, 2012–2017," Cisco Visual, May 2013.

[2] A. C. Begen, T. Akgul, and M. Baugher, "Watching video over the web: part 1: streaming protocols," *IEEE Internet Computing*, vol. 15, no. 2, pp. 54–63, 2011.

[3] T. C. Thang, Q.-D. Ho, J. W. Kang, and A. T. Pham, "Adaptive streaming of audiovisual content using MPEG DASH," *IEEE Transactions on Consumer Electronics*, vol. 58, no. 1, pp. 78–85, 2012.

[4] T. Stockhammer, "Dynamic adaptive streaming over HTTP: standards and design principles," in *Proceeding of the 2nd Annual ACM Multimedia Systems Conference (MMSys '11)*, pp. 133–144, San Jose, CA, USA, February 2011.

[5] K. Miller, E. Quacchio, G. Gennari, and A. Wolisz, "Adaptation algorithm for adaptive streaming over HTTP," in *Proceedings of the 19th International Packet Video Workshop (PV '12)*, pp. 173–178, IEEE, Munich, Germany, May 2012.

[6] Y. Zhou, Y. Duan, J. Sun, and Z. Guo, "Towards simple and smooth rate adaption for VBR video in DASH," in *Proceedings of the IEEE Visual Communications and Image Processing Conference (VCIP '14)*, pp. 9–12, IEEE, Valletta, Malta, December 2014.

[7] S. Akhshabi, S. Narayanaswamy, A. C. Begen, and C. Dovrolis, "An experimental evaluation of rate-adaptive video players over HTTP," *Signal Processing: Image Communication*, vol. 27, no. 4, pp. 271–287, 2012.

[8] C. Müller, S. Lederer, and C. Timmerer, "An evaluation of dynamic adaptive streaming over HTTP in vehicular environments," in *Proceedings of the 4th Workshop on Mobile Video (MoVid '12)*, pp. 37–42, New York, NY, USA, February 2012.

[9] C. Liu, I. Bouazizi, and M. Gabbouj, "Rate adaptation for adaptive HTTP streaming," in *Proceedings of the 2nd Annual ACM Multimedia Systems Conference (MMSys '11)*, pp. 169–174, San Jose, Calif, USA, February 2011.

[10] S. García, J. Cabrera, and N. García, "Quality-control algorithm for adaptive streaming services over wireless channels," *IEEE Journal on Selected Topics in Signal Processing*, vol. 9, no. 1, pp. 50–59, 2015.

[11] A. H. Duong, T. Nguyen, T. Vu, T. T. Do, N. P. Ngoc, and T. C. Thang, "SDP-based adaptation for quality control in adaptive streaming," in *Proceedings of the International Conference on Computing, Management and Telecommunications, (ComManTel '15)*, pp. 194–199, IEEE, DaNang, Vietnam, December 2015.

[12] S. Lederer, C. Mueller, C. Timmerer, C. Concolato, J. Le Feuvre, and K. Fliegel, "Distributed DASH dataset," in *Proceedings of the 4th ACM Multimedia Systems Conference, (MMSys '13)*, pp. 131–135, Oslo, Norway, March 2013.

[13] "H264/AVC video trace library," http://trace.eas.asu.edu/h264/.

[14] T. C. Thang, H. T. Le, H. X. Nguyen, A. T. Pham, J. W. Kang, and Y. M. Ro, "Adaptive video streaming over HTTP with dynamic resource estimation," *IEEE Trans. On consumer electronics*, vol. 58, no. 1, pp. 78–85, 2012.

[15] T. C. Thang, H. T. Le, A. T. Pham, and Y. M. Ro, "An evaluation of bitrate adaptation methods for HTTP live streaming," *IEEE Journal on Selected Areas in Communications*, vol. 32, no. 4, pp. 693–705, 2014.

[16] R. Dubin, O. Hadar, and A. Dvir, "The effect of client buffer and MBR consideration on DASH Adaptation Logic," in *Proceedings of the 2013 IEEE Wireless Communications and Networking Conference, (WCNC '13)*, pp. 2178–2183, IEEE, Shanghai, China, April 2013.

[17] G. Liang and B. Liang, "Effect of delay and buffering on jitter-free streaming over random VBR channels," *IEEE Transactions on Multimedia*, vol. 10, no. 6, pp. 1128–1141, 2008.

[18] Y. Kang, H. Chen, and L. Xie, "An artificial-neural-network-based QoE estimation model for Video streaming over wireless networks," in *Proceedings of the 2013 IEEE/CIC International Conference on Communications in China, (ICCC '13)*, pp. 264–269, IEEE, Xi'an, China, August 2013.

[19] S. Xiang, L. Cai, and J. Pan, "Adaptive scalable video streaming in wireless networks," in *Proceedings of the 3rd ACM Multimedia*

Systems Conference, (MMSys '12), pp. 167–172, New York, NY, USA, February 2012.

[20] Y. Liu and J. Y. B. Lee, "On adaptive video streaming with predictable streaming performance," in *Proceedings of the 2014 IEEE Global Communications Conference, (GLOBECOM '14)*, pp. 1164–1169, IEEE, Austin, TX, USA, December 2014.

[21] S. Akhshabi, A. C. Begen, and C. Dovrolis, "An experimental evaluation of rate-adaptation algorithms in adaptive streaming over HTTP," in *Proceedings of the 2nd Annual ACM Multimedia Systems Conference (MMSys '11)*, pp. 157–168, San Jose, CA, USA, February 2011.

[22] G. Ji and B. Liang, "Stochastic rate control for scalable VBR video streaming over wireless networks," in *Proceedings of the 2009 IEEE Global Telecommunications Conference, (GLOBECOM '09)*, Honolulu, HI, USA, December 2009.

[23] M. Xing, S. Xiang, and L. Cai, "Rate adaptation strategy for video streaming over multiple wireless access networks," in *Proceedings of the 2012 IEEE Global Communications Conference, (GLOBECOM '12)*, pp. 5745–5750, IEEE, Anaheim, CA, USA, December 2012.

[24] Z. Ye, R. EL-Azouzi, T. Jimenez, and Y. Xu, "Computing The Quality of Experience in Network Modeled by a Markov Modulated Fluid Model," 2014.

[25] Y. Xu, E. Altman, R. El-Azouzi, M. Haddad, S. Elayoubi, and T. Jimenez, "Analysis of buffer starvation with application to objective QoE optimization of streaming services," *IEEE Transactions on Multimedia*, vol. 16, no. 3, pp. 813–827, 2014.

[26] H. Thomas, E. Cormen Charles, L. Ronald, and S. Clifford, *Introduction to Algorithms*, MIT Press and McGraw-Hill, 3rd edition, 2009.

[27] Y. Mansour and S. Singh, "On the complexity of policy iteration," *UAI*, pp. 401–408, 1999.

[28] L. Rizzo, "Dummynet: a simple approach to the evaluation of networkprotocols," *ACM Computer Communication Review*, vol. 27, no. 1, pp. 31–41, 1997.

[29] D. M. Nguyen, L. B. Tran, H. T. Le, N. P. Ngoc, and T. C. Thang, "An evaluation of segment duration effects in HTTP adaptive streaming over mobile networks," in *Proceedings of the 2nd National Foundation for Science and Technology Development Confernce on Information and Computer Science, (NICS '15)*, pp. 248–253, Ho Chi Minh City, Vietnam, September 2015.

[30] L. Koskimies, T. Taleb, and M. Bagaa, "QoE estimation-based server benchmarking for virtual video delivery platform," in *Proceeding of IEEE International Conference on Communications (ICC '17)*, Paris, France, May 2017.

14

Revealing Traces of Image Resampling and Resampling Antiforensics

Anjie Peng,[1,2] **Yadong Wu,**[1] **and Xiangui Kang**[2]

[1]*School of Computer Science and Technology, Southwest University of Science and Technology, Sichuan, China*
[2]*Guangdong Key Lab of Information Security, School of Data and Computer Science, Sun Yat-Sen University, Guangzhou, China*

Correspondence should be addressed to Xiangui Kang; isskxg@mail.sysu.edu.cn

Academic Editor: Mei-Ling Shyu

Image resampling is a common manipulation in image processing. The forensics of resampling plays an important role in image tampering detection, steganography, and steganalysis. In this paper, we proposed an effective and secure detector, which can simultaneously detect resampling and its forged resampling which is attacked by antiforensic schemes. We find that the interpolation operation used in the resampling and forged resampling makes these two kinds of image show different statistical behaviors from the unaltered images, especially in the high frequency domain. To reveal the traces left by the interpolation, we first apply multidirectional high-pass filters on an image and the residual to create multidirectional differences. Then, the difference is fit into an autoregressive (AR) model. Finally, the AR coefficients and normalized histograms of the difference are extracted as the feature. We assemble the feature extracted from each difference image to construct the comprehensive feature and feed it into support vector machines (SVM) to detect resampling and forged resampling. Experiments on a large image database show that the proposed detector is effective and secure. Compared with the state-of-the-art works, the proposed detector achieved significant improvements in the detection of downsampling or resampling under JPEG compression.

1. Introduction

Resampling is a useful image processing tool, such as upscaling in consumer electronics, downscaling in the online store, social networking, and picture sharing portal. However, some people intentionally utilize the resampling to create tampered images and upload these images to social networks to spread rumors. Due to the abuse in image tampering, resampling forensics attracts researchers' attentions [1–12]. Resampling forensics can also be used to reveal the image's processing history or help people select the secure cover for stenography; for example, Kodovský and Fridrich analyzed how the parameters of downscaling affect the security of stenography [13]. Hou et al. utilized the resampling forensics for blind steganalysis [14]. Therefore, resampling forensics is of particular interest in the multimedia security field.

Early works [1–10] of resampling forensics were based on the periodical artifacts resulting from equidistant sampling and interpolating. These detectors [1–10] can provide reliable results in the uncompressed resampled images. However,

their detection accuracies significantly degraded in the case of resampling with JPEG compression. Recent works [11, 12, 15] utilized pattern recognition methods to detect resampling. These works extract the features at first and then perform classification by the machine learning tools. Feng et al. [11] exploited the normalized energy density as the characteristic of image resampling. They divided the DFT frequency spectrum of the second derivative of the image into 19 windows of varying size and then extracted the normalized energy density from each window to form a 19D feature. Li et al. [12] utilized a moment feature to reveal the position and amplitude distribution of resampling in the DFT frequency domain. They first divided the DFT frequency spectrum into 20 subbands with equal interval and then extracted the moment feature from each subband to form a 20D feature. For the sake of simplicity, we called the 19D normalized energy density feature [11] and 20D moment feature [12] as FE and FM, respectively. The machine learning-based detectors [11, 12, 15] get better results than periodical artifacts-based detectors [1–10] for the upsampling with JPEG compression. However, their performances on the downsampling with JPEG compression still need to be improved. Besides, the above detectors [1–12, 15] have not considered the existence of malicious adversary, a practicable challenge in real life. For instance, Kirchner and Böhme [16] proposed an antiforensic scheme by removing the periodic artifacts with irregular sampling and successfully defeated the periodicity-based approach [1–10]. In the sequel, we called the resampling antiforensics [16] as forged resampling for short.

The appearance of antiforensic technology has been drawing the researchers' attentions to the *security* of the forensics [17, 18]. Sencar and Memon [18] formally define the *security* and *robustness* of the forensics. They pointed out that the *security* concerns the ability to resist intentionally concealed illegitimate postprocessing, while the *robustness* concentrates on the reliability against legitimate postprocessing. In our previous work [19], we employed partial autocorrelation coefficient to reveal the artifacts caused by the forged resampling. Li et al. [15] utilized steganalytic model, SRM, [20] to detect forged resampling and obtained excellent performance.

For a test image, we have no knowledge whether it has been processed by resampling or forged resampling. To avoid missing detection, an alternative approach is that sequentially testing the image by the resampling detector and forged resampling detector. Only if two detectors both predict the image is innocent is the test image taken as an innocent image. To simplify the detection procedure, we propose an integrated detector which can simultaneously detect resampling and its forged resampling. As both the resampled image and forged resampled image are generated via interpolation, we employ the histogram and coefficients of AR model on multidirectional differences to capture the interpolation traces. Experimental results indicate that the proposed integrated detector is effective and secure.

The rest of this paper is organized as follows. Section 2 reviews the resampling forensics and the antiforensic scheme [16]. In Section 3, we introduce a new feature set for resampling forensics. The experiments are presented in Section 4. Section 5 concludes the paper.

2. Background

In this section, we first introduce the resampling and its periodical artifacts and then review the forged resampling scheme proposed by Kirchner and Böhme [16].

2.1. Resampling. The frequently used image resampling operation, including scaling and rotation, consists of two basic operations: (1) resampling, which is also called as spatial transformation of coordinates, and (2) intensity interpolation, which assigns pixel values to the transformed pixels.

Assume that we want to rescale a $r \times c$ image $I(x, y)$ to a $m \times n$ image $E(i, j)$. Generally speaking, 2D image scaling can be separated into two 1D scaling operations along the row and column, respectively. Intuitively, image I is first rescaled along the row to get an intermediate image B of size $m \times c$; then image B is rescaled along the column to get rescaled image E

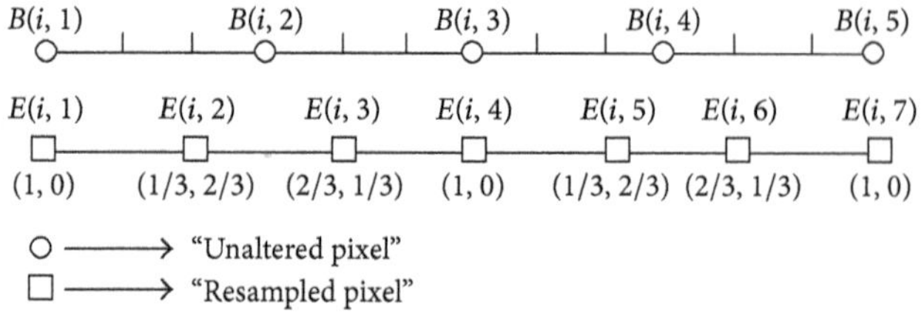

FIGURE 1: Example of the upscaling ($s = 3/2$, bilinear) process for the ith row of image B (the first line). The corresponding interpolated weights are shown in the bracket.

with size of $m \times n$. The whole scaling process can be formulated as

$$E = A^r I A^c = B A^c, \qquad (1)$$

where the matrix $A^r (m \times r)$ and $A^c (c \times n)$ determined by the scaling factor s and interpolation kernel embodies the rescaling process for the row and column, respectively. According to (1), we can simplify the discussions of 2D scaling to 1D scaling. As image rotation is similar to image scaling, we concentrate on the image scaling in the following.

In the resampling phase, for a scaling factor $s = v/h$ (the greatest common divisor of v and h is 1), the rescaling pixels are first mapped into the original pixel grid with equidistance h/v. Then the intensities of rescaling pixels are calculated by the weighted sums of neighboring original pixel intensities. The weights are determined by the interpolation kernel function, which uses the distances between the rescaled grid and its neighboring original grids as the input.

Due to equidistant sampling, the distance sequences are periodical; thus the interpolated weights are periodical and periodic correlation patterns between neighboring pixels are introduced. Figure 1 shows an example of upscaling ($s = 3/2$) with bilinear interpolation in the ith row of image B. It is shown that the interpolated weights emerge with periodicity equal to 3. In this case, the scaling matrix A^c is as follows:

$$A^c = \begin{bmatrix} 1 & \frac{1}{3} & 0 & 0 & 0 & \cdots \\ 0 & \frac{2}{3} & \frac{2}{3} & 0 & 0 & \cdots \\ 0 & 0 & \frac{1}{3} & 1 & \frac{1}{3} & \cdots \\ 0 & 0 & 0 & 0 & \frac{2}{3} & \cdots \\ \vdots & \vdots & \vdots & \vdots & \vdots & \vdots \end{bmatrix}. \qquad (2)$$

From matrix A^c, we can infer that the $3k$th ($k = 1, 2, 3, \ldots$) column is a linear combination of its 4 neighboring columns, which reveals that the correlations among adjacent pixels are periodical.

Early works [1–10] utilized periodical linear correlations to detect resampling. Popescu and Farid [1] revealed the periodical correlation by a probability map (p-map), which is estimated by the expectation maximum algorithm. For an automatic detector, the periodical artifacts were transformed

p-map   Fourier spectrum

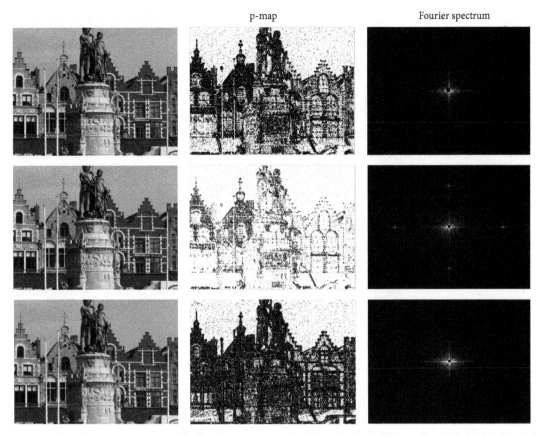

FIGURE 2: Top row: unaltered image, p-map, and its Fourier spectrum. Second row: upscaled image ($s = 3/2$, bilinear). Third row: forged upscaled image (*attack* 1, $s = 3/2$, bilinear, $\sigma = 0.4$).

as peaks in the frequency domain as shown in the middle row of Figure 2.

2.2. The Forged Resampling Scheme. As the equidistant sampling mainly results in the periodicity appearing in the resampled image, Kirchner and Böhme proposed two attacks to remove that periodicity [16].

(1) The first attack is based on geometric distortion with edge modulation (denoted by *attack* 1). To disturb equidistant sampling, the transformed pixel (i, j) was added by a zero mean Gaussian noise, whose standard variance σ controls the attack strength. That is, the transformed pixel (i, j) turned into a distorted pixel $(i + \varepsilon_1, j + \varepsilon_2)$, where $(\varepsilon_1, \varepsilon_2)$ is the Gaussian noise. Only geometric distortion severely degraded the visual quality, especially at the edge of the image. In order to improve the visual quality, the edge modulation was employed to tune attack strength. Particularly, the attack at the edge was weakened. After unequal sampling, the forged resampled image was obtained by applying the interpolation on the distorted pixel $(i + \varepsilon_1, j + \varepsilon_2)$.

(2) The second attack is dual-path approach (denoted by *attack* 2). This approach applied attacks to the low and high frequency components of the resampled image. In the low frequency path, Kirchner and Böhme applied a nonlinear 5×5 median filter to destroy linear correlations among neighboring pixels. In the high frequency path, they first obtained the

residual by subtracting a 5×5 median filtered version from its source image $I(x, y)$ and then applied *attack* 1 on the residual to get the distorted resampled residual. The final forged image is obtained by adding the filtered resampled image and distorted resampled residual.

Both attacks successfully concealed the periodicity in the resampled image; meanwhile they preserved the image's visual quality. Figure 2 demonstrates that an unaltered image (first row) and its forged resampled image (third row) have nearly the same p-map and corresponding Fourier spectrum, which indicates that the periodicity-based detectors [1–10] probably misclassify a forged resampled image as an unaltered image.

3. The Proposed Method

The proposed method aims at classifying the resampled image and forged resampled image from the unaltered image. Such a forensic problem can be formulated as the following hypothesis test:

H_0: the test image is an unaltered image

H_1: the test image is a resampled image or a forged resampled image

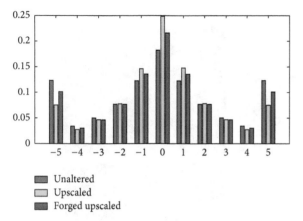

FIGURE 3: The average histogram for 1500 unaltered images, their corresponding upscaled images (s = 3/2, bicubic), and forged upscaled images (*attack* 1, s = 3/2, σ = 0.4, bicubic).

3.1. Traces of Interpolation.

Compared with unaltered image, due to interpolation, resampled and forged resampled image inevitably leave behind interpolation artifacts. We mainly focus on blurring artifacts and statistical changes of the relationships among neighboring pixels.

In the interpolation phase, the intensity of resampled pixel is a weighted sum of its adjacent original pixels. So, the interpolation is similar to a low-pass filter [11]. The blurring artifact is distinct in the upscaled and forged upscaled images. Figure 3 empirically shows the normalized histograms of the 1st-order horizontal difference ($I(x, y) - I(x, y + 1)$) estimated from BOSSRAW database [21] (please see Section 4 for more details about the database). It can be seen that the upscaled image and forged upscaled image have more bins than the unaltered image in the range of $[-1, 1]$. Because the antialiasing suppresses some high frequency components in the image, the downscaled image with antialiasing also shows slightly blurring artifacts [13]. To capture the blurring artifacts in the resampled and forged resampled image, we will employ the normalized histograms of the image difference as a feature subset.

The interpolation operation also changes the relationships of neighboring pixels. According to formula (1), an unknown scaled pixel is a linear combination of its adjacent l known original pixels, where l is kernel width. For a rescaled image, let us calculate the number of original pixels used to generate p consecutive rescaled pixels. First, the distance of these p rescaled pixels is $(p - 1)/s$, so there are $\lfloor(p - 1)/s\rfloor$ or $\lceil(p - 1)/s\rceil$ original pixels located among these p consecutive pixels, where $\lfloor\cdot\rfloor$ and $\lceil\cdot\rceil$ denote the floor and ceil function for the nearest integer. Second, the left (or right)

$l/2$ original pixels participate in the interpolation process for the starting (or ending) rescaled pixel. *So, we can infer that there are* $\lceil(p - 1)/s\rceil + l$ *or* $\lfloor(p - 1)/s\rfloor + l$ *original pixels used to generate p consecutive rescaled pixels.* For example, Figure 1 shows that 6 upscaled pixels $E(i, 1), E(i, 2), \ldots, E(i, 6)$ are generated by 5 original pixels $B(i, 1), B(i, 2), \ldots, B(i, 5)$. According to the above conclusion, we can infer that the relationship of p consecutive rescaled pixels reflects the relationship of $\lceil(p - 1)/s\rceil + l$ or $\lfloor(p - 1)/s\rfloor + l$ consecutive original pixels and of course differs from the relationship of p consecutive original pixels. For the forged rescaled image, due to irregular sampling, some forged pixels cluster closely in the original grid and other pixels located sparsely in the original grid, which also indicates that the forged rescaled image behaves different relationships among neighboring pixels from those of unaltered image. To capture the relationships of neighboring pixels, we will fit the image difference into an AR model and extract AR coefficients as a feature subset. The AR feature can characterize high-order correlations of adjacent pixels, but it has much smaller dimension than SPAM [22] (Subtractive Pixel Adjacency Matrix).

3.2. Multidirectional Differences.

As aforementioned, the interpolation is somewhat similar to low-pass filter [11] and thus causes significant statistical changes in the high frequency components of an interpolated image. In general, high frequency components (such as texture and edge) of a natural image are multidirectional. Accordingly, the changes caused by interpolation are also multidirectional. To capture these changes, we first design multidirectional high-pass filters to create multidirectional differences and then extract the proposed feature from these differences.

We employ the kernels of the 1st-order difference to derive multidirectional kernels. The kernels of commonly used 1st-order differences are shown as follows.

The Kernel of the 1st-Order Difference in the Horizontal (H), Vertical (V), Diagonal (D), and Antidiagonal (AD) Direction. It is given as follows:

$$
\overset{H}{\begin{bmatrix} 0, & 0, & 0 \\ 1, & -1, & 0 \\ 0, & 0, & 0 \end{bmatrix}}
\overset{V}{\begin{bmatrix} 0, & 1, & 0 \\ 0, & -1, & 0 \\ 0, & 0, & 0 \end{bmatrix}}
\overset{D}{\begin{bmatrix} 1, & 0, & 0 \\ 0, & -1, & 0 \\ 0, & 0, & 0 \end{bmatrix}}
\overset{AD}{\begin{bmatrix} 0, & 0, & 1 \\ 0, & -1, & 0 \\ 0, & 0, & 0 \end{bmatrix}}. \quad (3)
$$

We utilize combinations of horizontal (H), vertical (V), diagonal (D), and antidiagonal (AD) kernels to construct the multidirectional kernels as shown in the following.

Multidirectional Kernel Groups G(1)–G(3). They are given as follows:

$$
G(1)
$$

$$
\overset{H}{\begin{bmatrix} 0, & 0, & 0 \\ 1, & -2, & 1 \\ 0, & 0, & 0 \end{bmatrix}}
\overset{V}{\begin{bmatrix} 0, & 1, & 0 \\ 0, & -2, & 0 \\ 0, & 1, & 0 \end{bmatrix}}
\overset{H+V}{\begin{bmatrix} 0, & 1, & 0 \\ 1, & -2, & 0 \\ 0, & 0, & 0 \end{bmatrix}}
\overset{H+V}{\begin{bmatrix} 0, & 1, & 0 \\ 0, & -2, & 1 \\ 0, & 0, & 0 \end{bmatrix}}
\overset{H+V}{\begin{bmatrix} 0, & 0, & 0 \\ 0, & -2, & 1 \\ 0, & 1, & 0 \end{bmatrix}}
\overset{H+V}{\begin{bmatrix} 0, & 0, & 0 \\ 1, & -2, & 0 \\ 0, & 1, & 0 \end{bmatrix}}
$$

$$
G(2)
$$

$$
\begin{array}{cccccc}
D & AD & D+AD & D+AD & D+AD & D+AD \\
\begin{bmatrix} 1, & 0, & 0 \\ 0, & -2, & 0 \\ 0, & 0, & 1 \end{bmatrix} &
\begin{bmatrix} 0, & 0, & 1 \\ 0, & -2, & 0 \\ 1, & 0, & 0 \end{bmatrix} &
\begin{bmatrix} 1, & 0, & 1 \\ 0, & -2, & 0 \\ 0, & 0, & 0 \end{bmatrix} &
\begin{bmatrix} 1, & 0, & 0 \\ 0, & -2, & 0 \\ 1, & 0, & 0 \end{bmatrix} &
\begin{bmatrix} 0, & 0, & 0 \\ 0, & -2, & 0 \\ 1, & 0, & 1 \end{bmatrix} &
\begin{bmatrix} 0, & 0, & 1 \\ 0, & -2, & 0 \\ 0, & 0, & 1 \end{bmatrix}
\end{array}
$$

$$
G(3)
$$

$$
\begin{array}{ccccc}
H+D &
\begin{bmatrix} 1, & 0, & 0 \\ 1, & -2, & 0 \\ 0, & 0, & 0 \end{bmatrix} &
\begin{bmatrix} 0, & 0, & 0 \\ 1, & -2, & 0 \\ 0, & 0, & 1 \end{bmatrix} &
\begin{bmatrix} 0, & 0, & 0 \\ 0, & -2, & 1 \\ 0, & 0, & 1 \end{bmatrix} &
\begin{bmatrix} 1, & 0, & 0 \\ 0, & -2, & 1 \\ 0, & 0, & 0 \end{bmatrix} \\[4ex]
V+D &
\begin{bmatrix} 1, & 1, & 0 \\ 0, & -2, & 0 \\ 0, & 0, & 0 \end{bmatrix} &
\begin{bmatrix} 0, & 1, & 0 \\ 0, & -2, & 0 \\ 0, & 0, & 1 \end{bmatrix} &
\begin{bmatrix} 0, & 0, & 0 \\ 0, & -2, & 0 \\ 0, & 1, & 1 \end{bmatrix} &
\begin{bmatrix} 1, & 0, & 0 \\ 0, & -2, & 0 \\ 0, & 1, & 0 \end{bmatrix} \\[4ex]
H+AD &
\begin{bmatrix} 0, & 0, & 0 \\ 1, & -2, & 0 \\ 1, & 0, & 0 \end{bmatrix} &
\begin{bmatrix} 0, & 0, & 1 \\ 1, & -2, & 0 \\ 0, & 0, & 0 \end{bmatrix} &
\begin{bmatrix} 0, & 0, & 1 \\ 0, & -2, & 1 \\ 0, & 0, & 0 \end{bmatrix} &
\begin{bmatrix} 0, & 0, & 0 \\ 0, & -2, & 1 \\ 1, & 0, & 0 \end{bmatrix} \\[4ex]
V+AD &
\begin{bmatrix} 0, & 1, & 0 \\ 0, & -2, & 0 \\ 1, & 0, & 0 \end{bmatrix} &
\begin{bmatrix} 0, & 1, & 1 \\ 0, & -2, & 0 \\ 0, & 0, & 0 \end{bmatrix} &
\begin{bmatrix} 0, & 0, & 1 \\ 0, & -2, & 0 \\ 0, & 1, & 0 \end{bmatrix} &
\begin{bmatrix} 0, & 0, & 0 \\ 0, & -2, & 0 \\ 1, & 1, & 0 \end{bmatrix}
\end{array}
$$

$$(4)$$

Here "+" means the combination of two directional kernels.

From the 1st-order H or V kernel, the 2nd-order H, V, and H + V kernels (here "+" means the combination of two directional kernel) are derived to reflect the interpolation traces in both H and V directions. Similarly, the 2nd-order D, AD, and D + AD kernels are generated. We also consider the combinations between {H, V} and {D, AD} and obtain four kinds of kernel: H + D, V + D, H + AD, and V + AD. Finally, we have 28 2nd-order filter kernels in total. Following the above way, we can create higher-order kernels. However, the number of higher-order kernels increases sharply, which will increase computation burden in the feature extraction phase, so we only choose aforementioned 28 2nd-order filter kernels to create multidirectional differences.

Based on the kernel's direction, we divide all kernels into 3 groups (denoted by G(1)–G(3) in "*Multidirectional Kernel Groups G(1)–G(3)*"). It is noted that any kernel within a group can be obtained by rotating or flipping other kernels within the same group. We therefore specify that kernels within a group share the same pattern. Considering that spatial statistics in natural images are symmetric with respect to mirroring and flipping [22], we can average the feature sets extracted from the same group to reduce the feature dimension.

To further enhance the interpolation traces left in the high frequencies, besides the image itself, a high frequency spatial residual (denoted by $R^1(x, y)$) is created to construct multidirectional differences. To do this, we firstly divide the Discrete Cosine Transform (DCT) frequency into 3 subbands with equal interval and then select the high frequency subband as shown in Figure 4 to create a high frequency spatial residual $R^1(x, y)$ by the inverse DCT. The whole process can be formulated as

$$
S(u, v) = \mathrm{DCT}\,(I\,(x, y)),
$$
$$
R^1\,(x, y) = \mathrm{IDCT}\,(S\,(u, v) \cdot H\,(u, v)), \tag{5}
$$

where $H(u, v)$ is a high-pass filter. We empirically find that the type of $H(u, v)$ (such as Gaussian high-pass filter) and the partition of the subband have trifling impacts on the resampling detector. For the sake of conciseness, we employ the above proposed method to generate $R^1(x, y)$. For notation convenience, an image $I(x, y)$ is denoted as $R^0(x, y)$ in the sequel.

Each kernel shown in "*Multidirectional Kernel Groups G(1)–G(3)*" is convoluted with an image $R^0(x, y)$ and its high frequency residual $R^1(x, y)$ to generate the 2nd-order difference (denoted by $D(x, y)$). Finally, we get 56 kinds of differences. Inspired by the rich model for steganalysis [20], assembling the feature from the multidirectional differences is expected to be beneficial to the challenging forensic problem, such as detecting resampling in a JPEG compressed image.

3.3. The Feature Construction. In this subsection, we first extract the AR feature (FAR) and histogram feature (FH) from each image difference and then assemble FAR and FH extracted from 56 differences to construct the final feature set.

FAR is extracted based on the direction of $D(x, y)$. (1) For the differences derived from H kernel, as it is mainly used to reflect the variations in the horizontal direction, FAR is extracted in the horizontal direction. (2) Similarly, for the differences created by V kernel, FAR is extracted in

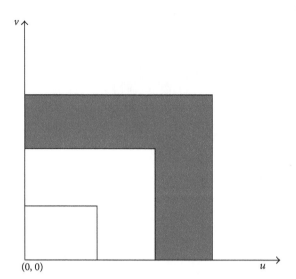

FIGURE 4: The high frequency DCT subband in red shaded region is used to create $R^1(x, y)$. The coordinate $(0, 0)$ is the DC coefficient.

the vertical direction. (3) For the differences created by other kernels shown in "*Multidirectional Kernel Groups G(1)–G(3),*" the AR coefficients are first extracted from the horizontal and vertical direction, respectively, and FAR are then obtained by averaging them.

Extracting FAR in the horizontal direction is as follows. First, concatenate all rows of $D(x, y)$ to generate a 1D sequence $z = [D(1,:), D^{(LR)}(2,:), D(3,:), D^{(LR)}(4,:), \ldots]$, where $D^{(LR)}(m,:)$ (m is the row index) is a left-right flipped version of the mth row. Then, input z into an AR model formulated to calculate AR coefficients [23]. Transposing $D(x, y)$, we can extract FAR in the vertical direction in the same way. The AR model can be formulated as

$$z(t) = -\sum_{k=1}^{p} a(k) z(t - k) + \varepsilon(t), \qquad (6)$$

where p, $a(k)$, $\varepsilon(t)$ represent the order, AR coefficients, and prediction error, respectively.

According to the symmetric distribution of the difference as shown in Figure 3, FH is calculated as follows:

$$FH = \left[h_0, \frac{(h_1 + h_{-1})}{2} \cdots \frac{(h_q + h_{-q})}{2} \right], \qquad (7)$$

where h_q (or h_{-q}) is the normalized frequency of the difference element which is equal to q (or $-q$).

To reduce the dimensionality, under the assumption that the kernels within a group belong to the same pattern, we average FAR and FH within the same difference group and denote them as FAR_i^k and FH_i^k (group index $i = 1, 2, 3$; residual index $k = 0, 1$). The proposed feature constructed from multidirectional differences (denoted by FD) is obtained as in (8) by concatenating the feature subset FD^k extracted from

$R^k(x, y)$. The dimensions of FAR_i^k and FH_i^k are p and $q + 1$, respectively. Thus, the total dimension of FD is $6 (p + q + 1)$.

$$FD^k = \left[FAR_1^k, FH_1^k, FAR_2^k, FH_2^k, FAR_3^k, FH_3^k \right],$$

$$(k = 0, 1), \quad (8)$$

$$FD = \left[FD^0, FD^1 \right].$$

We set the parameters p and q based on the distributions of AR coefficients and histograms for unaltered images and resampled images. Figure 5 shows the distributions of AR coefficients estimated from BOSSRAW database [21] (please see Section 4 for more details about the database).

For the sake of brevity, we only show the plots for FAR_1^0 and FAR_1^1. Recall that FAR_1^0 and FAR_1^1 are, respectively, extracted from the differences of $R^0(x, y)$ and the differences of $R^1(x, y)$. The subscript "1" represents the fact that the differences are generated by G(1) kernel groups. Both plots show that 12-order AR feature is able to distinguish the scaled or forged scaled image from the unaltered image, so we set $p = 12$. It is shown that FAR_1^0 and FAR_1^1 present different plot shapes, which indicates that they are complementary in the resampling forensics. The parameter q is empirically set as 5, because we observed that most of the difference elements fall within $[-5, 5]$, such as the images in the BOSSRAW database. With $p = 12$ and $q = 5$, the dimension of FD is 108.

The proposed detector is summarized as follows:

(1) Select the high frequency band of DCT as shown in Figure 4 to create the spatial residual $R^1(x, y)$.

(2) Create multidirectional differences by performing the convolution between $R^k(x, y)$ ($k = 0, 1$) and the kernels in "*Multidirectional Kernel Groups G(1)– G(3)*."

(3) Extract FAR and FH from each difference $D(x, y)$ and construct the proposed feature as (8).

(4) Feed the feature set extracted from the training images into SVM to train the proposed detector.

4. Experimental Results

We test the proposed detector on a composite image database which is comprised of 3000 never resampled images. The BOSSBase [21] and Dresden Image Database (DID) [24] are widely used in the image forensics. Their raw image source database is denoted by BOSSRAW and DIDRAW, respectively. We randomly select 1500 raw images from BOSSRAW and DIDRAW database, respectively, to create the composite database. Before further processing, all images are converted to 8-bit gray images.

The unaltered composite database is provided as the source database for creating resampled image database. We created three kinds of resampled database: upscaling, downscaling, and rotation. We also used the antiforensic method proposed by Kirchner and Böhme [16] to create three kinds of forged resampled database: forged upscaling, forged downscaling, and forged rotation. The commonly used parameters

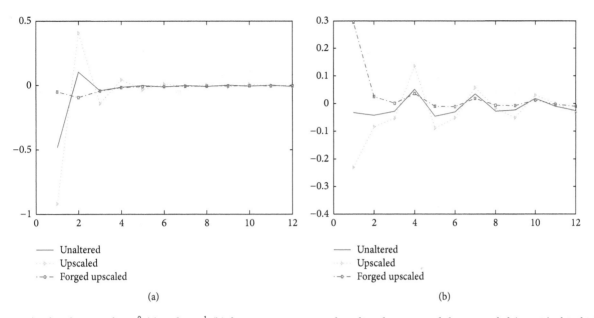

(a)   (b)

Figure 5: The distribution of FAR_1^0 (a) and FAR_1^1 (b) for 1500 uncompressed unaltered images and their upscaled ($s = 3/2$, bicubic) and forged upscaled (*attack 1*, $s = 3/2$, $\sigma = 0.4$, bicubic) versions. X-coordinate: the index of AR coefficient; Y-coordinate: averaged value of AR coefficient.

Table 1: Parameters used to create resampled image database.

Database	Parameters
Upscaling (3000 images)	Scaling factors: 1.2, 1.4, 1.6, 1.8
	Interpolation kernels: bilinear, bicubic, Lanczos3
Downscaling (3000 images)	Scaling factors: 0.6, 0.7, 0.8, 0.9
	Interpolation kernels: bilinear, bicubic, Lanczos3
Rotation (3000 images)	Rotation angle: 5°, 10°, 15°, 20°
	Interpolation kernels: bilinear, bicubic
Forged upscaling (3000 images)	Scaling factors: 1.2, 1.4, 1.6, 1.8
	Interpolation kernels: bilinear, bicubic, Lanczos3
	Attack type: *attack 1*, *attack 2*
	Attack strength (σ): 0.3, 0.4, 0.5
Forged downscaling (3000 images)	Scaling factors: 0.6, 0.7, 0.8, 0.9
	Interpolation kernels: bilinear, bicubic, Lanczos3
	Attack type: *attack 1*, *attack 2*
	Attack strength (σ): 0.3, 0.4, 0.5
Forged rotation (3000 images)	Rotation angle: 5°, 10°, 15°, 20°
	Interpolation kernels: bilinear, bicubic
	Attack type: *attack 1*, *attack 2*
	Attack strength (σ): 0.3, 0.4, 0.5

of resampling and forged resampling (depicted in Table 1) are used to generate various types of resampled images. We use the same number for each type in the resampled or forged database. For example, for 12 types of upscaling (four types of scaling factor, three kinds of kernel), we allot each one with $3000/12 = 250$ images. To preclude the influence from image resolution, unaltered, resampled, and forged resampled images are center-cropped to 512×512.

SVM with Gaussian kernel is employed as the classifier [25]. To avoid overfitting, we conducted a grid-search for the best parameters of SVM by fivefold cross validations on the training set. For training and testing purpose, we created several training-testing pairs. Each pair owns 6000 images, which is comprised by unaltered composite database and its altered version. Training is performed on a random 50% subset of the pair, and testing is performed on the remaining 50%. Hereafter, the same SVM setups are adopted unless particularly specified. The receiver operating characteristic (ROC) curves and the detection error P_e are used to evaluate the SVM-based detector's performance. In formula (9), FPR and TPR denote the false positive rate and true positive rate, respectively.

$$P_e = \min \frac{(\text{FPR} + 1 - \text{TPR})}{2}. \tag{9}$$

To the best of our knowledge, there are no related works which simultaneously detect the resampled image and forged image from the unaltered image. We compare our proposed FD-based detector with the state of the art in the resampling forensics: FE-based detector [11] and FM-based detector [12]. As FE-based detector [11] and FM-based detector [12] have captured some artifacts of interpolation, we suppose they may be effective in forged resampling detection. Additionally, FE detector and FM detector are SVM-based, so it is convenient to compare them with the proposed detector under same experimental settings. We also note that the steganalysis-based detectors [15, 26] have achieved excellent performances in the resampling detection. However, because of huge dimension (34761-D) of steganalysis feature, extracting the 34761-D feature and training the model by the SVM are very time-consuming, so we do not directly compare our method with the steganalysis-based detectors [15, 26].

TABLE 2: P_e (%) of each detector on detecting resampled images from unaltered images. Here "without" means without applying JPEG compression on test images. The best result is displayed by bold texts.

	JPEG compression	Proposed FD	FM [12]	FE [11]
Upscaled versus unaltered	Without	**0.17**	6.63	13.63
	QF = 95	**1.53**	10.60	14.53
	QF = 80	**11.53**	16.27	18.07
Downscaled versus unaltered	Without	**0.77**	14.87	12.93
	QF = 95	**4.37**	17.90	17.87
	QF = 80	**21.07**	29.50	29.70
Rotated versus unaltered	Without	**0.70**	14.57	23.30
	QF = 95	**3.13**	21.53	23.43
	QF = 80	**13.10**	30.20	28.67

TABLE 3: P_e (%) of each detector on detecting forged resampled images from unaltered images. Here "without" means without applying JPEG compression on test images. The best result is displayed by bold texts.

	JPEG compression	Proposed FD	FM [12]	FE [11]
Upscaled versus unaltered	Without	**0.13**	5.13	3.30
	QF = 95	**1.40**	8.20	6.90
	QF = 80	**6.10**	18.47	15.47
Downscaled versus unaltered	Without	**0.13**	11.33	16.60
	QF = 95	**3.70**	16.27	20.20
	QF = 80	**16.0**	32.10	30.80
Rotated versus unaltered	Without	**0.20**	8.93	8.13
	QF = 95	**0.90**	12.70	12.30
	QF = 80	**6.67**	26.40	27.47

In the following, we first evaluate the effectiveness of the proposed composite feature. Then, we show that the FD-based detector can not only detect resampled or forged resampled images from unaltered images as traditional method [11, 12, 26] but also simultaneously detect both resampled and forged resampled images from unaltered images. Finally, we give an example of splicing detection using the proposed detector.

4.1. Evaluating Effectiveness of the Composite Feature. The proposed feature FD is a composite of subset FD^k ($k = 0, 1$) as shown in (8). To verify that no subset is redundant, we compared FD with FD^0, FD^1 through detecting upscaled images from unaltered images. As aforementioned, the composite of FD^0 and FD^1 is expected to be beneficial for detecting resampling in a JPEG compressed image. To test FD's robustness against lossy JPEG compression, both unaltered and upscaled images are postcompressed by JPEG 80. With SVM testing, P_e of FD, FD^0, and FD^1 is 7.23%, 8.30%, and 10.57, respectively. This result means that FD yields lowest P_e, which indicates that the feature subset FD^0 extracted from the difference of image and FD^1 extracted from the difference of high frequency residual are collaborative in the resampling classification. In the following, we only reported the result of FD.

4.2. Detecting Unaltered Images from Resampled Images. In this subsection, the proposed detector is tested by distinguishing the unaltered image from the resampled image. To this end, we create 3 uncompressed training-testing pairs: upscaled versus unaltered, downscaled versus unaltered, and rotated versus unaltered and their corresponding JPEG 95 and JPEG 80 version.

Table 2 shows the results for three kinds of feature. Under the uncompressed scenario, the proposed FD-based detector achieves nearly perfect performance ($P_e < 1\%$) for the detections of upscaling, downscaling, and rotation. The FD-based detector performs much better than two other detectors, especially in the detection of downscaling or rotation. For example, in the detection of downscaling without JPEG compression, P_e of the FD-based detector is, respectively, 14.10

percentage points and 12.16 percentage points lower than that of the FM-based detector and FE-based detector. The ROC curves in Figure 6 again verify that the proposed detector has achieved great improvements in the resampling forensics. Under JPEG compression scenario, the FD-based detector also yields lowest P_e in JPEG 90 and JPEG 80 compressed training-testing pairs.

4.3. Detecting Unaltered Images from Forged Resampled Images. In this subsection, we test whether the proposed FD-based detector can resist the malicious attack [16]. The test is designed for distinguishing the unaltered images from the forged resampled images. The FE-based detector [11] and FM-based detector [12] initially do not aim at detecting the antiforensic scheme [16], but they have captured some artifacts of interpolation in the resampled image, such as energy density. Hence, we also test whether FE-based detector and FM-based detector can detect the interpolation artifacts hidden in the forged resampled image.

Table 3 shows the detailed results. Without JPEG compression, the FD-based detector achieves nearly perfect performance ($P_e < 0.2\%$), which indicates that FD-based detector can effectively resist the attacks from antiforensic scheme [16]. Figure 7 shows the corresponding ROC curves under the uncompressed scenario. It can be seen that the ROC curve of the proposed detector is always above that of other two detectors. The advantage of FD-based detector is prominent when FPR is low. For example, in the downscaling detection, the TPR of FD-based detector is 99.93% at FPR = 1%, which is about 59.53 percentage points and 87.63 percentage points higher than that of the FM-based detector and FE-based detector. The FE-based detector and FM-based detector have gotten good performances in the detections of forged upscaling and forged rotation. However, their performances deteriorate in the forged downscaling detections. Under JPEG compression scenario, the results in Table 3 indicate that the proposed FD-based detector also outperforms two other detectors.

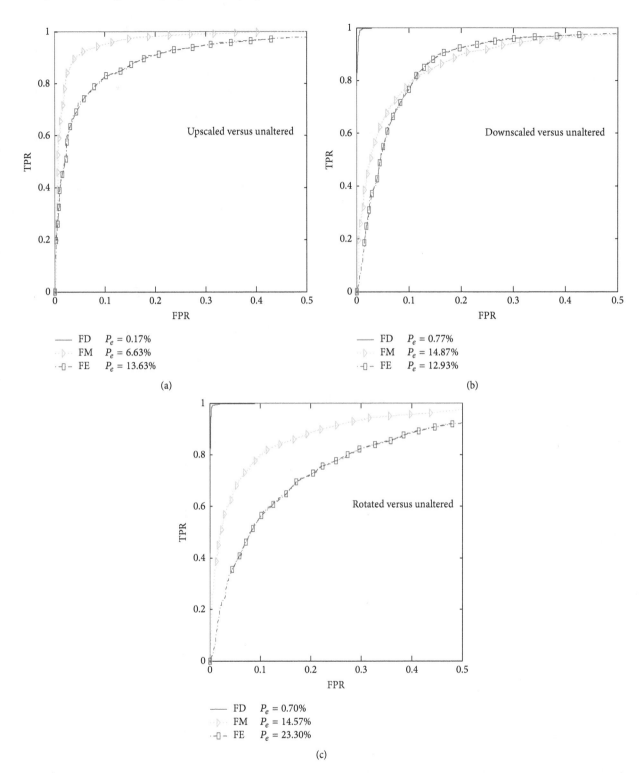

FIGURE 6: ROC curves showing detections of (a) upscaling, (b) downscaling, and (c) rotation under uncompressed scenario.

4.4. Detecting Unaltered Images from Resampled Images and Forged Resampled Images. In applications, we may have no prior knowledge about the test image. For a more practical detector, we train the SVM detector by unaltered images and "ALL" images including resampled images and forged images. Such a detector requires that the forensic features be distinguishable between heterogeneous images. To visually demonstrate the ability of FD, we map FD into a 2D space by linear discriminate analysis (LDA). Clear distinctions among three types can be seen in Figure 8.

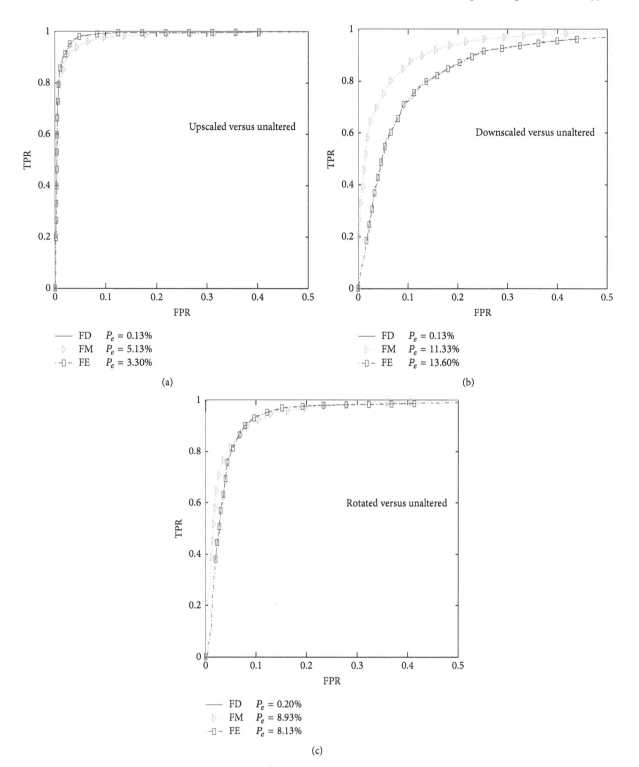

FIGURE 7: ROC curves showing detections of (a) forged upscaling, (b) forged downscaling, and (c) forged rotation under uncompressed scenario.

We create 3 training-testing pairs in this subsection as shown in Table 4. "ALL" class is comprised by 1500 resampled images and 1500 forged resampled images. We randomly select 500 upscaled images, 500 downscaled images, and 500 rotated images to compose the resampling class in "ALL"

database. The forged resampling class is formed by the same manner.

Table 4 gives the detailed results. Under the uncompressed scenario, it can be seen that FD-based detector can effectively distinguish the altered image ("ALL" class)

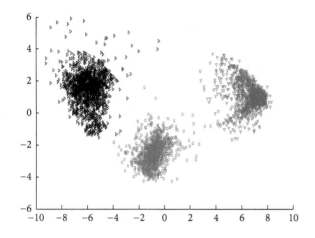

- ◦ Unaltered image
- ▷ Upscaled image
- ▽ Forged upscaled image

FIGURE 8: The 2D feature of FD (after LDA) estimated from 1500 uncompressed images of BOSSRAW database.

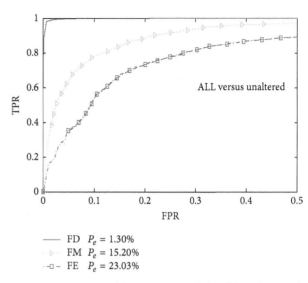

——	FD	P_e = 1.30%
▷···	FM	P_e = 15.20%
-□-	FE	P_e = 23.03%

FIGURE 9: ROC curves of detecting resampled and forged resampled image ("ALL") from unaltered image under uncompressed scenario.

TABLE 4: P_e(%) of each detector on detecting "ALL" images from unaltered images. Here "without" means without applying JPEG compression on test images. The best result is displayed by bold texts.

	JPEG compression	Proposed FD	FM [12]	FE [11]
ALL versus unaltered	Without	**1.30**	15.20	23.03
	QF = 95	**5.40**	21.90	26.63
	QF = 80	**20.33**	32.73	33.93

from the unaltered image, which indicates that the proposed feature captures the fingerprints of interpolation which are left in the resampled image and forged resampled image. Either under uncompressed or JPEG compressed scenario, the proposed FD-based detector performs the best. Figure 9 demonstrates that, with FPR = 1%, the FD-based detector achieves TPR = 98.3%, which indicates that the proposed detector is practical in the real applications.

4.5. An Example of Splicing Detection. In this subsection, we use the proposed detector to detect the spliced tampering. Since the location of the pasted object is unknown, the questioned image is divided into nonoverlapped blocks at first, and then each block is predicted by the proposed detector. The block size is set to be 64 × 64. Accordingly, the SVM detector is trained on 64 × 64 blocks. The training set is composed of 3000 unaltered images and 3000 "ALL" images as used in Section 4.3.

Figure 10(b) shows an example of spliced image. It is created by splicing two birds into Figure 10(a). To create convinced tampering, the forger may repeatedly employ the resampling to adjust visual quality. To simulate the real cases, the right bird in Figure 10(b) is first downscaled (scaling factor s = 0.8, bicubic) and then upscaled (s = 1.2, bicubic). The left bird is processed by antiforensic scheme using default

settings [16] (*attack* 2, σ = 0.4, s = 0.8, bilinear). Figures 10(b) and 10(c) show the tampering detection results for the uncompressed and JPEG 95 compressed tampering, respectively. The 64 × 64 block predicted as tampered is marked in red color. Although the proposed detector is only trained on the image blocks with a single scaling operation, it can locate most of the spliced region, including the region which underwent multiple scaling operations. As the edge of the inserted object is a composite of unaltered and altered block, some missing detections emerge in the edge of two pasted birds. Note that this tampered example is simple tampering. In real life, the forgers will adopt various ways to escape the detection of forensic tools. Generalized forensic tools, which can identify usual image operations and their combinations, may be useful in the detections of complicated tampered images.

5. Conclusion

In this paper, we have proposed a novel integrated detector for detecting image resampling and forged resampling, which simultaneously addresses the effectiveness and security concerns. We design multidirectional differences to extract the feature. To capture the traces of resampling and forged resampling, the feature is extracted from the coefficients of the autoregressive model and histograms. Experiments on a large composite image database show that the proposed detector is effective and secure and yields great improvements in the detection of downsampling or resampling under JPEG compression. The tampering detection results illustrate that the proposed detector is promising in practical applications. We have found that the lossy JPEG compression affects the performance of the proposed detector. The performance degrades with increasing JPEG compression ratio. Improving the detector's robustness against heavy JPEG compression is our future work.

(a)   (b)   (c)

FIGURE 10: An example showing (a) an unaltered image and tampering detection results for (b) uncompressed and (c) JPEG compressed (QF = 95) tampering. The red box of size 64×64 indicates that this box is predicted as tampered by the proposed detector.

Competing Interests

The authors declare that they have no competing interests.

Acknowledgments

This work was partially supported by NSFC (Grant nos. 61379155, U1135001, and 61303127), the Research Fund for the Doctoral Program of Higher Education of China (Grant no. 20110171110042), NSF of Guangdong province (Grant no. s2013020012788), and Doctoral Research Fund of Southwest University of Science and Technology (Grant no. 16zx7104).

References

[1] A. C. Popescu and H. Farid, "Exposing digital forgeries by detecting traces of resampling," *IEEE Transactions on Signal Processing*, vol. 53, no. 2, pp. 758–767, 2005.

[2] A. C. Gallagher, "Detection of linear and cubic interpolation in JPEG compressed images," in *Proceedings of the 2nd Canadian Conference on Computer and Robot Vision (CRV '05)*, pp. 65–72, IEEE, May 2005.

[3] B. Mahdian and S. Saic, "Blind authentication using periodic properties of interpolation," *IEEE Transactions on Information Forensics and Security*, vol. 3, no. 3, pp. 529–538, 2008.

[4] M. Kirchner, "Fast and reliable rescaling detection by spectral analysis of fixed linear predictor residue," in *Proceedings of the 10th ACM Workshop on Multimedia and Security (MM&Sec '08)*, pp. 11–20, Oxford, UK, September 2008.

[5] W. Wei, S. Wang, X. Zhang, and Z. Tang, "Estimation of image rotation angle using interpolation-related spectral signatures with application to blind detection of image forgery," *IEEE Transactions on Information Forensics and Security*, vol. 5, no. 3, pp. 507–517, 2010.

[6] M. Kirchner and T. Gloe, "On rescaling detection in recompressed images," in *Proceedings of the IEEE International Workshop on Information Forensics and Security*, pp. 21–25, 2009.

[7] D. Vázquez-Padín, C. Mosquera, and F. Pérez-González, "Two-dimensional statistical test for the presence of almost cyclostationarity on images," in *Proceedings of the 17th IEEE International Conference on Image Processing (ICIP '10)*, pp. 1745–1748, IEEE, Hong Kong, September 2010.

[8] D. Vázquez-Padín, C. Mosquera, and F. Pérez-González, "Prefilter design for forensic resampling estimation," in *Proceedings of the IEEE International Workshop on Information Forensics and Security (WIFS '11)*, pp. 1–6, Iguacu Falls, Brazil, November 2011.

[9] D. Vázquez-Padín and P. Comesaña, "ML estimation of the resampling factor," in *Proceedings of the IEEE International Workshop on Information Forensics and Security (WIFS '12)*, pp. 205–210, IEEE, Tenerife, Spain, December 2012.

[10] D. Vázquez-Padín, P. Comesaña, and F. Pérez-González, "Set-membership identification of resampled signals," in *Proceedings of the 5th IEEE International Workshop on Information Forensics and Security (WIFS '13)*, pp. 150–155, Guangzhou, China, November 2013.

[11] X. Y. Feng, I. J. Cox, and D. Gwenaël, "Normalized energy density-based forensic detection of re-sampled images," *IEEE Transactions on Multimedia*, vol. 14, no. 3, pp. 535–546, 2012.

[12] L. Li, J. Xue, Z. Tian, and N. Zheng, "Moment feature based forensic detection of resampled digital images," in *Proceedings of the 21st ACM International Conference on Multimedia (MM '13)*, pp. 569–572, ACM, Barcelona, Spain, October 2013.

[13] J. Kodovský and J. Fridrich, "Effect of image downsampling on steganographic security," *IEEE Transactions on Information Forensics and Security*, vol. 9, no. 5, pp. 752–762, 2014.

[14] X. Hou, T. Zhang, G. Xiong, Y. Zhang, and X. Ping, "Image resampling detection based on texture classification," *Multimedia Tools and Applications*, vol. 72, no. 2, pp. 1681–1708, 2014.

[15] H. D. Li, W. Q. Luo, X. Q. Qiu, and J. W. Huang, "Identification of image operations based on steganalytic features," *IEEE Transactions on Circuits and Systems for Video Technology*, 2016.

[16] M. Kirchner and R. Böhme, "Hiding traces of resampling in digital images," *IEEE Transactions on Information Forensics and Security*, vol. 3, no. 4, pp. 582–592, 2008.

[17] G. Cao, Y. Zhao, and R. Ni, "Forensic identification of resampling operators: a semi non-intrusive approach," *Forensic Science International*, vol. 216, no. 1–3, pp. 29–36, 2012.

[18] H. T. Sencar and N. Memon, "Digital image forensics," in *Counter-Forensics: Attacking Image Forensics*, Rainer Bohme and Matthias Kirchner, pp. 327–366, Springer, 2013.

[19] A. Peng, H. Zeng, X. Lin, and X. Kang, "Countering anti-forensics of image resampling," in *Proceedings of the IEEE International Conference on Image Processing (ICIP '15)*, pp. 3595–3599, IEEE, Québec, Canada, September 2015.

[20] J. Fridrich and J. Kodovský, "Rich models for steganalysis of digital images," *IEEE Transactions on Information Forensics and Security*, vol. 7, no. 3, pp. 868–882, 2012.

[21] P. Bas, T. Filler, and T. Pevný, "Break our steganographic system—the ins and outs of organizing BOSS," in *Proceedings of the 13th Information Hiding Conference*, pp. 59–70, Prague, Czech Republic, 2011.

[22] T. Pevný, P. Bas, and J. Fridrich, "Steganalysis by subtractive pixel adjacency matrix," *IEEE Transactions on Information Forensics and Security*, vol. 5, no. 2, pp. 215–224, 2010.

[23] S. Kay, *Modern Spectral Estimation*, chapter 7, Prentice-Hall, 1988.

[24] T. Gloe and R. Böhme, "Dresden image database for benchmarking digital image forensics," in *Proceedings of the ACM Symposium on Applied Computing*, pp. 22–26, 2010.

[25] C.-C. Chang and C.-J. Lin, "LIBSVM: a Library for support vector machines," *ACM Transactions on Intelligent Systems and Technology*, vol. 2, no. 3, article 27, 2011.

[26] X. Q. Qiu, H. D. Li, W. Q. Luo, and J. W. Huang, "A universal image forensic strategy based on steganalytic model," in *Proceedings of the 2nd ACM Workshop on Information Hiding and Multimedia Security*, pp. 165–170, Salzburg, Austria, June 2014.

15

Video Traffic Flow Analysis in Distributed System during Interactive Session

Soumen Kanrar[1,2] and Niranjan Kumar Mandal[2]

[1]*Vehere Interactive Pvt. Ltd., Calcutta, West Bengal 700053, India*
[2]*Vidyasagar University, West Bengal 721102, India*

Correspondence should be addressed to Soumen Kanrar; soumen.kanrar@veheretech.com

Academic Editor: Martin Reisslein

Cost effective, smooth multimedia streaming to the remote customer through the distributed "video on demand" architecture is the most challenging research issue over the decade. The hierarchical system design is used for distributed network to satisfy more requesting users. The distributed hierarchical network system contains all the local and remote storage multimedia servers. The hierarchical network system is used to provide continuous availability of the data stream to the requesting customer. In this work, we propose a novel data stream that handles the methodology for reducing the connection failure and smooth multimedia stream delivery to the remote customer. The proposed session based single-user bandwidth requirement model presents the bandwidth requirement for any interactive session like pause, move slowly, rewind, skip some of the frame, and move fast with some constant number of frames. The proposed session based optimum storage finding algorithm reduces the search hop count towards the remote storage-data server. The modeling and simulation result shows the better impact over the distributed system architecture. This work presents the novel bandwidth requirement model at the interactive session and gives the trade-off in communication and storage costs for different system resource configurations.

1. Introduction

An interactive video on demand (VOD) system requires smooth data streaming for the user irrespective of geographic location to access on demand video, such as movies, electronic encyclopedia, interactive games, and educational resources from the distributed storage servers through a high-speed network. The number of customer's requests increases exponentially in the local cluster domain. It brings a heavy load to the network system. The consequence is a high rate of customer request drop and huge bandwidth wastage. Next-Generation Network (NGN) provides multimedia services over broadband based networks, which supports high definition DVD quality multimedia data streaming content. The multimedia data streaming services are thus seen to be merging mainly in three areas such as computing, communication, and broadcasting. It has numerous advantages. More

exploration for the large-scale deployment of the storage system is still needed. The distributed system hierarchy of multimedia storage has focused on analyzing the system architecture. The distributed system hierarchy of multimedia storage becomes important due to the services supported by the high-speed networks, multimedia storage servers, and distributed multimedia file systems. A customer will be able to request a multimedia stream from anywhere and at any time. In response to a customer's request, local or remote storage system will deliver a high quality digitized multimedia data stream directly to the clients set-top-box over a local distributed network. The local cluster domain may store a complete or a partial set of multimedia data streams. As the overall VOD user population grows, newer local clusters are added to the distributed system, and the network capacities are sized to match the increased user population for that neighborhood. Clearly, it indicates the need for scalability of the distributed system hierarchy of a multimedia storage system. The remote site may be archival in nature, providing a permanent repository for all multimedia streams, or they may act as replicated servers such as mirrored sites. The remote sites may provide service to many user populations. The distributed system itself is a hierarchy of neighborhoods in the geographical region. If a request cannot be served from the local site, it may be directed to other remote sites. A storage container either local or remote has to reserve sufficient I/O and network bandwidths before accepting a customer's request. We define a server channel as the server resource required to deliver a multimedia stream, while guaranteeing a client's continuous playback. In general, the VOD service can be characterized as long lived session with a typical movie on demand service runs for 1 hour to 2 hours. Thus, sufficient storage and I/O bandwidth must be available, and we need a solution that efficiently utilizes the server and network resources. Class based admission control [1] was used in the "video on demand system" to get better performance. However, some level of planning and managing of the resource is required in the Internet-based [2, 3] video on demand to enhance the performance up to an optimum level. In fact, the network I/O bottleneck has been observed in many earlier systems, such as Network Project in Orlando [4] and Microsoft's Tiger Video Fileserver [5]. The multicast facilities of modern communication network [6–8] offer an efficient means of one to many data transmissions. Multicast techniques can also significantly improve the VOD performance by reducing the required network bandwidth greatly, so that the overall network load is reduced. In other ways the multicasting alleviates the workload of the VOD server and improves the system throughput by batching requests [9, 10]. In this paper, we present a new methodology to reduce the traffic load in the "distributed video on demand system" for different types of service request in interactive session. The types of the service requests in interactive session are like fast forward, pause, stop, or move backward. Tewari and Kleinrock [11, 12] have designed a simple queueing model to shape the number of replicas corresponding to the request rate and the driven content. Zhou and Xu [13] have shown the target jointly maximizing the average encoding bit rate in content transfer over the network. The overall average number of content replicas that is minimizing the communication load imbalances the storage servers [14]. The brief content placement for P2P video on demand systems is presented by Suh et al. [15]. Tewari and Kleinrock [11, 12] have designed a simple queueing based model to shape the number of replicas corresponding to the request rate of the content driven. LRU (least recently used) and LRFU (least recently and frequently used) based methods worked efficiently and classified the batches of content with respect to the hit count. They efficiently update the peer cache and proxy server cache in the mesh type network for content replicas [9, 10]. The user initiative huge traffic load to the video on demand network generally follows the Zipf like distribution to analyze the traffic load and shape of the load inside the on demand system [6–8]. Li et al. [16] proposed different types of batching request model. This model integrates both the user activity and the batching model. In this model the user requests

are batching and the effect of such batching is captured in a batching model. The user activity includes the various interactive modes like pause, move slowly, move fast, and so forth. The model is unable to describe the user initiative interactive operational mode. The video on demand system requires a uniform model that can be used to determine the requirements of network bandwidth at the user interactive session. The proper bandwidth requirement model at the interactive session gives the trade-off in communication and storage costs for different system resource configurations. This paper is structured as follows. Section 1 presents the brief literature survey for finding the problem in Introduction. We briefly represent the hierarchical architecture of the distributed system and the distributed database storage in Sections 2 and 3. Section 4 presents the session based multiuser model and single-user bandwidth requirement model. Section 5 illustrates the snap of the traffic flow model to this problem. Section 6 presents the parameter's description of the simulation environment and performance evaluation of the system. Section 7 presented broadly the related work on the interactive session and the related domain. The conclusion remark is followed by the references at the end of the document.

2. Distributed Architecture

Large-scale VOD system requires the servers to be arranged in a distributed fashion in order to support a large number of concurrent streams. The system architecture is hierarchical, and the local server can handle the requests from specific geographic zone. The local server in the hierarchy takes the requests from the cluster switch; if they cannot handle, then request proceeds for next level. This architecture provides the cost efficiency, reliability, and scalability of servers. Generally, servers are either tree based shaped [9] or graph structured [8]. The graph structured system often offers good quality of service for handling the requests, but the management of request, videos, and streams is complicated in the distributed system. The tree-shaped system can easily manage requests, videos, and streams, but it offers poorer quality of service than the former. In order to evaluate the effectiveness of distribution strategies in such a hierarchy, the authors of [2, 17] investigate how to reduce storage and network costs while taking the customer's behavior into account.

In the distributed system hierarchy of multimedia storage architecture, local proxy servers are installed at strategic locations in the network (closer to the clients). Remote clusters can communicate with the network's distributed storage and with its local proxy servers immediately. Each local cluster server can support a number of customers connected to it through a cluster switch. The customers are connected to the distributed database servers through the cluster switch, which acts as an interface between the client cluster and the database servers. The proxies are used to distribute the storage contained functionality within the network by using the concept of local proxy storage according to Figure 1. If the user cannot be served by the local storage server for any reason, such as a blockage in the

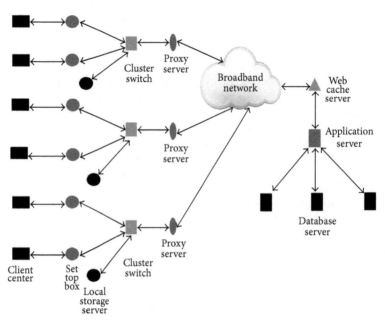

FIGURE 1: Distributed hierarchy system.

local network, or data is not available in the local storage, then the requesting user will be transported to the distributed multimedia storage. By locating the proxy server close to the user, it is expected that there will be significant reductions in the load on the system as a whole [6, 7]. Another advantage of the distributed local proxy video on demand system is that it can be expanded in a horizontal manner for system scalability and evolution. It can start from an initial two-level system (with a centralized multimedia server and one local proxy video server) to a system with as many local proxy servers as needed. The system is incorporated with the distributed multimedia storage system. The distributed system may utilize a lower than average network bandwidth and have a higher system reliability, but at the expense of significant amount of local storage systems.

3. Distributed Database Server

If the request is not served by the local storage then it will proceed to remote storage. The working structure of distributed storage is presented in Figure 2. The video on demand viewer sends the request simultaneously via the connected network. Here we present streams of request access from the particular video storage site. Initially, all requests from HTTP or HTTPs are forwarded to web cache memory. Now the web cache memory that has the content of the video stream is forwarded directly to the viewer. In case the web cache memory does not have the required content then the request is forwarded to application server in the list of application servers. The application web server is selected from the least loaded application server [4, 6]. The application web server searches the required video stream from a set of the well connected distributed database servers in Figure 2.

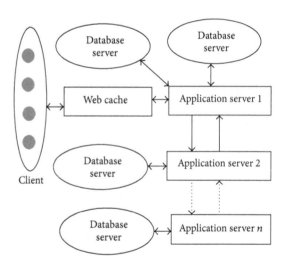

FIGURE 2: Distributed database server.

In the large-scale video on demand system, bandwidth optimization largely depends on the minimum hop counts in high demand stage or in a specific time or some of the days in a week [9]. The efficiency of the video on demand system depends on the "least recently and frequently used" (LRFU) cache updating policy at each server. LRFU policy is composed of the two dynamically growing cache memory blocks "least recently used" (LRU) and "least frequently used" (LFU) cache memory [9]. The performance of the audio video on demand system purely depends on the efficient cache replacement at the proxy server [10]. The initial submitted request pattern to the web proxy container is approximately presented by the Zif like probability distribution [4, 8].

4. Analytic Structure

The required bandwidth varies during the interactive session. Users use various modes of playing operation such as fast forward, skip, pause, and rewind. The required bandwidth continuously varies with the mode of user operation. In general, let p be the initial (prior) probability to select a channel according to the binomial distribution, the total available bandwidth $B_{(\Delta t)}$ (i.e., in the trunk) at session Δt and W is channel required bandwidth at that session, ($p \approx W/B_{(\Delta t)}$). In real time W (assuming) varies according to the user playing mode of operation within $(W_{\min}, W_{\max})$ such that $(W_{\min} \leq \cdots \leq W_{\min+t(i)} \leq \cdots \leq W_{\max})$ for the ith type of real interactive session; $t(i)$ is the bandwidth demand adjustment function. It initially, $W_{\max}$, is assigned to each channel, but in real time when a huge request is coming at a session, the channel is assigned with adjusted bandwidth or otherwise at least $W_{\min}$ is available. If this is impossible, then the request is buffered to the queue (at the 1st queue of the proxy server or any intermediate router) [18]. For connection, setup $W_{\min}$ is required and then bandwidth is assigned to the channel according to the user's requirement and the availability of the bandwidth. User requirement or required bandwidth is maximized and subject to condition of availability of the bandwidth from the trunk. During the phase of connection startup to connection closed, the user behavior goes through a number of major interactive sessions in a random fashion. We denote the different mode of operations like fast forward (I^1), play normally (I^2), play slowly or move slowly (I^3), rewind (I^4), pause (I^5), and so forth. So, for the case $I^i \geq I^j$ it seems to be $i \geq j$ according to the bandwidth requirement. Now, there is a possibility of more than one mutually exclusive outcome for each type of interactive operation during any session.

Let e_i for $1 \leq i \leq k$ be k mutually exclusive and exhaustive outcome with the respective probabilities p_i for user mode of operation (Exp i).

For example, p_1 is for fast forward, p_2 for play normal, p_3 for play slow, p_4 for rewind, and so forth. If e_1 occurs x_1 times, e_2 occurs x_2 times $\cdots e_k$ occurs x_k times assuming that e_i occurs x_i times for $1 \leq i \leq k$.

Now, m is the number of independent observations of any customer behavior in a session and then $\sum x_i = m$.

So for the Tth customer we get

$$P(X = X_T) = p(x_1, x_2, \ldots, x_k) = C p_1^{x_1} p_2^{x_2} \cdots p_k^{x_k}. \quad (1)$$

Here, C is the number of permutations of the events.

So, $C = \lfloor m / \lfloor x_1 \lfloor x_2 \lfloor x_3 \cdots \lfloor x_k$.

Hence,

$$p(x_1, x_2, \ldots, x_k) = \frac{\lfloor m}{\lfloor x_1 \lfloor x_2 \lfloor x_3 \cdots \lfloor x_k} p_1^{x_1} p_2^{x_2} \cdots p_k^{x_k}$$

$$\text{for, } 0 \leq x_i \leq m, \sum x_i \leq m \quad (2)$$

$$= \frac{\lfloor m}{\prod_{i=1}^{K} \lfloor x_i} \prod_{i=1}^{K} p_i^{x_i}.$$

This is true for "single customer" when the allocated bandwidth for that channel is $\geq W_{\max}$.

So $n \approx B_{(\Delta t)}/W_{\max}$ and $B_{(\Delta t)}$ is the total bandwidth of the trunk in ideal situation or scenario at session Δt (Exp ii).

n is the number of active links for corresponding users.

Hence every customer has an independent interactive mode of operational choice.

4.1. Session Based Multiuser Model. So, according to function (1) the distribution is

$$P(X_1 \cap X_2 \cap \cdots \cap X_n) = \prod_{T=1}^{n} P(X = X_T). \quad (3)$$

In an interactive session, different bandwidth is required for different service modes like pause, fast forward, rewind, play normally, or play slowly; that is, number of frame downloads by the user node varies, but the frame length is fixed for different interactive session. When the channel is assigned to the user, then at least minimum bandwidth y is assigned to the user for any interactive session. Consider $\Rightarrow W_{\min} \leq y \leq W_{\max}$.

It follows the probability distribution function

$$p_i = \frac{y - W_{\min}}{W_{\max} - W_{\min}}. \quad (4)$$

In a session, we get the mixed type distribution by (1), (2), and (3)

$$P(X_1 \cap X_2 \cap \cdots \cap X_n)$$

$$= \prod_{t=1}^{n} \frac{\lfloor m}{\prod_{i=1}^{K} \lfloor x_i} \prod_{i=1}^{K} \left[\int_{W_{\min}}^{W_{\max}} \left[\frac{y - W_{\min}}{W_{\max} - W_{\min}} \right]^{x_i} dy \right]. \quad (5)$$

Here, n is the total number of users in the video on demand system. m is the total number of interactive modes used by the particular customer in that session. k is the particular type of modes like pause, move forward, rewind, and so forth and x_i is the number of times in which modes are used by that user in that session.

4.2. Single-User Bandwidth Requirement Model. According to Expression (Exp i), i is any type of interactive mode of operation for any individual user. The modes of user operation are like pause, rewind, fast forward, move slowly, and so forth. Let b_i be the required bandwidth for particular interactive mode of operation in that session, $W_{\min} \leq b_i \leq W_{\max}$, $b_i > 0$, $i \in I^{>0}$.

If, in a session, there are possible L numbers of interactive modes, then the bandwidth requirement of the user mode of operation satisfies expression

$$W_{\min} \leq \max \{b_i\}_{i \in \{1, \ldots, L\}} \approx W. \quad (6)$$

In any interactive mode of operation in a session, there are multiple subsessions.

So the occurrence of that particular interactive subsession is

$$P\left(\frac{(X_i = b_i)}{(X_1 = b_1, \ldots, X_{i-1} = b_{i-1})} \right). \quad (7)$$

To evaluate (7), we require finding out the volume of the solid sphere in k dimension plane such that

$$P\left(\frac{(X_i = b_i)}{(X_1 = b_1, \ldots, X_{i-1} = b_{i-1}, X_{i+1} = b_{i+1}, \ldots, X_k = b_k)}\right). \quad (8)$$

b_i is the required bandwidth to continue and maintain the ith type active interactive mode and $c \geq 0$ is the very minimum bandwidth required for other passive interactive user modes of operation at the same session. So the reserved bits for other interactive service connectivity required ($c \approx W_{\min}$).

So expression (8) becomes

$$P\left(\frac{(X_i = b_i)}{(X_1 = c, \ldots, X_{i-1} = c, X_{i+1} = c, \ldots, X_k = c)}\right). \quad (9)$$

We can assume c as the required reserved bits for other interactive user modes of operation except ith type. In general, the k-dimensional volume of Euclidean ball of radius R in the k-dimensional Euclidean space is defined as $V_k(R) = (\Pi^{k/2}/\lfloor(k/2 + 1)\rfloor)R^k$ so for even and odd, we get $V_{2k}(R) = (\Pi^k/\lfloor k\rfloor)R^{2k}$ and $V_{2k+1}(R) = (2^{k+1}\Pi^k/\lfloor 2k+1\rfloor)R^{2k+1}$; here k is the number of interactive modes in a session.

Due to interactive mode of user operation at each session, the volume of the sphere is changing. Now we get inequality

$$V_k(R)$$

$$\approx \frac{\Pi^{k/2}}{\lfloor((k/2) + 1)\rfloor}c^{k-1}(W_{\max}) \ll \frac{\Pi^{k/2}}{\lfloor((k/2) + 1)\rfloor}(W_{\max})^k. \quad (10)$$

Expression (9) becomes

$$P\left(\frac{(X_i = b_i)}{(X_1 = b_1, \ldots, X_{i-1} = b_{i-1}, X_{i+1} = b_{i+1}, \ldots, X_k = b_k)}\right)$$
$$\approx \left[\frac{\Pi^{k/2}}{\lfloor((k/2) + 1)\rfloor}c^{k-1}(W_{\max})\right]^{-1}\int_{\mathbb{R}^k} dx_1 \cdots dx_k. \quad (11)$$

Here we focused on finding the bandwidth requirement for ith type of user service mode of operation.

Since $\int_{\mathbb{R}^k} dv = \prod_{i=1}^k (\int_{-\infty}^{\infty} dx_i)$ (integration by parts), allocated bandwidth for that user holds true with the following expression:

$$x_1 + x_2 + \cdots + x_k \leq W,$$
$$W_{\min} < x_i \leq W_{\max}, \quad 1 \leq i \leq k. \quad (12)$$

The interactive sessions are mutually independent for each customer; only one type of interactive session occurs, that is, ith type like pause or watch normally or move forward.

If a viewer opens more than one window, for example, one window is paused and another window is using service required except paused, then the service request will be multiplexed to single stream through that dedicated channel that was allocated to that viewer.

Expression (11) becomes

$$P\left(\frac{(X_i = b_i)}{(X_1 = b_1, \ldots, X_{i-1} = b_{i-1}, X_{i+1} = b_{i+1}, \ldots, X_k = b_k)}\right) \approx \left[\frac{\Pi^{k/2}}{\lfloor((k/2) + 1)\rfloor}c^{k-1}(W_{\max})\right]^{-1}$$

$$\cdot \int_{x_i=0}^{W_{\max}} \cdot \int_{x_{i-1}=0}^{[W-(x_1+\cdots+x_{i-2}+x_i+\cdots+x_k)]} \cdot \int_{x_{i+1}=0}^{[W-(x_1+\cdots+x_i+x_{i+2}+\cdots x_k)]} \cdot \int_{x_k=0}^{[W-(x_1+\cdots+x_i+\cdots+x_{k-1})]} f(x_1, \ldots, x_k)\,dx_k \cdots dx_{i+1}dx_{i-1}dx_i. \quad (13)$$

Here, $f(x_1, \ldots, x_k)$ is a k-dimensional integrand function related to k-dimension volume. If the user is active only in one interactive mode then, in special case, we can consider $f(x_1, \ldots, x_k) \approx (1)^k = 1$.

5. Traffic Flow Model

In distributed local proxy architecture, local proxy servers are installed at strategic locations in the network (closer to the clients). Remote viewer clusters can communicate with the networks of distributed primary storage servers and with its local proxy servers. Each local proxy server supports continuous streaming to the number of customers connected to it through a cluster switch. The customers are also connected to the distributed multimedia storage, that is, databases through the cluster switch and proxy server. This composition acts as an interface between the client cluster and the broadband network. The main idea of distributed video on demand (VOD) local storage (as shown in Figure 1) is to distribute the multimedia data functionality within the user cluster by using the concept of local proxy storage. If the streams cannot be served by the local storage due to reasons, such as blockage at the proxy to pull the required segment or chunk of video objects from the local multimedia storage, or the case of the unavailability of the video clips at the proxy server, then the request will be transported to the distributed database servers. To find the proxy server close to the user, it is expected that there will be significant reductions in the load on the system as a whole [6, 7]. Another advantage of the distributed architecture system is that it can be expanded in a horizontal manner for system scalability and evolution. It can start from an initial two-level system (with a centralized multimedia server and one local storage video server) to a system with as many local servers as needed. Compared with the centralized multimedia server system, the distributed system may utilize a lower than average network bandwidth. It has a higher system reliability, but at the expense of needing a significant amount of local storage to the architecture. The proposed model of the distributed video on demand architecture satisfies the basic requirements of the distributed networks. Let n be the maximum number of customer's requests, serviceable at the proxy server for a user centric cluster. Now R_d is the disk bandwidth and R_p is the client request playback rate including the interactive session at the local storage. Then the stream available at the proxy server will be served to the customer, if the condition still holds true, $n \leq \lfloor R_d/R_p \rfloor$. The request admission control test at the proxy server determines whether the proxy server is able to serve maximum n number of requests. The proposed methodology is used for proxy server. Proxy server has total bandwidth capacity with C ports. Let us have k classes of service requests for interactive operations; each class receives mean rate λ_i to the proxy server for $i = 1$ to k related to different service classes. Service requests are categories of fast forward with one frame, two frames, up to m number of frames, pause, move backward, and so forth. Initially the proxy server port capacities are divided into a number of sections with each section having port capacity C_j, for $j = 0$ to k, and $C_i \neq C_j$ if $i \neq j$. The overall proxy port capacity is $C = \sum_{j=0}^{k} C_j$. Initially, each section is assigned with specific category of the service requests. At any interactive session of time Δt the occupied size of the section of ports C_j for $j = 0$ to k can be changed dynamically. It totally depended upon the viewer's choice. So at any session of time Δt, if the request for a particular service class service finds that the specific preassigned section is blocked, then it will search for free port in other sections of the ports. This is mutual shareable port strategy. Request for the section "a" will be admitted to a section "b" with probability

$$p(a, b) = p\left(\frac{(b)}{(a = \text{blocked})}\right) = p_a^b. \quad (14)$$

For example, $\sum_{i=0}^{k} p_a^{(a+i)\bmod(k+1)} = 1$. So, request generates in viewer cluster and arrives at the connected proxy server with mean Poisson rate. Here the maximum ports occupancy for class i type of service request is Q_i for $i = 0$ to k. When a request for class "a" type of service arrives, check whether $Q_a > \text{occupancy}(C_a)$. For simplicity we consider port occupancy at the session Δt is $C_a^\#$ such that $\text{occupancy}(C_a) = C_a^\#$ for $a = 0, 1, \ldots, k$. If so, then a service request of "a" type of service request is admitted to the corresponding "a" section of port with probability p_a^a. Now, $p_a^a = (Q_a - C_a^\#)/Q_a$. So the

request is admitted and updates the port occupancy class as $C_a^\# = C_a^\# + 1$ at the session Δt. If $Q_a \leq \text{occupancy}(C_a)$, then checking continues into other port sections. This happens due to the sectional subnetwork between each proxy to the corresponding local storage in the "distributed video on demand system." This forms a compact topology. To admit the request to the VOD system, checking is continued into the other service section of the port while satisfying the condition $Q_{a+j} > \text{occupancy}(C_{a+j})$ for finding free port. If free port is available in the other section then the request is admitted by the proxy server and updates the probability p_a^{a+j} for $j = 0, 1, \ldots, k$ according to Lemma 1 and expression (17).

5.1. Lemma

Lemma 1. *A system will be compact if and only if the execution of any specific event fully depends mutually on other events in compound execution.*

Proof. In a compact system, the resources are shareable such as channel, link, and port; that is, we prove the converse case; let, $x_1, x_2, \ldots, x_n$ be n mutually dependent events. Here we show that compound execution $p(x_1, x_2, x_3, \ldots, x_{n-1}, x_n)$ depends on the occurrence of each specific event x_i, that is, $p(x_i)$ for $1 \leq i \leq n$. Now,

$$
\begin{aligned}
p(x_1, x_2, x_3, \ldots, x_{n-1}, x_n) &= p(x_2, x_3, \ldots, x_{n-1}, x_n) \\
&\cdot p\left(\frac{x_1}{(x_2, x_3, \ldots, x_{n-1}, x_n)}\right) = p(x_3, \ldots, x_{n-1}, x_n) \\
&\cdot p\left(\frac{x_2}{(x_3, \ldots, x_{n-1}, x_n)}\right) \\
&\cdot p\left(\frac{x_1}{(x_2, x_3, \ldots, x_{n-1}, x_n)}\right) = \cdots = p(x_n) \\
&\cdot p\left(\frac{x_{n-1}}{x_n}\right) \\
&\cdot p\left(\frac{x_{n-2}}{(x_n, x_{n-1})}\right) \cdots p\left(\frac{x_1}{(x_2, x_3, \ldots, x_{n-1}, x_n)}\right).
\end{aligned}
\quad (15)
$$

Hence this proves the system is compact. □

So according to Lemma 1 and compactness in the local subnetwork of "distributed video on demand system" we get the following expression:

$$
\begin{aligned}
&p\left(Q_a \leq C_a^\#, Q_{a+1} \leq C_{a+1}^\#, Q_{a+2} \leq C_{a+2}^\#, \ldots, Q_{a+j-1} \leq C_{a+j-1}^\#, Q_{a+j} > C_{a+j}^\#\right) \\
&= p\left(Q_{a+1} \leq C_{a+1}^\#, Q_{a+2} \leq C_{a+2}^\#, \ldots, Q_{a+j-1} \leq C_{a+j-1}^\#, Q_{a+j} > C_{a+j}^\#\right) \\
&\quad \cdot p\left(\frac{(Q_a \leq C_a^\#)}{(Q_{a+1} \leq C_{a+1}^\#, Q_{a+2} \leq C_{a+2}^\#, \ldots, Q_{a+j-1} \leq C_{a+j-1}^\#, Q_{a+j} > C_{a+j}^\#)}\right)
\end{aligned}
$$

$$\vdots$$

$$= p\left(Q_{a+j} \succ C_{a+j}^{\#}\right) p\left(\frac{\left(Q_{a+j-1} \le C_{a+j-1}^{\#}\right)}{\left(Q_{a+j} \succ C_{a+j}^{\#}\right)}\right)$$

$$\cdot p\left(\frac{\left(Q_{a+j-2} \le C_{a+j-2}^{\#}\right)}{\left(Q_{a+j-1} \le C_{a+j-1}^{\#}, Q_{a+j} \succ C_{a+j}^{\#}\right)}\right) \cdots p\left(\frac{\left(Q_a \le C_a^{\#}\right)}{\left(Q_{a+1} \le C_{a+1}^{\#}, Q_{a+2} \le C_{a+2}^{\#}, \ldots, Q_{a+j-1} \le C_{a+j-1}^{\#}, Q_{a+j} \succ C_{a+j}^{\#}\right)}\right)$$

$$= p_a^{a+j} \text{ (say)}.$$

$$(16)$$

By reversing the order we get

$$p\left(Q_a \le C_a^{\#}, Q_{a+1} \le C_{a+1}^{\#}, Q_{a+2} \le C_{a+2}^{\#}, \ldots, Q_{a+j-1}\right.$$
$$\left. \le C_{a+j-1}^{\#}, Q_{a+j} \succ C_{a+j}^{\#}\right) = p_a^{a+j}. \tag{17}$$

Now update the occupancy class by $C_{a+j}^{\#} = C_{a+j}^{\#} + 1$ for any particular $j = 1, \ldots, k$ according to Figure 3. Otherwise, the service request will not be admitted to the local system. If the request cannot be considered, then it is considered blocked for local networking system and the request is to be forwarded to the remote database server before discarding from the distributed system.

The request is forwarded to retrieve video content from the distributed data storage. The distributed data servers are presented in Figure 2. Let us consider p_s as the probability that s out of N video storage servers are active. Active means that the storage server has the required encoded video file, and the end-to-end link is live throughout the streaming at the session Δt. So, we get the expression $p_s = \binom{N}{s} \rho^s (1 - \rho)^{N-s}$. The event space is $\{0, 1\}$ with the probability $\{1/2, 1/2\}$ for ρ. Let $B_{(\Delta t)}$ be the aggregate stationary bit rate from the distributed server according to Figure 2 at session Δt. Now, $C_{(\Delta t)}$ is the equivalent capacity of networking with respect to bit streaming rate for the whole network according to Figure 1 at session Δt. The value of $C_{(\Delta t)}$ is obtained by computing the smallest positive integer k'. k' is the least positive integer number of servers that have the required video objects or chunk of the video stream. If L and M are two events such that $M = (B_{(\Delta t)} \le C_{(\Delta t)})$ and $L = \{$At least k' number data storage is currently streaming, out of the N data storage server at session $\Delta t\}$,

$$p\left(\frac{L}{M}\right) = \frac{p(M/L) p(L)}{p(M)}$$

$$= \binom{N}{k'+1} \rho^{k'+1} (1 - \rho)^{N-k'-1} + \cdots \tag{18}$$

$$+ \binom{N}{k'+r} \rho^{k'+r} (1 - \rho)^{N-k'-r} + \cdots$$

for $r \in I^{>0}$. So, $k' \le N$ is the selected number of minimum database servers from the N number of database servers.

There is at least k' number of servers that have the required segment. Now the search for video segments or stream generated a query and broadcast from the application server towards the database servers. So the optimization problem becomes concentrated to find the value of k'. In the next section, we present the video stream searching procedure to identify the storage location that is the database server IP address.

5.2. *Session Based Query Matched Algorithm.* Algorithm 1 runs at the application server.

6. Performance Analyses

The simulation parameters are considered according to the real life streaming scenario in distributed architecture. The parameter's values are summarized and presented in Table 1. For simplicity, we have considered that individual occupancy class of customers is contained in equal number of ports at every "sector of the proxy server." A sector of size n ports can be occupied by "occupancy class of customer." The size of "occupancy class of customer" is $(\gg n)$ during the multithreading operation evoked. The traffic arrival rate with different class of the service requests started from 1 Mb/s and ended at 10.5 Mb/s. The number of viewers for each client center is 20. Figures 4–7 present the performance of distributed video on demand system at the local network with respect to analytical methodology.

We have considered 1000 trials and mean of the data is presented in the flowing figures. Figure 4 presents the blockage in the "distributed video on demand system" with respect to the incoming "service requests" traffic flows from the 20 clusters towards the proxy server; here the first sector is blocked. The performance of the distributed system at the local network is evaluated with randomly generated probability set $p(a, b)$ for the different occupancy class of the service requests. At the first sector, that is, $(a = 1)$ and $2 \le b \le 20$, where sector $a = 1$ is blocked. Figure 5 presents the performance of the distributed VOD system with respect to the randomly generated probability set $p(a, b)$ for $a = 2$, $1 \le b \le 20$, and $b \ne 2$; here sector $a = 2$ is blocked.

The "request for service" traffic arrival rate to the proxy server varies within 1 Mb/second to 10.5 Mb/second with

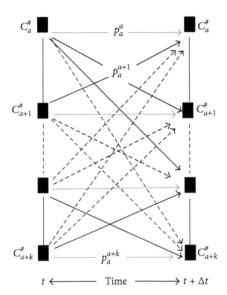

$$t \longleftarrow \text{Time} \longrightarrow t + \Delta t$$

FIGURE 3: Occupancy transition in a session.

TABLE 1: Simulation parameters.

Parameter	Value
Number of viewers per client cluster	20
Number of client clusters	10
Different service request arrival (minimum)	1 Mb/sec
Different service request arrival (maximum)	10.5 Mb/sec
Number of ports for each type service	10
Port access time	140 sec
Number of different service classes	20
Number of application servers	7 to 6
Number of database servers	3 to 5
Simulation time	460 sec
Unified parameter (k/n)	
k number of interactive modes used in a session	
n number of active channels used	
Set 1	0.2 to 1.0 step 0.2
Set 2	0.05 to 0.1 step 0.02

increment of 0.5 Mb/second. Figure 6 presents the performance of the distributed video on demand system at the proxy server, with respect to the randomly generated probability set $p(a,b)$. Now, $a = 3$, $1 \leq b \leq 20$, and $b \neq 3$; here sector $a = 3$ is blocked. Similarly Figure 7 presents the simulation graph when the sector $a = 4$ is blocked at the proxy server.

Figures 8 and 9 present the comparative study of system performance at the proxy server during the pull steam operation for different service requirement. The "pull data operation" draws raw data from every local storage to a connected proxy server in distributed architecture. The service requests are different types of service like fast forward, pause, and move backward. Figures 8 and 9 present the comparative graph at one proxy server. The pull operation retrieves multiplexed raw data stream from local storage to the connected proxy server. The plotted graphs are the system performance with and without proposed methodology of the service request handling. Both the figures have shown when the methodology of traffic handling is not used the blocking at the proxy server of "the distributed video on demand system" increases very rapidly. Figure 8 presents the comparative study of a blocked sector $a = 3$ at the corresponding proxy server. Figure 9 presents the comparative study of a blocked sector $a = 4$ at the corresponding proxy server. Both Figures 8 and 9 show that the blocking rate increases with an exponential growth without using the methodology.

When we use methodology, the blocking curve is below the threshold level. Clearly the "service of request" can be handled very efficiently by using the methodology at the proxy server for the distributed VOD system. On the other hand, when the load on the video on demand system decreases, this in turn will increase the overall system performance. The packet loss is clearly reduced efficiently by the methodology which enhances the system performance. In the 2nd part of simulation, we consider distributed database storage that is well connected to the application servers.

The service request is submitted to the proxy server but cannot be served from the connected local server. The service request proceeded further towards the web cache of the distributed database server. The simulation uses the stream search algorithm run at the application server.

In the 2nd stage of simulation, we consider seven application servers, and every application server is well connected with three database storage servers according to Figure 2. Similarly, we consider six application servers, and each application server is connected with five data storage servers in the next phase of simulation. We have considered 90% confidence level for acceptance. From Figure 10, we have noticed that 42000 numbers of user service requests well responded from hop count 4. Figure 11 shows that 51000 numbers of user service requests responded from hop count 3. So the balanced storing distribution of the video stream among the database servers reduces the searching cost and hence reduces the delay and packet drop. If we consider a rough estimate to measure the performance metric for the proposed methodology as the sum of the "number of requests served," that is, l_i multiply the hop counts h_i which gives $\sum_{i=1}^{n}(l_i * h_i)$, the expression gives the following performance metric score value according to Figure 10 that is 368000 and 317000 according to Figure 11. The score value directly depended on the number of computations to search the corresponding stream according to the proposed algorithm. The performance of the system increases as the score value decreases. In the third stage of simulation, we have considered the compact network where the data can be pulled for the user interactive session. The size of the request inside the network grows from 0 to 1000 in one minute, that is, 60 seconds presented in the horizontal axis. The vertical axis is the normalized traffic load with respect to maximum bandwidth on demand requirement, and the distributed network provides the amount at a session. We consider the unified demand parameter as ($\approx k/n$) at 90% confidence

```
(1) At t = t_s // t_s is the start time of the
                    // session
(2) Var Queue_of_finite_Size : integer
(3) While (t ≠ (t_s + Δt))
(4) {
(5) Initial node {S} // set of data base storage
                    // nodes
(6) Boolean matched_node_not_found ← True
(7) Q ← Queue of finite Size
(8) Begin
(9) Q ← push (S) // first in first out
(10) while (match_node_not_found) do
(11) {
(12)        v ← Pop (Q) // pop is queue operation
(13) For each {w} from single hop neighbor of v
(14)     {
(15)        If (query string ∈ w)
(16)        then
(17)            {
(18)            match_node_not_found ← False
(19)            return node ID of w
(20)            exit
(21)            }
(22)        else
(23)        Q ← Push (w) // Push is a queue operation
(24)     } // End for
(25) } // End Inner While
(26) t = t_s + Δt
(27) } // End Outer While
(28) Send("query matched node not found")
                            // To application Server
(29) End
(30) Stop
```

ALGORITHM 1

interval; according to (13) and expression *(Exp ii)*, k is the number of interactive modes used in a session and n is the number of active links for corresponding users. So, n depended upon the size of the network at that session. But, $n \approx B_{(\Delta t)}/W_{max} \Rightarrow$ parameters $\approx k(w_{max})/B_{(\Delta t)}$ and $B_{(\Delta t)}$ is the total bandwidth of the trunk provided in ideal situation or scenario at session Δt.

Figures 12 and 13 present the traffic load inside the distributed network for various stages of the user driven interactive session. We observed from the figures that the traffic load increases by the increases over the number of users who operates the user driven interactive mode of operation at any session. The unified demand parameter value increases from 0.2 to 1.0 with the step size 0.2 for a particular session. Figure 13 presents the normalized traffic load at that interactive session, for a number of peer nodes, presented in the distributed system.

The peer node is the representation of local storage or proxy servers or distributed storage in distributed system.

Similar type of results is presented in Figure 12 for the unified demand parameter value starting from 0.05 to 0.1 with step size 0.02 for another interactive session with the same set of distributed network environments. In both the cases, we

have considered the duration of the interactive session is 60 seconds and 1000 trials.

7. Related Work

Interactive operation on multimedia systems represents a key technology. It is evolving from viewer demand and research prototypes to commercial deployments. Supporting truly and efficiently interactive multimedia services require smooth providing of personalized, dedicated channels or sessions for each user. For this particular set of services, the user requires complete control over the session and has the freedom to explore the depth of both live and stored archive. Development of these interactive multimedia services requires solving a diverse set of technical problems, many of which are tractable. According to Little and Venkatesh, in the interactive services, virtual VCR capabilities and interfaces to view parallel media streams are the most crucial requirement for video on demand system [19]. The earlier work presented by Paxson and Floyd [20], on Poisson processes for analytic simplicity, and a number of traffic studies have shown that packet interarrivals are not exponentially distributed.

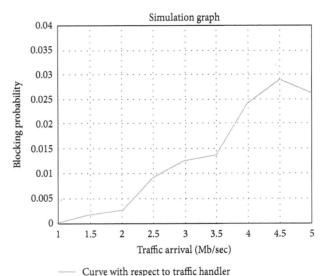

Curve with respect to traffic handler

FIGURE 4: Blocking probability versus arrival rate with respect to incoming service requests.

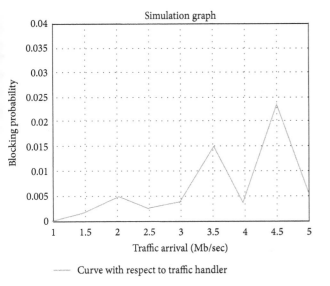

Curve with respect to traffic handler

FIGURE 5: Blocking probability versus arrival rate with respect to the randomly generated probability set.

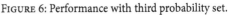

Curve with respect to traffic handler

FIGURE 6: Performance with third probability set.

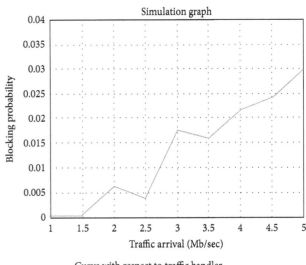

Curve with respect to traffic handler

FIGURE 7: Performance with fourth probability set.

In this work, authors considered 24 wide-area traces for investigating a number of wide-area TCP arrival processes. Basically, traces are analyzed: the network, date, duration, and packet (amount). For the analysis purpose tracer considered TCP connection interarrivals, TELNET packet interarrivals, and FTPDATA connection arrivals. The Pareto distribution plays a role both in TELNET packet interarrivals and in the size of FTPDATA burst. Huang et al. [21] mainly focused on the single video stream pull approach. The single peer only redistributes the video stream that it is currently using. This work shows that 95 percentile server bandwidth costs would have been reserved for single peer assisted employment that was instead used. The streaming sessions trace records that were generated by the same Windows Media Player (WMP). Chat application does not consume huge

amounts of traffic. This implies that catering to such users can be a promising way of attracting them, especially in low bandwidth environments. The chat traffic uses neither a well defined port nor a well defined protocol, but there exists a wide spectrum of protocols [22]. It is like IRC protocol used by IRC networks or their applet-based user interface equivalents: custom application protocols used by HTML Web chat systems running on top of HTTP. Diot and Gautier [23] describe the design, implementation, and evaluation of MiMaze. MiMaze is the multiplayers game with a distributed architecture using the multicast backbone for carrying IP multicast traffic over the Internet. It describes the design of dedicated transmission control mechanisms. MiMaze used distributed communication architecture based on the IP multicast protocol suite (RTP/UDP/IP). This work analyzed distributed interactive game on the multicast Internet. Zink

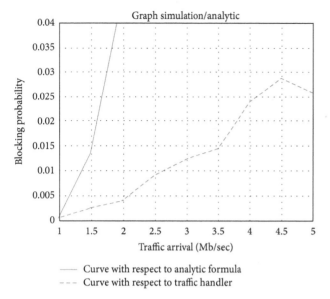

FIGURE 8: Comparison of service request from local storage with third probability set.

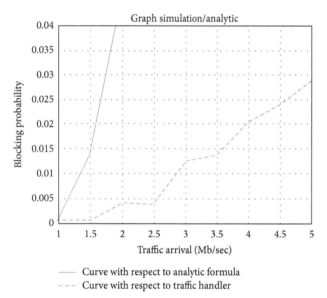

FIGURE 9: Comparison of request server from local storage with fourth probability set.

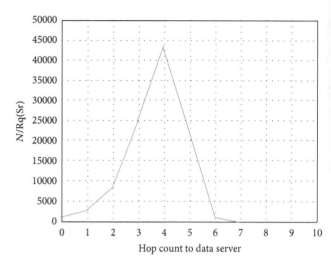

FIGURE 10: Service request served from database server to application server (orientation 1).

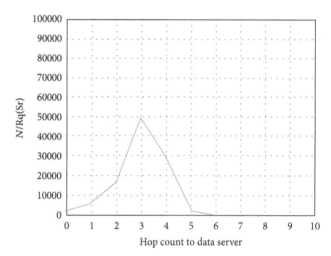

FIGURE 11: Service request served from database server to application server (orientation 2).

et al. [24] analyze the content distribution in YouTube. It is realized and conducts a measurement study of YouTube traffic for large university campus network. Based on these measurements, author analyzed the duration and the data rate during streaming sessions. For monitoring the YouTube traffic, a client retrieves a video stream from YouTube. The multithreaded catcher obtains YouTube usage statistics for a particular campus network. Monitoring is done through a two-step process. In the first step, the collected data analyze signaling traffic, that is, HTTP message exchange between the client and the YouTube web server. In the second stage, video streaming is monitored. It is TCP headers of the video data sent from the CDN (content driven network) storage server.

The traces are presented as follows: the trace length, user population, and content of local importance on the performance of different distribution architectures. The current tendency in Internet traffic is a shift from web traffic to P2P traffic. Many studies focus on the characterization of P2P traffic analysis [25, 26]. Kim et al. [27] propose a new method to identify current Internet traffic, which is a preliminary but important step toward traffic characterization. The traffic identification method is considered flow grouping in peer-to-peer (P2P) communication architecture. The video traffic is traces by the time-series graph based on the metrics traffic flows, packet, and byte, respectively. Broadband Internet service is popular in many parts of the world. Numbers of research studies have examined the characteristics of such traffic. Maier et al. [28] have considered a common assumption regarding residential traffic. The downstream dominates over the upstream; that is, most bytes are transferred to the local side. Indeed, the considered assumption has shaped and is

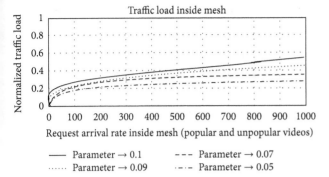

FIGURE 12: Normalized traffic load in interactive session (lower range of parameters).

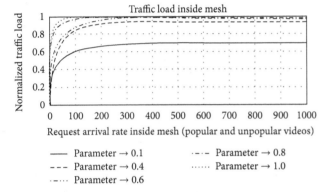

FIGURE 13: Normalized traffic load in interactive session (higher range of parameters).

ingrained in the bandwidth allocations of ADSL (asymmetric digital subscriber line) and cable broadband offerings. In the DSL session characteristics, Maier et al. study with a look at the behavior of the user's DSL sessions (periods of connection to the ISP's network). To trace the traffic, author used HTTP, Bit Torrent, eDonkey, SSL, NNTP, and RTSP protocols.

The performance of traffic monitoring and analysis systems highly depends on the number of flows as well as link utilization and the pattern of packet arrival. Kim et al. [29] examine the characteristics of recent Internet traffic from the perspective of flows. The authors used pipeline based real time traffic monitoring and analysis system architecture. In order to collect IP traffic trace data, authors considered "NG-MON" flow generator simulator and placed at the connection point of the network. The distribution of traffic flow duration and the distribution of the number of packets in flows are presented with the help of TCP and UDP protocols. The simulation result also presented the flow's density. In this work, author used bytes and packets as metrics. In the case of peer-to-peer IPTV communities, Silverston et al. [30] have considered P2P IPTV traffic. It provides useful insights into both transport and packet levels statistical properties of P2P IPTV. It is useful to understand the impact on network nodes and links. The data traffic is collected by peers within the community watching the 2006 FIFA World Cup. The collected data is analyzed on mesh based topological system (PPLive, PPStream, SOPCast, and TVAnts). The tracer plots the (PPLive, PPStream, SOPCast, and TVAnts) traffic with respect to the number of videos downloaded from the neighboring peers with respect to time. The tracer plots the joint probability density function (PDF) of the interpacket time (IPT) and packet size (PS) of the download traffic. The IPT of each packet is the time that elapsed between that packet and the previous one of the same sessions. Loguinov and Radha [31] analyzed the dynamics of a live streaming experiment that has been conducted between a number of unicast dial-up clients, connecting to the Internet through access points, and a backbone video server. The clients streamed low-bit rate MPEG-4 video sequences from the server over paths with a number of distinct Internet routers. The authors have considered client-server based architecture for MPEG-4 streaming on the Internet. The server was fully multithreaded to ensure that the transmissions of chunk video were performed at the target IP. The bit rate of each streaming session provides a quick response to clients' NACK requests. The streaming was implemented in bursts of packets (with the varying burst duration). The author considered six datasets, each collected from the different machine. The plots are mainly distribution of the number of end-to-end hops and average packet loss rates. The author analyzed the dynamics of a large number of TCP web sessions at a busy Internet server. Liang [32] systematically investigates the long term, online, time variable bit-rate (VBR) video traffic prediction. It is the key and complicated component for advanced predictive dynamic bandwidth control and frame allocation. Since in the Internet and other packet/cell switching broad-band networks (such as ATM), VBR video traffic will be a major part of the traffic produced by multimedia as sources, many researchers have focused on VBR video traffic prediction. Liang [32] traced the prediction of video frame by multiresolution learning neural network (NN) based model.

8. Conclusions

In this work, we have presented the three-phase simulation for distributed video on demand system for interactive session. The first stage of simulation according to the proposed methodology reduces the blockage at the proxy server for different types of service requests. It efficiently serves from the local server. If the requested video stream is not present at the local storage or the blockage is above some preassigned threshold then the service request proceeds further to distributed databases. The 2nd stage of the simulation results is presented to reduce the search hop counts for the required storage stream in "distributed video on demand system" by using the session based query search algorithm, which runs at the application server. In the third phase we have seen that the bandwidth requirement completely depended upon the number of interactive modes used by the user at any session. Increase in the number of users brings higher use of interactive modes that leads to the high bandwidth requirement at any session. The size of the network brings little impact to this scenario. The size of the network increases linearly, scalable with the number of peers' nodes in the network. The unified demand parameters do not depend upon the size of the network or the number of peer nodes. Furthermore, the single-user bandwidth requirement model for interactive mode at any session does not depend upon the number of peer nodes present in the distributed network. The simulation result also reflects the same scenario.

Competing Interests

The authors Soumen Kanrar and Niranjan Kumar Mandal declare that there is no conflict of interests regarding the publication of the paper.

Acknowledgments

The authors are grateful to Sharmista Das Kanrar from Bishop Westcott, Ranchi, India.

References

[1] P. Mundur, A. K. Sood, and R. Simon, "Class-based access control for distributed video-on-demand systems," *IEEE Transactions on Circuits and Systems for Video Technology*, vol. 15, no. 7, pp. 844–853, 2005.

[2] S. Annapu Reddy, "Exploring IP/VOD in P2P swarming systems," in *Proceedings of the Conference on Computer Communications (INFOCOM '07)*, pp. 71–75, Anchorage, Alaska, USA, May 2007.

[3] D. Agrawal, M. S. Beigi, C. Bisdikian, and K.-W. Lee, "Planning and managing the IPTV service deployment," in *Proceedings of the 10th IFIP/IEEE International Symposium on Integrated Network Management (IM '07)*, pp. 353–362, Munich, Germany, May 2007.

[4] L. Shi, Z. Gu, L. Wei, and Y. Shi, "Quantitative analysis of Zipf's law on web cache," in *Parallel and Distributed Processing and Applications*, vol. 3758 of *Lecture Notes in Computer Science*, pp. 845–852, Springer, 2005.

[5] G. Hasslinger and O. Hohlfeld, "Efficiency of caches for content distribution on the internet," in *Proceedings of the 22nd International IEEE Teletraffic Congress (ITC '10)*, pp. 1–8, Amsterdam, The Netherlands, September 2010.

[6] S. Kanrar, "Analysis and implementation of the large scale video-on-demand system," *International Journal of Applied Information Systems*, vol. 1, no. 4, pp. 41–49, 2012.

[7] S. Kanrar, "Performance of distributed video on demand system for multirate traffic," in *Proceedings of the International Conference on Recent Trends in Information Systems (ReTIS '11)*, pp. 52–56, Kolkata, India, December 2011.

[8] S. Kanrar, "Efficient traffic control of VoD system," *International Journal of Computer Networks & Communications*, vol. 3, no. 5, pp. 95–106, 2011.

[9] S. Kanrar and K. N. Mandal, "Dynamic page replacement at the cache memory for the video on demand server," in *Advanced Computing, Networking and Informatics—Volume 2*, pp. 461–469, Springer, 2014.

[10] S. Kanrar and K. N. Mandal, "performance enhancement for audio-video proxy server," in *Proceedings of the 3rd International Conference on Frontiers of Intelligent Computing: Theory and Applications (FICTA), 2014, Volume 1*, vol. 327 of *Advances in Intelligent Systems and Computing*, pp. 605–613, Springer, 2015.

[11] S. Tewari and L. Kleinrock, "On fairness, optimal download performance and proportional replication in peer-to-peer networks," in *Proceedings of the 4th International IFIP-TC6 Networking Conference*, Waterloo, Canada, May 2005.

[12] S. Tewari and L. Kleinrock, "Proportional replication in peer-to-peer networks," in *Proceedings of the Conference on Computer Communications (INFOCOM '06)*, Barcelona, Spain, 2006.

[13] X. Zhou and C.-Z. Xu, "Efficient algorithms of video replication and placement on a cluster of streaming servers," *Journal of Network and Computer Applications*, vol. 30, no. 2, pp. 515–540, 2007.

[14] S. Kanrar and N. K. Mandal, "Optimum storage finding in video on demand system," in *Proceedings of the IEEE 2nd International Conference on Signal Processing and Integrated Networks (SPIN '15)*, pp. 827–830, Noida, India, Feburary 2015.

[15] K. Suh, C. Diot, J. Kurose et al., "Push-to-peer video-on-demand system: design and evaluation," *IEEE Journal on Selected Areas in Communications*, vol. 25, no. 9, pp. 1706–1716, 2007.

[16] V. O. K. Li, W. Liao, X. Qiu, and E. W. M. Wong, "Performance model of interactive video-on-demand systems," *IEEE Journal on Selected Areas in Communications*, vol. 14, no. 6, pp. 1099–1109, 1996.

[17] G. M. Lee, C. S. Lee, W. S. Rhee, and J. K. Choi, "Functional architecture for NGN-based personalized IPTV services," *IEEE Transactions on Broadcasting*, vol. 55, no. 2, 2009.

[18] A. Dan, D. Sitaram, and P. Shahabuddin, "Scheduling polices for an on demand video server with batching," in *Proceedings of the 2nd ACM International Conference on Multimedia (MULTIMEDIA '94)*, pp. 15–23, San Francisco, Calif, USA, October 1994.

[19] T. D. C. Little and D. Venkatesh, "Prospects for interactive video-on-demand," *IEEE MultiMedia*, vol. 1, no. 3, pp. 14–24, 1994.

[20] V. Paxson and S. Floyd, "Wide area traffic: the failure of Poisson modeling," *IEEE/ACM Transactions on Networking*, vol. 3, no. 3, pp. 226–244, 1995.

[21] C. Huang, J. Li, and W. Keith, "Can internet video-on-demand be profitable?" *ACM SIGCOMM Computer Communication Review*, vol. 37, no. 4, pp. 133–144, 2007, Proceedings of the Conference on Applications, Technologies, Architectures, and Protocols for Computer Communications (SIGCOMM '07).

[22] C. Dewes, A. Wichmann, and A. Feldmann, "An analysis of internet chat systems," in *Proceedings of the 3rd ACM SIGCOMM Internet Measurement Conference (IMC '03)*, pp. 51–64, October 2003.

[23] C. Diot and L. Gautier, "A distributed architecture for multiplayer interactive applications on the Internet," *IEEE Network*, vol. 13, no. 4, pp. 6–15, 1999.

[24] M. Zink, K. Suh, Y. Gu, and J. Kurose, "Characteristics of YouTube network traffic at a campus network-measurements, models, and implications," *Computer Networks*, vol. 53, no. 4, pp. 501–514, 2009.

[25] S. Sen and J. Wang, "Analyzing peer-to-peer traffic across large networks," *IEEE/ACM Transactions on Networking*, vol. 12, no. 2, pp. 219–232, 2004.

[26] S. Saroiu, K. P. Gummadi, R. J. Dunn, S. D. Gribble, and H. M. Levy, "An analysis of internet content delivery systems," in *Proceedings of the 5th Symposium On Operating Systems Design And Implementation ACM SIGOPS Operating Systems Review (OSDI '02)*, vol. 36, pp. 315–327, December 2012.

[27] M.-S. Kim, Y. J. Won, and J. W.-K. Hong, "Application-level traffic monitoring and an analysis on IP networks," *ETRI Journal*, vol. 27, no. 1, pp. 22–41, 2005.

[28] G. Maier, A. Feldmann, V. Paxson, and M. Allman, "On dominant characteristics of residential broadband internet traffic," in *Proceedings of the 9th ACM SIGCOMM Internet Measurement Conference (IMC '09)*, pp. 90–102, November 2009.

[29] M.-S. Kim, Y. J. Won, and J. W. Hong, "Characteristic analysis of internet traffic from the perspective of flows," *Computer Communications*, vol. 29, no. 10, pp. 1639–1652, 2006.

[30] T. Silverston, O. Fourmauxa, A. Bottab et al., "Traffic analysis of peer-to-peer IPTV communities," *Computer Networks*, vol. 53, no. 4, pp. 470–484, 2008.

[31] D. Loguinov and H. Radha, "End-to-end Internet video trafficdynamics: statistical study andanalysis," in *Proceedings of the 21st IEEE Annual Joint Conference of the IEEE Computer and Communications Societies (INFOCOM '02)*, vol. 2, pp. 723–732, New York, NY, USA, 2002.

[32] Y. Liang, "Real-time VBR video traffic prediction for dynamic bandwidth allocation," *IEEE Transactions on Systems, Man and Cybernetics, Part C: Applications and Reviews*, vol. 34, no. 1, pp. 32–47, 2004.

Permissions

List of Contributors

Ran Li, Hongbing Liu, Yu Zeng and Yanling Li
School of Computer and Information Technology, Xinyang Normal University, Xinyang 464000, China

Chunnian Fan, Shuiping Wang and Hao Zhang
Jiangsu Engineering Center of Network Monitoring, Nanjing University of Information Science and Technology, Nanjing 210044, China
School of Computer and Software, Nanjing University of Information Science and Technology, Nanjing 210044, China

Yizhong Yang, Qiang Zhang, Pengfei Wang, Xionglou Hu and Nengju Wu
School of Electronic Science and Applied Physics, Hefei University of Technology, Hefei, China

Diego José Luis Botia Valderrama and Natalia Gaviria Gómez
Engineering Department, Universidad de Antioquia, Medell'ın, Colombia

Shanshan Li and Weiyang Sun
School of Information Engineering, Chang'an University, Middle Section of Nan'er Huan Road, Xi'an 710064, China

Yuan-Yu Tsai
Department of M-Commerce and Multimedia Applications, Asia University, Taichung 413, Taiwan
Department of Medical Research, China Medical University Hospital, China Medical University, Taichung 404, Taiwan

Niranjan Kumar Mandal
Vidyasagar University, West Bengal 721102, India

Hui-Lung Lee and Ling-Hwei Chen
Department of Computer Science, National Chiao Tung University Hsinchu, Hsinchu 300, Taiwan

Yanhui Zhu, Qiang Liu, Shengqiu Yi, Zhiqiang Wen, Qi Tong and Zhigao Zeng
College of Computer and Communication, Hunan University of Technology, Hunan 412007, China

Intelligent Information Perception and Processing Technology, Hunan Province Key Laboratory, Hunan 412007, China

Sanyou Zeng
Department of Computer Science, China University of Geosciences, Wuhan, Hubei 430074, China

Mengyu Xu, Zhenmin Tang, Yazhou Yao, Lingxiang Yao, Huafeng Liu and Jingsong Xu
Nanjing University of Science and Technology, Nanjing 210094, China

Debajyoti Pal and Vajirasak Vanijja
IP Communications Laboratory, School of Information Technology, King Mongkut's University of Technology Thonburi, Bangkok 10140, Thailand

Xuchao Lu, Li Song, Rong Xie, Xiaokang Yang and Wenjun Zhang
Institute of Image Communication and Network Engineering, Shanghai Jiao Tong University, Shanghai, China
Future Medianet Innovation Center, Shanghai, China

Thoa Nguyen, Thang Vu and Nam Pham Ngoc
Hanoi University of Science and Technology, Hanoi, Vietnam

Truong Cong Thang
The University of Aizu, Aizuwakamatsu, Japan

Anjie Peng, Yadong Wu and Xiangui Kang
School of Computer Science and Technology, Southwest University of Science and Technology, Sichuan, China
Guangdong Key Lab of Information Security, School of Data and Computer Science, Sun Yat-Sen University, Guangzhou, China

Soumen Kanrar
Vehere Interactive Pvt. Ltd., Calcutta, West Bengal 700053, India
Vidyasagar University, West Bengal 721102, India

Index

Printed in the USA
CPSIA information can be obtained
at www.ICGtesting.com
JSHW051411221024
72173JS00006B/1340